Case Studies in Clinical Linguistics

Case Studies in Clinical Linguistics

Edited by Michael Perkins and Sara Howard

Whurr Publishers Ltd
London

© 1995 Whurr Publishers Ltd
First published 1995 by
Whurr Publishers Ltd
19b Compton Terrace, London N1 2UN, England

British Library Cataloguing in Publication Data
A catalogue record for this book is available from the
British Library.

ISBN 1-897635-75-3 ✓

Printed and bound in the UK by Athenaeum Press Ltd,
Gateshead, Tyne & Wear

Preface

The need for a book of case studies in clinical linguistics has become increasingly apparent to us after a number of years of teaching applied clinical linguistics without a suitable set text. We have found that, often in spite of the benefit of numerous courses in linguistics, it is only by applying their linguistic knowledge in a detailed analysis of a language-impaired client in their care that students finally convince themselves – and often their supervising clinicians – that clinical linguistics is actually worth while.

The still rather sparing use made of linguistics by practising clinicians and the purported reason for this – namely lack of time – are two of the main reasons why both students and clinicians are sometimes reluctant to recognise the central role of clinical linguistics in the assessment and remediation of communication disorders. We hope that the case studies in this book will demonstrate the value of spending the necessary amount of time on clinical linguistic analysis, and that clinical results which could not have been achieved by any other means form a powerful argument for such time and expertise being routinely available where needed.

In addition to students training to become speech and language therapists, this book should also be of benefit and interest to practising speech and language therapists, remedial teachers, educational psychologists and other professionals involved with the language impaired; to academics teaching and researching in the area of speech and language pathology; and to theoretical and applied linguists.

We have been helped indirectly by various people in producing this book, but we would like to single out for special thanks our co-contributors for their enthusiastic participation in this venture and the clients whose cases are reported here. We are also grateful to David Crystal for his helpful and encouraging comments on an earlier draft. The influence of his pioneering work in clinical linguistics will be evident throughout the book.

Finally, we would like to express our gratitude to Justine Byrden for valour at mealtimes, and to Stefan Perkins for allowing access to the word processor in between computer games.

Michael Perkins
Sara Howard

Contents

Contributors

Richard Body
Head Injury Rehabilitation Centre, Sheffield

Monica Bray
Speech and Language Therapy Group, Leeds Metropolitan University, Leeds

Ian Crookston
Speech and Language Therapy Group, Leeds Metropolitan University, Leeds

Sue Franklin
Department of Psychology, University of York, York

Barry Heselwood
Speech and Language Therapy Group, Leeds Metropolitan University, Leeds

Sara Howard
Department of Speech Science, University of Sheffield, Sheffield

Deirdre Martin
School of Education, University of Birmingham, Birmingham

Kay Mogford-Bevan
Department of Speech, University of Newcastle upon Tyne, Newcastle upon Tyne

Rosemarie MorganBarry
National Hospitals' College of Speech Sciences, London

Julie Morris
Department of Psychology, Birkbeck College, London

Mark Parker
Head Injury Rehabilitation Centre, Sheffield

Michael Perkins
Department of Speech Science, University of Sheffield, Sheffield

Caroline Pickstone
Sheffield Children's Hospital, Sheffield

Oonagh Reilly
School of Speech Therapy, University of Central England in
Birmingham, Birmingham

Ray Wilkinson
National Hospitals' College of Speech Sciences, London

Amanda Willcox
North Durham Community Health Care, Durham

Acknowledgements

Chapter 3
Thanks to Pat Sullivan, Professor of Child Dental Health, University of Sheffield for information relating to Rebecca's dentition and occlusion.

Chapter 4
We would like to thank the following individuals for their past and ongoing involvement in Rachel's programme of assessment and management: Sheila Bone and Anne Crichton of the Department of Paediatric Communication, Sheffield Children's Hospital; Professor Pat Sullivan and members of the Orthodontic Department at the Charles Clifford Dental Hospital, Sheffield; Nancy Milloy; Kath Milner.

Chapter 5
We would like to thank Hilary Crane, speech and language therapist, who worked with C and provided all the case history and therapy information.

Chapter 7
The authors would like to thank N's family, and the staff at the school that N attended. The authors are also grateful to Durham Health Authority for funding this research.

Chapter 10
We are very grateful to JS and his family for all their time, effort and enthusiasm. We would also like to thank Debbie Lapin and Catherine Exley for referring JS to the study. Thanks to Dr Judy Turner who developed most of the tests described and to Andrew Ellis for helpful comments regarding the work. This research was supported by an MRC grant. The study forms part of the first author's doctoral thesis.

Chapter 11
The author would like to thank the patients, their families, and the

speech and language therapists of Frenchay Hospital for their help in the project from which these data were taken. The project is supervised by Rachel David, Pam Enderby and David Cox and is funded by a grant from the Stroke Association. I am grateful to Anthony Wootton and to Mick Perkins and Sara Howard for their comments on an earlier version of this chapter.

Part I
Preliminaries

Chapter 1
Introduction

MICHAEL PERKINS and SARA HOWARD

Why a book of case studies?

Clinical linguistics is a relatively new discipline. Although a number of books in this area have been published over the last 15 years, they have tended to focus either on the general principles of clinical linguistic analysis at different levels of language (e.g. Crystal, 1987a) or else on specific procedures involved in such analysis (e.g. Crystal, 1992). There is widespread feeling, however, that before clinical linguistics can make any significant headway as an applied science (for example, in establishing a serious typology of language disability based on linguistic principles), a great deal of linguistic analysis of a variety of language disorders first needs to be carried out. A related requirement is to demonstrate to speech and language therapists the practical validity and usefulness of clinical linguistics in the assessment and remediation of language disorders – in other words, to show that clinical linguistics actually works. One way of achieving both of these goals is to carry out – and publish – case studies. Although there are a number of single or group clinical linguistic case studies in print, they do not exist as a single coherent body of work, being mainly found either in conference proceedings (e.g. Grunwell and James, 1989) or in journals such as *European Journal of Disorders of Communication*, *Journal of Speech and Hearing Disorders*, *Clinical Linguistics and Phonetics* and *Child Language Teaching and Therapy*. The current volume will hopefully help to improve this situation.

We have several general related aims in this book:

1. First and foremost we want to make available within the covers of a single volume a wide-ranging set of clinical linguistic case studies, covering several different levels of linguistic analysis and demonstrating the application of more than one level of linguistic analysis in individual cases. As well as increasing the pool of knowledge on

3

language disorders, this should also enable practitioners such as speech and language therapists to see how clinical linguistics can be made to work for them.

2. Also with such practitioners in mind, we focus on single case studies which are 'client-driven', i.e. the analytical techniques chosen are determined by the nature of the client's problem and typically result in coherent interventional and remedial strategies. Some of the studies, for example, show how a programme of linguistic analysis and therapeutic management has developed over time, responding to a client's changing needs, with therapy and analysis complementing and informing each other. Our particular approach to the single case study is discussed in more detail in Chapter 2.

3. We aim to demonstrate the collaborative nature of applied clinical linguistics by illustrating the kind of service that speech and language therapists may reasonably ask of a linguist, without feeling that they need have specialist expertise in that area themselves.

4. Conversely, we hope that linguists will also benefit from such a series of practical demonstrations of how their theoretical knowledge and analytical skills can play an integral role in the assessment and remediation of language disorders.

5. Finally, an underlying motivation is our experience of the occasionally negative feelings – ranging from inadequacy and mistrust to outright hostility (!) – which speech and language therapists sometimes experience towards linguistics. Our approach will hopefully help to allay such feelings and illustrate the practical usefulness of linguistics for clinicians.

The approach outlined above contrasts with that of other books in this area. These can be divided into two different categories. First, there are those that focus on specific areas of linguistics, for example, syntax or phonology, and show how they can be used in the analysis of a variety of language disorders. For example, Crystal (1984, 1987a, 1992), Crystal et al. (1989), Grundy (1989), Ball (1989) and McTear and Conti-Ramsden (1992) all focus either on general principles of clinical linguistic analysis, or else on specific procedures involved in such analysis. Some include case study material, but with the exception of Crystal et al. (1989) where case studies are integral, such material tends to be included only incidentally or merely for illustrative purposes. The second approach is to discuss the symptomatology of specific types of language pathology and suggest the kinds of linguistic analysis from which they might benefit, but without going into detailed and comprehensive coverage of the actual application of these analyses. This is evident, for example, in Grundy (1989) and Leahy (1989), both of which focus on the language disorders themselves, rather than on their specific manifestation in individual patients. Once again, any case study material included is merely incidental rather than the main focus of interest. In contrast to both of these approaches we instead give the case studies themselves centre stage.

Format and organisation

Parts II and III of the book each comprise five single case studies. Part II focuses on children with communication disorders and Part III on acquired disorders in adults. We have tried as far as possible to use the following general format for each case study:

Background
• Case history
• The problem
• Theoretical background
• Initial hypotheses

Analysis
• Data collection
• Analytical frameworks
• Analysis and discussion
• Follow-up investigations and analyses

Implications
• Remedial implications
• Theoretical implications
• Methodological implications.

Inevitably, however, there are differences of emphasis, organisation and focus as a result of the unique nature of each case and the specific aims of the investigators. There are other formats we could have used (for example, Crystal, 1987b) but this one enabled us to focus on the interrelationships of four areas that we regard as having central importance: theory, analysis, methodology and therapy:

Theory

Each study aims to show how a particular case can be illuminated by current theoretical models in both linguistics and other relevant disciplines.

Analysis

All studies include detailed linguistic analysis. In addition, we aim to demonstrate the value of multilevel linguistic analysis. To this end, several of the cases included are of a complex nature where a number of interrelated problems combine to produce speech or language which appears particularly difficult to explain – a situation that, in our experience, is more common than is often assumed.

Methodology

Here we are concerned with issues such as what kind of data to collect, how to collect them, how to transcribe and code them and how to analyse them.

Therapy

Finally, each case study seeks to show how an appropriate choice of theory, analysis and methodology can have a direct effect on intervention and remedial outcome.

Each of these related areas is considered in detail in Chapter 2.

A fairly wide range of communication disorders is covered in Part II and Part III, although it is not intended to be comprehensive. We have tried to find cases that provide an opportunity to say something new, either because of the nature of the disorders themselves or because of the nature of the analytical approaches applied to them. Much of what has been published on communication disorders has focused either on grammatical disability – using procedures such as the Language Assessment, Remediation and Screening Procedure (LARSP: Crystal et al., 1989) – or on phonological disability – using procedures such as PACS (Phonological Assessment of Child Speech – Grunwell, 1985b). Although both these types of disability feature in several cases, they are always part of a more complex problem and not the exclusive focus of interest. We are well aware that one inherent danger in adopting such an approach is that it risks giving the impression that clinical linguistics is of use only for complicated or unusual cases – which is, of course, entirely false. We trust, however, that the general usefulness of the analytical methods described and their applicability to simple and common cases as well as the complex and unusual ones will be self-evident.

Finally, when describing language disorders we feel that it is important to provide plenty of transcribed speech and language data, not just for illustrative purposes but to allow other researchers and therapists to make comparisons with data from their own clients. We therefore make no apology for the numerous data samples which appear throughout the book.

Overview

The main chapter in Part I – Principles of clinical linguistics – provides an overview and update on the field of clinical linguistics. We consider what clinical linguistics is, who does it, why they do it and how they do it. We also address issues such as: the reciprocal relationship between linguistic theory and clinical practice, and between their respective practitioners; the client-driven and data-driven single case methodology adopted in Parts II and III of the book; the importance of carrying out an adequate transcription of clinical data; and one way in which current developments in computational linguistics could revolutionise the study of communication disorders.

In Parts II and III the chapters are organised roughly according to the main linguistic 'level' they consider, starting with phonetics and ranging through phonology, grammar and semantics to pragmatics.

In the opening study in Part II, Sara Howard uses perceptual and instrumental phonetic analysis retrospectively to examine the changes in a child's speech production following electropalatographic therapy for misarticulated fricatives. Although the therapy achieved its aim of correcting the misarticulated segments, other significant changes gradually occurred which only became auditorily apparent after a number of months. Retrospective instrumental analysis, however, revealed a process of gradual change taking place long before this.

In Chapter 4, Sara Howard and Caroline Pickstone show how clinical phonetic and linguistic analysis played a critical role in the diagnosis and treatment of a complex speech disorder presenting in a child with cleft palate. The study shows how close phonetic transcription facilitated an initial phonological analysis but also suggested a number of subsequent instrumental analyses, each of which informed the clinical process in different ways.

In the following chapter Deirdre Martin and Oonagh Reilly use two contrasting approaches to analyse the language performance of a child with severe communication problems resulting from a central auditory perception deficit. Partly because of the severity of the case, analyses based on theoretical frameworks drawn from the literature on central auditory processing proved inadequate, whereas a cognitive neuropsychological approach enabled a more coherent and illuminating analysis which was better able to identify promising intervention strategies.

The study by Monica Bray, Barry Heselwood and Ian Crookston in Chapter 6 analyses the language of a boy with Down's syndrome at several different levels and considers their interplay. They conclude that his linguistic problems result from: difficulties at the conceptual level which cause his language to be disjointed and oddly phrased; from difficulties with the rhythmic organisation of articulatory gestures; from an inability to initiate utterances easily; and from poor control of pitch and vocal quality because of inadequate respiratory support. Over and above these, he also has problems with processing different levels simultaneously.

In the final chapter of Part II, Amanda Willcox and Kay Mogford-

Bevan describe the successful remediation programme of a child initially diagnosed as having a 'semantic–pragmatic' disorder. Over a 10-month period, the child's conversational behaviour in a variety of different contexts was repeatedly analysed using categories drawn from conversation analysis, and a range of intervention activities building on the analyses were devised and carried out. Not only did the targeted behaviours improve, but there was also considerable generalisation to other non-targeted areas.

Part III starts with a study by Rosemarie MorganBarry which presents a phonological analysis of a dysarthric speaker, showing how abnormalities at both the segmental and prosodic levels conspire together to reduce intelligibility in dysarthric speech. She then shows how these findings can be used to inform the process of clinical management.

In Chapter 9 Sara Howard and Rosemary Varley describe the use of perceptual and instrumental phonetic analysis to aid in the diagnosis of an unusually severe case of acquired apraxia and they discuss some of the implications of the case for traditional assumptions about the nature of acquired apraxia.

The study by Julie Morris and Sue Franklin in Chapter 10 is an investigation of an aphasic man with multilevel problems. A cognitive neuropsychological analysis made it possible to identify the separate components of his language difficulties, and one of these – an auditory discrimination deficit – was targeted for detailed analysis and remediation. The patient was reassessed to evaluate the effectiveness of the therapy programme and results demonstrate that the improvements seen following therapy are specific to the area of language processing targeted and not simply part of a general improvement.

In Chapter 11, Ray Wilkinson demonstrates the usefulness of conversation analysis in the investigation of aphasic language. A detailed analysis is carried out on a 5-minute section of a conversation between a therapist and an aphasic patient, focusing, in particular, on how the sequential placement of specific utterances can cause problems for both interactants, and the knock-on effect this can have on successful repair completion. The value of this type of analysis using natural conversation is further illustrated by a comparison with the same patient's performance in a picture description task where his conversational difficulties are less in evidence.

In the final chapter of Part III, Mick Perkins, Richard Body and Mark Parker present an analysis of topic bias and repetitiveness in the language of an adult with closed head injury which considers the relationship of factors such as utterance sequence, semantic cohesion, prosody and conversational repair. The analysis suggests that rather than being the result of cognitive inflexibility, as has usually been assumed in such cases, in this instance at least the tendency continually to revert to a fixed set of conversational topics is better seen as a repair strategy used to compensate for impaired memory. A subsequent programme of intervention based on this analysis achieved considerable success.

Chapter 2
Principles of clinical linguistics

MICHAEL PERKINS and SARA HOWARD

In this chapter we will consider what clinical linguistics is, who does it, why they do it and how they do it.

What is clinical linguistics?

Clinical linguistics gradually emerged as a coherent subdiscipline of applied linguistics, particularly in the UK, during the 1970s and 1980s. The fact that it emerged at all is in large measure the result of the pioneering work of David Crystal, and his influence is very apparent in the way it has developed since. Strange as it may seem now, linguistics was not always considered to have a major role to play in the study of communication disorders.* Such a role, as argued, for example, in Crystal (1972), first gained wide acceptance in the early 1970s and the study of linguistics soon became a compulsory part of training programmes for speech and language therapists throughout the UK. The publication of the textbook *Clinical Linguistics* (Crystal, 1981) was an important milestone. As Perkins (1982, p. 87) noted in a review: 'the term "clinical linguistics" . . . has now been accorded official status, as it were, in the title of Crystal's book and the internal coherence of the sub-discipline itself is recognized in the fact of a single volume being devoted to it'. Specific areas of clinical linguistics have subsequently been accorded similar status by being incorporated in the titles of books, e.g. clinical phonetics (Shriberg and Kent, 1982), clinical phonology (Grunwell, 1987) and clinical pragmatics (Smith and Leinonen, 1992). *Clinical Linguistics and Phonetics*, the only journal to date to focus exclusively on this area, first appeared in 1987, and the International Clinical Phonetics and Linguistics Association (ICPLA) was established in 1991.

---

*The same cannot be said for phonetics which has always played a central role. The issue of whether clinical phonetics should be regarded as a subdiscipline of clinical linguistics or as a separate discipline in its own right is discussed in Ball (1988a).

A definition of 'clinical linguistics' broad enough to be acceptable to many of its practitioners would be something like 'the application of theoretical and descriptive linguistics to speech and language pathology and remediation'. Some, however, prefer a somewhat narrower emphasis. Crystal has always seen clinical linguistics as having a practical goal, and has defined it as 'the application of the theories, methods and findings of linguistics (including phonetics) to the study of *those situations where language handicaps are diagnosed and treated*' (our italics) (Crystal, 1984, p. 30). In other words, clinical linguistics is seen primarily as an applied discipline which is only ultimately justified if it can be shown to contribute to remedial progress. Others, in contrast, adopt a broader view. Ball and Kent (1987), in their editorial in the first issue of the journal *Clinical Linguistics and Phonetics,* argue for a definition of clinical linguistics which also includes the contribution that the study of clinical data can make to linguistic theory. In practice, the analysis of language disability from a linguistic perspective often raises issues of a theoretical nature as is apparent throughout this book. There is, furthermore, also ample evidence in this volume that in addition to the theoretical implications raised by the careful study of clinical data, there is also much to be learned about the methodology of language study in general. Thus although we share Crystal's concern with the practical outcome of clinical linguistic analysis, we do not see this as being incompatible with theoretical and methodological concerns.

Theory and practice

We have just noted that we regard the relationship between linguistic theory and description on the one hand, and practical clinical concerns on the other, as being a mutually influential one. Any clinical linguistic analysis or therapy programme presupposes some theoretical basis no matter how impoverished and unacknowledged, and any insightful analysis of clinical data will invariably raise issues that have potential theoretical implications for language in general. Grodzinsky (1994), for example, notes that a linguistic theory that purports to provide an account of how grammatical knowledge is represented in the brain must also be capable of accounting for the patterns observed in aphasia, and this must ultimately be the case for levels of language other than grammar and for disorders other than aphasia.

Unfortunately for practitioners such as speech and language therapists, however, theoretical models of language inevitably involve a high degree of abstractness. Generative linguistic theory, for example, attempts to represent our underlying knowledge of language, but the extent to which such representations have psychological validity and relate to language use is far from clear. Cognitive–neuropsychological models as discussed in Chapters 5 and 10 have the advantage of representing psychological processes underlying language use rather than mere knowledge of language, but even here the relationship between the modelled representation and the purported process itself remains unclear.

Although theorists and practitioners may be interested in the same phenomena, their aims are quite different. Theorists are only ultimately interested in clinical linguistic behaviour to the extent that it may confirm or disconfirm their hypotheses about the nature of language. Speech and language therapists, on the other hand, are only interested in linguistic theory – at least in their remedial role – to the extent that it may be of some clinical use. Nevertheless, the theoretical needs of speech and language therapists are very real. Theory is needed to provide answers to questions such as:

- How is language organised and represented in the brain?
- How is language produced and understood?
- How does a given instance of abnormal language differ from a target norm?
- In cases of language loss, what has been lost, and therefore what needs to be replaced?
- In cases of developmental disorder, what forms and functions still need to be acquired, and in what order?

The fact that current linguistic theory can provide only partial and provisional answers does not render the questions any less crucial.

Two further problems with the application of linguistic theory to clinical practice are (1) which theory and model to choose from a range of possible contenders, and (2) the fact that theories are constantly changing. With regard to (1), we can do no more than keep abreast of theoretical developments in our area of interest – certainly no easy task – and bear them in mind in our encounters with communication disorders. All the case studies in this book are client-driven, which means that our starting point is the client's disability and that the choice of a particular theoretical framework is guided by the extent to which it promises to illuminate the case of the individual in question. This is admittedly not the approach that a linguistic theorist would take, but it nevertheless has an eminently respectable pedigree in the applied sciences as we shall see in the section below on methodology. The difficulties inherent in problem (2) are apparent in the large back catalogue of articles which made use of theoretical frameworks that are now superseded or outmoded. This does not mean that such articles no longer have anything of value to offer, but they are certainly less likely to be consulted now. Unfortunately, the shelf life and clinical usefulness of any clinical linguistic publication is likely to be adversely affected by the extent to which it nails its colours to a particular theoretical mast.

Given the difference in aims between linguistic theorists and clinicians and the abstract and constantly changing nature of linguistic theory, it is hardly surprising that many clinical linguistic tools are rather cautious in their theoretical claims. To take one example, the Language Assessment, Remediation and Screening Procedure or LARSP (Crystal et al., 1989), one of the most successful clinical tools for describing and assessing grammatical disability, is unashamedly theory neutral and in particular makes no claims to be generative. Salkie (1990, p. 95) offers the following rationale:

> There may be a more illuminating way to explain why Crystal et al make their choice to opt for a non-generative framework. If I have an electrical problem with my car, I go to a car mechanic rather than a theoretical physicist. The physicist's information would be more scientifically correct, but for my purposes the intuitive practical knowledge of the mechanic is more useful. Crystal's adoption of a tried and tested grammatical framework is rather like my choice of a car mechanic rather than a physicist: the grammar has, so to speak been tested in the workshop rather than in the more rigorous setting of a laboratory, but that is good enough for certain purposes.

To illustrate some of the problems with applying linguistic theory to clinical practice we will briefly consider developments in several areas of linguistic theory over recent years and see to what extent they have been able to meet the practical needs of clinicians.

Phonetics and phonology

The assessment and treatment of phonological disorder over the last 20 years have been firmly grounded on segmental linear models of phonology, with process-based frameworks such as Metaphon (Dean et al., 1990) and PACS (Phonological Assessment of Child Speech – Grunwell, 1985b) proving much more popular than the generative and distinctive feature-based clinical approaches explored in the 1970s (Pollack and Rees, 1972; Smith, 1973; McReynolds and Engmann, 1975; Compton and Hutton, 1978). However, the development of these segment-based approaches to clinical phonological analysis has taken place at a time when theoretical phonetics and phonology have been moving away from models of speech production and phonological organisation which are based on the linear arrangement of strings of speech segments, and the notion of segment in particular has come under attack. Dissatisfaction with the inability of linear phonological models to deal with notions such as stress, tone, assimilation, nasality, etc. which have significant and systematic relationships that spread across traditional segment boundaries, and the increasing recognition of the importance of the phonological unit of syllable which, again, linear-based approaches deal with unsatisfactorily, led to the development of a number of new phonological frameworks which can be broadly described as 'non-linear'. (For reviews of the area see Durand, 1990 and Goldsmith, 1990.) Non-linear phonologies attempt to capture segmental and prosodic relationships between phonological units such as word, syllable, feature, etc. by a hierarchy of autonomous but interlinked tiers of representation. These approaches have been applied fruitfully to the area of phonological development (Spencer, 1986; Bernhardt, 1992a) but are only just beginning to be applied in the field of speech disorders. The limited theoretical discussions of clinical applications of non-linear approaches have yet to be translated into the kinds of assessment and management materials which are at present readily available for process-based clinical phonology. Nevertheless the literature so far points to an exciting and influential new trend which may illuminate and explain aspects of speech disorder not made transparent by process phonology (Spencer, 1984; Bernhardt, 1992b; Bernhardt and Gilbert, 1992; Bernhardt and Stoel-Gammon, 1994). Another development in theoretical phonetics and phonology which is yet to have a significant impact on speech pathology is the growing interest in models that seek to unite the areas of phonetics and phonology to produce more unified accounts of the ways in which the two areas interrelate and can inform each other (Kingston and Beckman, 1990; Docherty and Ladd, 1992). This in turn may have implications for our notion of phonological disorder and its relation to disorders of articulation and phonetics. An influential paper by Hewlett (1985) addresses this area and challenges the traditional classification of speech problems into disorders of articulation and phonology.

Grammar

The most influential theory of grammar is currently Chomsky's 'principles and parameters' (also referred to as 'government and binding') theory of universal grammar (UG) (compare Chomsky, 1986). Using this model it has been argued, for example, that the fact that English-speaking individuals with Broca's aphasia often omit noun and verb inflections, whereas Italian-speaking individuals with Broca's aphasia never do so, can be explained by attributing to each group a different initial setting for the 'stem parameter' (Leonard and Frome Loeb, 1988). Grodzinsky (1990) and Tait and Shillcock (1993) characterise agrammatism in similar terms, and Frome Loeb and Leonard (1988) likewise describe specific language impairment in children as a failure to set parameters appropriately. It is difficult to see, however, what practical use clinicians are to make of descriptions that are based on constructs (e.g. 'parameter') which are highly abstract and of only putative psychological reality. Some are also sceptical about the value of using clinical data to test specific hypotheses within the theory of principles and parameters. As Salkie (1990, p. 93) remarks:

No one has yet found a child who has a problem specifically with the Binding Principle or some other identifiable principle of UG. Similarly, adults with brain damage seem to have more general problems rather than losing just one part of UG. We should not expect precise claims within generative grammar to be confirmed, then, by work in speech pathology.

Pragmatics

Pragmatics is playing an increasing role in language pathology and therapy and categories from a number of theoretical frameworks are in common use – for example, speech act theory (e.g. Lucas, 1980), Grice's maxims of conversation (e.g. Damico, 1985), relevance theory (e.g. Happé, 1993), discourse analysis (e.g. Joanette and Brownell, 1990) and conversation analysis (e.g. Lesser and Milroy, 1993). Partly as a result of the relative lack of rigour in pragmatic theory in general (compared, for example, with syntax and phonology) and partly because of the range of theoretical categories available, clinical pragmatic assessment frameworks tend to make rather eclectic and piecemeal use of theoretical pragmatic notions. A good example of this is Prutting and Kirchner's (1987) Pragmatic Protocol which contains a disparate checklist of pragmatic skills selected from a range of frameworks with little mention of their theoretical status or of the way each relates to the others. It is perhaps significant that conversation analysis, which is currently attracting a great deal of interest among speech and language therapists (see, for example, Chapters 7, 11 and 12), differs from the other frameworks mentioned above in being data-driven and in avoiding as far as possible the imposition of preconceived theoretical categories.

Psycholinguistics

One area of psycholinguistics that many speech and language therapists have recently found useful in clinical work – particularly in the assessment and treatment of aphasia – is cognitive neuropsychology (see, for example, Lesser and Milroy (1993) and Chapters 5 and 10 in this volume). As noted earlier, cognitive neuropsychology is of greater potential relevance to speech and language therapists than various other theories of language in that, instead of representing underlying knowledge, it models the psychological processes that underly language production and comprehension. In addition, it focuses on processing in *individuals* rather than attempting to identify properties of language that are universal, as in the case of chomskian generative grammar. Although some remain sceptical about the direct application of cognitive–neuropsychological models in remediation (e.g. Caramazza, 1989), Lesser and Milroy (1993) in a review of over 30 case studies conclude that such remediation can indeed be effective, a finding that is certainly borne out in Morris and Franklin's case study in Chapter 10. Although the extent to which the model directly represents actual processes is still not fully known, the fact that the match is good enough to affect remedial outcome is the main argument for its use by clinicians.

To focus, finally, on the application of clinical linguistics, summaries are provided by Crystal (1984) and Grunwell (1985b, 1993) of the aims of clinical linguistic analysis and of the contribution such analysis can make to clinical practice. Each argues that the careful and systematic description of the client's communicative behaviour provides a means of assessing that behaviour in relation to linguistic and, where appropriate, developmental norms. Equally, they both suggest, clinical linguistic analysis can reveal the systematic and communicative status of the client's linguistic patterns in their own right, regardless of considerations of target norms. They further suggest that the descriptive and analytical processes should aid differential diagnosis and the categorisation of the client's behaviours according to different identifiable types of linguistic deficit and disorder.

The information derived from the analysis should also facilitate the formulation of specific treatment aims and strategies and both authors make the important observation that careful analysis carried out at different points during the assessment and management process allows the identification and evaluation of changes in the client's communicative behaviour over time. This critical issue is taken up by Howard et al. (1995) who point out that, in accord with present and developing health care practices, the careful and accurate description of the client's behaviour and of changes over time may contribute to a number of procedures which are related to but not actually part of therapeutic management programmes themselves. An obvious example is the necessity for the kind of information linguistic analysis can provide in the growing areas of clinical audit and outcome and efficacy measures. Further relevant areas include assessment of clinical need and client prioritisation for limited therapeutic resources and the provision of information for medical advice (i.e. 'statementing') for children. Thus clinical linguistic analysis and description can be seen to have an important and developing role both inside and outside the treatment room.

Clinical linguistics as a collaborative enterprise

Just as there is no single unequivocal definition of the term 'clinical linguistics', so there is a similar lack of consensus about the term 'clinical linguist'. Indeed, it is probably a pointless exercise to attempt a rigid and prescriptive answer to the question 'What is a clinical linguist?' and is rather more fruitful to address the question 'Who *does* clinical linguistics?'. The answer to this will, of course, be that a range of people 'do' clinical linguistics in various forms and for various purposes. They share a common interest in the broad field of communication disorder, but will have different professional and academic backgrounds, different areas of specific interest, and different skills, knowledge and aims. Viewed as a continuum we could place academic linguists with a particular theoretical interest in aspects of communication disorder at one end of the continuum, and practising speech and language therapists for whom clinical linguistics forms a part of their broader professional knowledge base at the other end. In between these two groups there will clearly be many other individuals who possess a range of types and levels of academic and professional experience which our simplistic model fails to capture in detail. Probably most people would use the term 'clinical linguist', if at all, to refer to the academic linguist rather than the speech and language therapist, and for the purposes of this discussion we will follow that convention with the proviso that we see them as only one category of a range of individuals who 'do' clinical linguistics.

Historically, many academic clinical linguists have developed that role by virtue of academic involvement with a speech and language therapy training course, often teaching linguistics and its clinical applications to speech and language therapy students and carrying out research in the area. Thus they are linguists who, by their specialisation in the field of communication disorder, become 'clinical linguists'. Unlike speech and language therapists their background does not qualify them to treat clients with disorders of communication, but their background will typically provide them with a more extensive knowledge of linguistics than the speech and language therapist. They are generally interested in the ways in which aspects of communication disorders can be described and/or explained using linguistic frameworks and concepts and in how communication disorders can inform the study of language in general. Speech and language therapists, on the other hand, are professionally qualified to provide appropriate management for clients with communication disorders, and their linguistic knowledge and expertise forms only a part of the broad interdisciplinary content of their training. Typically they will see clinical linguistics as part of the 'tool-kit' which helps them fulfil their primary aim which is the effective assessment, description and management of a wide range of multifaceted disorders.

Thus we see two groups of individuals with overlapping interests and some overlap of knowledge and skills, but who can generally be said to possess complementary and mutually beneficial abilities. This is further reflected in the ways in which members of each group develop further specialisation in the area of communication disorder. If clinical linguists specialise, it will typically be in a particular area of linguistics (e.g. clinical pragmatics, clinical phonetics) whereas speech and language therapists specialise in the management of a particular client group (e.g. cleft lip and palate, hearing impairment, closed head injury) or a particular disorder (developmental speech disorders, dysfluency, acquired dysarthria).

Having described the two broad categories of individuals involved in the practice of clinical linguistics, let us move on to consider the relationship between their respective disciplines, i.e. clinical linguistics and speech and language therapy. An obvious but important observation is that both fields are of relatively recent origin in comparison, for example, with medicine. Clinical linguistics has emerged as an identifiable subdiscipline of linguistics only over the last 20 years as the importance of its contribution to speech and language therapy has been increasingly recognised. However, speech and language therapy itself is also a comparative newcomer in the field of health care and education. It has only been recognised as a professional body in the United Kingdom for 50 years, having developed gradually as a discipline over the last century or so. In comparison with the medical profession they are both very young. In 1982 Crystal suggested that the present emergent state of research in speech and language therapy was not unlike that of pathological medicine nearly a century ago. The intervening years have seen a huge amount of research undertaken in speech and language therapy and related areas, but in comparison with the established and ongoing body of research in medicine the analogy still holds true.

Both clinical linguistics and speech and language therapy continue to develop rapidly in a variety of ways and this is reflected in an expansion of the therapists' clinical remit, with ensuing implications for the management of time and resources. Besides ongoing developments in theory and practice in the better established areas such as phonology and grammar, the developments we have discussed above in areas such as pragmatics and conversation analysis, together with the rapid expansions in the theory and applications of cognitive neuropsychology, all provide the speech and language therapist with valuable new frameworks for clinical assessment and analysis, some of which have direct application to clients whose difficulties may traditionally have fallen outside the accepted remit of the therapist. A further development with significant implications for time and resources is the growing acknowledgement of the importance of viewing each client as a potentially unique case and thus the necessity of making full and detailed descriptions of individual patterns of skills and deficits, rather than falling back on broad diagnostic categories which might well prove superficial and misleading. Thus, more than ever before, the speech and language therapist is faced with the tension between the demands and opportunities presented by theoretical developments and the practical constraints of finite time and resources in the clinical context.

This expansion comes at a time of radical re-evaluation and reorganisation of models of health care provision and of educational practice, so it is an appropriate time to take stock and to reassess the roles and aims of the closely linked areas of clinical linguistics and speech and language therapy. For practitioners working in the field of communication disorder, we suggest that the ability to describe and analyse communicative behaviour accurately and to identify significant features and patterns is a fundamental necessity which is the starting point of all that follows in the clinical process: management, re-evaluation, outcome and measurements of efficacy. In a full appraisal of the client, the therapist will, of course, draw on knowledge from a wide range of disciplines, but, in making an assessment of the client's communicative behaviour, clinical linguistics will be the central focus.

Given the evident complexities of disorders of communication and the time-consuming and demanding nature of clinical linguistic analysis, and given the practical constraints within which the speech and language therapist must work, how can we best ensure that the requisite standard of analysis is observed? There is an obvious dilemma here: the time necessary to carry out appropriate assessment and analysis is growing in relation to theoretical developments in the field but the number of clients being referred to the speech and language therapy service is also growing and at present there is no commensurate growth in resources. We feel very strongly – and this position is amply supported by the case studies in this book – that the time taken to carry out assessment and analysis in the initial stages of client care and also as an ongoing feature of management is a fundamental necessity which should actually save time in the longer term by leading to more finely targeted and effective management. As Crystal (1984) observes:

A day devoted to linguistic analysis early on in the case may seem trivial by comparison with the overall amount of time devoted to a patient in subsequent months.

The College of Speech and Language Therapists in the UK appear to support this position in their discussion of the necessity of careful prioritisation of provision of care within the wider context of the rights of every individual to have equal access to the speech and language therapy service:

This will, at times, mean that some clients do not receive a service. The College does not believe that the alternative strategy; i.e. allocating a scarce resource across a greater number of clients, thereby diluting the service, resulting in clinical inefficiency, poor outcomes and low staff morale, to be an appropriate one.

The College of Speech and Language Therapists (1991, p. 253)

At present the student speech and language therapist receives a broad-based interdisciplinary training covering, among other things, speech and language pathology, the biomedical sciences, psychology, linguistics, education and clinical practice. This provides the necessary basis for working in this complex field, but at the same time the limitations of the training are also recognised. The practising therapist is not expected to be capable of doing everything to a specialised level. In spite of following courses in, for example, neurology and audiology, the therapist who requires detailed information about a client in either of these areas can refer the client on for specialist advice and assessment according to a well-established mechanism. Indeed, within the field of communication disorders, the therapist may seek specialist advice in a number of ways. As well as the kind of referral described above, advice about particular client groups and disorders is available from specialist speech therapists and specialist clinical advisers. As well as seeking advice to facilitate management the therapists may feel it appropriate in certain cases to refer the client for treatment to a specialist therapist who can offer a particularly high level of skill and knowledge in the appropriate area.

However, of all the aspects of client assessment and management, it is striking that such a fundamentally important and central discipline as clinical linguistics offers no formal route for the therapist to seek further advice or help. There are perhaps two particularly significant reasons for this. One is the relatively recent incorporation of linguistics into the training and practice of speech and language therapy. The other relates to its central role in the work of a therapist. It seems that at some tacit level there is the assumption that the speech and language therapist should be able to do all the necessary clinical linguistic analysis and assessment incorporating an appropriate level of theoretical knowledge and practical detail across all client groups and disorders and across all areas of linguistics. We have noted, however, that clinical linguists themselves would generally not claim to have specialist knowledge in all areas of clinical linguistics and that it is accepted that therapists need a reservoir of knowledge spanning a large number of disciplines and can only be expected to develop specialist knowledge of particular areas of communication disorder. Thus it would seem an unreasonable and, in fact, impossible demand to place on an individual therapist to possess specialist knowledge in all areas of clinical linguistics. And yet in any clinical caseload, generalist or specialist, there will be many clients for whom specialist clinical linguistic analysis is essential to successful management. What we are identifying here is a growing need for some formalised and accepted avenue for the speech and language therapist to seek specialist clinical linguistic advice in much the same way as specialist advice is available for other aspects of communication disorders.

In 1984 Crystal wrote:

In a sense, the present-day speech therapists and remedial language teachers are in the position of these old doctors, having to do their own pathological analysis of speech samples. I would like to think there will come a day when much of the mechanical load will be taken off 'I''s back, by the provision of automatic analysis techniques – techniques of analysis using microprocessors, techniques of remediation using interactive instrumentation.

Although there have been encouraging signs of development in these areas over the last decade, even the universal availability of clinical instrumentation (a position that is in practical terms a long way off) will not fulfil the therapist's need for specialist clinical linguistic advice across a broad spectrum of areas.

How this advice might best be provided is a contentious subject. Clearly in some way or other it would cost both time and money, but an initial outlay should be recouped in the time and money saved by improvements in clinical practice. Should such a service be located within the existing frameworks of the speech and language therapy service or of academic departments involved in training and research in communication disorders? Either way, it could clearly not be achieved by adding to any existing individual's workload, but would entail the creation of extra posts within the field and extra investment in instrumentation. Should we then be advocating the setting up of a whole new service comparable to the kinds of pathology departments devoted to the analysis of blood, tissue, etc., which we take for granted in other areas of the health service? How should such a service operate in relation to the multidisciplinary team in which speech and language therapists work?

These are not idle questions. As the profession of speech and language therapy continues to develop and expand these issues are closely tied to critical issues such as efficacy and clinical audit, models of service delivery, the ongoing debate about specialists and generalists, the role and remit of the profession and, not least, the benefits that speech and language therapy can provide to the population of individuals with disorders of communication.

In discussing similar issues more than a decade ago, Crystal (1984, pp. 118 *et seq.*) remarked on the lack of individuals with 'the right blend of linguistic and clinical experience' and suggested that collaboration was 'the only real solution'. We have argued here that it is virtually impossible for any individual to command sufficient linguistic and clinical expertise to deal satisfactorily with the whole range of communication disorders. In the absence of the services we have suggested above, it remains the case that the best way of furthering our knowledge and providing appropriate management for clients is, as Crystal suggested, through the collaboration of linguists and therapists, each bringing complementary skills and knowledge to the process of assessment and analysis.

All of the case studies in this book are based on such a combination of contributions from the areas of speech and language therapy and clinical linguistics. Most are the result of collaboration between individuals with different academic and professional backgrounds. Single authors are either linguists with a dual qualification in speech and language therapy or speech and language therapists with specialist knowledge of an area of linguistics. The case studies are also based on a commitment to spend time at the outset on detailed assessment and analysis. Each of them demonstrates the value of this approach in terms of the efficacy of the subsequent management. Our maxim is 'spending time saves time' which, we feel, ought to be popular with clinicians and managers alike.

Methodology

In this book we adopt a single case methodology where each case study is both client-driven and data-driven. We will consider each of these points in turn.

As a research methodology, the single case study approach has become popular in recent years as a reaction against large group studies which are more interested in what subjects have in common than in how they differ. Interest in language universals, a legacy from the chomskian revolution in the 1960s, has been increasingly supplemented particularly in studies of child language acquisition (e.g. Bates et al., 1988, 1995) and aphasia (e.g. Ellis and Young, 1988) by an awareness of individual differences. In addition to their role in pure research, single case studies of aphasia using a cognitive neuropsychological approach have proved to be effective in diagnosis, assessment and remediation (e.g. Pring, 1986; Howard and Hatfield, 1987; Morris and Franklin in Chapter 10). The single case approach makes the assumption that the allocation of a patient to a syndrome or some other general diagnostic category is only a first step, and that to address the patient's specific remedial needs it is necessary to obtain a clear picture of their unique individual characteristics. The growing awareness of the vast range of individual differences in both the normal and language-impaired population has led many to conclude that the very notion of syndrome itself is perhaps premature (e.g. Caramazza, 1985). As Crystal (1984, pp. 76 *et seq.*) observes:

> the individual differences stand out, at the expense of the common features. We can see the trees, but not the wood. Indeed, at present we are only at the stage of realizing that there is a wood. And it will be years before the main pathways are traced through it.

Any single case study that aims to affect remedial outcome must by definition be client-driven. We have already noted our agreement with Crystal that the ultimate justification for clinical linguistic analysis is the contribution it can make to the practical needs of the communication impaired, and indeed our own experience amply confirms that for the academic linguist the necessity of giving client needs priority over the study of a linguistic phenomenon for its own intrinsic interest can be not only rewarding but also intellectually stimulating with spin-offs for theory and description in general.

Our third requirement for the case studies in this book – namely, that they be data-driven – might be regarded by some as less essential and therefore merits rather more discussion.

One of the results of Chomsky's revolution in the late 1950s and the 1960s was to shift the focus of mainstream linguistics away from the analysis of raw linguistic data and towards the consideration of the underlying knowledge that made such data possible. Linguists who collected and analysed language corpora were dismissed as mere taxonomists whose interest was in linguistic performance rather than competence. Native speakers' intuitions about the grammaticality of language structure came to be seen as more important than consideration of the utterances that people actually produced. Although this change in emphasis made it possible to appreciate better the role and nature of genetic linguistic endowment, it dealt a serious blow to what was referred to as 'corpus linguistics'. It took another revolution in the 1980s and 1990s – this time a technological one which enabled the processing of massive corpora of language by computer – to restore the fortunes of linguistic data analysis by identifying numerous previously unknown features of language that could not have been discovered any other way (see, for example, Sinclair, 1991).

In addition to the incidental fact that it is once again respectable from a theoretical perspective to study real language data, there are two further compelling reasons why this is even more essential in the case of disordered language*. First, one of Chomsky's indirect contributions to speech and language therapy is the generally accepted assumption that a disordered language system is still a rule-governed one, and one of the aims of the therapist is to establish what these rules are, i.e. what forms are licensed or generated by the patient's impaired linguistic system. Unlike in the study of normal language, one is usually unable to rely on the patient's intuitions to do this, and there are no clearly established linguistic norms for specific types of language disorder as there are for normal language. In the study of disordered language, therefore, one has no choice but to analyse the client's linguistic performance. Clinical linguistic descriptions can only be observation-based, as opposed to intuition-based, in the first instance. This does not mean that one should not use linguistic data to generate and

---

*These two points are taken from a more extensive argument for the study of corpora of disordered language made in Perkins (1995).

test hypotheses about a disordered language system – merely that contrary to what Chomsky has for so long maintained for normal language, one cannot do without an initial sample of data.

The second reason is the proven benefits from a long tradition of studying language data from another population whose linguistic intuitions are also notoriously hard to tap – namely, children. It has long been generally accepted that the best way to study children's language is through the collection of either spontaneous or elicited spoken discourse. Diary studies of normal child language date back well over a century (e.g. Darwin, 1877) and the practice was further developed in the 1960s by Brown using transcriptions of tape-recorded data (Brown, 1973). This general approach strongly influenced the development by Crystal and colleagues (see Crystal, 1992) of the linguistic 'profiling' of both children and adults with impaired speech and language. Profiles of a patient's grammatical system (LARSP), semantics (Profile In Semantics – PRISM), segmental phonology (Profile in Phonology – PROPH) and prosody (Prosody Profile – PROP) are obtained by collecting, transcribing and analysing a sample of spontaneous speech.

In spite of this preliminary focus on language data, the data-driven case study methodology need not be divorced from theoretical rigour and good scientific practice. The use of primary linguistic data to generate hypotheses which are subsequently tested through reanalysis of the same or further data samples is widely accepted both as a research methodology (see Bloom, 1991) and as an effective basis for remediation (see Crystal, 1984, pp. 104 *et seq.*). Bloom (1991, pp. 45 *et seq.*) describes one instance of the hypothesis-testing procedure:

> . . . a tentative description was made of a portion of the recorded data, and then successively larger and larger portions of the data were examined in order to test the consistency and regularity of the original description. Repeated passes through the recorded data, then, consisted of successive hypothesis testings: As questions were generated, the data were examined in order to answer the questions; the questions were revised; the data re-examined in order to answer the revised questions; and so on.

The advantages of such an approach are that it avoids to a large extent the imposition of preconceived descriptive categories on the data, and can inform therapy by providing testable predictions about a client's linguistic performance.

A further related methodological stance which is evident in many of the case studies in this book is that of taking a holistic and multilevel view of the client's disorder. It has become increasingly apparent since the publication of a seminal paper by Crystal (1987c) that many actual instances of disordered communicative behaviour may result not from a specific impairment of, say, the syntactic or phonological system but from the interplay of a whole range of subsystems. So, for example, a child with limited syntactic ability may also exhibit poor phonological performance when attempting to produce utterances of a given degree of syntactic complexity, as a result of processing overload. Crystal (1987c, p. 20) refers to this notion as 'bucket theory' where language processing capacity is likened to a bucket in which 'an extra "drop" of phonology (syntax, semantics, etc.) may cause the overflow of a "drop" of syntax (semantics, phonology, etc.)'. Others, particularly in the area of fluency disorders, explain the same phenomenon in terms of a 'demands-capacities' model whereby fluency breakdown is attributed to external and/or internal demands which exceed the speaker's cognitive, linguistic, motoric and/or emotional capacities (Starkweather and Gottwald, 1990; Karniol, 1992). Whatever term is used to describe it, the notion is certainly an extremely useful one and is much in evidence throughout this book.

Finally, we would like to comment on the fact that the case studies in this book make very little use of formal or standardised tests and assessments. This is not to disparage their worth or their role in the assessment process, but it is in recognition of their inherent limitations. Formal tests and assessments are often very successful in identifying the specific skills and deficits which they are designed to test. But they do no more than that. Any individual test can only provide limited information about a narrow range of linguistic abilities and an over-reliance on test scores and results for the purposes of diagnosis and management may prove inadequate or even downright misleading. Formal speech and language tests and assessments have a valuable contribution to make in the initial stages of the investigative process. They can be used as a starting point to suggest directions for further exploration and hypothesis formation (Howard et al., 1995). However, as a result of the dual constraints of time and resources, speech and language therapists may sometimes feel compelled to rely too heavily on the results of formal assessments, without the necessary further investigation. At times this may be to the detriment of effective therapy. We would point to the studies in this book as evidence for using a careful (albeit time-consuming) data-driven approach which is responsive to the individual differences and particular needs of each client and which respects the complexity of communication disorders. We believe that the closer one looks at data and the more detailed the analysis, the less adequate off-the-shelf procedures appear for providing an accurate picture of a client's individual skills and deficits. Quite obviously, compromises between what is theoretically advisable and what is clinically practical have to be made, but at a time when there are growing pressures on increasingly stretched resources, we must be careful that the compromise is not at the expense of effective assessment and consequent effective management.

Transcription

We have not tried to impose a single consistent transcription format for the contributions to this book for three reasons. First, there is considerable variation in the type of linguistic information that each case study wishes to highlight, ranging from fine phonetic distinctions which can only be captured through the use of acoustic instrumentation to broad pragmatic functions which may apply to whole utterances or even a series of utterances. Second, a number of theoretical and descriptive frameworks are used many of which include their own idiosyncratic conventions. Third, there is as yet no universally agreed set of principles and conventions for transcribing spoken language. Some progress has been made recently in outlining a comprehensive set of such principles (e.g. Edwards, 1993) and a great deal of care and consultation has gone into the impressively comprehensive Text Encoding Initiative Guidelines (Sperberg-McQueen and Burnard, 1994) which attempt to provide a standardised transcription and coding system for electronically readable spoken and written language, but whether these will be influential, acceptable and accessible enough to provide a new universal standard remains to be seen.

As the case studies in this book make use of a variety of transcriptional levels and techniques, and particularly because a number of them employ detailed phonetic transcription and discuss its advantages and limitations in relation to individual cases, we discuss the subject of transcription in some detail here to obviate the necessity for repetition of similar ground in a number of chapters.

Our general principle in these case studies is to start by making a close observation and detailed transcription of the client's communicative behaviour and not to begrudge the time and effort this entails. The very good reason for this is that the resulting transcription is the attempt to capture the essential and significant aspects of the client's communicative behaviour. The word 'significant' is of course important here, because until further analysis is carried out we may not be able to tell which aspects of the behaviour are actually clinically and communicatively significant. Thus, in reality, our initial observations and transcriptions will attempt to capture the behaviour in as much detail as possible in the hope that in doing so we will have captured that which is relevant and important. Thus we share the sentiments of Kelly and Local (1989, p. 26) who say of detailed phonetic transcription for phonological purposes:

> Our view is that it is not possible to have too much phonetic detail. Part of the reason for this claim is our belief that at the beginning of work on language material we can't, in any interesting sense, know beforehand what is going to be important.

Quite obviously, to make this commitment is to commit a great deal of time to this initial stage of investigation. Crystal (1984) observes that it is transcription that will take the largest share of time in a linguistic assessment. We have already argued the case for spending time and effort on linguistic assessment and analysis and our earlier observations apply equally to the act of transcription. Such time is well spent because the validity of all subsequent analyses and the success of treatment programmes based on the conclusions drawn from the analyses will be directly linked to how accurately the transcription reflects the client's actual behaviour.

A dilemma emerges at this point between our knowledge that in the first instance we can't know what is going to be relevant and the certainty that the more ambitious our transcription is in terms of range and detail the more time-consuming it is going to be, even for relatively small amounts of data. Added to this is the fact that linguists generally advise collecting as much data as possible in as wide a variety of contexts and elicitation conditions as possible (Crystal, 1984; Müller, 1985). Different authors suggest, for example, that a phonological analysis requires an absolute minimum of between 100 and 250 single words plus a sample of connected speech (Grunwell, 1985b; Lambert, 1989; Crystal, 1992). And this is good advice, because we know that analyses based on small amounts of data may well prove to be inadequate reflections of the client's true abilities and limitations and may also fail to identify significant variability within the sample. To use our time as economically and yet effectively as possible we need at the outset to make some provisional decisions about the aims and scope of our transcription and the kinds and levels of detail we are going to attempt to capture. These will vary with each client, depending on the severity of the disorder, on the level of intelligibility, on any provisional diagnosis and on the various kinds of background information already available. Thus, for example, if we are interested in analysing conversational ability our transcription may well be orthographic rather than phonetic for the most part, but with prosodic variables such as pitch and stress levels, tempo, duration and location of pauses and intonational contours all marked, and attention also paid to non-verbal phenomena such as gesture, posture and gaze, and contextual and ethnographic information (Edwards, 1991, 1993). Some transcriptions made for the purpose of grammatical analysis will need some level of phonetic transcription, for example, to distinguish utterances that are grammatically, though not prosodically, ambiguous. Others, for example, Siren and Wilcox's study in 1990 of the grammatical abilities of a 3-year-old child with hearing impairment, claim that orthographic transcription is sufficient. Transcriptions for the purposes of conversation analysis will need to capture phenomena such as speaker overlap, complete versus incomplete speaker turns, interruptions, hesitations, etc. For the investigation of most speech disorders, on the other hand, the focus of attention will be on the close impressionistic phonetic transcription of the utterances produced by the client with less attention usually paid to how these utterances fit into a larger framework of interaction.

Should we decide to carry out a close phonetic transcription, there are still further decisions which need to be made. How much and what kind of detail are we interested in? Are we going to concentrate on 'segmental' aspects of speech production or is our transcription going to attempt to capture prosodic information such as speech rate and rhythm, stress patterns, pitch changes, pauses, etc.? What about voice quality? And how far should we attempt to note the situational and linguistic contextual variables present in the sample?

Crystal (1981, p. 16) observes:

> One measure of the success of a transcription is the extent to which it supplants the tape from which it derives: if we have made a transcription at the right level *for our purposes* [our emphasis] it should be unnecessary to have to refer back to the tape in carrying out our analyses later.

Already then, it looks as though we are beginning to compromise on the levels of transcriptional detail for some clients, but we would strongly argue the necessity in these cases of being constantly open to the need to revise our methods according to our ongoing observations.

The last 15 years have seen a number of significant developments in the area of the transcription of disordered speech, arising out of a recognition by phoneticians and speech and language therapists alike that the transcription conventions provided by the International Phonetic Alphabet (IPA) (1993) were inadequate for capturing many aspects of abnormal speech production. This is not, of course, surprising, nor is it a criticism of the IPA which was designed to transcribe normal adult speech across the languages of the world and not to transcribe the speech production of speakers whose speech reflects a wide range of unusual and abnormal exploitations of the possibilities offered by the human vocal organs.

There have been a number of attempts at recognising and dealing with those aspects of disordered speech not catered for by judicious use of the IPA. In the USA, Bush et al. (1973) (cited in Ingram, 1976), for example, produced quite an extensive range of diacritics aimed at transcribing the speech of young children, including a detailed section devoted to the notoriously tricky area of immature and/or aberrant fricative production, and Shriberg and Kent (1982) also give detailed suggestions for the transcription of atypical speech. Ohde and Sharf (1992, p. 333) propose a symbol system for disordered speech based on the American transcription tradition, reflecting:

> . . . an effort on the part of American scholars to develop a practical system by avoiding the use of special characters, supplementing basic symbols with

diacritics rather than new characters, and seeking to provide characters for American English rather than for universal coverage.

In the UK, a working party of linguistics and speech pathology lecturers was set up in 1977 to investigate the problems experienced by academics and practising speech and language therapists alike in the transcription of disordered speech and to offer some solutions. This resulted in the publication in 1983 of a major selection of additional symbols known as RAPS (recommended additional phonetic symbols) or PRDS (the phonetic representation of disordered speech). At the 1989 IPA Congress at Kiel, the importance of the transcription of disordered speech was further recognised by the establishment of the Working Party for Pathological Speech and Voice. Their work resulted in the development of the symbol set known as ExtIPA (extensions to the IPA) (Duckworth et al., 1990) and since then further suggestions and revisions have taken place (Bernhardt and Ball, 1993; Ball et al., 1994) all aimed at facilitating the transcription of both segmental and non-segmental aspects of disordered speech production.

Even with the aid of these recent developments, capturing a detailed and accurate record of the client's speech and language is still a daunting task which is fraught with well-documented pitfalls at every step. As Shriberg et al. (1987, p. 171) observe:

> Narrow phonetic transcription is a data reduction activity requiring technical knowledge, auditory perceptual skills, and a positive attitude.

A problem at the outset for the transcriber of disordered speech is that of how best to collect a data sample. Should transcription be carries out live *in situ* or should the transcriber make use of audio or video recordings? There seems to be general agreement that a combination of live transcription and subsequent transcription or checking of the same data from a recording of some sort is the most useful way to proceed. Even then, Grunwell (1985b), among others, cautions that reference to the recorded data should take place as soon as possible after the recording session and preferably within the following 24 hours. The advantages of the live situation in terms of the superior quality of both auditory and visual information is, of course, to be weighed against the transience of the speech events. Amorosa et al. (1985) argue that live transcription unsupplemented by audio or video recordings cannot provide a reliable basis for even the most superficial of phonological analyses of developmental speech disorders. Audio and video recordings, on the other hand, allow the transcriber the opportunity to listen to the data as often as is felt necessary to achieve a satisfactory transcription. Both types of recording, however, also have their drawbacks. In general, video recordings cannot deliver an appropriate level of sound quality, although of course they can capture important visual information about speech production. Conversely,

audio recordings give a much better quality of sound signal, but the listener is unable to exploit visual aspects of the speaker's utterances.
Even with the generally superior sound quality which audio recordings
provide over video recordings, some studies suggest that this sound
quality is not always adequate and that transcriptions made from audio
recordings are sometimes less accurate than 'live' transcriptions
(Stephens and Daniloff, 1977; Daniloff et al., 1980), although of course
recording quality has improved since these studies took place and continues to improve, with, for example, the more widespread availability
of DAT recorders. As there is no clear evidence in favour of any one of
these different transcription procedures (Shriberg and Kent, 1982), as
we have noted, a combination of live and recorded data sampling is
usually recommended.

Whatever the type and level of transcription and for whatever purpose it has been made, its reliability and validity are crucial to further
analysis and interpretation. This is an issue which has attracted much
debate over recent years. Many research studies, for example, report a
reassuringly high level of inter-transcriber agreement, but Pye et al.
(1988) and Shriberg and Lof (1991) point out that this may be an over-
simplification stemming from the fact that many studies claiming high
inter-transcriber agreement only use two transcribers. Where the transcriptions from three transcribers are compared reported agreement
falls to between 26% and 78%. Theoretically, of course, a greater number of transcribers should increase the number of inter-transcriber dis-
agreements, but should also increase the ultimate accuracy of the
record. Many of the case studies in this book have been able to exploit
the skills of more than one transcriber. Practically, in the clinical situation, however, the luxury of more than a single pair of eyes and ears is
a rarity.

Pye et al. (1988) put forward a number of factors which are related
to transcriber agreement and judgements of reliability in the transcription of immature or abnormal speech. Both the type and severity of the
speech disorder and the resultant levels of unintelligibility are important. The greater the severity of the disorder and the higher the level of
unintelligibility, the greater the disagreement between transcribers. The
type of speech sample is also significant: it is easier to reach agreement
on the transcription of single words than on the transcription of spontaneous speech. These factors appear to be related to the observation
of Ollers and Eilers (1975) that the perceived meaning of an utterance
will affect its transcription. This may be the case even to the extent, as
they note (1975, p. 301), that:

> The listener may perceive elements which are *not* present in the acoustic
> signal, and/or he may fail to perceive elements which *are* present.

This observation has clear implications for the transcription of the kinds of data from speakers with disordered speech production, which is often elicited from picture material precisely because this provides the transcriber with a known target utterance. The frequency of the occurrence of particular segments in the speech sample also has an effect on transcriber agreement, as does the level of phonetic detail aimed at in the transcription. Shriberg et al. (1984) and Pye et al. (1988) also note that, as well as the number of transcribers in a group transcription session affecting the overall agreement and reliability, the perceived relative status of individual transcribers with regard to academic background, training, experience, etc. as well as personality differences, can result in a tendency to defer to particular transcribers.

Nevertheless, the use of consensus or composite transcription techniques, whereby a number of transcribers attempt to reach agreement in the production of a 'final version' (either informally or using particular explicit procedures) is generally held to be a valuable means of helping to ensure the accuracy of the data (Shriberg et al., 1984, 1987; Amorosa et al., 1985; see also Pye et al., 1988).

As we have noted, although most of the case studies in this book have benefited from using a range of methods of data collection and transcriptions based on the auditory and visual perceptions of more than one individual, it is generally the case that considerations of time and resources prevent the involvement of more than one speech and language therapist in the collection and transcription of clinical data. If there are so many reservations about the reliability of transcribed data and if consensus transcription is generally put forward as a partial solution to the problems, is it worth the individual speech and language therapist expending large amounts of time and effort in making careful transcriptions of clinical data? The answer here must be strongly in the affirmative. A number of authors attest to the worth of transcription for a range of communication disorders (Crystal, 1984; Grunwell, 1985b; Kelly and Local, 1989; Shriberg and Lof, 1991). Indeed, the very act of transcription, regardless of how accurately one transcribes, makes the transcriber pay very close attention to the speech and language data, thus usually prompting a number of testable hypotheses about the client's abnormal communicative behaviour.

Given the reservations that exist about the reliability of transcription, particularly at the narrow phonetic level, it is sometimes useful to make use of instrumental techniques as a means of further analysis. Information gained in this way may then be compared with transcribed data. Popular techniques include spectrography (to gather acoustic information about the speech signal), nasometry (useful for investigating oral–nasal resonance and airflow ratios) and electropalatography (which captures information about lingual–palatal activity). For full reviews of the clinical applications of these and other techniques, see Code and Ball (1984) and Baken (1987).

Instrumental analysis can provide information about articulatory activity which is not auditorily perceptible and can help to characterise phenomena that are perceptible to some extent but that are particularly difficult to transcribe. The latter might include precise statements about voicing and voice-onset time, nasalisation and oral–nasal resonance, voice quality and durational aspects of speech production. Instrumental analysis may reveal that there is a clear mismatch between auditory perceptions and acoustic and articulatory events or that apparently perceptually equivalent pieces of speech have different acoustic and articulatory bases. Indeed the mismatch between what is revealed by perceptual analysis and by instrumental analysis reflects the distinction drawn by Hewlett (1985) between speaker-oriented and listener- or data-oriented perspectives on disordered speech. He argues that in some cases a speaker may be intending to preserve phonological contrasts and, significantly, may be signalling them by consistent articulatory strategies and yet the listener may still fail to perceive them. The listener who is making a close phonetic transcription of disordered speech is arguably a listener *par excellence* in terms of a listener-oriented perspective on the data and yet there may still be aspects of the data that elude transcription. Instrumental analysis, on the other hand, can sometimes get nearer to revealing the speakers' intentions by revealing auditorily imperceptible aspects of the data and thus more closely reflects a speaker-oriented perspective. Both perspectives are, of course, useful in considering the communicative effects of disorders of speech.

Thus, for example, Kent and Rosenbek (1983) used spectrographic techniques to identify and measure significant features of dyspraxic speech production including voice-onset time and segment and utterance durations which would have been difficult, if not impossible, to capture using transcription alone. Macken and Barton (1980) and Maxwell and Weismer (1982) also measured voice-onset times and were able to demonstrate that children were producing consistent but auditorily imperceptible differences between voiced and voiceless targets. Hambly and Farmer (1982) measured vowel durations to show that children who were deleting final consonants were nevertheless using vowel length differences to maintain a consistent distinction between words with target voiced and voiceless consonants. Using electropalatography, Hardcastle et al. (1985), Hardcastle and Edwards (1992) and Gibbon et al. (1993) all provide data on lingual–palatal contact patterns which illustrate both auditorily imperceptible articulations and mismatches between auditory impressions and articulatory events. Findings like these have important implications for clinical diagnosis and management of disorders of speech.

Future directions for clinical linguistics

One of the objectives of this book of single case studies is to move us one small step further towards the distant goal of establishing a comprehensive typology of language disorders based on their linguistic characteristics. This goal may appear to sit uneasily with an approach that deliberately focuses on the language disorders of individuals rather than the language-disordered population as a whole. The reason for this is that, until enough individual cases of language disability have been described and analysed in systematic linguistic detail, we will not have enough information to make generalisations and establish diagnostic groups and subgroups. But how many more case studies will need to be carried out? How long will it take? Is there any way of speeding up the process? We will end this chapter by offering a tentative proposal that addresses these questions*.

Every day a large number of speech and language therapists as a matter of routine record and transcribe their clients' language as part of the ongoing assessment and remediation process. They are highly skilled transcribers, as is ensured by the rigorous training they receive in applied linguistics and phonetics. The vast majority of transcripts go no further than the client's case notes and will be seen by no more than a handful of people at most. Although these transcripts play an important role in the treatment of individual patients, it is frustrating to consider the many further uses to which they could be put if only it were possible to incorporate them in an easily accessible machine-readable database.

There is one such database – the Child Language Data Exchange System (CHILDES) which was established in 1984 as a child language archive for use by the academic research community (see MacWhinney, 1991) – but to date it only contains two corpora of aphasic language and six corpora of disordered child language, none of which is particularly large. Apart from this there are a few machine-readable corpora of disordered language to which access is rather more restricted (e.g. Menn and Obler, 1990; Fletcher and Garman, 1994; Perkins and Varley, 1995; the SALT Reference Database in Miller and Chapman, 1982–1993) but that appears to be it. No doubt there is also a vast amount of transcribed and coded disordered language data which exists either as hard copy or on computer files in a range of formats throughout the world to which access is virtually impossible for technical, copyright or ethical reasons.

To create a database of disordered language a standardised transcription and coding format would be essential. The current push towards standardisation and wider availability in the electronic media –

*The following proposal was first outlined in Perkins (1995).

as exemplified in the Text Encoding Initiative (TEI) guidelines referred to above – suggests a possible way forward. If TEI-conformant software could be developed which was specifically geared towards the needs of speech and language therapists, it should ultimately be possible to create a cumulative online read/write database of disordered language corpora. The software needs of speech and language therapists are the following:

1. It should make it possible to transcribe in a straightforward way the phonetic, phonological, grammatical, semantic, pragmatic and discourse features found in disordered language systems.
2. It should incorporate a classification system to enable the subcategorisation of each transcript according to both linguistic and medical criteria.
3. It should be user-friendly and relatively easy to learn.
4. Once learned, it should take no longer to use than transcription and coding by hand.
5. It should produce hard copy appropriate for inclusion in a patient's case notes.

Linguistic classification of language disorders could be cross-referenced and made compatible with the standardised classification system currently being developed by the British medical establishment (the 'Read' codes).

If it did prove possible to create a database along these lines, what use would it be to clinicians? Recent work on normal language corpora by computational linguists has shown that if the corpus is sufficiently large and representative it is possible to identify structural patterns and regularities which are not otherwise apparent. If it were possible to categorise disordered language varieties according to such criteria, this could have important diagnostic implications. To take a fairly straightforward example, the correlation between word and structure frequencies and register type is well established in normal corpus variety studies (see Svartvik, 1992). As yet, we know very little about such phenomena in impaired language, but the limited evidence available suggests that such information could prove extremely useful in differential diagnosis. For example, a relative lack of productivity is a common feature of language disorders (see Perkins, 1994) and it is well known that closed-class words – the most frequent words in normal language – are relatively rare in agrammatic aphasia. Once detailed statistical characterisations of this type have been established for large corpora, it becomes possible to identify a range of defining characteristics on the basis of relatively small samples. Multifeature/multidimensional approaches developed for the analysis of text types and genres (see Biber and Finegan, 1991) are able to represent reliably various linguistic characteristics of a text based only on a thousand-word sample. Procedures such as these hold out great promise for clinical linguistics. For example, the ability to make even a broad diagnosis of a patient's disorder based simply on the computational analysis of a transcribed thousand-word sample would mean an enormous saving in time, money and personnel.

Looking beyond purely practical concerns, corpus studies could play an important role in the theoretical study of language disability. One important insight into the nature of normal language that has received a great deal of support from corpus studies is that, in addition to a generative grammar and a lexicon, a speaker's linguistic competence must also incorporate a large number of semiproductive phrases and sentences (see Altenberg, 1993). Much current linguistic theorising on aphasia, however, fails to take account of this and characterises linguistic deficits solely in terms of generative grammatical competence and lexis (e.g. Grodzinsky, 1990). The existence of disordered language corpora large enough to enable the type of collocational analysis carried out by Sinclair and colleagues (e.g. Sinclair, 1991) could have far-reaching implications for theoretical models of language disability.

A large, widely accessible, ever-increasing, read/write database into which speech and language therapists entered all their transcribed and coded data as a matter of course could eventually serve the various needs of speech and language therapists who might wish to enquire about the type of medical condition that may have given rise to a particular sample of language. It could also serve the needs of medical professionals who might want to know what type of linguistic behaviour was typically found in a particular medical condition, and of clinical linguists and researchers who might wish to establish linguistic norms for the whole range of speech and language disorders.

Part II
Developmental
Communication Disorders

Chapter 3
Intransigent articulation disorder: using electropalatography to assess and remediate misarticulated fricatives

SARA HOWARD

Background

Introduction

This case study reports on the use of electropalatography (EPG) to treat a young girl's intransigent misarticulation of sibilant fricatives.* Also, significantly, it uses perceptual and instrumental analyses to examine the widespread phonetic repercussions throughout the child's sound system of treatment of isolated misarticulated segments. Unlike the other case studies in this book, where detailed clinical linguistic analysis preceded and accompanied therapy, some of the analysis presented here was carried out retrospectively in an attempt to explain the unexpected changes that took place during the course of the treatment programme.

Case history

Rebecca was a 10-year-old girl whose otherwise normal speech and language skills were marred by difficulties with the correct articulation of alveolar and postalveolar fricatives and affricates. She had already received therapy for her speech between the ages of 4 and 7, so her previous speech and language therapy notes allow a more detailed summary than would otherwise have been available about her early speech development and about her early development generally.

Rebecca had a history of normal development in all areas other than speech and language. She had no significant health problems and no record of hearing problems. She had been bottle-fed and was weaned at 5 months. Her mother reported that she had shown a marked lack of interest in the teat while being bottle-fed, but that there were no feeding problems once she moved onto solid foods. Rebecca at 4 years,

*A shorter version of this work was published as Howard (1994).

during her first contact with the speech and language therapy service, was a rather reserved and clingy child and was felt by her mother to be somewhat in the shadow of her very extrovert, confident, older sister. Rebecca's mother was also concerned that her speech production might have been affected by a long-term thumbsucking habit.

Rebecca's mother's recollections suggested a picture of delayed expressive language development: Rebecca was said to have been a very quiet baby. First words were late and she didn't begin to produce two-word utterances until well after the age of 2;0 years. However, formal language assessments carried out at 4;0 years indicated that her expressive and receptive language were by that time in advance of chronological age and she produced plenty of spontaneous speech in the clinical situation.

At 4;0 years Rebecca's problem appeared to be with her sound system. She presented with a delayed phonological system which was significantly reducing her intelligibility. Analysis of her speech using a natural process framework suggested that the reduction in her system of phonological contrasts could be described by reference to three main phonological processes: stopping of most fricatives and affricates, context-sensitive voicing and cluster reduction. Her target alveolar segments were said to be dentalised and variably interdental and more unusual features of her speech included variable backing of the postalveolar affricates (/tʃ, dʒ/ → [k, g]) and the realisation of intervocalic fricatives in syllable initial within-word (SIWI) and syllable final within-word (SFWW) positions (Grunwell, 1985b) as [h]. Her imitative skills were poor. In stimulability testing (where she was given explicit verbal instructions about segment production, rather than just being provided with a model to imitate) Rebecca produced /tʃ/ as [t] but /dʒ/ as [g]. /s/ and /z/ were produced as [θ] and /ʃ/ as [h̪].

Rebecca had weekly individual therapy from 4;4 to 4;7 years followed by a series of review appointments and home programmes over the next 2 years, particularly addressed at the production of alveolar fricatives and the establishment of consonant clusters. During this period, lingual fricatives and affricates emerged and it was noted that these were usually dentalised or interdental and variably laterally released. At 7;6 years Rebecca was judged to have only minor residual dentalisation of alveolar fricatives and minor articulatory immaturities affecting postalveolar fricatives and affricates which her speech and language therapist felt would resolve spontaneously. At this point she was discharged from speech and language therapy.

The problem

At the age of 10 years Rebecca requested a referral to a speech and language therapist because she was unhappy about her production of 's'.

She attended for a reassessment of her speech with her mother, but was able to sum up her problem and her reasons for seeking help herself:

> I can't say 's' properly and when I listen to my speech on a tape-recorder it sounds babyish. I'd like to sound more grown-up and I'd like to do readings and drama at school. I never get picked for things like that and I think it's because of my speech.

She was reassessed by a speech and language therapist, with a clinical phonetician observing the session.

At 10;9 years, Rebecca's expressive and receptive language skills were normal but she appeared to have a number of difficulties related to speech production. She had normal hearing and intelligence and was motivated but rather quiet and withdrawn. Oral examination and consultation with an orthodontist suggested that she had a class 2 incisor relationship with edge-to-edge contact of the lateral incisors and a reduced overbite, possibly linked to her long-term thumbsucking habit (Bloomer, 1971; Foster, 1990).

A perceptual reassessment of Rebecca's speech production was made using speech data from spontaneous conversation produced during quite a lengthy discussion between the speech therapist and Rebecca about her motivation for seeking therapy, and also from single word data from the Sheffield Computerised Articulation Test (SCAT) (Eastwood, 1981). The data were transcribed *in situ* by the phonetician and a video recording of the session enabled later consensus transcription and discussion by the phonetician and therapist together. Oral motor, imitation and stimulability abilities were also assessed during the session.

This reassessment of Rebecca's speech skills revealed a pattern of more pervasive misarticulation than her reported inability to produce /s/ appropriately. All of her target alveolar segments – /t, d, n, l, r, s, z/ – were visibly either dentalised or interdental and all of her lingual–palatal fricatives and affricates – /s, z, ʃ, ʒ, tʃ, dʒ/ – were misarticulated in various ways, including the aforementioned dentalisation, but also with variable lateral release of friction. Although /s/ and /z/ were sometimes interdental Rebecca appeared to make them distinct from /θ, ð/ which were consistently markedly interdental and produced with central release of air. The alveolar lateral and postalveolar median approximants, /l/ and /r/, were, unusually, both realised as lateral approximants, but consistently contrasted by place of realisation: /r/ was visibly interdental, [l̪], whereas /l/ was dentalised, [l̪]. This rather small visual distinction had even less auditory impact and thus from a listener perspective (Hewlett, 1985) the phonological contrast was neutralised. Close inspection of the data also revealed visible right-sided asymmetry of lingual and labial movements and some right-sided mandibular lateral movement during speech. Rebecca's voice quality was palatalised and it was felt that she maintained a fairly close mandibular setting for speech production overall with noticeable lowering and some instability and lateral movement of the jaw for interdental segments (Laver, 1980). She did not, however, have an interdental lingual setting at rest as is often seen in speakers with a dentalised sound system.

Although Rebecca's oral motor skills were satisfactory, in imitation and stimulability testing she was unable to produce anything approaching an appropriate grooved alveolar fricative, even when provided with detailed instructions and a number of different strategies. It was felt that she would benefit from visual feedback to aid her self-monitoring in speech production and it was therefore decided to offer her treatment using EPG. Our assessment had revealed a number of speech production difficulties in addition to those reported for /s/. However, Rebecca had requested that we help her with 's' and as this seemed a reasonable place to start, she was offered therapy to overcome her misarticulation of the voiced and voiceless alveolar fricatives /s/ and /z/. It was felt that further therapy could be offered for the remaining misarticulated segments at a later date.

Theoretical background

Articulatory and acoustic characteristics of /s, z, ʃ, ʒ, ʧ, ʤ/

The English alveolar and postalveolar fricatives and affricates – /s, z, ʃ, ʒ, ʧ, ʤ/ – are complex segments in articulatory terms, both in the timing and location of lingual–palatal gestures and in the coordination of lingual activity with egressive respiratory activity required to produce the auditory effect of friction. The fricatives – /s, z, ʃ, ʒ/ – and the fricative release phase of the affricates – /ʧ, ʤ/ – require that the egressive airstream escapes along a central groove in the tongue. This groove is usually produced by the lateral margins of the tongue making contact either with the lateral edges of the palate or with the inner surfaces of the upper molars. Some speakers make this lateral lingual contact by resting the lateral edges of the tongue between the upper and lower teeth. A central groove is thus formed between these areas of closure.

The alveolar and postalveolar fricatives are characteristically distinguished from each other by both groove width and location of the narrowest point of the groove (sometimes referred to as the point of maximum constriction – e.g. Hoole et al., 1989). Typically, alveolar fricatives have a narrower groove (about 5–8 mm in width) than /ʃ, ʒ/ (about 6–12 mm) and the grooves are located at different points in the oral cavity, usually in the region of the alveolar ridge for /s, z/ and behind the alveolar ridge, towards the front of the hard palate, for /ʃ, ʒ/

(Flege et al., 1988; Fletcher, 1989), although there is a range of inter-speaker variability which will nevertheless result in acceptable sound-ing fricatives (Hoole et al., 1989). Groove width and location are closely interrelated in distinguishing /s, z/ (narrow groove, anterior location) from /ʃ, ʒ/ (wider groove, more posterior location), although it seems that where a potential conflict arises, for example, where a wider than normal groove occurs in the alveolar region, location effect overrides groove width effect in the listener's perception of the identity of the segment so that, in this example, the segment would be identi-fied as an alveolar fricative. Hoole et al. (1989) and Stone et al. (1992) note that lingual grooving extends posteriorly behind the point of max-imum constriction and suggest that characteristically different patterns of posterior grooving form a further significant factor in distinguishing /s, z/ from /ʃ, ʒ/. Fletcher (1989) and Gibbon (1994) confirm, from palatographic data, Gimson's (1989) observation that speakers produce the fricative elements of the postalveolar affricates at the same location as their postalveolar fricatives. Speakers may also vary as to whether the tongue tip or blade is the major articulator for /s, z/ production, that is to say whether during the articulation of these segments the tongue tip is raised to the alveolar ridge (apical articulation) or located immedi-ately behind the lower incisors, with the blade of the tongue raised to achieve the alveolar constriction (laminal articulation) (Bladon and Nolan, 1977). The rear surfaces of the teeth appear to be a significant sound source in /s, z/ production (Fant, 1960; Catford, 1977) and Fletcher (1989) suggests that the vertical face of the rear edge of the alveolar process has a similarly important function in the auditory effect of /ʃ, ʒ/.

These different articulatory gestures and lingual palatal contact pat-terns appear to have robust acoustic correlates. [s, z, ʃ, ʒ] are classed as sibilant fricatives, differing from the non-sibilants [f, v, θ, ð, h] in having higher intensity levels and their peaks of acoustic energy occurring in lower frequency bands. For normal adult male speakers voiceless alveo-lar fricatives show peaks of energy in the 4000–8000 Hz region, where-as their postalveolar counterparts have peaks extending across the region from about 2000 Hz up to 6000 kHz (Fry, 1979), for children these ranges are shifted upwards by approximately 2000 kHz (Daniloff et al., 1980).

Although traditional accounts of median fricative production assume a symmetrical central groove, asymmetry in lingual–palatal fricatives has been revealed by a number of instrumental techniques: EPG (Hamlet et al., 1986; Hiki and Itoh, 1986; Marchal and Espesser, 1989), airflow patterns, lingual pressure recordings (McGlone and Profitt, 1973, 1974) and ultrasonic imaging (Stone et al., 1992). The asymmetry tends to be characterised by greater lingual contact of the left side of the palate (Hamlet, 1988; Marchal and Espesser, 1989).

Although Stone et al. (1992) suggest a relationship between the asymmetrical palate shape of their subject and the asymmetrical patterns of his articulations, other studies tend to play down any obvious link between palatal shape and asymmetry (Hiki and Itoh, 1986; Hamlet, 1988). It seems that asymmetry of lingual activity is a feature of normal speech production, but that in some fricative misarticulation patterns this tendency may increase to a degree which contributes to the auditory effect of abnormality (McGlone and Profitt, 1973; Howard et al., 1994).

The acquisition of alveolar and postalveolar fricatives and affricates

In acquiring the sound system of their native language, children have to develop both phonological and articulatory skills. At the phonological level, the child must develop an internal representation of the sound system which contains, among other information, the appropriate system of functionally contrastive segments, i.e. phonemes, for the language in question. Part of this knowledge for English will include the understanding that /s, z, ʃ, ʒ, ʧ, ʤ/ are separate phonemes which must be appropriately selected and produced to indicate the child's desired linguistic meaning. The child learns that inappropriately selected or unsuccessfully articulated speech segments may result in a frustrating loss of intelligibility. Grunwell (1987) suggests that /s/ emerges as a functionally contrastive unit between the ages of 2;6 and 3;6 years, although production of the forms may be phonetically variable. Thus the child may well acquire some of these segments at the phonological level, i.e. have acquired the knowledge that they are significant, contrastive units, before developing the requisite articulatory skills to produce them successfully. If articulatory skills are particularly poor or immature, the child may not be able to signal an appropriate perceptible contrast between segments or may achieve segments which are auditorily distinct from each other but which are not yet phonetically close to the adult target segments. In other words, the child cannot yet successfully articulate the phonological contrasts he or she knows to exist: together with phonological knowledge, the child needs to develop articulatory ability.

The task for children learning to articulate the sibilant fricatives and affricates is that of achieving a particular complex of articulatory gestures to produce centrally grooved tongue configurations with lateral closure of appropriate width and depths at different points in the vocal tract and to coordinate these lingual gestures with laryngeal, velic and mandibular adjustments and activity and an appropriate airstream. Not surprisingly, the correct articulation of alveolar and postalveolar fricatives and affricates is achieved relatively late in the child's acquisition of his or her sound system, although immature articulations of the

segments will typically have been incorporated to function at a phonological level rather earlier in the scheme of things. The picture is one of
gradual refinement over time of the complex of articulatory gestures
required to achieve the appropriate segments (Prather et al., 1975,
Ingram et al., 1980). Moskowitz (1975) notes that children's early realisations of /s/ indicate difficulties in achieving both appropriate place and
manner of articulation and that the gradual refinement of production is
based on both the perceptual and the physiological information available to them as they produce speech segments. Perceptual feedback
provides the speaker with knowledge about the acoustic effects of articulatory movements. Physiological and proprioceptive feedback provides information about motor movements.

Ingram (1975) suggests that the acquisition of /s/ can be seen as a
series of interlinked stages: at first the segment is omitted and words
containing it may actively be avoided; during the next stage /s/ is produced as a homorganic stop [t, d]. In the third stage of development,
friction begins to emerge and before a stable pattern of production is
established /s/ may be variably dentalised or palatalised. Hale et al.
(1992), in an examination of the development of oral–motor control,
claimed a dentalised contact point for all alveolar segments in a striking
84% of their 8-year-old subjects, but as this included lingual contact
with the back of the *lower* incisors their results may give a somewhat
misleading impression. Accurate production is usually acquired
between 4;0 and 5;0 years. /ʃ/, /tʃ/ and /dʒ/ also emerge around 4;0–4;6
years (Gibbon, 1994), whereas /z/ and /ʒ/ appear later, becoming established only between 5;0 and 6;0 years, which is in keeping with the
general observation that voiced fricatives are acquired later than their
voiceless counterparts. This pattern of development appears to be common, although Ingram notes that individual speakers may vary in the
exact order of acquisition of particular segments. Ingram (1975) and
Faircloth and Faircloth (1970) note significant differences in production across different contexts: different words, word positions, phonetic context, isolated words versus connected speech.

The acquisition of the alveolar and postalveolar fricatives can thus
be seen to be a gradual process, whereby the phonological contrast is
signalled by the child before she or he is able to produce completely
accurate articulations of the segments in question. Increasing refinement of oral motor control results in phonetically accurate productions
and this process is usually completed between the ages of 4;0 and 6;0
years.

Misarticulated fricatives

The alveolar and postalveolar fricatives and affricates, in particular /s/
and /z/, are also vulnerable to misarticulation in a number of ways.

Traditionally there are three common categories of misarticulation of /s/ and /z/: dentalisation or interdentalisation, where the tongue tip makes contact with or protrudes between the front teeth – [s̪] [z̪] [ʃ̪] [ʒ̪]; lateralisation, where the grooved, central friction is replaced by friction resulting from air released around one or both sides of the tongue – [ɬ] [ɮ]; and palatalisation or retraction, where the central groove is produced inappropriately posteriorly in the oral cavity – [ʂ] [ç] [ʐ] [j] (Daniloff et al., 1980). Both dentalised and retracted realisations appear to be common developmentally and many will resolve spontaneously, in contrast to lateral misarticulations which do not improve without therapy (Stephens et al., 1986). This suggests that, up to the age of 7 years or thereabouts, children with dentalised or palatalised speech may be described as having delayed articulatory development which may resolve spontaneously, but that children of any age with lateralised realisations of the alveolar and postalveolar fricatives and affricates are more accurately described as having disordered, rather than merely delayed, articulatory development which will require speech therapy if the child is to attain normal articulatory patterns.

Traditional accounts of dentalised misarticulations of [s, z] have regarded the problem as that of the phonemic substitution of /θ/ for /s/ (Van Riper and Irwin, 1958; McGlone and Profitt, 1973) but more recent studies have identified clear articulatory and acoustic differences between misarticulating children's dentalised productions of /s/ as [s̪] and their realisations of the dental fricative /θ/, which correspond to differences between normal /s/ and /θ/ (Weismer and Elbert, 1982; Behrens and Blumstein, 1988; Baum and McNutt, 1990), suggesting that the problem is not one of phonological substitution, but of a delay in the development of the fine articulatory control required to produce adult-like /s/.

Many factors have been implicated in the delayed or abnormal development of alveolar and postalveolar fricatives and affricates. A summary provided by Gibbon and Hardcastle (1987) includes the following: general articulatory immaturity; delayed language development; emotional problems; hereditary factors and a cluster of factors relating to the structure and function of the articulators – jaw position; habitual tongue position at rest and in speech, size and shape of palate and occlusion and dental abnormalities. Factors relating to structure and function of the articulators have been examined by a substantial number of studies, but it must be noted that this area is notoriously fraught with pitfalls relating to the collection and interpretation of data because of the difficulty of controlling for the multitude of variables involved.

Habitual low forward lingual settings at rest have been linked to misarticulations of alveolar targets (Garliner, 1981; Langer, 1981; Hale et al., 1992) but the evidence is not conclusive (Lebrun, 1985).

Mandibular setting has also been implicated: more open jaw positions during speech appear to be linked to dentalised misarticulations, whereas lateralised misarticulations relate to closer jaw settings (Wilcox et al., 1985).

There have been numerous studies linking dental and occlusal abnormalities to abnormal speech patterns, although until recently studies have tended to lack accurate phonetic description or transcription of the misarticulations reported (e.g. Rathbone and Snidecor, 1959; Snow, 1961). Anterior open bite has frequently been associated with dentalised fricative articulations whereas large overjet may be linked to retracted realisations of /s/ and /z/ (e.g. Bloomer, 1971; Laine, 1986). Shape and size of the palate have also been linked to misarticulation of speech sounds, particularly /s/ and /z/. Using EPG, Itoh et al. (1980) claim that for their subjects it was possible to predict which speakers would misarticulate the Japanese phonemes /s/, /ʃ/ and /ç/ by reference to spatial relationships within their oral cavities. Hiki and Itoh (1986) also used EPG to identify consistent relationships between palatal dimensions and articulatory patterns. Length of palate is another factor that has been linked to patterns of misarticulation (Laine et al., 1987): shorter palates were linked to dentalised or interdentalised realisations of /s/ whereas palates that were longer than normal could be related to retracted realisations. They also found that speakers with abnormally narrow palates were susceptible to fricative misarticulation.

Therapy for misarticulated fricatives and affricates

Misarticulations of fricatives and affricates are seldom offered therapy at an early age for a number of reasons. Often early phonological difficulties take priority in treatment provision and as fricatives and affricates develop relatively late they are not viewed as appropriate targets for early therapy. Furthermore, as many cases of misarticulated fricatives resolve spontaneously, often therapists understandably prefer to wait and see if this takes place. Those cases where this does not occur provide a client population of somewhat older children with well-established misarticulations which, particularly in the case of lateralised realisations, may well prove resistant to therapy (Gibbon and Hardcastle, 1987).

Traditional therapeutic approaches often start by assessing the child's ability to discriminate auditorily between their own misarticulations and normal productions, before moving on to the use of various imitation and stimulation activities which provide both verbal and graphic information about the target articulatory postures. This is more easily achieved for dentalised fricatives, where the problem and solution are relatively easily monitored visually, than for [ɬ] and [ɮ] where there is no visual feedback. Added to this, the possible variations of width and location of lingual contact patterns found in different later-alised fricatives means that accurate instructions on the articulatory modifications required are difficult to estimate. Some lateralised misar-ticulations respond to conventional techniques such as encouraging the child to achieve the necessary lateral lingual closures by gently bit-ing the lateral margins of the tongue between the teeth and thus facili-tating central release of airstream (Gourlay, 1988). Myofunctional therapy has also been suggested, to correct orofacial muscle imbal-ances claimed to contribute to patterns of misarticulation (Langer, 1981). However, a significant number of lateralised fricatives do not respond to such approaches. Some of these cases may be more success-fully treated using therapy techniques which provide the speaker with visual feedback about the nature of lingual–palatal contact patterns.

Electropalatography is an instrumental technique which can provide this feedback and there are a number of reports of its successful use in the treatment of intransigent fricative misarticulation (Gibbon and Hardcastle, 1987; MorganBarry, 1989; Gibbon et al., 1991). EPG pro-vides visual feedback about the nature of lingual contact patterns in speech and non-speech activities.* The speaker wears an artificial acrylic palate which covers the palatal region inside the upper teeth, from immediately post-dental to the margins of the soft palate. Sixty-four electrodes are arranged in eight rows from front to back along the palate: the first three rows correspond to the alveolar region, the next three to the region of the hard palate and the final two to the edge of the soft palate. These electrodes are triggered by contact made by the tongue and the patterns of contact are displayed in real time on a com-puter screen and can be recorded and stored or printed out for future examination. Thus EPG can capture objective information about lingual activity of a kind not routinely available because intraoral lingual activi-ty is not generally visible.

EPG therapy programme

EPG therapy

MorganBarry (1989) and Gibbon et al. (1989, 1991) provide guidelines for the selection of appropriate clients for EPG therapy and about factors that are contraindications. Rebecca was offered therapy because she emerged as a strong candidate when assessed according to this information. She was of a similar age to other children who had successfully responded to EPG therapy for fricative misarticulation (Gibbon and Hardcastle, 1987; MorganBarry, 1989; Gibbon et al.,

---

*For detailed accounts of the Reading EPG2 and EPG3 systems and their clinical applications, see Hardcastle et al. (1989a, 1991).

1991) and had no other problems in addition to her speech production difficulties. She had normal hearing and normal intelligence and was easily able to grasp the concept of EPG therapy. She had good attention skills and was very motivated to change her articulatory patterns. There were no orofacial abnormalities to prevent the palate fitting satisfactorily and Rebecca was able to tolerate it and accommodate to its presence well. A further positive indicator for Rebecca was the strong support and motivation of her family, which was utilised both within the clinical sessions and, importantly, in home practice aimed at skill stabilisation and generalisation away from the EPG.

Rebecca had dental impressions taken from which the artificial palate could be manufactured. Two palates were produced, one for use with the EPG which contained the appropriate electrodes and wiring, and a further plain 'training plate', which was worn by Rebecca before therapy to become accustomed to wearing an artificial palate and to allow her speech patterns to accommodate to its effects (Hardcastle et al., 1989a).

Résumé of therapy programme and data collection

EPG and video data of Rebecca's speech production were collected at five points during the treatment programme. There was an initial intensive block of therapy for /s, z/ production in the form of five sessions which took place over a single week. Data were collected at the beginning of the first session (data point 1 or DP1) and at the end of the final session of the block (data point 2 or DP2). Rebecca's speech was reviewed after 6 weeks (data point 3 or DP3) and again after 6 months (data point 4 or DP4). The final data collection took place at a session 10 months after the original block of therapy (data point 5 or DP5).

Intensive therapy block

Rebecca attended for five 1–1.5 hour sessions each morning for a week. The therapy took place in a half-term holiday, at Rebecca's request, both because she did not want to miss school and because initially she was a little reluctant to tell her friends that she was having speech therapy. Rebecca was accompanied to all the sessions by her mother who was present at the beginning and end of each session but, by design, sometimes withdrew from parts of the session. A speech and language therapist and a clinical phonetician worked with Rebecca and collected data during the sessions.

At the beginning of the first session EPG and video recordings were made of Rebecca producing a list of 37 single words containing the sibilant fricatives and affricates in a variety of phonotactic and phonetic contexts (see Appendix). Each item was produced in three positions: syllable initial word initial (SIWI); syllable initial within-word (SIWW) and syllable final word final (SFWF) (Grunwell, 1985b) with a variety of open/close, front/back vowels. /s/ and /z/ were also recorded in a variety of initial and final consonant clusters. EPG recordings for comparative purposes were made of two female speech and language therapists judged as having perceptually normal articulation producing the same word list. After the recording of Rebecca's production of the word list had been made, part of the first session was spent increasing her intra-oral awareness and supplying her with information about the vocal organs and basic phonetic concepts and terminology. This would provide her with a metalinguistic vocabulary and awareness which could be exploited during therapy. Diagrams were used and were linked to the plaster cast models of both Rebecca's and the therapist's oral cavities. These, in turn, were linked to a demonstration of EPG representation of speech sounds by the therapist and finally Rebecca's own exploration of the link between speech–sound production and EPG feedback by her own production of sounds she could produce appropriately – /t, d, n, k, g, ŋ/. At this stage, as a check on and reinforcement of Rebecca's knowledge, she explained the terms and concepts to which she had been introduced to her mother who had withdrawn from and then returned to the session.

Therapy could now focus on /s/ production. Rebecca's auditory discrimination of a normal /s/ from lateralised and dentalised variants modelled by the therapist was assessed and found to be very good. This distinction was then linked to EPG patterns for normal and misarticulated variants produced by the therapist.

Lingual contact patterns for a normal /s/ have some degree of permissible inter- and intraspeaker variability but, as shown in Figure 3.1, they are typically characterised by lateral lingual–palatal contact at both

```
   66          67          68          69          70          71          72
 00.000      00.000      00.000      00.000      00.000      00.000      00.000
000..000    00...000    00...000    00...000    00...000    000..000    000..000
00...000    00...000    0....000    0....000    0....000    00...000    00...000
0.....00    0.....00    0.....00    0.....00    0.....00    0.....00    0.....00
0......0    0......0    0......0    0......0    0......0    0......0    0......0
0......0    0......0    0......0    0......0    0......0    0......0    0......0
0......0    0......0    0......0    0......0    0......0    0......0    0......0
0......0    0......0    0......0    0......0    0......0    0......0    0......0


   73          74          75          76          77          78
 00.000      00.000      00.000      00.000      00.000      00.000
000..000    000..000    00...000    00...000    00...000    00...000
00...000    00...000    00...000    0....000    0....000    0....000
0.....00    0.....00    0.....00    0.....00    0.....00    0.....00
0......0    0......0    0......0    0......0    0......0    0......0
0......0    0......0    0......0    0......0    0......0    0......0
0......0    0......0    0......0    0......0    0......0    0......0
0......0    0......0    0......0    0......0    0......0    0......0
```

Figure 3.1 Typical lingual–palatal contact patterns for a normal /s/.

sides of the palate and a point of maximum groove constriction located in the alveolar region.

This lateral contact may not appear complete according to the EPG data even for normal speakers as the lateral seal may be made at least partially by the edges of the tongue making contact with the upper side teeth which will not, of course, show up in the EPG data (Figure 3.2). The lateral contacts help to form a central lingual groove for the escape of the egressive airstream and for /s/ and /z/ characteristically this groove is at its narrowest in the alveolar region.

For dentalised and palatalised/retracted variants the central groove is maintained but the point of maximum constriction is shifted relatively further forward or back in the oral cavity. Lateral fricatives, on the other hand, are produced when the escape of air takes place over one or both sides of the tongue because part of the tongue is forming a central obstruction to the airstream. Although the lateral fricative referred to in the IPA is described as an alveolar segment, implying central obstruction formed by the tip or blade of the tongue making contact with the alveolar ridge, the obstruction is not limited to this place of articulation and lateral friction can result from a range of places of articulation and a range of widths of closure.

Rebecca was able to see and describe the different lingual contact patterns for an alveolar median fricative, /s/, and an alveolar lateral fricative, /ɬ/, modelled by the therapist and then to compare these with her own dentalised and lateralised realisation of /s/.

At this stage Rebecca was asked to attempt to copy the pattern of lingual closure for /s/ as a static pattern without an airstream. For Rebecca, whose habitual articulation of /s/ was typically both dentalised *and* lateralised, there was the dual task of achieving a central groove and also

```
  202        203        204        205        206        207        208
 000..0     000..0     000..0     000..0     000..0     000..0     000..0
0000..00   0000..00   0000..00   0000..00   0000..00   0000..00   0000..00
000...00   000...00   000...00   000...00   000...00   000...00   000...00
00.....0   00.....0   00.....0   00.....0   00.....0   00.....0   00.....0
0.......   0.......   0.......   0.......   0.......   0.......   0.......
........   ........   ........   ........   ........   ........   ........
........   ........   ........   ........   ........   ........   ........
........   ........   ........   ........   ........   ........   ........


     209        210        211        212        213        214
    000..0     000..0     000..0     000..0.    000..0     000..0
   0000.000   0000.000   0000.000   0000.000   0000.000   0000.000
   000...00   000...00   000...00   000...00   000...00   000...00
   00.....0   00.....0   00.....0   00.....0   00.....0   00.....0
   0.......   0.......   0.......   0.......   0.......   0.......
   ........   ........   ........   ........   ........   ........
   ........   ........   ........   ........   ........   ........
   ........   ........   ........   ........   ........   ........
```

Figure 3.2 Lingual–palatal contact patterns for a variant of normal /s/ showing absence of lateral lingual contacts.

attempting to retract the tongue tip to the alveolar ridge. This was facilitated by asking Rebecca to make the alveolar grooved constriction with the tongue tip. After some instruction and encouragement from the therapist as Rebecca produced increasingly close approximations to the pattern, Rebecca was left on her own with the EPG for a short time to experiment by herself. She was quickly able to produce the requisite pattern and the task of adding an airstream to the pattern followed the same format: the therapist provided a model and verbal instruction and encouragement during Rebecca's initial attempts and then left Rebecca to practise and experiment on her own for a short time. In this way, by the end of the first session Rebecca was able to produce /s/ in isolation and was encouraged to alternate it with her own lateralised realisation to obtain maximum intraoral and auditory feedback about the differences between the two articulations.

Over the course of the next four sessions, therapy was carefully structured in a series of graded steps moving from the articulation of [s] versus [ɬ] in isolation through a variety of increasingly complex contexts: CV; VC; VCV; SIWI in CVC structures; SFWF in CVC structures; initial clusters; final clusters; short phrases; reading passages; conversation. During this process /z/ was introduced and Rebecca had very little problem in adding vocal fold vibration to her productions so practice included both voiceless and voiced target segments.

At each stage in this process Rebecca was encouraged to self-monitor and to discuss the processes involved and she was given time on her own during the sessions to experiment and to consolidate learning. Encouraging proprioceptive, kinaesthetic and auditory self-monitoring permitted the gradual withdrawal of the visual cues provided by the EPG at each stage of the process, and it was emphasised that this was a crucial part of the therapy which would help Rebecca to generalise her new skills to everyday speech. Rebecca was also encouraged to explain ideas, aims and progress to her mother as a reinforcement to the learning process and she took home set tasks every night, which she and her mother carried out assiduously.

By the end of the week's block of therapy, Rebecca could produce /s/ and /z/ appropriately in all contexts in conscious, careful speech, although there was some variability if speech became more rapid and less careful. Both she and her mother were pleased with this result and Rebecca herself appeared to be more confident and outgoing, although this must have partly been a consequence of increasing familiarity with the staff and surroundings of the clinic. At the end of the final session further EPG and video recordings were made of Rebecca producing the word list.

Rebecca was offered a review session to take place 6 weeks later to assess how well her improvements had been maintained and had, hopefully, generalised to everyday communication.

Data analysis

For DP1 and all subsequent data points, analysis took the form of consensus transcription and discussion by the therapist and phonetician of the video recording of Rebecca's production of the word list, followed by consideration of the EPG data.

Data point 1: pre-EPG therapy

The auditory analysis of R's sound system at DP1 suggested that the dentalisation of alveolar targets noted in her previous case history was accompanied by variable lateralisation. Alveolar fricatives – /s, z/ – were visibly dentalised and at times there was asymmetrical right-sided lingual protrusion interdentally, but the auditory impression of these segments was variably of laterally released friction. Postalveolar fricatives – /ʃ, ʒ/ – were transcribed as lateral fricatives which were *not* dentalised. Postalveolar affricates – /ʧ, ʤ/ – proved difficult to transcribe in terms of the place of the closure phase although auditorily the fricative phase was clearly laterally released. Consensus transcription and discussion limited the location of closure to the alveolar to palatal region, but both a degree of variability and transcriber disagreement and uncertainty meant that place of articulation was not more closely specified. Target alveolar plosives, nasals and lateral approximants – /t, d, n, l/ – were also visibly dentalised, although auditorily somewhat difficult to categorise and R's postalveolar voiced median approximant – /r/ – was also realised as a lateral approximant, with an apparent phonological distinction between /l/ and /r/ being realised by a strategy of dentalising the former and interdentalising the latter.

EPG recordings confirmed the auditory impression of R's alveolar and postalveolar fricatives. /s/ and /z/, as shown in Figure 3.3, show a complete band of contact across the first and variably the second rows of the palate, corresponding to the alveolar region immediately post-dentally. However, lingual contact was visibly extended in front of the anterior margin of the palate onto at least the rear of the upper teeth, so the actual width of the band of contact was wider than indicated by the EPG data. Lateral lingual contact extends typically only as far back as row 4 of the palate, suggesting possible lateral release of air posterior to this contact. /ʃ/ and /ʒ/ (Figure 3.4) are characterised by a fairly broad band of complete closure extending over rows 3–5 of the palate, in the postalveolar/palatal region. Thus /s, z/ and /ʃ, ʒ/ *are* distinguished from a speaker perspective by different places of closure, but unfortunately from a listener perspective the lateral friction means that the distinction is neutralised in auditory terms. EPG recordings of the affricates /ʧ/ and /ʤ/ (Figure 3.5) reveal an initial phase of fairly broad complete closure in the alveolar region. This band of closure then

```
   190      191      192      193      194      195      196
 000000   000000   000000   000000   000000   000000   000000
0000..00 0000..00 0000.000 0000.000 0000.000 0000.000 000..000
00.....0 00.....0 00.....0 00.....0 00.....0 00.....0 00....00
0......0 00.....0 0......0 0......0 0......0 0......0 0......0
........ .......0 .......0 .......0 .......0 .......0 .......0
........ ........ ........ ........ ........ ........ ........
........ ........ ........ ........ ........ ........ ........
........ ........ ........ ........ ........ ........ ........

   197      198      199      200      201      202      203
 000000   000000   000000   000000   000000   000000   000000
000..000 000..000 000..000 000..000 000..000 000..000 000...00
00....00 00....00 00....00 00.....0 00.....0 00.....0 0......0
0......0 0......0 0......0 0......0 0......0 0......0 0......0
.......0 .......0 .......0 .......0 .......0 .......0 .......0
........ ........ ........ ........ ........ ........ ........
........ ........ ........ ........ ........ ........ ........
........ ........ ........ ........ ........ ........ ........
```

Figure 3.3 Rebecca's typical lingual–palatal contact patterns for /s/ and /z/ at DP1.

```
   276      277      278      279      280      281      282
 ......   ......   ......   ......   ......   ......   ......
...0.... ...0.... ...0.... ...0.... ...0.... ...0.... ...0....
0000000. 000000.. 000000.. 000000.. 000000.. 000000.. 00000...
00000000 00000000 00000000 00000000 00000000 00000000 00000000
00000000 00000000 00000000 00000000 00000000 00000000 00000000
0.....00 0.....00 0.....00 0.....00 0.....00 0.....00 0.....00
0.....00 0.....00 0.....00 0.....00 0.....00 0.....00 0.....00
0....... 0....... 0....... 0....... 0....... 0....... 0.......

   283      284      285      286      287      288
 ......   ......   ......   ......   ......   ......
...0.... ...0.... ...0.... ...0.... ...0.... ...0....
00000... 00000... 00000... 00000... 00000... 0.000...
00000000 00000000 00000000 00000000 00000000 00000000
00000000 00000000 00000000 00000000 00000000 00000000
0.....00 0.....00 0.....00 0.....00 0....00 0.....00
0.....00 0.....00 0.....00 00....00 00....00 00....00
0....... 0....... 0....... 0....... 0......0 0......0
```

Figure 3.4 Rebecca's typical lingual–palatal contact patterns for /ʃ/ and /ʒ/ at DP1.

moves back to occupy a place of articulation very similar to that of Rebecca's laterally released postalveolar fricatives – /ʃ/ and /ʒ/. Thus the closure and fricative release phases of the Rebecca's affricates are not homorganic. This may reflect the normal articulation of postalveolar affricates as described by Gimson (1989) where the fricative portion of the segment involves not only homorganic friction as the tongue tip is slowly released from the rear of the alveolar ridge, but also friction that occurs as a result of the raising of the front of the tongue, behind the stop stricture, towards the hard palate. Alternatively it may illustrate a degree of conflict in the whole gesture as described for various abnormal realisations of postalveolar affricates by Gibbon (1994). The EPG contact patterns for Rebecca's /t, d, n/ show bands of contact variably

```
     121        122        123        124        125        126        127
  ......     ......     ......     ......     ......     ......     ......
  ........   .00000..   .00000..   .00000..   .00000..   .00000..   .0000...
  00......   0000000.   0000000.   0000000.   0000000.   0000000.   0000000.
  00....00   000..000   000.0000   000.0000   00000000   00000000   00000000
  00....00   00....00   00....00   00....00   00....00   00...000   00...000
  00....00   00....00   00...000   00...000   00....00   00....00   00....00
  00...000   00...000   00...000   00...000   00,,.000   00...000   00....000
  000..000   000..000   000.0000   000.0000   000.0000   000.0000   000..000
```

```
     128        129        130        131        132        133        134
  ......     ......     ......     ......     ......     ......     ......
  ..0.0...   ........   ........   ........   ........   ........   ........
  0000000.   000000..   .00000..   .0000...   .0000...   .0000...   .0.00...
  00000000   00000000   00000000   00000000   00000000   00000000   00000000
  000..000   000..000   00000000   00000000   00000000   00000000   00000000
  00....00   0.....00   0.....00   0.....00   0.....00   0.....00   0.....00
  00...000   00...000   00....00   00....00   0.....00   0.....00   0.....00
  00...000   00...000   00...000   00...000   00...000   00...000   00....000
```

```
     135        136        137        138        139        140        141
  ......     ......     ......     ......     ......     ......     ......
  ........   ........   ........   ........   ........   ........   ........
  .0..0...   .0..0...   ,0......   .0......   ........   ........   ........
  00000000   00000000   00000000   00000000   00000.00   00000.00   00000.00
  00000000   00000000   00000000   00000000   00000000   00000000   00000000
  00....00   .00...00   .00...00   .00.0.00   .00.0.00   .00.0000   .0000000
  0.....00   0.....00   0.....00   0,....00   0.....00   0.....00   0.....00
  00...000   00...000   0.....00   0.....00   0.....00   ........0   ........0
```

```
     142        143        144        145        146        147        148
  ......     ......     ......     ......     ......     ......     ......
  ........   ........   ........   ........   ........   ........   ........
  ........   ........   ........   ........   ........   ........   ........
  00000.00   00000.00   000..000   00...000   00...000   00....00.   .0......
  00000000   00000000   00000000   00000000   000..000   00....00   0.......0
  .0000000   .00.0.00   .0....00   ......00   ........0   ........0   0.......0
  0.....00   0.....00   0.....00   0.....00   ........0   0.....00   0.......0
  .......0   ......,.0   ......,0   .......0   0......0   0......0   0......0
```

Figure 3.5 Rebecca's typical lingual–palatal contact patterns for /tʃ/ and /dʒ/ at DP1.

restricted to the alveolar region or extending over almost the entire palate to make a very broad closure which appears to be the product of a variable and unrefined lingual gesture. This, in turn, may explain our difficulties in attempting to transcribe these segments. Other than the variability in these plosive and nasal articulations, the EPG recordings reveal a set of very consistent articulatory patterns.

Other aspects of Rebecca's speech noted at this point include a pronounced labial asymmetry in fricative articulations, an overall palatalised voice quality and an overall, somewhat tense, close jaw setting with noticeable rather unstable lowering for individual interdental segments.

Data point 2: end of EPG therapy block

EPG and video recordings made on the final day of the block of therapy illustrated that the desired grooved alveolar articulations for /s/ and /z/ had been achieved, as shown in Figure 3.6. Auditorily these segments now sounded normal. EPG recordings show the groove achieved for central release of air and significantly also reveal an extension of lateral

```
      131       132       133       134       135       136       137
     0.....     00....    00..00    00..00    00..00    00..00    00..00
    00....00  000..000  000..000  000..000  000..000  0000.000  000..000
    00....00  00....00  00....00  00....00  00....00  00....00  00....00
    0......0  0......0  0.....00  0.....00  0.....00  0.....00  0.....00
    0......0  0......0  0......0  0......0  0......0  0......0  0......0
    0......0  0......0  0......0  0......0  0......0  0......0  0......0
    0......0  0......0  0......0  0......0  0......0  0......0  0......0
    0......0  0......0  0......0  0......0  0......0  0......0  0......0
```

```
      138       139       140       141       142       143
     00..00    00...0    00...0    00....    0.....     ......
    000..000  000..000  00...000  00....00  00....00  0......0
    00....00  00....00  00....00  0.....00  0......0  0......0
    0.....00  0......0  0......0  0......0  0......0  0......0
    0......0  0......0  0......0  0......0  0......0  0......0
    0......0  0......0  0......0  00.....0  00.....0  00.....0
    0......0  0......0  0......0  0......0  00.....0  00.....0
    0......0  0......0  0......0  0......0  0......0  0......0
```

Figure 3.6 Rebecca's typical lingual–palatal contact patterns for /s/ and /z/ at DP2.

lingual contact, particularly on the right side of the palate. The auditory impression at this point was that none of the other misarticulated segments in R's speech had changed in any perceptible way. From a clinical perspective the outcome of the intervention appeared to have been very successful. Both perceptual and instrumental evidence demonstrated that the segments targeted by therapy had indeed undergone the required change. Given this outcome and given the constraints on staff time and resources, there seemed little justification in allocating precious clinical time to a more detailed analysis of the EPG data for those segments that had not been targeted in therapy and which perceptually appeared unchanged.

However, when Rebecca's articulation of her sound system showed significant deterioration 6 months after the original block of therapy, retrospective analysis of the EPG data from earlier data points was undertaken. EPG recordings made at DP2 reveal consistent changes in the lingual–palatal contact patterns of other target alveolar and postalveolar segments, in addition to the changes undergone by /s/ and /z/. The postalveolar fricatives, /ʃ/ and /ʒ/, although still laterally released and generally lacking any route for central escape of air, now show a pattern of significant reduction of the broad band of postalveolar contact, with a changed back gradient indicating a grooved configuration beginning to develop behind the complete contact (Figure 3.7). On occasions, the band of contact is not complete for the duration of the segment and there is the possibility of brief central escape of air accompanying the perceived lateral release, as shown in Figure 3.8. /tʃ/ and /dʒ/ are still laterally released, but the closure phase is now visibly retracted (Figure 3.9). The alveolar plosives and nasal – /t, d, n/ – show quite variable contact patterns at this point; there are significantly

```
     166        167        168        169        170        171        172
   ......     ......     ......     ......     ......     ......     ......
  ........   ........   ........   ........   ........   ........   ........
  ..0.....   ..0.....   ..0.0...   ..0.0...   ..0.0...   .00.0...   .00.0...
  000000..   000000..   000000..   000000..   000000..   000000..   000000..
  000.0000   000.0000   000.000.   000.000.   000.000.   000.000.   000.000.
  00....00   00...000   00...000   00...000   000..000   000..000   000..000
  00....00   00....00   00,,,,00   00....00   00....00   00....00   00....00
  0......0   0......0   0......0   0......0   0......0   0......0   0......0
```

```
     173        174        175        176        177        178
   ......     ......     ...ii#     ii..       ii#i#i     ......
  ........   ........   ........   ........   ........   ........
  .00.0...   .00.0...   .00.0...   .00.0...   .00.0...   .00.0...
  000000..   000000..   000000..   000000..   000000..   000000..
  000.000.   000.000.   000.000.   000.000.   000.0000   000.000.
  000..000   000..000   000..000   000..000   000..000   000..000
  00....00   00....00   00....00   00....00   00....00   00....00
  0......0   0......0   0......0   0......0   0......0   0......0
```

Figure 3.7 DP2: the development of posterior lingual grooving for /ʃ/ and /ʒ/.

```
     249        250        251        252        253        254        255
   ......     ......     ......     ......     ......     ......     ......
  ........   ........   ........   ........   ........   ........   ........
  ........   ........   ........   0.......   0.......   0.......   0.......
  00......   00......   000.....   000.....   000.....   0000....   0000....
  00....00   000..000   000.0000   000.0000   000.0000   000.0000   000.0000
  0.....00   0.....00   0.....00   0.....00   00....00   00....00   00....00
  0.....00   0.....00   0.....00   0.....00   0.....00   0.....00   0.....00
  0.....00   0.....00   0.....00   0.....00   0.....00   0......0   .......0
```

```
     256        257        258        259        260        261
   ......     ......     ......     ......     ......     ......
  ........   ........   ........   ........   ........   ........
  0.......   0.......   0.......   0.......   0.......   ........
  0000....   0000....   000.....   000.....   000.....   00......
  000.0000   000.0000   000.0000   000.0000   000..000   00....00
  00....00   00....00   00....00   0.....00   0.....00   0.....00
  0.....00   0.....00   0.....00   0.....00   0.....00   0.....00
  0......0   0......0   0.....00   0......0   0......0   0......0
```

Figure 3.8 DP2: /ʃ/ token showing lack of former complete band of lingual–palatal contact.

fewer instances of the very broad closure patterns found at DP1 and some retraction of the band of complete closure.

Thus close examination of the EPG data for the lingual–palatal contact patterns for alveolar and postalveolar segments as a whole reveal consistent, significant changes which are auditorily imperceptible except in the case of /s/ and /z/.

Data point 3: 6 weeks post-therapy

When a review of R's speech was carried out 6 weeks after the original block of therapy, further changes were noted in R's articulatory patterns

```
   154      155      156      157      158      159      160
 ......   ......   ......   ......   ......   ......   ......
 ........ ........ ........ ........ ........ ........ ........
 ........ ........ ........ ...00... .......0 0....... 00......
 ........ 0....... 00...... 000..00. 0000000. 0000000. 0000000.
 .......0 00....00 00....00 000..000 000.0000 000.0000 000.0000
 .......0 0......0 0......0 0......0 0......0 0....00 0.....00
 0......0 00.....0 00....00 00....00 00....00 00....00 00....00
 00....00 00....00 00....00 00....00 00.....0 00.....0 00.....0

   161      162      163      164      165      166      167
 ......   ......   ......   ......   ......   ......   ......
 ........ ........ ........ ........ ........ ........ ........
 00..0... 00..0... 00..0... 00..0... 00..0... 00..0... 00..0...
 0000000. 0000000. 000000.. 000000.. 000000.. 000000.. 000000..
 000.0000 000.0000 000.0000 000.0000 000.0000 000.0000 000.0000
 0.....00 0.....00 0.....00 0.....00 0.....00 0.....00 0.....00
 00....00 00....00 00....00 00....00 00....00 00....00 00....00
 0......0 0......0 0......0 0......0 0......0 0......0 0......0

   168      169      170      171      172      173      174
 ......   ......   ......   ......   ......   ......   ......
 ........ ........ ........ ........ ........ ........ ........
 00..0... 00..0... 00..0... 0....... ........ ........ ........
 000000.. 000000.. 0000000. 0000000. 0000000. 000..0.. 00......
 000.0000 000.0000 000.0000 000.0000 000.0000 000..000 00...000
 0.....00 0.....00 0.....00 0.....00 0.....00 0......0 0......0
 00....00 00....00 00....00 00....00 00....00 00....00 00.....0
 0......0 0......0 0......0 0......0 0......0 0......0 0......0

   175      176      177      178      179      180      181
 ......   ......   ......   ......   ......   ......   ......
 ........ ........ ........ ........ ........ ........ ........
 ........ ........ ........ ........ ........ ........ ........
 00...... 0....... ........ ........ ........ ........ ........
 00....00 0.....00 0......0 0......0 0......0 ........ ........
 0......0 0......0 0......0 0......0 0......0 0......0 ........
 0......0 0......0 0......0 0......0 0......0 0......0 0......0
 0......0 0......0 0......0 0......0 0......0 0......0 0.......
```

Figure 3.9 Rebecca's typical lingual–palatal contact patterns for /tʃ/ and /dʒ/ at DP2.

both from auditory impression and from examination of the EPG record-ings. /s/ and /z/ had maintained an auditorily normal alveolar grooved articulation. EPG recordings show maintenance of a central groove, although this now showed more variability of contact pattern across different tokens of the same segment and also showed a degree of asym-metry of lingual contact not present in the recordings at DP2 which were characteristically very symmetrical. As noted earlier, however, a degree of such lingual asymmetry is common in normal speakers and does not affect perceptual judgements of normality. At this stage Rebecca's speech therapy notes refer to a 'huge' reported change in her confi-dence and her self-perception and self-image.

However, retrospective analysis of the EPG data revealed further changes in Rebecca's speech production. Greater variability had now developed in the production of /ʃ/ and /ʒ/. They were still sometimes laterally released, although the band of complete contact was now con-sistently narrower and there were more instances of incomplete con-tact permitting central release of air. Alveolar plosives and nasals and postalveolar affricates remained similar in their lingual–palatal contact patterns to those revealed by EPG in DP2.

Rebecca herself had noted that her postalveolar fricatives were beginning to sound different and at this point she was introduced to the target lingual–palatal contact patterns, as shown by EPG, for /ʃ/ and /ʒ/, with discussion of the similarities and differences between normal lingual contact patterns for /s, z/ and /ʃ, ʒ/.

Data point 4: 6 months post-therapy

Six months after the original block of therapy, it was intended to offer Rebecca another block of therapy focusing further on the production of the postalveolar fricatives that had been introduced earlier. However, when Rebecca attended for an initial review session, it became apparent that in the intervening period auditorily significant and detrimental changes had taken place in her speech production and it was felt that further treatment was contraindicated at this point. EPG and video recordings were made of Rebecca producing the word list and also producing quite a large number of items from the Sheffield Computerised Articulation Test (Eastwood, 1981). As she had been aware of the previous improvements in her speech production so Rebecca was now aware of and visibly disappointed by the deterioration in her speech. She was given reinforcement, through EPG, of the lingual contact patterns and their corresponding articulatory movements for alveolar grooved fricatives. No further intervention was offered until requested.

At this point detailed perceptual and EPG analysis was carried out, which revealed the marked changes in Rebecca's realisations of all target alveolar and postalveolar segments. /s/ and /z/ now showed great variation in realisation across different tokens. Although in some instances a normally grooved alveolar fricative was achieved, at other times Rebecca reverted to her previous lateralised and dentalised articulation. At times this dentalisation was so marked that there was virtually no remaining trace of the underlying target alveolar on the EPG recording and only minimal evidence of lateral lingual contact (Figure 3.10). The affricates – /tʃ/ and /dʒ/ – were also variably articulated. Some tokens showed something approximating to Rebecca's original pattern for these segments which was of an initial complete alveolar closure moving back to a postalveolar closure with lateral friction. Other tokens showed patterns of greatly reduced lingual–palatal contact which is variable and asymmetrical. The alveolar plosives and nasals showed similar variability of lingual–palatal contact patterns with corresponding detrimental effects on the auditory impression of R's speech. Some realisations of /t, d, n/ again show very broad closure patterns. Place of closure stricture varied from interdental to postalveolar. The EPG recordings of some tokens illustrated a phase of lingual–palatal stricture producing affrication both before and after the closure phase, and this was audible in the video recordings of the particular items. An

```
  145      146      147      148      149      150      151
 .....O   ....OO   ....O.   ....O.   ......   ......   ......
 .......O .......O ........ ........ ........ ........ ........
 O......O O......O .......O .......O ......OO ......OO ......OO
 O....... O......O O......O O......O O......O O......O O......O
 ........ ........ ........ ........ ........ ........ ........
 ........ ........ ........ ........ ........ ........ ........
 ........ ........ ........ ........ ........ ........ ........
 ........ ........ ........ ........ ........ ........ ........

  152      153      154      155      156      157      158
 ......   ......   ......   ....O    ......   O.....   O.....
 ........ ........ ........ ........ ......OO .......O ........
 ......OO ......OO ......OO ......OO ......OO .......O O......O
 O......O O......O O......O O......O O......O O......O O......O
 ........ ........ ........ ........ ........ ........ ........
 ........ ........ ........ ........ ........ ........ ........
 ........ ........ ........ ........ ........ O....... O.......
 O....... O....... O....... O....... O....... O......O O......O
```

Figure 3.10 Lingual–palatal contact patterns for a dentalised /s/ at DP4.

example of friction occurring before complete closure for /t/ is shown in Figure 3.11.

Significantly, at this point, whereas most alveolar and postalveolar articulations had deteriorated, /ʃ/ and /ʒ/ were produced with a consistently appropriate postalveolar grooved configuration, which consequently fell within normal limits in terms of auditory impression.

Data point 5: 10 months after original therapy

Ten months after the original block of EPG therapy for /s/ and /z/ Rebecca's speech was reviewed and further data collected. At this point the auditory impression of R's speech was of a startling and significant improvement in all alveolar and postalveolar articulations. EPG recordings confirmed this improvement. /s/ and /z/ were now once again consistently produced as alveolar grooved fricatives with lateral lingual–palatal contact. /ʃ/ and /ʒ/ maintained the appropriate lingual–palatal contact patterns shown at DP4. The alveolar plosives and nasal – /t, d, n/ – were now almost always produced with the band of complete closure appropriately confined to the alveolar region. The postalveolar affricates – /tʃ/ and /dʒ/ – still showed some variability both auditorily and in terms of their EPG contact patterns. Sometimes the fricative phase had audible lateral release but now in many cases there were appropriate configurations of lingual–palatal contact: a phase of complete closure in the postalveolar region followed by a phase of central release of air, corresponding to the fricative phase of the segment. Rebecca was pleased and cheerful about her speech production and no further intervention was subsequently offered or requested.

```
    151        152        153        154        155        156        157
 ......     ......     ......     ......     ......     ......     ......
 ........   ........   ........   ........   ........   ........   ........
 O.......   O.......   O.......   O.......   O.......   O.......   O.......
 O.......   O.......   O.......   O.......   O.......   O.......   O.......
 O.......   O.......   O.......   O.......   O.......   O.......   O.......
 O.......   O.......   O.......   O.......   O.......   O.......   O.......
 O......O   O......O   O.......O  O......O   O......O   O.......   O.......
 O......O   O......O   O.......O  O......O   O......O   O......O   O......O

    158        159        160        161        162        163        164
 O.....     O.....     OO...O     OO...O     OO...O     OO...O     OOO..O
 O.......   OO......   OO.....O   OO.....O   OO.....O   OO.....O   OO.....O
 O.......   O.......   O.......   O......O   O......O   O......O   O......O
 O.......   O.......   O.......   O.......   O.......   O.......   O.......
 O.......   O.......   O.......   O.......   O.......   O.......   O.......
 O.......   O.......   ........   ........   ........   ........   ........
 O.......   O.......
 O......O   O.......

    165        166        167        168        169        170        171
 OOO.OO     OOO.OO     OOO.OO     OOO.OO     OOOOOO     OOOOOO     OOOOOO
 OO.....O   OO.....O   OO.....O   OO....OO   OO....OO   OOO...OO   OOO...OO
 O......O   OO.....O   OO.....O   OO.....O   OO.....O   OO.....O   OO....OO
 O.......   O......O   O......O   O......O   O......O   O......O   O......O
 O.......   O.......   O.......   O......O   O......O   O......O   O......O
 ........   ........   ........   ........   ........   O.......   O.......
 ........   ........   ........   ........   ........   ........   O.......
 ........   ........   ........   ........   ........   ........   O.......

    172        173        174        175        176        177        178
 OOOOOO     OOOOOO     OOOOOO     OOOOOO     OOOOOO     OOOOOO     OOOOOO
 OOO...OO   OOO...OO   OOO...OO   OOO..OOO   OOO...OOO  OOO...OOO  OOO..OOO
 OO....OO   OO....OO   OO....OO   OO....OO   OO....OO   OO....OO   OO....OO
 O......O   O......O   O......O   O......O   O......O   O......O   O......O
 O......O   O......O   O......O   O......O   O......O   O......O   O......O
 O.......   O......O   O......O   O......O   O......O   O......O   O......O
 O.......   O......O   O......O   O......O   O......O   O......O   O......O
 O.......   O......O   O......O   O......O   O......O   O......O   O......O
```

Figure 3.11 Fricative phase before complete alveolar closure is achieved in /t/ production at DP4.

Implications

Most accounts of misarticulated sibilant fricatives describe three categories of misarticulation: dentalisation, lateralisation, and retraction of some sort such as palatal, palatalised or retroflexed realisations (Daniloff et al., 1980; Ohde and Sharf, 1992). Rebecca, however, showed an unusual pattern of a combination of dentalisation *and* lateralisation. Thus the therapeutic task in remediating her alveolar fricatives had the dual aims both of facilitating the retraction of the tongue tip from a dental to an alveolar place of articulation and of helping her to achieve release of airstream through a central lingual groove. Whereas it is more difficult to predict whether or not spontaneous improvement will take place with immature dentalisation of alveolar targets, the literature suggests that lateral misarticulations will not improve without therapy (Stephens et al., 1986). In a case such as Rebecca's, where there is a grosser overall misarticulation involving both dentalisation *and* lateralisation, it may have been possible to predict at an earlier age that she would need therapy to facilitate correct articulation of the sibilant fricatives and affricates. Rebecca's sound system at age 10 years contained a number of problems but could best be defined as an articulatory rather than a phonological disorder. The misarticulations were related in manner and a combination of perceptual and instrumental analysis showed that, even when the auditory distinction between target phonemes was not clearly signalled to the listener, Rebecca was indeed signalling intended phonological distinctions by the use of distinct articulatory gestures.

In choosing to target therapy on the misarticulation of /s/ and /z/, the focus of main attention, both during the therapy sessions and in the perceptual and instrumental analysis of the data, was confined to these segments until the point where it became obvious that Rebecca's sound system as a whole was undergoing articulatory changes. However, to explain these widespread and unsought changes in Rebecca's speech over the 10 months following the original block of EPG therapy, it was necessary to re-examine her original sound system holistically, rather than viewing the misarticulated segments as being unrelated to the system as a whole. Rebecca had originally presented with a palatalised voice quality and a generally close jaw setting, combined with a class 2 dental malocclusion and a reduced overbite. Her sound system did not contain any grooved lingual–palatal fricatives and there was lateral (and variably dentalised) realisation of a significant number of normally median segments: /s, z, ʃ, ʒ, ʧ, ʤ, r/. When producing interdental realisations of alveolar targets there was visible lowering of the jaw and some indication of instability of mandibular control shown by variable asymmetrical lateral mandibular movement, which echoed asymmetry of the lips and tongue in speech production. This may link to the claim by Wilcox et al. (1985) that there is a positive relationship between lateral misarticulations and close jaw setting. These observations suggest that Rebecca's speech was habitually produced with a high tongue body and that her preferred articulatory gesture for alveolar and postalveolar segments was that of raising that high tongue body into a stricture of complete closure. This was a successful strategy for the production of /l/ but not, obviously, for the remaining alveolar and postalveolar segments.

To correct the misarticulation of /s/ and /z/ required the introduction of the ability to produce a central lingual groove and this, in turn, involved the radical adjustment of long-term habitual lingual and mandibular settings. Introducing this grooved articulation appears to have radically affected her kinaesthetic and proprioceptive experience of speech production and to have triggered changes throughout her speech, in particular affecting the subsystem of alveolar and postalveolar segments which were already interrelated by the nature of their misarticulated realisations. Close analysis of the data reveals that this process of change was a gradual one which had already begun taking place at the end of the original block of EPG therapy. Although consistent patterns of articulatory change can be identified by instrumental analysis, they were not identifiable by means of auditory and visual perception.

The perceptual analysis of Rebecca's speech was based on video recordings and on live observation of her speech production, although regrettably there were no audio recordings made of the early EPG therapy sessions. There are various well-documented advantages and disadvantages of transcription using these different conditions. Although it is virtually impossible to capture enough accurate detail from the fleeting speech signal in the live situation, this nevertheless provides the best auditory and visual quality of the data. Audio and video recordings allow repeated observation of the data, but the former lacks important information on visual aspects of speech production whereas the sound quality of the latter may be inferior to audio recordings. Certainly the visual information available in the video recordings of Rebecca's speech was extremely valuable in later analysis and it is debatable how much audio recordings would have improved the transcription of those aspects of her speech production that were revealed by instrumental means.

In this way, the technique of electropalatography was a doubly valuable one in this study. First, its visual feedback provided Rebecca with the necessary information to correct her previously intransigent misarticulation of /s/ and /z/. This, happily, proved to have a markedly beneficial effect on her self-confidence, showing how important it is to provide effective therapy for those misarticulations that are often referred to as 'minor' because they do not have pervasive phonological effects on the speaker's sound system and thus on intelligibility. Second, EPG provided the means for a detailed analysis of Rebecca's speech production which revealed a significant number of important articulatory features that had proved difficult or impossible to capture by transcription alone; indeed, it explained the difficulties transcribers had with some segments, in particular those with very broad bands of closure which gave conflicting visual and auditory impressions. It would have been useful to have had the opportunity to make further instrumental investigations of aspects of Rebecca's speech production. Spectrography could have provided more information about how articulatory behaviour was reflected in the acoustic signal and it would have been beneficial to the study to have had an objective method of measuring mandibular setting and activity in speech production.

It is significant that in this case study the detailed phonetic analysis of Rebecca's alveolar and postalveolar subsystem took place retrospectively, rather than as an ongoing accompaniment to the therapy for /s/ and /z/. Indeed, typically it would be considered unusual to devote significant amounts of staff time to phonetic analysis in a case of articulation therapy of discrete segments. However, if Rebecca's sound system had been examined in detail and also viewed from a more holistic perspective from the outset, it might have been possible to predict some of the unexpected but significant changes to her speech production, although it is debatable whether prediction could have permitted prevention of the undesirable changes. Speech and language therapists are accustomed to seeing phonological therapy as affecting a whole sound system; indeed it is a cornerstone of phonological therapy that discrete changes will generalise throughout a system and that change to a particular segment can trigger changes to related segments. It is not, however, usual to adopt the view that articulation therapy for discrete misarticulation of individual sounds could have significant pervasive effects throughout the speaker's sound system as a whole. This, nevertheless, is what occurred with Rebecca. Although the degree of change and of detrimental auditory effect was particularly significant in this case, it is likely that detailed perceptual and instrumental analysis of the speech production of other individuals who have received articulation therapy for discrete sounds would also reveal similar if not as marked changes.

Appendix: EPG word list

peace	a zoo	razor	pots
peas	a shore	washer	pods
fish	a chalk	measure	balls
peach	a jaw	nature	walks
age	horse	major	warts
a sea	paws	a stop	wards
a zip	Porsche	a spot	bags
a sheep	a torch	a Scot	
a cheep	a gorge	a slop	
a jeep	racer	the tops	
a saw			

Chapter 4
Cleft palate: a perceptual and instrumental investigation of a phonological system

SARA HOWARD and CAROLINE PICKSTONE

Background

Introduction

This study examines the articulatory and phonological abilities of Rachel, a 6-year-old girl with a repaired cleft palate.* At the time of the investigation she had received speech therapy treatment over several years, but although some changes in speech production had taken place, overall there had been little significant improvement and it was felt that her speech was remarkably resistant to treatment.

Case history

Rachel was born 11 weeks pre-term, with a central cleft of the hard and soft palate. Although there had been very little babbling, her expressive and receptive language appears to have developed satisfactorily, in contrast with her speech, which at the age of 6 still presented as a significant problem. Rachel, in common with many cleft palate patients (Russell, 1989a; Stengelhofen, 1989), had a history of mild-to-moderate conductive hearing impairment, resulting from chronic infections of the middle ear. Ventilation tubes or grommets were inserted at the age of 3 years and reinserted at 4 years, and significant improvements in auditory ability were reported. T tubes were inserted at 5;11 years and once again improvements in hearing levels were reported, although auditory discrimination for some speech sounds remained inconsistent. Surgical repair of the cleft palate took place at 2;2 years, and at 5;5 years a pharyngoplasty was carried out with the aim of reducing

*A somewhat different version of this study was published as Howard (1993) in *Clinical Linguistics and Phonetics*.

65

nasal emission during speech. Unfortunately the pharyngoplasty failed to bring about the hoped for improvement. Assessment for oral apraxia and apraxia of speech had not suggested a pattern of significant problems with volitional oral movements. Also the nature of Rachel's difficulties was not consistent with a pattern of congenital suprabulbar paresis (Worster–Drought syndrome) (Rain, 1993), although both had been suggested at different stages as possible aetiologies.

The problem

The immediate puzzle presenting was of a child with extremely abnormal speech production and an apparently severely reduced phonological system which was proving very resistant to therapy, who nevertheless achieved a surprisingly high level of intelligibility after only a brief period of listener 'adjustment'. Rachel was a sociable child and a confident communicator who appeared to be largely unaware of the severity of her speech production problems because her family and friends and those with whom she came into regular contact, such as teachers and therapists, were able to understand her spoken language fairly easily. Her mother, in fact, commented that she often found herself forgetting that Rachel had a speech disorder. This was in marked contrast to the reactions of those individuals, speech and language therapists included, who, after coming into contact with Rachel for the first time, always remarked on the severity of her speech problems and the initial unintelligibility of her speech.

We were interested to identify the nature of Rachel's speech disorder and, given its severity, to explain why so many people found her so intelligible. One of our main aims was to clarify whether Rachel's speech was the result of a primary articulatory problem where articulatory constraints limited her ability to signal target phonological contrasts, or whether, particularly in view of her history of hearing impairment, it illustrated an interrelationship of articulatory problems and disordered or delayed phonological development. From the point of view of a listener, Rachel's phonological system was clearly inadequate and phonetically distant from the target system. Rachel could signal only a very limited number of phonemic contrasts in a manner that corresponded to normal speech patterns. Other contrasts appeared to be absent or, at best, signalled by distorted or deviant speech segments. It was felt that detailed and integrated phonetic and phonological analyses of Rachel's sound system could help in the formulation of a principled therapeutic management programme, while at the same time providing insight into the relationships between articulation and phonology in disordered speech. As will become apparent from our treatment of the data, we felt that only an analysis that undertook to examine the data in what some might consider an unusual amount of detail could illuminate the complex articulatory and phonological relationships which resulted in Rachel's sound system.

Theoretical background

The severity and intractability of Rachel's speech disorder was striking even in comparison with the general client population of children with cleft palate. Indeed, it is estimated that as many as 50–60% of children with cleft lip and/or palate will develop acceptable sounding speech without the need of speech and language therapy (Grunwell and Russell, 1988; Albery, 1989). Even so, at any one time in the UK there will be approximately 15 000 children with cleft lip/palate who *do* require help from a speech and language therapist (Enderby and Philipp, 1986) and for some of these children disentangling the articulatory and phonological components of their disorder can pose a real challenge. At an articulatory level, speech production problems may pervade each of the subsystems of articulation, phonation and resonance as a result of structural, sensory and kinaesthetic abnormalities and deficits caused by the cleft palate itself, and also sometimes by subsequent surgery. Cleft palate children experience problems in achieving and coordinating movements of the lips, tongue, velum and vocal folds such that both segmental and prosodic aspects of speech may be affected. Thus there may be articulatory problems in producing target segments with certain places and manners of articulation (in particular lingual–palatal obstruents), resonatory problems as evidenced by audible nasal emission of air and hyper- or hyponasality and phonatory problems both in signalling voiced–voiceless contrasts at the segmental level and in overall voice quality and pitch. However, at the same time, children with cleft palate may suffer from phonological delay or disorder resulting from difficulties with the internal representation and organisation of the sound system. The large number of children with cleft palate whose auditory input has been disturbed from an early age by chronic and often fluctuating conductive hearing impairment may be particularly vulnerable to phonological difficulties (Shriberg and Smith, 1983; Bamford and Saunders, 1990; Russell and Grunwell, 1993).

As both articulatory and phonological difficulties may have the same end result of unintelligible speech, it is not always easy to disentangle the two and to identify the basis of the speech disorder. But this, of course, is a crucial part of the intervention process, because a speech disorder that has a primarily articulatory basis will require and respond to a different therapeutic approach from a phonological disorder and speech that is the result of a combination of articulatory and phonological factors will require yet a different plan of management, even if each type of disorder causes very similar problems for the listener.

It is important to consider both the speaker and the listener in the investigation of the effects of disordered speech and in the mid-1980s considerable debate centred on the value of speaker-oriented versus listener/data-oriented analyses of disordered speech. Hewlett (1985) argued in favour of a speaker-oriented approach, where importance was placed on the speaker's intended production, irrespective of whether this intention was realised in the actual speech production. Hewlett notes, for example, that 'What is relevant in a case like the pronunciation [tɪn] for the word *din* is whether the speaker's intention was to produce a /d/ or a /t/'(p. 158). As Rachel has had marked hearing impairment, it seemed likely that at least part of her problem could be the result of deficits in the organisation, rather than the realisation, of her phonological system. In other words, it may have been that rather than the listener being unable to interpret her intended contrasts, she was in fact not attempting to signal the full range of adult phonemes. On the other hand, Rachel's speech also had many of the characteristic features associated with cleft palate, e.g. a lack of lingual–palatal articulations, glottalisation of target obstruents, consonants, hypernasality and abnormalities of phonation – which can cause the neutralisation of phonological contrasts and the breakdown of intelligibility, but which can be presumed to result primarily from articulatory constraints. As Hawkins (1985) remarks, a subject with disordered speech may indeed be aware of phonological contrasts which he or she is unable to signal, or may be signalling contrasts in such a way that the listener cannot perceive them. If this proved to be the case with Rachel's speech, one would be able to argue that she did not have problems at the organisational phonological level, but that implementation problems reduced her ability to signal her phonological contrasts to the listener. This would be consistent with Hewlett's (1988, 1990) 'two-lexicon' theory of phonological processing and phonetic production, where an 'input lexicon' contains perceptual representations of single words represented in terms of their auditory–perceptual features. These representations are then mapped by a series of realisational rules onto articulatory representations in the output lexicon. Hewlett suggests that, in the case of abnormal speech, a speaker might possess correct phonological representations in the auditorily/perceptually based 'input lexicon' (e.g. representing *string* as /strɪŋ/), but as a result of, for example, the structural anomalies of the vocal tract associated with cleft palate, would be forced to devise different motor programmes to execute production. This would entail compensatory articulatory strategies resulting in a different phonological representation in the 'output lexicon'. This representation, Hewlett argues, would consequently prove difficult to change, even if the physical anomalies originally causing it were then removed, for example, by surgery.

Harris and Cottam (1985) also provide support for examining data from the perspective of speaker intention rather than listener interpretation, and like Hewlett (1985) and Beresford (1987) argue for explanatory rather than merely descriptive approaches. On the other hand, Crystal (1981), Grunwell (1985a) and Milroy (1985) have all sounded a note of caution regarding the validity of proposing explanatory power or psychological reality for phonological models, although Grunwell, highlighting the importance of interaction between articulatory and phonological levels, has suggested that detailed and exhaustive phonetic and phonological analyses might form the basis for explanatory, speaker-oriented models, at least at the level of the single case study and, indeed, suggests that the PACS framework although basically descriptive in nature could be used to formulate explanatory theories.

Initial hypotheses

The following are two initial hypotheses that we wished to test, based on a first brief exposure to Rachel's speech:

1. Rachel has an intact speaker-oriented phonology: her internalised phonological representations are adequate, but articulatory constraints operating presently or in the past have limited her ability to realise these satisfactorily.
2. Rachel's high level of intelligibility is the result of her recourse to subtle, subphonemic cues which she uses to signal target phonological contrasts.

Analysis

Data collection and analytical frameworks

The first step in trying to disentangle the complex articulatory and phonological relationships in Rachel's speech was to collect a sample of speech and carry out a detailed phonetic transcription to form the basis for a phonological analysis. The absolute necessity of detailed transcription at this initial stage in clinical phonological analysis has considerable support (see Chapter 2), based on the premise that in disordered speech all phonetic information may have phonological implications, and that every case will differ and may make use of phonetic parameters in unusual ways to signal phonological contrasts.

Accordingly, high-quality audio and video recordings of Rachel's speech were made, simultaneous with live transcription by a clinical phonetician and a speech therapist. Samples of both the production of words in isolation, and of connected speech in free conversation and picture description were collected. At this stage it was noted, not surprisingly, that Rachel's speech was somewhat better in the production of words in isolation, so it was decided, at this preliminary stage at least, to base the phonological analysis on this part of the data as being representative of Rachel's optimal phonological performance, and arguably the best reflection of her phonological competence. The data were transcribed using IPA and ExtIPA symbols, and further annotations and comments where necessary. This material formed the basis for an initial phonological analysis of Rachel's speech.

For such an analysis it was decided to use the PACS framework (Grunwell, 1985b) for the following reasons. First, it is an assessment that includes a variety of specific procedures designed to elucidate the data from different perspectives which, as Grunwell states, allows the user to 'select procedures appropriate to the specific child's speech to be analysed'. Second, while allowing for a developmental perspective, PACS also provides a framework for analysing phonological disorders where the speech is not usefully characterised by comparison with developmental patterns. Third, it is a framework where the inclusion of phonetic data at a number of points in the different analyses allows for the identification of phonetic relationships underpinning phonological contrasts and for the forming of hypotheses regarding the articulatory constraints on the sound system. As well as providing a description of Rachel's phonological abilities, it thus has potential explanatory power.

The PACS analysis

Although a full PACS (Phonological Assessment of Child Speech) analysis was carried out, only selected sections will be discussed here. This is because Rachel's speech did not conform readily to patterns of developmental delay, and a natural process analysis such as that provided in PACS was therefore not helpful in its description. As Rachel's speech appeared markedly abnormal, but in a consistent, patterned way, the task of our analysis was to identify and attempt to explain these patterns.

Phonetic inventory

As shown in Figure 4.1, Rachel's speech included quite a wide range of phones, with a preponderance of 'front' (labial and labiodental) and 'back' (uvular, pharyngeal, glottal) articulations and a noticeable lack of lingual–palatal obstruents. We were interested in establishing which of these phones were potentially contrastively significant, which were non-contrastive variants, and also which could be identified as being the products of previous therapy rather than Rachel's spontaneous attempts at sound production.

It is worth echoing at this point Kelly and Local's (1989) remark that 'some phonological treatments of children's speech reduce the primary

	Labial	Dental	Alveolar	Post-Alveolar	Palatal	Velar	Glottal	Other
Nasal	m m:							N N: Nʰ
Plosive	b b̃ p̃ʰ b̥						ʔ ʔʰ	p̚ʔ
Fricative	f̃ff ff θ θ̃ v̰ v̥ v̶			ç̃ ç̃ ç̰ ç̃h		h	ɧ ç̃ɟ ɧ ç̃ɬ ɧ̃
Affricate								ʔç̃
Approximant	w w̃ ʋ̰ ʋ			j j:				ʔj
Other	⊙							oʔ

Marginal Phones: f̬ ç̰̃ h̝ ɰ ʟ (ɹ?)

Figure 4.1 Phonetic inventory.

phonic data inappropriately'. It is, indeed, sometimes a temptation at this stage in the analysis to 'clean up' and 'phonemicise' the data, either for economy of time or because the analyst's listener-oriented perspective appears to justify it. In Rachel's case, however, this would be singularly unhelpful because it is not yet possible to distinguish between phonetic variants that are merely random or contextually determined and others that may well be significant, contrastive segments in Rachel's speaker-oriented phonological system.

Phonotactic possibilities

A comparison of the phonotactic structure of Rachel's sound system with that of the adult target system reveals an almost complete match. Rachel is acknowledging and signalling, by various articulatory strategies, each position in which a segment occurs in an adult target word, thereby implying knowledge of the phonological structure of English words. This is in accord with her teacher's observations that Rachel's reading and writing skills are appropriate for her age. Thus, even in complex clusters each element of the cluster is marked by a corresponding segment in Rachel's speech, even though these segments may be auditorily and articulatorily distant from the target form, for example:

glasses	/ˈglæsɪz/	[ˈɴwæ̃ç̃ə̃ç̃]	CCVCVC	–	CCVCVC
string	/ˈstɪɪŋ/	[ˈfŋwɪɴ]	CCCVC	–	CCCVC
soldier	/ˈsəʊldʒə/	[ˈç̃əʊʟʔjə]	CVCCV	–	CVCCV

Systems of contrastive phones/feature contrasts

The first of these two procedures provides a clear polysystemic summary of how Rachel's wide range of phones is used to contrastive effect
at various places in structure, as shown in Figure 4.2.

Syllable Initial Word Initial

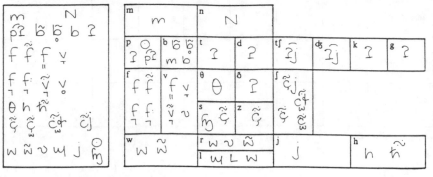

Syllable Initial Within Word

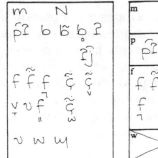

Syllable Final Word Final

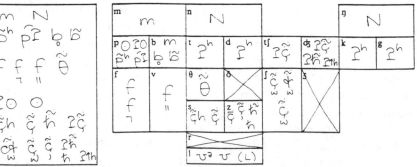

Figure 4.2 Systems of contrastive phones and contrastive assessments.

The second (Figure 4.3) shows Rachel's contrastive performance at a more generalised level, i.e. that of broad, phonetically based phonological feature categories.

By examining the results from these two procedures together it is possible to gauge Rachel's success at maintaining contrasts between broad classes of sounds based on feature contrasts such as place and manner of articulation, and also discover how contrasts were then marked between individual segments.

The four following sections contain a detailed examination of manner, place of articulation and voicing contrasts and provide significant information regarding the articulatory underpinning of Rachel's sound system.

Manner of articulation 1: nasal–oral

The ability to signal a clear distinction between oral and nasal segments is, of course, fundamental for satisfactory phonological development and one that is acquired early in the speech of normally developing children. In articulatory terms it is dependent on ability to raise and lower the velum and to coordinate velic movements with other articulatory gestures. The appropriate velic action is necessary to valve the egressive airflow through the nasal or oral cavities to achieve clearly audible contrasts between those segments with nasal airflow and those with predominantly oral airflow. The latter may not require complete velic closure but there must be a clear and consistent difference in airflow ratios between the two types of segment (Laver, 1980b).

Feature Contrasts

		SIWI	SIWW	SFWF
Nasal	– Plosive	✓	m N – p̃ʔ O ʔ b̥ b̥	m N – p̃ʔ b̥ b̥ b̥ʔ	m N – ʊ ʔ ʊ pʰ pʔ
Stop	– Fricative	✓	O p̃ʔ b ʔ – f ʰ̃j θ h ̃ʔ etc.	p̃ʔ b ʔ – f ʊ ʔ etc.	pʰ O b – f ʰ̃ ʔ etc.
Stop	– Affricate	✓	ʔ – ʔj̃	ʔ – ʔj̃	ʔʰ – ʔ ʔ̃ etc.
Fricative – Affricate		✓	h̃j ʔ̃ etc. – ʔj̃	ʔ̃ f etc. – ʔj̃	ʔ̃ F θ etc. – 2 ʔ̃
Stop	– Approximant	✓	p̃ʔ ʔ O ʔ – ʊ ʊ ʊ (J̃) j	p̃ʔ ʔ ʔ dc – ʊ ʊ L	ʔʰ – L
Fricative – Approximant		✓	f̃ ʔ θ h̃ etc. – ʊ (ʊ) j	f ʊ ʔ ʊ – ʊ ʊ w L	fʰ̃ θ ʔ̃ etc. – L
Labial	– Lingual	✓	m O b etc. – ʔ̃ L j etc	m b p̃ʔ – ʔ̃ L etc	m p̃ʰ O – ʔ̃ L etc.
Alveolar – Velar		✗	ʔ N – ʔ N	ʔ N – ʔ N	ʔʰ N – ʔʰ N
Alveolar – Post-Alveolar		?	possibly contrasted by labialisation	? : ʔ̃ – ʔ̃
Alveolar – Dental		✓	ʔ̃ h̃ – θ	ʔ̃ – ʊ	ʔ̃ – θ̃
Voiced	– Voiceless	✗	only occasional target voiced	evidence of voicing obstruent	evidence of voicing ʔ̃
Med. Approx. – Lat. Approx.	✓	ʊ (J̃) ʊ L	ʊ, ʊj – L	
Other Features					

Figure 4.3 Feature contrasts.

Rachel, however, in common with many children with a cleft palate (Russell, 1989a; Stengelhofen, 1989), has and has had problems preventing nasal escape of air during the production of target oral segments. At a non-segmental level, this nasal escape gives a general overlay of increased nasality to her habitual voice quality, but at the segmental level nasal escape has more serious consequences for the production of oral obstruents because of the reduction in difference between airflow ratios and the concomitant reduction in oral air pressure for target oral segments. We expected that Rachel would possess the phonological contrast oral:nasal, but that articulatory constraints would make its realisation problematic.

An examination of the data shows that in Rachel's speech nasals in all contexts are fully nasal and are generally contrasted successfully with oral segments by various means, thus maintaining the broad oral–nasal contrast. It is illuminating to examine in more detail how this contrast is expressed in terms of individual segments.

Given the problem of nasal escape, one way of achieving an adequate plosive is to ensure that plosion takes place before loss of air can occur nasally, by substituting a glottal plosive and this is a strategy which Rachel, in common with many cleft palate speakers (Grunwell and Russell, 1988; Albery and Grunwell, 1993), uses frequently.

For alveolar and velar segments her contrast is between a uvular nasal and a glottal plosive, so that although the contrast is between an oral and a nasal segment, neither actually corresponds to the target sound, for example:

letter	[ˈɥeʔə]	nose	[nəʊç̃]
ladder	[ˈɥæʔə]	ring	[ʊɪɴ]
sugar	[ˈç̃ʊʔə]	fine	[f̟:aɪɴ]
down	[ʔaʊɴ]	penny	[ˈp͡ʔɛnɪ]
dog	[ʔɒʔʰ]	singing	[ˈç̃ɪnɪɴ]
cat	[ʔæʔʰ]	teaspoon	[ʔiç̃ɓuɴ]

For bilabials, the picture is more complex and appears to be the result of two separate factors: the established preference of cleft palate speakers for 'front' and 'back' articulations (Grunwell and Russell, 1988; Russell, 1989b) and the effect of a significant amount of previous speech therapy aimed at achieving a satisfactory voiceless bilabial plosive, for example:

pig	[ʘɪʔʰ]	mud	[məʔʰ]
pen	[ʔɛɴ]	mum	[məm]
tap	[ʔæʔʘ]	mouth	[maʊθ:]
paper	[p͡ʔeɪp͡ʔə]	thumb	[θəm]
big	[mɪʔʰ]	jam	[ʔjæm]

baby   ['ɓeɪbɪ]   hammer   ['h̃æmə]

bike   [maɪʔʰ]/[ɓaɪʔʰ]

As with target alveolars and velars, Rachel sometimes substitutes a glottal plosive for a bilabial segment. Helpfully for the listener (or observer!), she also sometimes gives an additional visual clue by co-articulating a bilabial closure [p̂ʔ]. Where a glottal plosive is not used, Rachel has the problem of nasal escape of air during oral articulations and this can be seen in various realisations of target plosives [ɓ, p̃ʰ, m] while others appear to achieve fully oral status. Here we have a continuum of sounds with differing oral–nasal airflow ratios. Some of these will prove difficult for the listener to identify correctly. Some target bilabial plosives will transgress categorical hearing boundaries by a wide margin and thus be identified inappropriately as bilabial nasals; others will occur on the margins of perceptual categories and thus prove difficult to identify. The rather more unusual realisations of [ʘ, ʘʔ] for /p/ were not noted in earlier transcriptions of Rachel's speech and thus appear to be the product of speech and language therapy aimed at replacing [ʔ] with /p/, where Rachel attempts to mimic a strongly audible voiceless bilabial plosive by using a velaric air stream mechanism.

In spite of much variability in these realisations, there is actually remarkably little overlap between oral and nasal segments and Rachel can be seen to be maintaining at least a rudimentary contrast between the two. Her realisations suggest that there is a degree of velopharyngeal incompetence, but also that there *is* some velic movement to control airflow partially

We decided that Rachel's velopharyngeal competence and the nasality of her speech should be examined in more detail and the instrumental investigations we carried out are reported later.

Manner of articulation 2: the stop:fricative:approximant continuum and the stop:affricate continuum

The articulatory basis of these classes of broad feature contrasts is that of differences of stricture along an open–close continuum and, in the case of stop versus affricate, of timing of release of closure. As with the nasal–oral contrast, Rachel is almost always successful in signalling these contrasts in terms of feature classes, although significantly, in terms of actual segments used, there is once again little correspondence between her segments and those of the target system.

All of Rachel's attempts at target plosives are realised by some sort of stricture of complete closure, usually plosives with the occasional ejective or nasal. In contrast, almost all of her fricative segments are realised by some sort of friction. Often this is achieved by or accompanied by nasal friction. Rachel distinguishes affricates from stops and fricatives, and acknowledges their structural nature by marking both the stop and fricative element of the affricate: the former, consistent with her realisation of alveolar stops, by use of a glottal plosive, the latter either by some kind of friction or by a palatal approximant. All the target approximants in the data are realised by various types of approximant. This, then, is evidence of a clear distinction at the phonological level being realised in a consistent manner within certain articulatory constraints.

A selection of words from the data illustrates these contrasts in word initial position:

tap	[ʔæʔʰ]	sock	[çɒʔʰ]	go	[ʔəu]
down	[ʔauɴ]	shop	[c̃jɒpʰ]	yes	[jɛʔ]
chair	[ʔjeə]	zipɪ	[ç̃ʔⵔ]	why	[waɪ]
jam	[ʔjæm]	cup	[ʔʊʔʰ]		

Thus it can be seen that Rachel has various articulatory strategies for maintaining these broad feature contrasts of manner of articulation. This is one of the aspects of her sound system which has a positive effect on her intelligibility, in spite of her actual segmental realisations being auditorily so distant from the target system.

Place of articulation

Contrasts of place of articulation within the oral cavity constitute a very significant gap within Rachel's sound system, resulting in the potential neutralisation of a number of important segmental distinctions. As already noted, in common with many cleft palate speakers (Grunwell and Russell, 1988; Russell, 1989b) Rachel displays a predisposition towards 'front' and 'back' articulations. Although she produces labial and labiodental articulations, there is little evidence in her speech production of segments requiring strictures of close approximation in the alveolar-to-velar region. Her tendency before therapy had been to back most target oral consonants to uvular, pharyngeal and glottal places of articulation. Therapy aimed at facilitating fricative production has apparently met with more success for segments with a clear visual element, i.e. /f, v, θ, ð/, than for strictures made less visibly within the oral cavity, i.e. /s, z, ʃ, ʒ/. These target alveolar and postalveolar articulations, although having been effectively brought forward from previous pharyngeal realisations, are misarticulated with minimal evidence of contrasts, although the labialisation of some of Rachel's realisations of target postalveolar fricatives may constitute a significant attempt to signal an alveolar–postalveolar contrast. Target lingual–palatal plosives and affricates typically remained 'backed' to glottal realisations.

Examples from the data illustrate the problems:

baby	[ˈbeɪbɪ]	paper	[pˀeɪpˀə]	Daddy	[ʔæʔɪ]
toy	[ʔɔɪ]	kick	[ʔɪʔʰ]	dog	[ʔɒʔʰ]
cat	[ʔæʔʰ]	bucket	[ˈbʊʔɪʔʰ]	sugar	[ç̃ǁʊʔə]
tap	[ʔæʔʘ]	Sue	[ç̃u]	shoe	[ç̃u]

Voicing

As with the overlay of nasality which at times interfered with the clarity of Rachel's nasal–oral distinction, here it is difficult in the first instance to distinguish the effect of Rachel's voice quality from her ability to mark the voicing of segments. Habitually, Rachel's voice quality is high-pitched and very breathy which reduces the perceptible contrast between voice and voicelessness. Thus the impression is of a variable rather than a consistently signalled contrast. Closer investigation of individual segments, however, reveals a more complex picture.

With regard to plosives, a contrast is usually marked for bilabials, but there is no apparent contrast for alveolar and velar targets. For fricatives generally, Rachel displays significant difficulty in combining friction with voicing. For some fricatives and for affricates, Rachel appears to achieve a voiced segment by using a more open stricture to produce an approximant, e.g. /v/ as [ɣ, ʋ], thus transgressing the boundary between different manners of articulation. This example is, however, a successful strategy in phonological terms because there is no danger of overlap at this point in the system with any other segment. Another articulatory strategy used by Rachel to signal a phonological contrast between /f/ and /v/ is relative force of articulation, such that target /v/ can alternatively be realised as [f] in contrast with a relatively weakly articulated [f̡] for target /f/. Examples of these strategies are shown below:

pig	[ʘɪʔʰ]	bib	[ɓɪɓʰ]	dig	[ʔɪʔʰ]
baby	[ˈbeɪbɪ]	tea	[ʔi]	key	[ʔi]
letter	[ˈɯe̞ʔə]	ladder	[ˈɯæʔə]	go	[ʔəʊ]
Sue	[ç̃u]	zoo	[ç̃u]	chair	[ʔjɛə]
watch	[wɒʔç̃]	jam	[ʔjæm]	fridge	[fʊɪʔh̃]
four	[f̡ɔ]	a van	[ə ˈfæɴ]	cover	[ʔʊʋə]
feather	[ˈf̡eʋə]	laughing	[ˈɯæfɪɴ]		

At this stage there is a lack of clear evidence of the presence of an established contrast, so we cannot be sure that this is not a phonological problem from the speaker's point of view. It may be, however, that once again Rachel's problems are at an articulatory level but with listener-oriented phonological consequences. We have already noted the likelihood that reduced oral airflow makes the production of oral obstruents difficult, and this combined with laryngeal setting may conspire against a clear voiced–voiceless contrast. It was further felt that Rachel's voice quality and consequent difficulties with voicing distinctions might be linked to a complex dynamic interaction of laryngeal, lingual and velopharyngeal function (Boone and McFarlane, 1988) and this was an area that we decided to explore in more detail instrumentally.

Summary: multiple loss of contrasts and the phoneme /z/

The overall conclusion to be drawn from Rachel's PACS is of a sound system where there is a lot of relatively consistent and controlled articulatory activity occurring simultaneously along several phonetic parameters to achieve phonological contrasts, but with the net effect that very few adult target consonants are realised. Instead what is produced appears to be a complex system of articulations designed to contrast target phonemes within the bounds of certain articulatory constraints which may be present now or may, critically, have been present when Rachel was originally attempting to construct a phonological system (see Hewlett, 1990). This suggests an intact internalised phonological system, arguing against a phonological disorder from the speaker-oriented perspective, and begins to explain why Rachel's deviant sound system is still surprisingly intelligible even though there are problems of listener adjustment and the sound system is inadequate from a listener/data driven perspective.

If we take a single phoneme, /z/, from the target system and examine its various realisations in Rachel's speech, we can capture the essence of her speech disorder, for example

Syllable initial word initial   [ç̃]
Syllable initial within-word   [ç̃, ç̃]
Syllable final word final   [ç̃, ç̃, ç̃, ɦ, ɦ̃]

Rachel's problems stem from the simultaneous interaction of multiple constraints which may be structural, sensory or kinaesthetic in origin, and which affect each of the subsystems of articulation, phonation and resonance. Problems with nasal emission, voicing and lingual stricture combine to produce various phones which are both auditorily and articulatorily distant from the target and which also overlap with realisations of other target phonemes. These problems reduce her ability to signal phonological contrasts clearly and unambiguously to the listener, even though she herself is aware of such contrasts and appears to be attempting to signal them by various compensatory strategies. It may be that the listener's gradual unconscious adjustment to these strategies accounts for Rachel's surprisingly high levels of intelligibility.

So far our hypotheses regarding the nature of Rachel's speech disorder had been based on our auditory perceptions of her speech production. However, we now decided that further instrumental investigations would be useful, both in checking the validity of our perceptual observations and in investigating the presence of any further strategies present in her speech which served contrastive functions but which we had not been able to perceive consciously.

Follow-up investigations and analyses

As a result of auditory perceptual and phonological analyses, a number of areas emerged as being worthy of further investigation to provide us with more information about Rachel's articulatory and phonological abilities. Various instrumental techniques could augment (or correct!) our transcriptions and provide objective measurement of aspects of speech production which were difficult or impossible to capture by means of auditory perception. The following techniques were chosen:

1. Nasometry: to investigate velopharyngeal function and oral–nasal airflow relationships.
2. Electropalatography: to investigate the presence and character of lingual–palatal contact patterns in Rachel's speech.
3. Oral stereognosis: to investigate intraoral sensory and kinaesthetic awareness at a non-speech level.
4. Lateral cineradiography: to provide information about the activity of the tongue, soft palate and larynx, and their dynamic interrelationships.
5. Spectrography: to measure selected acoustic dimensions of the speech signal to assess for the presence of any intended phonological contrasts not discernible at the level of auditory perception.

A number of further assessments and investigations were subsequently carried out and the results are discussed below.

Nasometry

Our initial strategy to examine the actions of the soft palate in Rachel's speech was via nasoendoscopy. Huskie (1989) suggests this as a useful technique to provide more information about velopharyngeal function during speech and non-speech activities. A nasoendoscopy was attempted by an ENT surgeon but unfortunately the attempt was frustrated because Rachel's nasal passages proved too small to allow access to the nasoendoscope.

Nasometry, however, proved to be a more successful technique for gathering information about nasal–oral airflow relationships in Rachel's speech, in spite of being unable to provide the detailed visual information about soft palate function which would have been available using nasoendoscopy. The Exeter Nasal Anemometer was used to assess Rachel's speech production in single words and short phrases. Some of the utterances selected for assessment contained both oral and nasal target segments, whereas others contained only oral targets. The anemometer provides information about the comparative degrees of oral and nasal emission of air, although it does not claim to measure nasal resonance. Gross nasal emission of air was recorded for most target fricative segments. Our hypothesis, however, that Rachel was attempting to signal a consistent contrast between oral and nasal stops was confirmed. Comparing her attempts at target tokens of /p/, /b/ and /m/, we could see that, although almost all realisations of the oral stop targets were nasalised abnormally, none appeared to have the degree of nasality of target /m/. However, the degree of contrast along a nasal–oral continuum was significantly reduced in comparison with those contrasts of a normal speaker with the result that in some cases phonemic boundaries were blurred or transgressed.

Given the visual feedback of the instrumentation, Rachel was quickly able to modify her articulations by reducing the nasality of target oral obstruents. This was dependent on the visual cues and Rachel, at this stage, found it impossible to achieve the same articulatory modifications without such feedback. However, the results strengthened our view that Rachel did have a significant degree of potential velopharyngeal activity and control, which with the appropriate therapy could form the basis for the appropriate articulation of a nasal–oral contrast at the phonological level.

Electropalatography

Phonetic transcription of Rachel's speech had suggested a typical cleft palate profile of a dearth of obstruent articulations in the alveolar to velar region. Target alveolar and velar plosives appeared to be realised as glottal plosives, and alveolar and velar nasals were typically retracted to a uvular point of articulation. The only segments that suggested patterns of lingual–palatal contact were the palatal fricatives which we had transcribed as Rachel's realisations of some tokens of target alveolar and postalveolar fricatives. We wanted to establish if there was any evidence of lingual–palatal activity which we had been unable to perceive auditorily, such as co-articulatory movements that were masked auditorily by glottal plosives or any silent articulatory activity and also to examine in more detail Rachel's realisations of /s/, /z/, /ʃ/ and /ʒ/.

Electropalatography (EPG) is a technique that provides information about lingual–palatal contact patterns in the region from the alveolar ridge to the margins of the soft palate. In this investigation we used the

Reading EPG 2 model. The patient is fitted with an artificial acrylic palate wired with 62 touch-sensitive electrodes. This enables real-time visual representations of lingual contacts which can be displayed but also stored and printed for further analysis. Hardcastle and Edwards (1992) and Gibbon et al. (1993) provide examples of EPG's ability to capture detailed information about lingual activity which is not discernible by perceptual analysis. This includes co-articulatory activity, silent articulations and unusual lingual–palatal contact patterns. Hardcastle et al. (1989b), Gibbon and Hardcastle (1989), Yamashita et al. (1992) and Dent et al. (1992) have all demonstrated its usefulness in the investigation and remediation of speech disorders arising from cleft palate.

To obtain an EPG palate Rachel had upper and lower dental impressions taken and from these an EPG palate was made and fitted. The dental impressions and the EPG palate itself showed that Rachel had a very short and very flat palate with hardly any discernible ridge in the alveolar region and considerable disruption from postsurgical scarring. There were no fistulae in Rachel's oral cavity and manufacture of the artificial palate was not made more difficult, as is sometimes the case with cleft palate subjects, by the presence of any abnormally positioned teeth.

EPG recordings were made of Rachel producing words containing target alveolar and velar plosives, and alveolar and postalveolar fricatives in isolation and in short phrases. For the target plosives our auditory impression for both alveolar and velar targets was of a glottal plosive. Significantly, EPG recordings showed that in no case was there evidence of any simultaneous lingual contact in the alveolar-to-velar region. This confirmed that Rachel was not producing co-articulated segments (e.g. [t͡ʔ] [k͡ʔ], etc.] and that the glottal plosives were not masking lingual–palatal contacts for these target segments. The evidence suggested rather that Rachel was actually unable to coordinate and maintain the requisite lingual movements for alveolar and velar plosive articulations.

EPG also provided us with the means to check for the presence of subtle differences in the articulation of Rachel's alveolar and postalveolar fricative segments. We had already noted that Rachel seemed to be signalling a phonemic contrast between the two places of articulation by labialisation of target postalveolar fricatives. EPG data, however, failed to show any discernible differences in lingual contacts between the two. Both alveolar and postalveolar target fricatives were realised by a fricative stricture with a fairly broad central groove and a wide band of side tongue contact from postalveolar to the front of the velar region as shown in Figure 4.4. It was interesting to note that, given the visual feedback provided by EPG, Rachel was able at least to achieve co-articulated alveolar–glottal and velar–glottal realisations of target

```
    706          707          708          709          710          711
  ......       ......       ......       ......       ......       ......
 ........     ........     ........     ........     ........     ........
 .......0     .......0     .......0     .......0     .......0     .......0
 0.....00     0.....00     0.....00     0.....00     0.....00     0.....00
 0.....00     0.....00     0.....00     0.....00     0.....00     0.....00
 00....00     00....00     00....00     00....00     00....00     00....00
 000..000     000..000     000..000     000..000     000..000     000..000
 00...000     00...000     00...000     00...000     00...000     00...000


    712          713          714          715          716          717
  ......       ......       ......       ......       ......       ......
 ........     ........     ........     ........     ........     ........
 .......0     .......0     .......0     .......0     .......0     .......0
 0.....00     0.....00     0.....00     0.....00     0.....00     0.....00
 0.....00     00....00     00....00     00....00     00....00     00....00
 00...000     00...000     00...000     00...000     00...000     00...000
 000..000     000..000     000..000     000..000     000..000     000..000
 00...000     00...000     00...000     00...000     00...000     000..000
```

Figure 4.4 Typical lingual–palatal contact patterns for Rachel's /s, ʃ, z, ʒ/.

plosives and could fairly consistently make non-speech lingual contacts upon request at various places along the palate. Thus, as with the results of the nasometry investigations, once again visual feedback appeared to be a significant aid to Rachel's sound production.

Oral stereognosis

As Rachel appeared to have such severe problems in achieving lingual–palatal articulations, we carried out some testing as a means of gaining more information about oral sensory function. This involved assessing Rachel's ability to identify the shape of small objects by intra-oral manipulation, without the aid of visual feedback. A set of small wooden tokens of 10 different simple shapes (e.g. cross, circle, square, star) were placed one at a time on Rachel's tongue, without her seeing them. She then had 15 seconds to identify each shape from a matching array presented on the table in front of her. Of the 10 shapes presented Rachel was only able to identify one (the circle) correctly, although over the course of several weeks she demonstrated a learning ability that resulted in her being able to identify all 10.

Deutsch (1984) and Edwards (1984) point out that the literature fails to demonstrate a clear link between speech disorder and lack of ability in oral stereognosis tasks. Research in the 1970s and 1980s provided conflicting evidence with some studies, suggesting that no difference existed between subjects with disordered speech and normals on oral form discrimination tasks (e.g. Catalanotto and Moss, 1973), and others suggesting that there was a significant link (e.g. Arndt et al., 1977). Of possible significance for Rachel's speech are studies by Hochberg and Kabnecell (1967), Andrews (1973) and Pressel and

Hochberg (1974), all of which report evidence of reduced performance on oral stereognosis tasks in cleft palate speakers.

The literature suggests that oral stereognosis skills develop gradually with age, with a particular gain from approximately 8 years onwards, but also that children younger than 8 can generally reliably identify a number of simple shapes. In the light of this information it is difficult to rate the significance of the fact that Rachel performed very poorly on an oral stereognosis assessment, correctly identifying only one out of a selection of 10 shapes. These results may, however, illustrate lowered levels of palatal and tongue tip sensitivity which would relate to her difficulties in producing lingual obstruents in the anterior oral cavity.

Lateral cineradiography

Lateral cineradiography was chosen as a minimally intrusive way of illustrating some aspects of simultaneous lingual, velic and laryngeal activity (see Ball, 1984). A brief recording was made of Rachel producing some short phrases and this provided useful information about the dynamics of the tongue, velum and larynx and about their interrelationships during speech production. As well as giving us a clear lateral view of the flattened shape of Rachel's palate, this technique provides a number of important insights into the dynamic relationships of various articulators.

It was noted that the tongue tip was never raised, either during speech or during short gaps between speech. The body of the tongue was held generally in a humped position towards the back of the oral cavity, with the root retracted towards the rear pharyngeal wall. The recording provided a clear explanation as to the lack of lingual contacts shown on EPG recordings. The back of the tongue was seen to achieve contacts in the uvular and pharyngeal regions but no lingual contacts were observed in more anterior parts of the oral cavity.

Significantly, posterior lingual movements seemed to be involved in a dynamic relationship with velic closure. We could observe that there was a good deal of velic movement during speech, but that actual closure of the velopharyngeal port only seemed to be achieved when posterior movement of the back of the tongue appeared to have been employed to add impetus to velic raising. The other significant observation from this investigation was of marked raising of the larynx for all speech production in comparison with its position at rest.

These observations confirmed our suspicion that Rachel's overall voice quality and certain crucial aspects of her segmental production were the result of a complex interrelationship of lingual, velic and laryngeal activity. As Stengelhofen (1989) points out, in cleft palate speech it is not easy to disentangle the articulatory, phonatory and resonatory dimensions of the client's speech production and this, in turn, raises the significant issue of the possible pervasive effects across these different subsystems of any therapeutic attempts to modify activity in any single area.

Spectrography

Harris and Cottam (1985) present evidence in a single case study of a child using subtle articulatory differences to mark phonological distinctions, and a number of studies (e.g. Macken and Barton, 1980; Weismer et al., 1981; Hambly and Farmer, 1982; Maxwell and Weismer, 1982; Smit and Bernthal, 1983) have used instrumental analysis to show how phonetic parameters such as voice-onset time (VOT) and vowel length have been used contrastively in both normal speech development and child speech disorder in ways that would not be readily discernible to the listener. Thus we return to the importance of the speaker's intended production, irrespective of the success of his or her actual realisation in conveying a phonological contrast to the listener (Hewlett, 1985).

To identify any such markers used in Rachel's speech, a spectrographic analysis of certain aspects of Rachel's speech was carried out, looking in particular at alveolar and velar plosives, where we had noticed a significant neutralisation of contrasts from an auditory perspective. Although these markers might not be significant or functional from the point of view of the listener, they would provide important evidence as to the nature of Rachel's internal phonological representations and could help to establish her speech disorder as being caused by articulatory constraints on phonological production, rather than a phonological problem per se.

For target alveolar and velar plosives, Rachel's consistent realisation was a glottal plosive typically with some degree of aspiration – [ʔʰ]. Thus at an auditory level the phonological contrasts between both voiced and voiceless targets and between targets at different places of articulation were neutralised and a potential four-way contrast – /t, k, d, g/ – was collapsed into a single phone. Spectrographic analysis was used to investigate the presence of any subtle methods by which Rachel might be marking intended distinctions which were not readily perceptible by the listener.

Vowel durations

In British English there is a significant difference in the lengths of vowels which is related to the nature of the following consonant (Kaleri-Wick, 1965, in Gimson, 1989). Vowels are consistently relatively longer preceding lenis consonants than fortis consonants. To investigate whether Rachel was marking this distinction in any way, we made recordings of her producing a number of minimal sets of target words containing the following short vowels – /ɪ, æ, ɒ, ʊ/ – followed by the lingual–palatal plosives – /t, k, d, g/. Although no significant differences in vowel duration emerged for place of articulation (i.e. Rachel did not appear to be using vowel durations to mark a distinction between alveolar and velar targets), significant vowel length differences emerged for fortis/lenis consonant contrasts, i.e. /t, k/ versus /d, g/.

Kaleri-Wick gives an average length value for short vowels preceding fortis consonants of 103 ms as compared with an average of 172 ms preceding lenis consonants. The average of Rachel's short vowel lengths preceding /t/ and /k/ was 132 ms compared with an average preceding /d/ and /g/ of 176 ms. Thus her vowel lengths preceding lenis consonants are virtually identical to Kaleri-Wick's estimates, although her values for vowels preceding fortis consonants are somewhat longer than those given by Kaleri-Wick which may reduce their perceptual contrastive value; she is, however, still clearly maintaining a significant distinction which echoes the distinction produced by normal speakers. For some vowels, we noticed occasional overlaps in length values for the fortis/lenis contrasts suggesting a degree of inconsistency in Rachel's realisations, but overall the measures showed a very robust result.

Slight differences of average lengths emerged between different vowels. Thus /ɪ/ was relatively the shortest vowel and /ɒ/ the longest. As Rachel has a northern British accent her realisation of /æ/ as [a] does not correspond to the quality of the standard British pronunciation which Kaleri-Wick suggests is the longest of the short vowels. For each individual vowel, in spite of relative length differences with other vowels, the length differences preceding fortis and lenis consonants were maintained.

Duration of plosive closure phases

In normal adult speech consistent differences in the durations of the closure phases of plosive consonants are maintained between fortis/voiceless and lenis/voiced targets. As Fry (1979, p. 122) notes:

> . . . the silence is likely to last something between 70 and 140 ms, being shorter in the voiced sounds than in the voiceless.

Measurements of the closure phases were made of the glottal plosives by which Rachel realised target /t, k, d, g/ and, as with the vowel duration measures, significant differences emerged. Mean durations of closure phases for /t/ and /k/ were 133 ms and 136 ms respectively, whereas closure phases for /d/ and /g/ had mean values of 48 ms and 55 ms. Thus closure phase durations for voiceless targets fall appropriately at the top end of the values suggested by Fry, whereas the durations for their voiced counterparts actually fall below the bottom end of that range. Thus a contrast is not only maintained but actually somewhat exaggerated.

Both of the durational measures made provide evidence that Rachel is aware of and is attempting to mark important phonological distinctions even though the strategies she uses are not successful from the listener's point of view in signalling contrasts. Such findings strengthen our view that Rachel's internal phonological representations and organisation are satisfactory and that the phonological neutralisations evident in her speech are the result of complex articulatory constraints on speech production.

Implications

Theoretical and methodological

The analysis of Rachel's sound system highlighted the importance of distinguishing between a speaker-oriented perspective and a listener-oriented perspective in the investigation of disordered speech, between the speaker's *intended* productions and the auditory effect of his or her *actual* productions. Both perspectives are important in planning programmes of remediation. The data supported the conclusions of Hewlett (1985) and Harris and Cottam (1985) in revealing a sound system where the realisation of the speaker's intact internalised phonological system was constrained by articulatory limitations. As satisfactory phonological contrasts were not realised by the usual target segments, there was a reduction of intelligibility and, indeed, a 'phonological' problem from the listener's point of view. Using Hewlett's three-way distinction of articulatory, phonetic and phonological speech disorders, Rachel's problems can be defined as an articulatory disorder that has phonological implications for the listener.

While recognising the limitations of Rachel's present sound system for signalling phonological contrasts successfully to a listener, it is very important to acknowledge both the appropriateness of her internalised phonological system and the complexity of the compensatory strategies used to make phonological contrasts within the limits of her articulatory abilities. Although Rachel's speech is auditorily distant from the target system, it is nevertheless a complex and consistent system in its own right with its own subtle marking of target contrasts.

The data analysed in this study support Hewlett's suggestion in his 'two-lexicon' model of speech production, whereby compensatory articulatory strategies to realise phonological contrasts may result in inappropriate representations becoming 'fossilised' in the speaker's 'output lexicon', even if the child possesses the correct phonological representation in the 'input lexicon'. This would lead to a sound system particularly resistant to remediation.

Of fundamental importance to the analysis of complex speech disorders is the relationship between the articulatory and phonological levels, and the concept of the articulatory underpinning of phonological contrasts. These relationships were revealed by detailed transcription and instrumental analysis. The study underlines the importance of making a close phonetic analysis of the primary data. If a considerable amount of time had not been spent on detailed transcription of the data, the subtleties of Rachel's speech could not have been identified. By resisting the temptation to clean up or 'phonemicise' the data at this stage, small and seemingly insignificant phonetic details were not obscured. In some cases it was these details that emerged as significant markers of Rachel's phonological system. Our instrumental analyses were also valuable in revealing a number of features of Rachel's speech which had been difficult or impossible to identify by transcription alone and thus in illustrating Rachel's underlying system of phonological contrasts.

It was also crucial to the analysis to keep in mind the old observation that in speech everything happens at once, and that in Rachel's speech this translates as 'all articulatory constraints operate simultaneously'. Rachel's speech is thus the product of multiple articulatory impairments and compensatory strategies which have effects at both the segmental and non-segmental levels.

Clinical

The results of our analyses revealed a sound system severely disrupted by the interaction of deficits in each of the subsystems of speech production: articulation, phonation and resonance. There was clear evidence, however, that Rachel's internal representation and organisation of the phonological system was appropriate and that her speech disorder had an articulatory rather than a phonological basis. The fact that she was using a number of unusual articulatory strategies with the intention of signalling consistent phonological contrasts provided an explanation of her ability to communicate so effectively and with such a high level of intelligibility with her family and friends, whereas to strangers she presented as highly unintelligible even given contextual information. As we have noted, her mother was so well attuned to her daughter's sound system that she found it difficult to monitor Rachel's difficulties. This had the unfortunate consequence of making it unrealistic to use her as the key person to work alongside speech and language therapists with Rachel, in spite of her willingness to be involved. As the need for long-term and intensive speech therapy emerged, the approach that evolved was to use one main speech and

language therapist consistently over the entire management programme, backed up by a team of further speech and language therapists
offering intermittent specialist input and with the very considerable
help of a Child Care Assistant who was able to work with Rachel in a
mainstream school setting on a daily basis.

The differential diagnosis pointed to the need to take a strongly
articulatory approach in therapy. In working with cleft palate children,
as Stengelhofen (1989) notes, it is often difficult to decide where to
start to remediate a sound system with multiple and interrelated
deficits.

Hypernasality and nasal emission formed a very intrusive component in Rachel's speech. They appeared to be linked to a habitually
retracted tongue body setting used as a compensatory strategy to aid
velic closure but which had the added detrimental effect of constrain-
ing lingual–palatal contacts in the anterior part of the oral cavity. These
observations suggested to us that tackling the problem of soft palate
function and coordination should be an early focus of therapy.
However, in spite of the fact that Rachel could modify her velic function for speech production purposes given visual feedback such as that
provided by the Micronose,* she was unable to maintain such modifications in the absence of the visual feedback. Furthermore, our hopes of
the early introduction of a palatal training aid (Stuffins, 1989) into the
management programme were thwarted, in spite of the best efforts of
our orthodontic colleagues, because her palate was so small and shal-
low at this stage that the difficulties of keeping the requisite dental
prosthesis in her mouth were simply too great.

Thus, although the results of our analysis suggested that ideally
early therapy should concentrate on soft palate control, difficulties in
implementing such a programme led to a shift towards therapy aimed
at articulatory skills. In the initial stages of this programme the focus
was on intraoral sensory and kinaesthetic awareness and on oral–motor
movements at the non-speech levels. Only when an appropriate baseline of non-speech skills had been developed was the emphasis shifted
to speech–sound production.

Assessment of, and work on, oral sensory awareness followed the
framework suggested by Milloy (1991):

- Awareness of oral space
- Awareness of different textures
- Awareness of temperature
- Awareness of air pressure and direction, and nasal versus oral
  airstreams
- Awareness of air vibration from articulatory movements.

*Manufactured by S.C.I. Instruments, Great Shelford, Cambridgeshire, UK.

As there are few normative data on intraoral sensory perception in children, this was an area of exploration and discovery for both Rachel and ourselves as therapists. We aimed to promote intraoral awareness by giving Rachel the metalanguage to talk about the vocal organs and about speech–sound production and we found her increasingly perceptive metalinguistic abilities invaluable in the therapy process. We experimented with techniques such as proprioceptive, neuromuscular, facilitation, oral stereognosis and texture recognition which would also prove useful once she could tolerate an artificial palate and thus the possible introduction of therapeutic techniques such as EPG, a palatal training appliance and use of a textured artificial palate to give kinaesthetic feedback about lingual contacts. Observations and discussion revealed that Rachel experienced difficulty in 'chasing' food particles around her mouth and this extended our area of work.

Rachel's difficulties in extending her oral motor skills remained acute at the outset of our management programme, in spite of the fact that she had had work on oral–motor movements from an early age. Given Rachel's history of hearing impairment and also our observations of her positive response to visual feedback during instrumental assessment sessions, we felt that a strongly visuomotor approach would be most effective. As her phonological system was intact, we needed to provide her with the necessary information and feedback to help her to achieve the appropriate articulatory movements for the production of normal speech sounds. Even with encouragement to use visual and kinaesthetic cues, Rachel's progress was initially slow and was very dependent on tasks being broken down into very simple component skills. When this work was developed to include a strong emphasis on intrapersonal monitoring, the resultant growth in her skills became much more rapid. The combination of emphasis on the ability to self-monitor with use of visual feedback and a concomitant development of metalinguistic skills (using, among other things, mirrors, myofunctional techniques (Garliner, 1981) and articulograms (Stephens and Elton, 1986)) was extremely effective. There were major gains which included a growth in Rachel's confidence and in her willingness to experiment with oral movements using techniques of movement sequences and programmes which might best be described as a sort of oral aerobics programme. This aimed to achieve single movements and then to build these into first repetitive and then sequenced patterns, all of which were supported by visual feedback from a mirror.

With any child who needs long-term therapy, management is usually implemented in stages and careful consideration needs to be given to the hierarchical ordering of the skills to be facilitated. Therapy may not necessarily follow a developmental pattern or even what appears at first glance to be a logical sequence. This was the case with therapy for Rachel's production of actual speech sounds. Rachel's very limited success with imitation at the single sound level, coupled with fears of exacerbating failure-avoidance behaviour, meant that new speech skills were incorporated into the programme because they were relatively more easily achieved, rather than because they were developmentally early sounds or even because of the potential functional impact on intelligibility. This is exemplified by the fact that one of the first new contrasts to be reliably established in Rachel's system was that of the dental fricatives, /θ/ and /ð/.

As therapy has progressed, Rachel has gradually extended her repertoire of individual sound segments, with a consequent increase in her intelligibility and in the acceptability of her phonological system from a listener's point of view. Her oral cavity has now developed to adequate proportions to allow the consistent retention of an artificial palate which has opened up new therapeutic possibilities both using EPG to provide visual feedback for consonant articulations requiring precise lingual–palatal contact patterns, and also the use of a palatal training appliance to help to control unwanted nasal emission of air. In the near future we plan to provide Rachel with an EPG palate with integral palatal training loop (Goldstein et al., 1994) and are very optimistic about its potential effects on Rachel's articulatory abilities.

A further important question raised by the results of our investigations has been the possible beneficial impact of the earlier application of detailed clinical phonetic and phonological analysis to Rachel's speech difficulties. Had such analyses taken place earlier in management, could more appropriate intervention have begun earlier and thus perhaps have prevented some of the educational sequelae resulting from the severity of her speech disorder? The reality is often that it is precisely the pattern of long-term, intractable difficulty and resistance to therapeutic management which may be the spur to further assessment of the type and detail undertaken here. The timing of such assessments needs to be considered carefully to obtain maximum benefit for the client and also to respond flexibly within the context of ongoing management.

Chapter 5
Global language delay: analysis of a severe central auditory processing deficit

DEIRDRE MARTIN and OONAGH REILLY

Introduction

This is a case study of a child, C, who at 4 years of age presented with virtually no verbal receptive or expressive language. C was being seen by a speech and language therapist in a language unit attached to a mainstream primary school. He was referred by his therapist to the Clinical Unit at the University of Central England, Birmingham, for a 'second opinion' of his difficulties and for guidance about future management for speech/language intervention and accessing the educational curriculum.

The assessment process for C at the Clinical Unit was intensive and relatively short – one day. However, it was based on the compilation and selection of information from C's case notes taken by his speech and language therapist, medical notes from the paediatrician and audiologist, school reports from the nursery and unit teachers, and a video of C with his therapist. The information was interpreted, in C's case, through two theoretical frameworks which are critically discussed with a view to showing which could better interpret C's difficulties and indicate preferred intervention.

This chapter describes and critically examines the process of appraising the nature and degree of C's disorder, suggesting strategies for intervention and development for C and involving other disciplines in this process.

Background

Case history

C, an only child, was born 10 weeks pre-term and was subsequently on a ventilator for 3 months. He also suffered a brain haemorrhage and hydrocephalus, which is successfully controlled by a fitted shunt. There was no further developmental medical history available.

He was referred for speech and language therapy at 2;9 years and received monthly therapy for 6 months. He then received a 2-week multidisciplinary assessment, aged 3;3 years. This was followed by weekly therapy for approximately 4 months. He also received home teaching on a weekly basis from a preschool teacher. C started nursery at 3;7 years and has been receiving daily therapy in school since then. His nursery school teacher reported that C's 'non-language skills were within normal limits'. As a result of his severe language problems C had a statement of special educational need.

At the time of the multidisciplinary assessment, results of C's hearing tests proved inconclusive. He responded to 'go' at 50 dB and to 'tick tock' at a whisper. The audiologist felt that C had a hearing loss of only 40 dB, if at all. C's mother felt that he was not deaf, whereas his nursery school staff felt that he had or had had some hearing loss. His speech and language therapist believed it was more likely that speech sound did not have any meaning for C.

C did not understand any spoken language. In fact, he did not always turn to his name. He seemed to understand some facial expressions and gestures. C communicated by facial expression, pointing with accompanying vowel sounds and patting and pulling the adult to what he wanted. His mother reported that at home he said 'no' [ɒ], 'yes' [ɛ], 'look' [ʊ] and 'up' [ʌ]. When looking at pictures or books, C would point and use vowel sounds as though mimicking, counting or reading aloud. He also mimicked talking on the telephone. C used the Makaton sign for TOILET when he needed to go and had also been seen to sign COAT when the other children in the nursery went to get theirs at playtime.

Regarding his oral motor skills, C could blow bubbles and copy lip movements. He could copy tongue protrusion but had difficulty with elevation and lateral movement. There were no reported difficulties with feeding or swallowing and he did not drool. As for gross motor skills, C joined in physical education with his peers from the mainstream school, and he was able to run, jump, climb and balance as they did. He could throw, catch and kick a large foam ball. His fine motor skills were developing. He was able to copy over a model and was beginning to copy under a model. If he was unsure of a letter he did not attempt it. He could colour, trace and use scissors appropriately for his age. He could also use a glue spreader appropriately and paints, using a variety of colours. As yet his drawings and paintings did not reflect much meaning.

Socially, C was a happy little boy who did not seem to become frustrated by his inability to speak or understand verbally. He managed to make his needs known through a very limited communicative repertoire. At nursery, when C was about 3;9 years old, his teacher reported that 'he is aware of the other children and takes his clues from them as to what is required. He conforms well to the routine of the unit'.

C maintained good eye contact and was pleased by praise. Yet this praise needed to be highly visual, such as a sticker or star, because he did not seem to appreciate a hug. He could dress himself at home and before and after physical education at school, although there were some difficulties, such as turning his clothes the right way around, shirt buttons and his coat zip. He could also wash himself and go to the toilet on his own.

In the nursery, C enjoyed playing in the home corner and for the most part he played appropriately. He played well with the other children, and enjoyed making them laugh by his actions. He played cooperatively with the other children using the Brio train and cars. He took turns happily in adult-supervised table games. He was able to do large floor puzzles and looked around for the piece he needed.

C could match and sort objects which shared some salient feature. He was able to sort by shape and colour. He had learnt the Makaton sign for ONE and TWO and could put the correct numeral by the set of that number. He had not yet mastered THREE.

Early data collection – video details

Before assessment in the Clinical Unit, the three most recent speech and language therapy reports were submitted, together with a 'pre-assessment video', which comprised the following five tasks:

Task 1: comprehension at a one-word level. Selection of five objects in a basket with the request 'Put the X in the basket'.

X was accompanied by the Makaton sign and the basket was pointed to. Once C understood the task, the request was reduced to a single word, X. A score of 11/15 was obtained. C imitated most of the signs made by the therapist during this task. One word (SHOE) was presented without the sign on four occasions. C responded by randomly choosing objects until he found the correct one. Upon each choice he would point to the object and look to the therapist for confirmation.

Task 2: oral–motor skills. C was offered sugar strands to lick off a spatula.

He was able to protrude his tongue, but not move it upwards or laterally towards the target in a discrete movement. This suggests some difficulties with volitional motor control, but it was too short an exercise to hypothesise about the specific nature of the difficulty.

Task 3: picture to picture matching – colour to black and white outline. Picture outlines of objects were mounted on a board, some distance from the therapist who held a selection of colour pictures that matched the outlines. C had to indicate which picture he needed to match to an outline. A score of 11/11 was obtained. C identified them all by signing, accompanied by vocalisations such as [m] or [ə] with rising intonation. This suggests that C had an internal representation of each object in the form of a sign.

Task 4: picture labelling. All picture labels began with /b/. Six of eight were correctly signed; five of eight were accompanied by [bə] except for BIRD which was produced as [bʌbʌbʌ]. This demonstrates some of the progress made in therapy. He was starting to link sign with spoken output and could produce [b] for some /b/ initial words.

Task 5: sound imitation (stimulability). C was asked to imitate isolated phonemes and one consonant–vowel structure. The task was repeated. The following results were obtained:

[b]	→	[b]
[a]	→	[ə]; [æ]
[bu]	→	[b]; [u]
[m]	→	[bə]
[g]	→	[æ]; [æ æ]
[aʊ]	→	[aʊ]

This demonstrates that C was using visual cues to help him imitate sounds. He achieved visually obvious sounds such as [b], [aʊ], but could not achieve aspects such as manner, for example, [m] → [b], or velar placement, [g] → [æ], which are either not visible or less visible. When sounds were combined, he picked up on one of the two phonetic segments – either the bilabial plosive [b] or the high round vowel [u]. In both cases the visual element of labiality of the segments may have been significant for C.

Conclusion

Overall this video demonstrated that C had some internal representations, based on the visual mode. He demonstrated an understanding of single words when accompanied by sign and also expression of these words using sign. Although he vocalised often, these were usually open vowel sounds or [mː], all accompanied by rising intonation. Already it was noticeable that (1) C did not understand all the signs he had been exposed to and (2) he partially understood one particular word (SHOE) without sign. (This was a goal of therapy and was chosen because of its lip-rounding pattern.)

The problem

C presented as a child with some degree of brain damage which might well be the organic cause of his problems. Socially, C was managing in his home and unit environments and displayed acceptable and cooperative behaviour with adults and peers.

At the various levels of motor ability, C seemed to be developing within normal limits, albeit on the slower side, except that he showed specific difficulty with certain lingual movements for speech. More important is that both his drawings and speech sounds reflected little meaning.

C's conceptual development appeared to be at a level substantially below his peers. He could categorise by two fundamental salient features only. We are aware that we have very little evidence to support this because C had such difficulty expressing himself verbally and non-verbally through signing, drawing and play. He may, in fact, have had conceptual development within normal limits for his age but was unable to demonstrate this.

C did communicate but only succeeded within the limited range of his abilities to understand and to make himself understood. He appeared to have a severe language acquisition problem in that verbal sounds had very little meaning for him, either for understanding or for expressing his needs and this could not easily be related to a substantial acuity loss. Interestingly, C seemed to be able to attach slightly more meaning to symbols visually and gesturally.

The picture emerging of C from the above description could match that of a child with a hearing impairment who also has moderate learning difficulties. However, we felt that there were sufficient indications that this would be an incomplete match. Further investigation might clarify this or present us with a different clinical picture of C.

Theoretical background

The literature which seeks to describe and explain C's difficulty comes from two main areas: central auditory processing and, to a lesser extent, cognitive neuropsychology. It has to be said that there is not much discussion in the literature on cases in children as severe as C, although in the literature on adult acquired disorders there is more information.

The literature on central auditory processing (CAP) will be discussed first. Keith (1981) summarises the debate in the field of CAP deficit as being about two hypotheses – an auditory deficit (acoustic level) versus a verbal mediation deficit (linguistic level). Duchan and Katz (1983) refer to this as the bottom-up versus top-down debate.

The verbal mediation deficit hypothesis (top-down model) represents

the view 'that most language processing must be done using higher
level linguistic and cognitive knowledge, applying them to the fuzzy
and uninformative signal' (Duchan and Katz, 1983, p. 34). It is argued
that paucity of information in the acoustic signal necessitates abstract
processing at phonological, syntactic and semantic levels. This is supported by evidence that higher order knowledge influences speech perception.

Proponents of the auditory perception deficit hypothesis (bottom-
up model) agree that *some* linguistic processing is necessary to explain
the speed and efficiency of auditory processing, but argue that the role
of the acoustic signal has much more significance than being 'fuzzy and
uninformative'. Other auditory perceptual skills are involved, such as
sequencing and memory. Thus the child is relying on acoustic information and cognitive/psycholinguistic strategies to process unknown or
difficult linguistic information.

What then is the relationship between CAP and cognitive and linguistic functions? Keith (1981) suggests that the abilities involved in
auditory perception such as auditory memory and discrimination of
phonemes are not fundamental to language learning but emerge with
the acquisition of language. A disorder of CAP does not necessarily
cause difficulties in learning or language and Kamhi and Beasley (1985,
p. 10) note that :

> central auditory processes, rather than being discrete are in fact highly inter-
> active . . . deficits in these processes might not be causally related to a lan-
> guage or learning disorder but instead be symptomatic of these disorders.
> That is, deficits in CAP might be the result and not the cause of language or
> learning disorder.

What then are the identifying features of a CAP disorder, and can we
identify the type of language or learning disorders that may give rise to
CAP disorders?

There are several degrees of severity of CAP disorder. The very mild
disability would be shown in the child who could learn in a mainstream classroom although have difficulty in discussion, because of the
rapidity of conversational exchange and the abstractness of language
content. The spectrum then seems to run through to the child who
appears to have difficulty developing any language at all. There is usually a history of auditory acuity problems, shown by inconsistent pure-
tone audiometry results which may also be incompatible with
electrophysiological testing results. Furthermore, there may be inconsistent results from speech audiometry. However, testing involving
speech and language with this disorder is fraught with controversy.
Would the child with a CAP disorder perform poorly on a speech/lan-
guage task because of auditory perception problems or because of linguistic processing problems? This controversy – in fact the bottom-up/

top-down polemic – has raised much debate about the use of speech/language assessments such as the Illinois Test for Psycholinguistic Abilities (ITPA, Kirk et al.,1968) with this population group. There seems to be agreement that, when speech/language assessment procedures are used, they probe the linguistic functioning of the child rather than auditory perception.

One explanation about the severe and chronic nature of the low acuity performance of these children is that there may be either immature development of the auditory pathways as described by Keith (1981) or morphological changes which may have taken place within the auditory pathways as reported by Byers Brown and Edwards (1989, p. 120). It is suggested that this is a sort of defence mechanism against the 'babble of meaningless noise'.

Keith (1981) identifies the following fundamental auditory abilities:

- localisation of sound
- ability to perceive rapid acoustic transitions in speech
- ability to perform primitive imitative speech tasks not requiring comprehension
- manipulation of intersensory information, and abstract thought.

Perceptual deficiency in these fundamental perceptual abilities may impede language acquisition, but children with a CAP disorder may also have problems at higher levels of *symbolic* and *conceptual* behaviour as noted by Johnson (1981). She also observed that children with this disorder cannot profit from intrasensory stimulation and may have problems with gesture and pantomime, performing better when pictures, objects and other figures accompany the auditory stimulation.

The relationship between linguistic and cognitive functioning – or dysfunctioning – could be interpreted according to the weak form of the cognition hypothesis by Cromer (1979), which argues that the relationship between linguistic and cognitive processing is both autonomous and contingent. An autonomous relationship includes the development of the metalinguistic abilities identified and assessed by the ITPA which develop alongside and support language development although not being causal to language development. We have already noted that this is controversial in CAP disorders. A contingent relationship is identified in models that have as their basis a semantic system matched to knowledge of the world. Such models have been discussed by Ellis and Young (1988) and Kay et al. (1992) and are the basis of psycholinguistic analysis of language processing in adults. These models are discussed later.

Although this present discussion is an attempt to clarify CAP theoretically, clinically the problem cannot be so clearly distinguished, because there is a range of terms describing the clinical presentation of CAP such as 'auditory perceptual disorders' and 'central auditory dysfunction'. Furthermore, it seems that the severe form of CAP mirrors verbal auditory agnosia (VAA: Rapin and Allen, 1987).

Verbal auditory agnosia, also known as auditory verbal agnosia and word deafness, has been identified in both children and adults. Travis (1971, p. 1226) describes it occurring in adult language disorders and as being 'disturbances in the recognition of sounds'. He recommends that assessment should be through the ability to imitate sounds or to indicate the source of the sound. Lees and Urwin (1991) note that children with verbal auditory agnosia have no comprehension in the auditory channel and as such present initially as deaf, but a hearing test usually confirms normal hearing. Communication prognosis is poor and alternative communication, usually signing, is necessary. A similar description is offered by Byers Brown and Edwards (1989, p. 120):

> . . . superficially these children may appear to be deaf . . . they show little response to auditory stimuli whether linguistic or environmental . . . prognosis for development of spoken language is poor.

In the literature these descriptions usually follow discussion of auditory perceptual difficulties. Consequently, it seems that CAP and VAA may be conditions that are related by lying along the same spectrum and severe CAP cases may be referred to as verbal auditory agnosia.

What is clinically dismaying about these discussions in the literature of VAA is that they are so brief. We hope that this description of C's performance on the tasks described below will be helpful to clinicians in their appraisal and management of severe non-verbal cases.

An unsatisfactory model for interpreting the problem

The hypotheses concerning CAP – whether the disorder is from an auditory deficit or from a verbal mediation deficit – do not constitute an integrated theory. These hypotheses account for C's auditory abilities affecting his language development, and they offer some explanation for the development of his visual and gestural skills. However, the relationship between language deficit and cognitive development remains unclear. Furthermore, the range of terms that may be used to identify this problem are not exclusive or distinguishing, other than in terms of severity of manifestation, for example, verbal auditory agnosia. The CAP framework has no predictive strength which means that we are unable to hypothesise outcome, except in the broadest terms such as 'prognosis for development of spoken language is poor' (Byers Brown and Edwards, 1989, p. 120). Within the CAP framework, depending on which of the two hypotheses one preferred – top-down or bottom-up – intervention would tend towards either developing auditory skills or developing language skills.

We feel that this is an unsatisfactory situation and would seek an alternative approach which offered a cohesive theory and model to interpret C's problem in an integrated way. We would also want from this approach a more specific prediction of outcome and remediation indicators which would offer cohesive rather than contrastive lines of intervention, linked to a central model. One such approach which is gaining considerable attention in the field of child language disability is one borrowed from work with adult language disability – the cognitive–neuropsychological approach.

The cognitive–neuropsychological model

The cognitive–neuropsychological approach to acquired language impairment and, in particular, the models developed by Ellis and Young (1988) and Kay et al. (1992) are a good example of the usefulness of applying findings from research on acquired disorders to the paediatric domain. These models are particularly relevant in C's case because they deal with the processing of single words, spoken and written, and C was at the single-word processing stage. They may also be extended to include the processing of single gestures and signs.

The adult cognitive–neuropsychological processing model is based on what is known as the *modularity hypothesis* which holds that: 'our mental life is made possible by the orchestrated activity of multiple cognitive processors or *modules*' (Ellis and Young, 1988, p. 10). It is hypothesised that there are modules for processing all neuropsychological stimuli, such as face recognition, recognising written words or voice recognition. The central tenet of the modularity hypothesis is that every module engages in its own form of processing independently of the activity in other modules, except those with which it is in direct communication. Brain injury can affect the operation of some modules although, at the same time, leaving the operation of other modules intact (Ellis and Young, 1988, p. 11). This is the explanation for *double dissociation behaviour* which means that clinical evidence should show the independent functioning of modules. One frequently quoted example is that in the field of visual behaviour, visual facial recognition skills are not dependent on reading behaviour. Thus if reading skills were impaired, facial recognition skills should remain unaffected. Applying this model to C, one could investigate whether such a double dissociation were present in C's language behaviour, and whether in fact the modules had developed sufficiently.

Two features of modules that are generally accepted are that each module operates independently and that each module processes one sort of information input. Clinicians and researchers note that impairment can eliminate the processing ability of the module. Consequently, in C's case the absence of a skill could be the result of a very early neurological impairment inhibiting the development of some (language) modules.

There is some controversy over whether cognitive modules are part of human genetic endowment, or whether certain modules are more likely to develop as a result of cultural learning, as in the case of modules involved in processing literacy skills. It is also claimed, less controversially, that modular processing is 'transparent' – i.e. the impaired or disrupted module could be observed through the disturbed or pathological behaviour. If C had several modules which were not fully functioning or might not even have developed, how much would observation of his behaviour lead us to identify specific module disruption?

Although the cognitive–neuropsychological model originated in work with normal adults and is being validated on adults with acquired disorders, we would like to apply it to C's case to identify where C's strengths and weaknesses might lie, and suggest a way forward for intervention.

The model we will refer to was developed by Kay et al. (1992) (Figure 5.1). It includes a semantic system, i.e. a cognitive body of knowledge of the world that is accessible/matched to semantic reference, which is informed by input (auditory and visual) and generates output (eventually speech and writing). The input is analysed by auditory and visual processes and there is auditory (speech) and visual (written) output through a 'buffer' which includes the neuromuscular coordination process.

There are also conversion systems which are systems processing the levels of representation: auditory to phonological, orthographic to phonological and phonological to orthographic. The following discussion aims to describe those features of the model that are relevant to C and then to suggest how it might be modified to explain and possibly predict outcomes in C's case.

The model is designed to show input modalities in the upper half of the diagram and output in the lower half. In the original model there are only three input modalities: the spoken word, the written word and objects or pictures. We will introduce a fourth, gesture, to portray C's system more accurately. This aspect of the system encompasses exactly the same modules as for other input modalities but is of course for gesture.

The semantic system

Nearly all the modules connect with the semantic system whose development involves the establishment of non-verbal representations as well as the words that access them. In C's case we need to ascertain whether (1) the representations are being established; (2) they are of both the verbal and non-verbal type; (3) if they are of only one type, i.e.

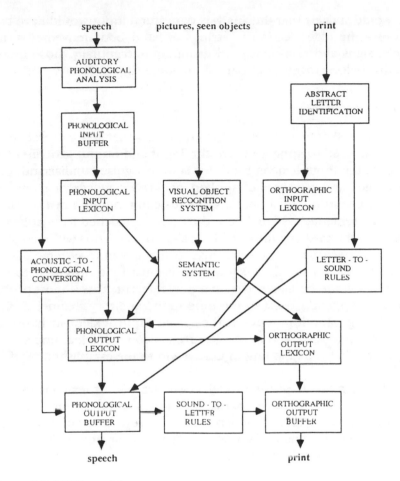

Figure 5 1 PALPA model.

non-verbal, why; and (4) if the non-verbal representations are limited, there is evidence of generally slow learning skills or that the modules involved in the language system are not processing properly or fully.

Analysis systems

The first 'level' of processing is that of analysis of auditory, visual and gestural input. The auditory analysis system 'extracts individual speech sounds from the speech wave' (Ellis and Young, 1988, p. 223). This process may be impaired by acuity or perceptual problems. The visual analysis system is thought to have three functions:

> . . . to identify letters in written letter strings, eg. words and non-words, to encode each letter for its position within its word, and to group perceptually those words which belong together as part of the same word.
>
> *Ellis and Young (1988, p. 224)*

We would suggest that the analysis of gestural input would have two functions – the identification of strings of hand–body movements, for example, signs and non-signs, and grouping perceptually those movements that belong together as part of the same sign.

Input and output lexicons

The next 'levels' of processing in the auditory, visual and gestural channels that we need to apply to C are the input and output lexicons. The function of the input lexicon modules is to recognise familiar auditory, visual or gestural strings, i.e. spoken or written words or signs. To interpret these strings meaningfully, the lexicon modules must transmit them to the semantic system where they can be matched to established referents. In the case of a non-word, or sign, the lexicons will recognise this without necessarily any reference to the semantic system. With a string that is a new word, or sign, then it must be transmitted to the semantic system to be matched with a new referent. This is most probably what is happening most of the time in the auditory channel during child language development. In the visual input lexicon it happens when learning to read, and in the gesture lexicon when learning a signing system. What is happening in C's system to the establishment of an input lexicon?

On the output side of the model, there are output lexicons for the auditory, visual and gesture channels. The semantic system activates these lexicons to select the correct lexical referent, whether it be spoken, written or signed. High-frequency words or signs will be more easily activated than lower frequency ones. In cases of developing language where there may be no lexical item for a referent, then a word or sign may be activated which is phonologically, orthographically or gesturally similar to the target. By way of an example, a 5-year-old child said: 'every play has an interview' (interval). Further, it may also be possible to see that the child's representation in the input lexicon has affected the output lexicon representation. For example, one 7 year old asked: 'You know the word "essay", S stands for story but what does A stand for?' (where 'essay' seemed to be represented as 'SA').

Visual object recognition system

C seemed to depend a great deal on processing visual information. According to Kay et al. (1992) the visual object recognition system has a direct input into the semantic system and is differentiated from other visual input, such as print. Other models (Ellis and Young, 1988) discuss it separately, possibly because this processing function does not handle single *words*. Although this processing component may remain distinct from the linguistic processing modules, it may offer important perspectives on C's restricted processing abilities. In C's case, we need to establish what the processing relationship is between the module for visual object recognition and the modules for processing visual communication, such as signing and print. Could this be the main system through which C was building up his semantic core of symbolic representations?

Initial hypotheses

We have discussed two of the approaches found in the literature which could help us to interpret C's difficulty. We need to point out that when we were working with C we only considered a CAP and VAA approach. It was later, when we appreciated the limitations of this approach, that a cognitive–neuropsychological approach was considered. Hence, our hypotheses and tasks were constructed within the CAP framework. We will present them as originally formulated and will then discuss them from the perspective of the cognitive–neuropsychological model.

The disorders of CAP and verbal auditory agnosia manifest on several levels of disability. Consequently, we decided to appraise on all these levels. We advanced the following four hypotheses about C's levels of disability.

Hypothesis 1

In line with the hypotheses in the literature of CAP, we would predict that C would show a low auditory acuity together with low linguistic processing skills.

Hypothesis 2

We would predict that C has some cognitive dysfunction as a result of his early brain trauma and consequently his symbolic and conceptual abilities would be below normal for his age (Johnson, 1981).

Hypothesis 3

In line with Keith's (1981) and Johnson's (1981) observations, we would predict that C would have difficulty manipulating multisensory information and would perform better with visual stimulation.

Hypothesis 4

With little auditory processing, we would predict that C would have severe speech production deficits even on primitive imitation tasks (Keith, 1981).

Analysis

Data collection

The following data were collected on the same day – a total of 1.5 hours spent in one-to-one contact with either one of the authors, interspersed with breaks. The session was observed via a video link by the other therapist, his mother and other professionals. The video was further analysed following the assessment day. The afternoon session was spent in discussion with C's mother, his teacher, therapist and the two authors, pooling together ideas and views as to the nature and treatment of C's difficulties and strengths.

Assessment tasks

Assessment comprised 11 tasks which have been grouped here according to the hypotheses that they address. Many of the tasks relate to more than one hypothesis (H) as shown below:

1. Teaching of a new Makaton sign (H2).
2. Picture–line drawing matching (H1, H2, H3).
3. Comprehension of single words and signs (H1, H3).
4. Visual sequencing (H3).
5. Oral–motor imitation (H4).
6. Imitation of single sounds (H4).
7. Small doll pretend play (H2).
8. Further comprehension of single words (no signs) (H1).
9. Kim's game (H2).
10. Sound–symbol representation (H2, H4).
11. IBM Speech Viewer (H4).

Hypothesis 1

Hypothesis 1 predicts that C would show low auditory acuity skills together with low auditory linguistic skills, and is addressed in part by task 3 (which will be discussed below under hypothesis 3) and task 8.

Task 8: further comprehension of single words (no signs)

This was presented at the end of task 7 (symbolic play) to substantiate earlier findings of task 3. Following a pretend play session, toys were spread out on the table, and C was asked by 'teddy' to put single items away in a box. C put a random selection of toys away, none in response to the command. In fact C was more interested in 'shooting' teddy, perseverating with an earlier behaviour.

The results of this task, and those of task 3 below, suggest that C had great difficulty processing linguistic information at the one-word level, if it was presented in the auditory mode alone, substantiating part of hypothesis 1. Auditory acuity can only be established based on information from other sources, notably the results of hearing tests and also observational descriptions by C's mother and professionals involved. C's mother did not believe that her son was deaf. This was supported by his therapist's observations, and by later audiology reports (see below).

Hypothesis 2

Hypothesis 2 predicts that C's symbolic and conceptual abilities would be below normal for his age, and is tested by the combination of tasks 1, 2, 7, 9 and 10.

Task 1: teaching a new sign

This was carried out to observe C's learning and generalisation abilities, particularly his capacity to retain and use new signs as a potential form of augmentative communication. C had already been taught some Makaton signs by his therapist. Part of this whole assessment was to ensure that such a system would be functionally useful to C. For this to happen, C needed to be able to retain signs over time, and recall and use them in other contexts. The sign for flower was introduced by producing real flowers from a bag, while saying and signing FLOWER.

C demonstrated good imitation of the sign. He did not produce the sign when a flower was produced, but as an imitation of the author's modelling. This task was repeated three times during the day. First with 'What's in the bag?' accompanied by the appropriate Makaton signs, although context and facial gestures rendered these redundant. C did not respond to this question on the first two occasions. Then, one by one, flowers were removed from the bag, and on the second occasion C spontaneously signed FLOWER as it was produced from the bag. On the third occasion, C responded to 'What's in the bag?' with the sign for flower – before any flower had been produced from the bag.

This suggests that C had internalised the concept and sign for flower *and* was able to recall and use it appropriately in this instance. C's ability to maintain the sign could not be monitored in this one-off assessment and it was noted that the task required much repetition before success was attained. One would expect a 4 year old normally to learn more quickly in this situation.

Task 2: picture–line drawing matching

The aim here was to observe C's level of symbolic understanding and his ability to generalise from task to task because picture–line drawing matching had also been used as a task in clinic with C's therapist. It also provided a context in which to encourage C's spontaneous use of signs. Picture outlines were mounted on a board some distance from C. The author held colour pictures to match. C had to indicate which colour picture matched which outline. The pictures used were based on the items used previously in this task in C's local clinic. We wished to find out whether C's internal representations were stable enough to accommodate this change in context and slight change in representation.

C was able to match all pictures to the appropriate line drawing, and spontaneously produced some signs, notably: TEDDY, CUP, BOAT, HOUSE, BALL, APPLE.

C imitated the following signs – TOOTHBRUSH, CAR – but did not sign BABY, CHAIR (instead, pointing to the picture) or SHOE, BOOT, JUMPER (pointing to what he was wearing).

These pictures were chosen as the signs had been worked on previously by C's therapist. C still had a limited vocabulary of signs at his disposal – only six spontaneous, two imitated and five pointing (to object or picture). No problems in matching picture to line drawings were evident, which does not support hypothesis 2 at this level of task. However, Cooper et al. (1978) note that children between 2 and 3 years can match small toys to pictures. Although this task is at a slightly higher level, one would expect it to be well within the attainment of a 4 year old.

Of note in this task was C's passive nature. Each picture was initially placed face down. In spite of modelling by the author ('What is it?' plus sign for 'what') C made no attempt to guess or turn the picture over, or to imitate the 'what' sign. When there was no BlueTack on the picture so C could not stick it to the board, he did not gesture or show in any way that the picture would not stick, or that he needed the BlueTack, nor did he reach for the BlueTack himself.

Obviously there are many related factors involved here, one being that it was a new situation with a new adult. However, C's family and the professionals involved confirmed this to be typical of C's overall functional communication skills. C's limited pragmatic skills are discussed later.

C's output of those signs he clearly recognised did not occur spontaneously in about half the occurrences. This may have been part of his passive nature, or a habitual inhibition, or a specific difficulty with signing.

Task 7: small doll pretend play

The object here was to gain an indication of C's pretend play on the assumption that symbolic or pretend play develops in parallel to language development (Ogura, 1991). A large selection of small doll material was given to C in a box. One author remained with C for part of the time, sometimes modelling play or directing C. She then left C for a short time while monitoring him on the video.

C took all the toys out of the box and explored them. He rolled the car backwards and forwards and put a doll on the toilet. He was directed to feed the doll. He did this briefly, by holding the fork to the doll's mouth. He also banged the fork on the plate and combed the doll's hair with a toy comb. When left alone with the toys, C looked bewildered, and did very little with the toys – rearranging them on the table. On the author's return, C used a toy soldier to 'shoot' her. He perseverated on this and became highly excited. He could not be distracted away from this, even when directed to use the soldier to shoot other toys rather than the author. When other toys, e.g. a teddy bear, were introduced, C tried to shoot them also. His preference appeared to be for physical turn-taking games – even enjoying 'peek-a-boo' with teddy. He showed little enthusiasm in manipulating the toys functionally, and no true symbolic actions were noted, for example, *pretending* to eat.

The development of both symbolic and functional play is closely related to language development (e.g. Vygotsky, 1986). The nature of the toy material used means that C's *functional* play (Lewis et al., 1992) was assessed rather than his symbolic play. This is at a lower level in the hierarchy of the development of symbolism. Symbolic play and language are related in that both depend on and contribute to conceptual development. For example, one needs the concept of 'chair' to play with a toy chair appropriately. One also needs the relevant concepts to be able to use words. Although this situation is far from ideal for measuring C's pretend play, it does suggest that C's pretend play skills were limited for his age (Jeffree and McConkey, 1976).

Task 9: Kim's game

The aim of task 9 was to encourage spontaneous signing within a structured situation. 'Teddy' hid one of three objects. C was required to indicate which of the three objects had been hidden. This produced no spontaneous signing, even though all the objects had signs that were familiar to C. It could be that C had difficulty in remembering the hidden object, or in recalling the appropriate sign from his semantic system, or as mentioned above, because of a specific difficulty with producing signs.

Task 10: sound–symbol representation

This provided further assessment of symbolic abilities within the context of (1) sound production (task 10a) and (2) sound discrimination (task 10b).

Task 10a: imitating sounds through visual symbols. Pictures of a ball, drum and coke can were used to represent the phones, [b,d,k] respectively. These phones were chosen because they were already present in C's phonetic inventory. One of the authors presented the picture and produced the phoneme, accompanying it with a gesture associated with the sound action. For example, opening the ring pull of a coke can to symbolise the phone [k]. Although this was initially a teaching session where C was not expected to produce the sounds, he did imitate them:

>   [k] – [fi]
>   [b] – [b]
>   [d] – [ø] [g]

He was then able to produce [b] when the 'b' picture was held next to the author's mouth, [g] when the 'd' picture was held there. On returning to the 'b' picture, C perseverated with [g] but changed it to [b] on a cue from the author for lip closure. Certainly, C appeared to understand the nature of this task – that the pictures represented sounds – and this was built upon in task 10b.

Task 10b: the above activity changed to make the task a discrimination one. Two pictures were placed in front of C. The author produced one of the phonemes and C had to point to the picture that matched the phoneme. C sat smiling and laughing and made no attempt to point to a picture. He then yawned and the task was discontinued. C appeared to have no understanding of this discrimination task. Although he may have been tired as indicated by his yawn, he may also have been bored, the auditory presentation holding no stimulus for him. He did appear to understand task 10a – that the pictures represented sounds. We cannot tell if his performance problems were caused by a difficulty associating a specific sound with its representation (i.e. input), or in producing the sound when shown the stimulus picture (i.e. output) or both.

Conclusion

C's pretend play and use of signs were limited, given his age and exposure to sign. It seems that his symbolic development was delayed. His slowness to learn signing (see also task 1) may suggest a delay in conceptual development. Ascertaining the intellectual functioning of a child with a severe speech and language disorder has always been challenging. As Johnston (1992, p. 108) notes:

> When we observe children who have normal non-verbal IQs and serious language delays, they in fact seem to be lacking the conceptual knowledge, the representational abilities and the reasoning patterns that would be expected for their age.

Hypothesis 2 is substantiated for the tasks given.

Hypothesis 3

This hypothesis predicts that C might have difficulty manipulating multisensory information, and would perform better when the stimulus was visual. It is tested by task 2 (which has already been discussed above), task 3 and task 4.

Task 3: comprehension of five single words versus words and signs

This task aimed to compare C's comprehension of signs and words versus words only, i.e. auditory channel supported by visual channel versus auditory channel only.

Task 3a. Same pictures as in task 2 above (picture–line drawing matching), mounted on a board some distance from C. C was asked 'Give me the . . .', accompanied by the signs for GIVE and the picture in question. This was stimulating both the auditory and visual channel. (Result: 5/5 correct.)

Task 3b. As above, but C was asked for two items, 'Give me X and Y', together with the appropriate signs. C remembered only the first of the two words. He was more interested in the nature of the task – pulling the pictures off the board and concerning himself with the remaining BlueTack.

Task 3c. As above, but auditory channel only. 'Give me' was omitted because the nature of the task was now learned and C was expected to respond to the auditory request, for example, TEDDY. (Result: 1/5.) SHOE was the only word recognised. This had been previously worked upon by his therapist because of its distinctive lip-rounding. Apart from this, the auditory channel appeared to have no meaning for C. He pointed to pictures randomly. At one stage he imitated the target BALL but did not choose the appropriate picture.

In this task it is clear that C was very reluctant to use signs to communicate. When only two pictures remained, the context was such that C did not need to comprehend the words when the author asked 'Which one next?'. C responded by pointing. Even when given signed alternatives he would only point and not imitate any of the signs. When only one picture remained, C was asked 'What is it?'. He was then turned to face away from the picture. He seemed unable to respond to this and insisted on turning round to point. Finally, C pointed to his foot saying [bu] (boot). There was therefore some minimal ability to store and recall auditory representations, although this was a very rare occurrence.

Task 4: visual sequencing

The rationale here was to observe C's capacity for sequencing and remembering visual information. Ten cards with pictures of objects on them were presented to C. Matching master cards with two pictures placed left to right were used as the target. First, the task was demonstrated to C by matching two of the ten single pictures to the double master card. Once C understood the task, the master card was placed face down and, by pointing, C was asked to select two of the ten single cards which matched – in sequence – the two hidden on the master card. (Result: 2/4.) C always correctly chose the first of the two pictures, and on two occasions remembered two in sequence. C's attention was poor – he needed constant direction to the task in hand. He was also slow to respond – which had been noted in task 3 above. Paradoxically, slowness to respond makes the task more difficult because he was obliged to hold the visual image of the master card in his memory for longer. Alternatively, C may have been slow to respond because he had a restricted memory capacity, i.e. he had forgotten the target pictures and had to scan each alternative individually, requiring constant direction to the task.

C achieved 2/4 which was better than his performance of remembering two signs. It is probable that he was more successful with pictures because these are permanent and can be rescanned, whereas signs are transitory and rely more on memory recall. C's performance on this task was still less than age appropriate, and this implies that visual compensation may have been limited by memory constraints.

This collection of tasks addressed hypotheses 1 and 3. It is clear that C responded best when he had both an auditory and visual input and less well to auditory input alone. He made minimal use of lip shape cues, such as BOOT versus TEDDY. Furthermore, as two of the items were SHOE and BOOT, it was quite probable that he *guessed* SHOE because it had a similar lip shape to BOOT.

C's performance on this task offers some support for hypothesis 3 in that visual stimulation helped him, but it does not explain why he did not use the natural cues available to him such as lip shape. As suggested above, C coped better with visual stimuli that were permanent. Lip shape is transitory and, overall, C's visual skills, although superior to his auditory skills, cannot be considered age appropriate. C's performance on this task also goes some way to supporting hypothesis 1 because his auditory channel capacity was obviously very weak.

Hypothesis 4

This hypothesis predicts that C would display severe speech production deficits and is tested by tasks 5, 6, 10 and 11.

Task 5: oral motor imitation

This aimed to assess C's oral agility and to collect any evidence that may point to a motor speech disorder. C's tongue and lip movements were assessed by: direct imitation, imitation in a mirror and somaesthetic feedback. C could imitate isolated movements, such as tongue-tip elevation, but performance was variable, particularly when sugar strands were introduced for somaesthetic feedback. C would make whole head movements rather than discrete tongue movements and would resort to using his fingers to retrieve sweets from the side of his lips or upper and lower lip. He did, however, demonstrate control of both oral and nasal airstreams using an oral–nasal shelf (Nuffield Dyspraxia Programme, Connery et al., 1992). C became very tired and this task was discontinued, and a full motor assessment was not completed. Consequently, the results of this are inconclusive. Connery et al. (1992) suggest that most 4 year olds are able to perform the Nuffield oral–motor assessment, which was similar to this assessment. At 4;4 years, it seems that C had difficulties with this task, but further assessment would need to be completed to clarify the full extent of the difficulties.

Crary (1993) suggests that single facial postures or movements alone are not a sufficient assessment of potential oral apraxias. We therefore cannot say that C has an oral apraxia, but we do suspect that he has some difficulties with primitive, oral imitation tasks. It is interesting that C became tired on this task which was less than 5 minutes in duration and occurred not long after a break in the session. This may be indicative of C's perceived difficulties with this type of task. However, hypothesis 4 cannot be substantiated on this evidence alone.

Task 6: imitation of sounds in isolation

The aim of this task was to observe C's ability to produce sounds in isolation through imitation. C was asked to imitate the following sounds in isolation: /p,b,t,d,k,m/. Results:

[p, b]: correct
[m]: correct lip shape, but no voicing or audible nasal airstream.
*[t] – [χi]: following no response initially
*[d] – [çi]
*[k] – [fi; fiu]

*A strip of paper was introduced to encourage airstream and plosion. This greatly affected C's productions because at first he attempted to blow rather than produce the sound. He then produced a constriction in the palatal region which has been transcribed as a palatal fricative. This shows a recognition of the presence of a consonant. C's productions may have been different if the strip of paper had not been introduced. C was tired by this stage and the task was discontinued.

Task 10: described above

A further task of sound–symbol representation was presented to C. We noted that C was unable to produce [d] at all and perseverated with [g] before changing it correctly to the target [b].

Task 11: IBM Speech Viewer

The aim here was to observe C's output abilities in the context of cause and effect using computer images. C was encouraged to babble (reduplicated) to move images on a computer screen. He quickly appreciated that he had vocal control over the images on the screen. He could imitate [bbbbbbb] but was unable to maintain it, changing to [g] and back to [b] . When he increased speed, he lost articulatory clarity and it became [b w ə ə]. When the consonant modelled by one of the authors was changed, C was unable to follow and change too. However, after repeated modelling of the prolonged vowel sound [u], C did change gradually from a [b] to a prolonged schwa [ə].

As C had a very limited spontaneous vocal output, only vowel-like sounds when excited, and was severely limited performance on all of these tasks, hypothesis 4 is substantiated.

Overall findings in relation to the hypotheses

C's performance on the above tasks has been considered in relation to the literature on CAP, and information provided by his mother, speech and language therapist, support teacher and paediatric audiologist.

With the exception of hypothesis 1, referring to C's auditory acuity, all the hypotheses have been substantiated. C had very severely limited auditory linguistic skills (hypothesis 1) which were in part compensated for by visual skills (hypothesis 3), but still restricted because he was slow to learn and use signs *and* make use of speech reading (Silverman and Kricos, 1990). Hypothesis 2 finds support from C's reduced symbolic and conceptual abilities, for example, representations in drawing, play, sound symbols and slowness in learning a sign system. Finally, C's output through speech was severely restricted for his age, substantiating hypothesis 4.

Cognitive–neuropsychological analysis

Scrutiny of the data may suggest to the reader that this is a child with a relatively straightforward diagnosis of hearing impairment and general learning difficulties – hence his slowness in learning to sign. However, as speech and language therapists, the authors responded to their clinical intuition, and those of C's therapist that he did not fit this clinical picture. We did not believe that the evidence supported the notion that his hearing and/or learning difficulties caused his severe language disorder.

An alternative framework for hypothesising was offered by the CAP/VAA literature. However, CAP is a deficit-based description. It does not and cannot identify C's strengths, or offer pointers for remediation. It became clear that a further framework would be needed to interpret C's performance. Consequently, the cognitive–neuropsychological model was studied as a viable alternative framework. It offers a processing model which allows points of breakdown to be identified as well as strengths and weaknesses in performance, which can then be utilised in a programme of therapy.

Visual channel

C's responses to matching object–picture and picture–picture tasks were likely to show how well developed his visual object representations are. C performed correctly on these tasks suggesting that he has appropriate representations in his visual object recognition system as shown in Figure 5.2.

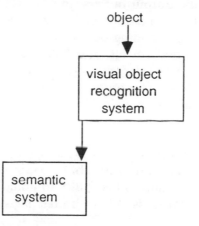

Figure 5.2 A model of the visual channel.

Processing the written word

The full model (see Figure 5.1) depicts quite a complicated network for the successful functioning of reading. The written word is first processed by the module for visual analysis which connects both with the input lexicon and with grapheme–phoneme conversion. The input lexicon in turn has connections with both the semantic system and output lexicon which connects with the grapheme output buffer. There is also the direct connection between visual analysis and the grapheme output buffer (copying) and between the written word and the grapheme output buffer (external feedback).

In C's case there is evidence of written copying skills developing, although his free drawing was very limited in symbolic content. There is also evidence that C was 'reading' single words from flash cards. He was matching flash cards and identifying words when they were read from flash cards. Yet, he did not verbalise. We would suggest that C had not developed the modules for literacy as described above, because he had almost no phonological representations on which to base visual output lexicon. Rather, we would argue that C was using his intact visual object recognition system to recognise visual configurations on flash cards. The ability to recognise single words in this way is a feature of young children, some as young as 2 years of age. It is known as the sight vocabulary phase (Harris and Coltheart, 1986). It soon disappears and does not seem to be a linked to later 'whole word' reading skills.

Imitation

The model shows that imitation, or copying, occurs when the stimuli from the analysis modules bypass the semantic system and the lexicons and directly trigger the output buffers. In C's case he had some imitation skills. His auditory imitation skills were assessed and showed a very restricted ability, performing best with highly visual sounds, such as labials and lip-rounded vowels, and falling away considerably with less visual sounds, such as velars and non-lip-rounded vowels. It could also be that C had motor programming problems at the speech output buffer level. This would have a similarly inhibiting effect on his imitation skills.

He had some written copying skills which again indicate a bypassing of the lexicon and semantic system while showing oculomanual dexterity. This dexterity is also seen in his ability to dress himself and in his physical education skills and in his ability to imitate sign. When C was assessed he showed that he is able to imitate signs better after several repetitions.

These observations suggest that C had imitation skills that seemed to rely heavily on visual input and were weakest when relying only on auditory stimuli. Although quite dextrous, he may have had motor programming difficulties at the speech output buffer level.

Auditory channel

C's language development was very restricted. Although his hearing was difficult to assess, it seems that his acuity was sufficient for language development. His failure to develop auditory analysis skills to any substantial degree, and barely at all for language, suggests that, according to the wider model for processing single words, the modules for auditory phonological analysis and phonological input lexicon had failed to develop. It is unclear whether the failure of one causes the failure of the other, i.e. the failure to analyse auditory phonological stimuli inhibits the development of the phonological input lexicon, or whether the two modules develop contemporaneously, with a mutually stimulating and supportive relationship. The same could be said about the failure in development of C's phonological output lexicon. It is not clear whether this is a resultant relationship or contemporaneous with the other phonological processing modules.

Gesture channel

C was able to imitate the gesture used to signal FLOWER. This implies the ability to analyse the gesture visually and to use it. By adapting Kay et al.'s model (1992) to encompass gesture, this imitation ability can be represented by:

- input through the sign into the module for gesture–visual analysis
- through to the module for visual-gesture conversion
- which links through to the gesture output buffer.

The sign was taught by repetition of the gesture with the object it depicted. It encouraged a network to develop between the visual object recognition system and gestural–visual analysis to develop a visual input representation (or lexicon) that fed into the semantic system. Eventually, C produced the sign, FLOWER, spontaneously, when presented with a flower. This shows that gestural–visual input went through the semantic system and formed a gesture output representation which connected to the gesture output buffer which facilitated the making of the sign (Figure 5.3).

It is questionable whether C had both a gesture output lexicon *and* a gesture output buffer. Research into acquired disorders in signing suggests that both these modules may occur for gesture. Poizner et al. (1984, p. 262) report cases of sign aphasia without apraxia. However, within a developmental framework, we cannot assume the existence of such modules, yet anticipate that, within 'normal' individuals, they gradually develop.

C's spontaneous signing was poor, and was possibly the result of inadequate representations in the semantic system or inadequate development of the gesture output lexicon. Input was limited to the visual mode–object recognition and gesture visual analysis, which has implications for any developing lexicon. It is difficult to ascertain the level of breakdown, whether it was in the semantic system or in the gesture output lexicon. However, inadequate development of the

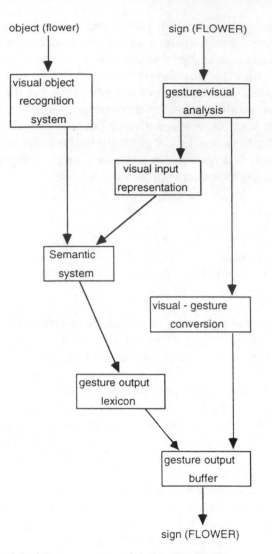

Figure 5.3 A model of C's processing of the sign FLOWER.

semantic system is bound to inhibit development of the gesture output lexicon. Gesture output as a structured, systematic lexicon could not be assumed in this child.

C's signs were often inaccurate but generally interpretable, and this was partly the result of a delay in fine motor development. This in itself would inhibit the development of a gesture output buffer.

Pragmatics

It is difficult to assess the level of C's communicative intent. The literature in acquired signing disorders suggests there are parallels between sign aphasias and aphasias of spoken language. Ellis and Young (1988) discuss the view that individuals with 'Broca's' aphasia have clear communicative intentions and know the meanings they wish to convey, whereas those with 'Wernicke's' aphasia may lack a clear communicative intention – which reveals itself in 'unfocused, incoherent gesturing'.

C was a passive child, suggesting reduced communicative intent. Consider particularly that he could understand the therapist when she signed, yet still did not use signs spontaneously. We have discussed above the possibilities of deficit at the output levels according to this model, but the model does not address – nor does it claim to – the wider, pragmatic components of communication.

Follow-up investigations and analyses

Six months after C's assessment, a questionnaire was sent to his therapist, asking for an update following his assessment. C was now 5;1 years and from the information received, the following was of note.

Hearing

C's hearing had been assessed twice using brainstem auditory evoked response. The first report noted that 'no really convincing responses were recorded up to 90 dBHL'.

This suggests that C had a hearing loss of 90 dB. Even though he had been ill on the morning of the assessment, this should not have affected the reliability of the assessment. However, it was felt that such a loss did not concur with the clinical impression and a re-test was arranged. The results of this show a 50-dB loss. To add to the confusion it is also recorded that C's performance 'when wearing hearing aids . . . reported a bigger hearing loss than when *not* wearing hearing aids' (Speech and Language Therapist's report, October 1992).

Byers Brown and Edwards (1989, p. 120) observe that '. . . despite very thorough audiological investigation, some of the children (diagnosed as having VAA) have later been found to have varying degrees of sensorineural deafness'. They speculate that certain morphological changes take place as a defence mechanism against the 'babble of meaningless noise'.

As there is no consensus of opinion or results of audiological investigation, we cannot be conclusive about the status of C's hearing. It is probable that there is some level of hearing impairment, whether brought about by morphological changes or more probably congenital – in the light of C's medical history. However, if the problem were purely one of hearing, then one would expect C's symbolic development to have developed to a higher degree, and in particular gesture to have been accepted by C as a useful means of communication.

Visual skills

C had started to learn to 'read' and was 'particularly interested in the written word' (Class teacher's report, October 1992). He was able to match words and could recognise his own written name and those of other children in the class. He could match the following eight words to an object or picture, and could make the correct Makaton sign when shown the written word: DOG, TRAIN, MAN, BOY, GIRL, MILK, BISCUIT, SWEETS.

His teacher noted that he had to be taught the concept of these words because he did not seem to realise that the sign referenced all examples of the category, i.e. the word for DOG referenced all dogs. This is an illustration of underextension in vocabulary development. He still had difficulty handling two words or signs together.

This supports our earlier view that C had difficulty in concept development and in processing information beyond one element at a time.

Understanding signs

C understood the Makaton signs for 51 words. He seemed to have some conceptual difficulty in differentiating some signs: MUM/WOMAN, DAD/MAN, BOY/GIRL. He seemed to interpret them as being like himself, PERSON. Similarly, he confused the signs for CAT/DOG. He was also unable to differentiate pictures of them, possibly perceiving them as the category ANIMAL. This aspect of C's vocabulary development reflects similar processes to those found in normal early vocabulary development, in particular, overextension and an absence of synonym development.

C continued to struggle with two-word level signing. For example, his attention needed to be drawn to watching both signs in the sequence 'NO X'. His comprehension of signs was not reliable at the two-word signing level.

Signing expression

C could use signs to label items he saw around him, yet he only used three signs to request communicatively: TOILET; COAT (to go out to play); HOUSE (to play in the home corner). Occasionally he would respond to forced alternatives, such as: 'Do you need a PENCIL or a SCISSORS?'

Spoken language

In teaching activities, C could make recognisable attempts at several words in response to the question: 'What's this?' However, he communicated by using a range of sophisticated facial expressions accompanied by pointing and indeterminate vowel sounds. Prosody remained largely intact and appropriate. C's mother reported that he said 'a lot more at home' but this had not been observed at school.

Social and cognitive development

Socially, C remained a 'happy little boy who does not seem to become frustrated by his inability to speak or verbally understand' (Teacher's report, October 1992). Gross and fine motor skills were developing appropriately for his age, but his drawings and paintings did not reflect much meaning. C was assessed by an educational psychologist when he was 4;9 years, and on a non-verbal IQ inventory C scored commensurate with his chronological age. This was in line with his therapist's opinion of his functioning.

Implications

Theoretical

The importance of having a coherent theoretical framework to interpret C's problem was highlighted earlier in the chapter. C's problem was wide-ranging across the language-processing spectrum and his profile of skills varied considerably, from almost no auditory analysis skills to word identification ('reading') skills.

The implications for relying solely on the CAP theories to interpret C's problem would have been very constricting. They did not form a cohesive approach and the separate hypotheses showed that it was possible to have contrasting intervention programmes with no predictions of outcome. Further, there were a variety of disorder 'labels' which did not contrast sufficiently with each other to be clinically meaningful. The CAP approach could not meet the demands placed on it by the range and severity of C's difficulties. However, CAP is a recognised field of disorders and the theories and hypotheses may be useful and pertinent in other cases.

Using the cognitive–neuropsychological model to interpret a child's difficulties must be approached with caution. This theory has been developed from the study of established language-processing mechanisms in normal adults and adults with language disruption. There have, however, been several positive implications of using this type of model with a child. First, there is the potential in the model to address C's range of difficulties and to view them in juxtapositional perspective. This is very important in C's case because of his different abilities across modalities. Second, a degree of mapping is possible between the child's observed processing skills and the model. It is not possible always to be certain how established these lines of processing are or whether they are uni- or bidirectional in their operation. Third, the model reflects a coherent theory of language processing, which facilitates predictions and hypotheses about the child's untested skills and future abilities. It also indicates preferred lines of intervention as well as contraindicating others.

Finally, one important implication for the cognitive–neuropsychological model which has been highlighted in its application to C is that there is a need to develop the processing framework for the gestural modality. This would not only be necessary for other children like C but is necessary for adults for whom gesture is a feature of their language processing difficulties.

Remedial

First, analysis showed that C's greatest processing ability lay in his visual skills. Second, because analysis showed that C's auditory analysis was very weak, working on auditory processing seemed to be contraindicated in the initial stages of intervention. Consequently, intervention preferred to avoid the auditory–verbal approach and to support the visual skills, namely gesture and word recognition. Gesture was developed as the medium of communication, and input was partly through the gestural modalities and expected output from C was through gesture. C's ability to recognise the printed word allowed input through the visual recognition system.

C had some imitation skills, particularly in signing and these were exploited in therapy, more so than oral imitation skills. However, oral work continued and after several months C successfully began to articulate word approximations.

In C's language processing system it seems that he had very restricted development of the lexicon modules, both for input or output. Developing the representations in the lexicon modules depends on developing his signing skills, i.e. his gesture imitation skills, his gesture output buffer, his gesture input lexicon and his semantic system. It seemed that by increasing the input through the visual channel, which C could more successfully process, the representations in his lexicon and semantic system increased. It could be hypothesised that these meaningful representations stimulated development through to the auditory modules (auditory analysis, auditory input lexicon) and oral programming module (speech output buffer). This is also possibly the direction of development in normal language acquisition.

Thus, developing the representations in C's semantic system is a fundamental and long-term aim of intervention. Developing the semantic system entails laying down representations, verbal (signed) or nonverbal, through whatever channel functions most successfully for the child. In C's case this was the visual channel. Without these representations, C would not be able to develop the lexicons in the language processing model. The development of the semantic system is also linked with the development of his cognitive system. C's cognitive development would lie beyond the role of the speech and language therapist and there are implications for involving the educational psychologist, support teacher and the classroom teacher.

C also needs intervention to develop his output. He needs specific work on his imitation skills both gesturally, written copying and oral movements. As he develops a wider range of expressive communication, it will become clearer whether he needs intervention and support for any pragmatic difficulties.

Methodological

All speech and language assessments are constrained in some way by time and resources. The assessment process described in this chapter is no different. As a 'one-off' assessment, certain factors must be taken into account which may have compromised the data and the advantages must be appreciated as they contribute to understanding C's difficulties.

Reliability of performance. C's performance was likely to vary across time and with different people. However, his performance on the day of the assessment was considered, by those who know him, to be consistent with his usual abilities. The 'round-table' discussion aimed to mitigate some of the problems caused by this. Those present could offer information regarding the child's performance in other contexts.

Time constraints. Although a whole day was set aside for assessment and discussion, a 4-year-old child can only cope with so much adult attention and demands on his performance. Ideally, this would be spread across more than one session. Time constraints also affect the flexibility to follow-up new hypotheses which often evolve during the assessment process and through discussion and data analysis.

Interdisciplinary team. This type of assessment procedure relies substantially upon other professionals, in C's case his therapist, class teacher, the audiology team, the paediatrician, the educational psychologist. His mother also formed part of the team. The procedure is dependent on the collation of as much data as possible from case history information and audiological and medical examinations, to class teacher reports and therapy session notes. Therapists and teachers have commented that it gives them an opportunity to take stock of the child's case and to gain a fresh perspective on results of investigations and progress so far. The clinical importance of this opportunity should not be overlooked.

Round-table discussion enhances the data collection and facilitates a multidisciplinary approach. It enables the child to be viewed as an individual where his functioning can be explored in relation to his many different environments.

Video transcription. In clinical circumstances, it is normally not possible to complete a detailed video transcription. This was the case for the two video recordings made of C. Repeated analysis of the video recordings showed that there were discrepancies in our observation records. At times it seemed that we had observed what we had wished to perceive. We were able to identify and rectify some of these misperceptions which is one of the advantages to working with video data. Consequently, without detailed initial transcription, misperception must always remain an area of potential methodological weakness.

Video data also offer an opportunity to evaluate objectively not only the child's performance but also the clinician and/or teacher working with the child. This has important implications for the teacher and/or therapist to modify their intervention techniques and strategies.

Chapter 6
Down's syndrome: linguistic analysis of a complex language difficulty

MONICA BRAY, BARRY HESELWOOD and IAN CROOKSTON

Background

Introduction

I'm Down's boy . . . I always got jobs about speaking people.

Paul is a young boy with Down's syndrome who is very talkative and happy to be both initiator and respondent in conversations. He converses on a wide range of topics such as television and video programmes, holidays, foods and activities, and tries hard to convey his messages as can be seen from this excerpt:

Paul is talking to Monica and describing himself from the point of view of his teacher
P   . . . so a bit silly asking me and the question's wrong
M   a bit silly at swimming?
P   yeh
M   and very strong?
P   the answer's wrong
M   what's strong?
P   the answer
M   the answer's strong?
P   no, answer's wrong
M   wrong, the answers wrong, oh I've got it now

These interchanges take time and effort and often the interlocutor will give up before fully understanding what Paul has to say. Paul still persists but, as he becomes more mature and aware, he may not be prepared to try as hard. It has been found that adults with learning difficulties will tend to be acquiescent and try to appear more linguistically

123

competent than they are (Edgerton, 1967; Leudar, 1989). This appears to be a factor in their lack of initiation of language and their lack of either using or requesting repairs (Leudar et al., 1981). If we are to maintain Paul's keenness to communicate, we need to understand better why he has so much difficulty and how we can improve the exchanges between himself and others so that they are more rewarding for both parties.

General information and development

Paul was born in 1982. The pregnancy was complicated by placental insufficiency in the third trimester and his birth was induced at 38 weeks. The Down's syndrome was detected straight away and his parents were informed within 24 hours. They were led to believe that Paul would have little chance of developing far and that they would be unwise to raise their expectations of him. He was a healthy baby except for regular upper respiratory tract infections in winter, and over the first year he grew and thrived.

During this year, Paul learned to sit up and move about. He was happy and smiling, he ate well, he seemed interested in everything, could pick up and manipulate toys and objects, and was making a lot of vocalisations.

In these early years, all development seemed to be occurring well. Paul was crawling early in his second year though it took him from 18 months to nearly 2;6 years to master walking securely. He was found to have a squint and possible short-sightedness for which he received corrective spectacles. His hearing had been checked and found to be within normal limits in spite of his continuing upper respiratory problems. He was using a wide range of sounds, words and gestures for communication and was a keen participant in conversational exchanges.

At 2;7 years, Paul's situational understanding was good and he was using about 20 intelligible words and 20 Makaton signs. Play had moved beyond the purely exploratory into relational and simple pretend. Paul was walking securely and attempting to kick a ball and climbing up and down stairs. He was very sociable and approached and interacted with adults and other children.

Overall Paul's development was slow but seemed to be following normal patterns in all areas. Paul attended MENCAP nursery and was also enrolled in his local nursery. His family were stimulating his development on all levels, helped by a Portage visitor, and he was responding positively and seemed set to continue with this slow but progressive development.

Language development

Paul's mother had been a careful diary recorder over the years and much of what can now be said about his early language is based on her painstaking work. A number of formal tests were also used with Paul: the Symbolic Play Test (Lowe and Costello, 1976) and the Reynell Developmental Language Scales (Reynell, 1977) in his early years, and the Language Assessment, Remediation and Screening Procedure (LARSP: Crystal et al., 1989) and the Test for Reception of Grammar (TROG: Bishop, 1989) later. This gathering of data was used to describe and chart Paul's language acquisition but not as a basis for understanding his specific problems.

Comprehension

Situational understanding had always been good, but linguistic comprehension was fairly slow to develop. At 4;0 years Paul had a language score on the Reynell of 2.01 and a standard score below the norms. Little change appeared to take place in the Reynell scores over the years so that at 5;10 years Paul still only had a language score of 2.07. Some of this lack of change may well be related to the nature of the Reynell test. Paul seemed unable to make the leap from section 7 (attributing action to an object) to section 8 (knowledge and use of words related to colour, size, position). Studies on young children with Down's syndrome have suggested that they have particular difficulty with concepts of number and colour (Cornwell, 1974; Gelman and Cohen, 1988). There is also a pervading difficulty with memory, particularly in relation to sequential information (Gibson, 1978), and to information presented auditorily as opposed to visually (Pueschel, 1988). It is not surprising therefore that a test such as the Reynell, which relies on cognitive development of this nature, gives little useful information on the actual linguistic skills of children such as Paul.

Expression

Paul's expressive language skills showed steady development through the early stages where he was moving from single word use to two- and three-word combinations. At this point, development plateaus with less expansion taking place at clause level than at phrase level. It is interesting to note the divergence between Comprehension and Expression on the Reynell test at 5;10 years where expression leaps forward so that Paul shows a deviation from the norm of only –1. This appears to be related to Paul's developing vocabulary and ability to combine words. A LARSP analysis at the same age gives a clearer picture of his difficulty in using words productively in sentences and shows most of Paul's utterances still at stages 2 and 3. Miller (1988) has noted that children with Down's syndrome are superior in their lexical–semantic ability to their grammatical ability and Paul exemplifies this dichotomy.

Phonology developed slowly but steadily in the early years, with Paul achieving a full phonetic inventory and using these sounds contrastively.

He has had more difficulty in development of structural aspects than systemic ones and at 12 years will still delete weak syllables and final consonants, but not consistently. Paul's speech is often unintelligible and this can only partially be explained by looking at phonological or motor development in isolation. A dysarthria profile (Robertson, 1982), while showing that Paul had some difficulty controlling exhalation, showed articulation to be in the fair to normal range. A more detailed investigation of how he produces speech is called for.

Down's syndrome

Paul's speech and language development needs to be put into the context of his syndrome. What part does the syndrome play in creating and/or perpetuating the difficulties he is having?

In Down's syndrome brain weight and configuration are affected with a noticeably small cerebellum and brain stem (Kemper, 1988), and progressive neural development is unlikely to proceed normally (Courchesne, 1988). This then has an effect on physiognomy and physiology leading to the characteristics of Down's syndrome as we know them. Courchesne suggests that abnormal neural activity exists in sensory and cognitive systems, with auditory–sensory messages showing abnormalities of timing. The cortical neurons selectively affected by the syndrome appear to be ones linked to the capacity to filter, integrate, select and store incoming information (Courchesne, 1988). Modulation of auditory as well as somato- and visuosensory information by the cerebellum is likely to be affected by its size and its cell abnormalities. Dustman and Callner (1979) found a difficulty of damping incoming information, in their sample of 66 people with Down's syndrome. This would make learning difficult as selective listening would be a problem. In fact this difficulty with inhibition of incoming stimuli would have a major effect on attention and memory.

As a possible consequence of cerebellum size and abnormal brain function, muscular hypotonia, and abnormal emergence and dissolution of reflexes occur in Down's syndrome (Henderson et al., 1981). In motor ability, as well as in cognitive ability, the research suggests that individuals with Down's syndrome are motorically less able than their peers without the syndrome and fall further and further behind as they get older (Cunningham, 1988).

Skeletal growth is also retarded in the early years (Barden, 1985). The maxilla is shorter and narrower with a consequently narrowed and distinctly shortened palate, poorly developed sinuses, a relatively narrow nasopharynx and a larynx high in the neck (Smith and Berg, 1976). Such structural difficulties are liable to have an effect on voice quality and resonance. It is unclear from the literature whether enlarged tongue size is a feature of the syndrome but the reduced proportions of the oral and nasopharyngeal cavities, and the bunched 'loaf' shaping and lack of grooving of the tongue (Lemperle, 1985) are likely to create difficulty with tongue positioning.

In spite of all these factors, the language of people with Down's syndrome is extremely variable, ranging from some individuals with near normal syntax and phonology to others who have few if any adequate forms of communication.

Summary

In summary it seems that Paul has developed and must maintain his linguistic system while having to deal with difficulties of attending to and memorising incoming auditory information, controlling motor output and coping with structural differences that are likely to distort outgoing acoustic information. Crystal (1987c) suggests that the linguistic system is similar to a bucket which has only a finite capacity – when one level of language is demanding all the organism's attention and capacity, other levels 'overspill' and become less adequate. For Paul we could hypothesise that, by having to expend so much effort on dealing with systems that are not functioning very adequately, he has only limited capacity for language development. Certain language levels are likely to be more demanding than others and for Paul development of longer and more complex utterances is dependent on articulatory–phonetic skills and grammatical skills, both of which are difficult for him.

To explore this hypothesis we will need much better information on what Paul is saying and how he is producing speech. We will therefore need to start from a careful linguistic description of his language behaviour and reflect on the psycholinguistic issues that emerge from analysis of the data.

Analysis

Data collection

Paul's language skills had been charted on a regular basis through the years, but now a corpus of spontaneous utterances was needed for analysis. This was collected on audio-recorder in Paul's home on numerous visits and on video-recorder in the more formal university setting. Paul was recorded story telling (an activity that he particularly enjoys), saying nursery rhymes, doing some basic reading, picture naming, attempting some particular linguistic tasks (to be described in the remediation section) and in general conversation. Paul is a keen communicator and there was never any difficulty in getting him to talk.

The data were orthographically transcribed and the content was

checked with Paul's mother if it was difficult to understand. This orthographic transcription was used to look at sentence length and structure. Many of the utterances were then transcribed in narrow phonetic
script.

Analytical frameworks

In investigating and analysing Paul's language we have looked to psycholinguistic processing models such as that of Levelt (1989) which
draws on earlier well-known models such as that of Garrett (1980). The
features of Levelt's model that we shall be basing our discussion on are
as follows.

Conceptualiser

This formulates the content of the message to be produced, and is not
specifically involved with any level of linguistic form, but with something like 'thought' in its everyday sense.

Formulator

This performs two partially separate processes on the output of the
conceptualiser:

1. Grammatical encoding, creating a syntactic structure to express the
   message. This contains the meanings of words but not their phonological forms.
2. Phonological encoding, adding phonological forms to the words in
   the syntactic structure.

   The output of the formulator is thus a phonological string of some
kind.

Articulator

This converts the phonological string into an executable set of instructions for the articulatory organs.

Levelt (1989) accepts the implication of such cascaded models of production that downloading must be stepped, i.e. that as soon as part of
a message is available in its conceptualised form, the part must be
passed to the formulator, and similarly from the formulator to the
articulator. Furthermore, the processors must have the potential to
function simultaneously: while utterance segment n is passing through
the articulator, segment $n+1$ is passing through the formulator, and
segment $n+2$ through the conceptualiser. Otherwise, as Levelt puts it

(1989, p. 27) 'speaking would be more like playing chess: an overt move now and then, but mostly silent processing'. The articulator would have to go silent until the next utterance had been conceptualised and formulated.

It is important also to consider some account of speech monitoring during production. Speakers with no language difficulty are aware of what they are saying and, for example, can correct slips of the tongue very quickly after producing them. On an auditory level, monitoring involves the sound waves created by the speaker going to the speaker's own ear and thence into his or her speech comprehension system.

It is possible to use this model as a way of attempting to understand some of the problems Paul has in organising and producing coherent sentences. We can also bear in mind the monitoring process when theorising about the difficulties he has in monitoring and correcting his own output.

As Paul finds maintaining the rhythm of his speech such an effort, as thorough an investigation as possible was carried out on the rhythmic aspects of his speech adopting a framework suggested in Heselwood et al. (1995). This assumes the rhythm group to be the planning frame for articulation and is similar in principle to suggestions in Selkirk (1984), Chiat (1989), Caplan (1992) and Levelt (1993).

Analysis and discussion

In the introductory section of this chapter, the focus of the investigation of Paul's language was on the identification of levels of linguistic ability and their similarities to and differences from expected norms. This information was obtained by use of available tests and gave a somewhat limited picture of Paul's abilities and disabilities. The use of these tests gave no indication of how Paul was attempting to produce messages and why certain difficulties were arising, therefore a more indepth consideration of Paul's utterances was needed. Narrow phonetic transcription and interpretation was undertaken by the two authors who are linguists, and hypotheses arose from discussion of the data by the linguists in conjunction with the speech and language therapist.

Dysfluency

Although it is obvious from listening to Paul that he produces hesitancies, revisions, broken words and repetitions, a careful analysis of what makes him appear so dysfluent compels us to focus on two particular symptoms – pauses and repetitions. Relating these to Levelt's processing model allows us to suggest why Paul may be so highly dysfluent.

Some examples follow which show these features; the bracketed dots represent (unfilled) pauses.

a [nəː] next wednesday (.) next Wednesday before (.) before
   my birthday
b I like [əL] (.) I like about the planets
c no yeah (.) and then I got some (..) some teddy
d [vaḥ] (..) I need to think (.) I (.) I need to think (.) I need
   to think before (.) before (.)before my party start
e nope (.) perhaps he didn't understand (.) him (..) because
   he speak in Chinese
f the end of (.) the end of our school (.) is very little
g no (.) it's lotsa (.) lots fields (.) another end of (.) school (.)
   is (.) being built (.) for school people work
h erm (.) monks (.) monks (.) monks (..) monks are orange
   people (.) [vɪdʒ] people

The context in which this sample of conversation was collected was
a relaxed conversation between Paul and a student. True, the student
was asking a number of questions that demanded a response from
Paul, but this type of output is not uncommon in all the examples we
have collected from many different environments. Paul's pauses and
repetitions do not appear to be related to psychological stress. We must
therefore look at what may be happening in Paul's utterance planning
to help us understand his dysfluency.

Pauses. An interesting feature to note is the lack of filled pauses ('um',
'er', etc.) in Paul's speech. Most of Paul's pauses are unfilled. Why this
plethora of unfilled pauses? An unfilled pause results from the articulator finishing its job and new material failing to arrive from the formulator. But this does not give us the real locus of the problem: it could
either be that the formulator is lagging in producing formulated material or that the formulator itself has no material because of delay in the
conceptualiser.

Second, the near-absence of filled pauses is quite striking in data
from a particularly hesitant speaker. Speakers normally fill a considerable proportion of their pauses, probably for the sake of keeping the
conversational 'floor', because a silence can be taken as an invitation to
the interlocutor to begin (Levinson, 1983). We must therefore ask what
processing underlies filling a pause? The phonetic transcription of the
main English pause filler [əː] might suggest that it is purely an articulatory matter: a possible account would be that the articulator empties,
material fails to appear from the formulator, and the articulators stay
switched on, so to speak, in a neutral configuration, until further formulated material arrives.

However, even a cursory cross-linguistic look at pause fillers shows
this account to be inadequate. The Scottish English pause filler is [eː],
many African speakers of English use [iː], and most strikingly, the

Japanese pause filler is [ano:]. A pause filler always seems to be made up of phones that are possible realisations of phonemes in the speakers' language or accent. It is therefore a phonological word of the language, one that can be greatly prolonged compared with the articulation of other phonological words.

In planning terms, the pause filler must therefore be triggered one level higher than suggested in the above initial account. Material from the conceptualiser fails to arrive in the formulator, and the gap is filled by the phonological word that fills pauses. This implies a further type of simultaneous processing: while an utterance stretch is being conceptualised, the formulator is retrieving the pause filler from the lexicon and passing it to the articulator.

Paul's lack of filled pauses may therefore be attributed to a reduced ability for simultaneous processing: the processing load of retrieving a filler while conceptualising a message is too much. The few pause fillers that Paul does use are at the beginning of a conversational turn, followed by a silence, so no simultaneous processing is necessary: Paul could formulate a pause filler, and then conceptualise his message during the silent pause that always follows that filler.

We would argue, then, that pause fillers involve a lexical-retrieval task, albeit a minimal one, while the conceptualiser is working, and one of Paul's particular difficulties is in having to conceptualise while lexical-retrieval and/or syntactic planning is in progress.

Repetitions. One possible account of planning which allows for repetition is as follows:

1. A stretch of formulated message is *copied* down to the articulator. A copy therefore remains in the formulator.
2. The articulator articulates the formulated message.
3. Synchronously with (2), a fresh planning stretch is passed from the conceptualiser to the formulator, which clears out the copy of the old formulated stretch.
4. Failing (3), (1) may happen again with the old planning stretch.

In such a model, repeating is a way of filling pauses. Work by Yairi (1981) with young non-fluent children suggests that repetitions of small units – words and part-words – can be considered to be a signal to the listener that the turn needs to continue. The benefits of using this type of pause filler are twofold: it makes it possible to fill much longer pauses than would be appropriate for a pause-filling word, and it avoids the lexical retrieval of the pause filler.

An alternative model for explaining repetition might be that the speech comprehension system has stored the speech output so as to monitor it. When the conceptualiser fails to provide material for the formulator and the articulator is waiting, the formulator takes what is

in the speech comprehension system and passes that down. The underlying failure is still in the conceptualiser.

The overall picture thus emerges that Paul has particular difficulty in
conceptualisation, i.e. in thinking out what to say. This is not to say that
there are no difficulties in formulation or articulation. There clearly are
many difficulties in the latter, some of which will be considered later.
Also, the blanket absence of the third person singular verb agreement
affix indicates at least one deficiency in the formulator or the grammatical knowledge on which the formulator draws. We submit, however,
that the dysfluencies identified above point more strongly to the conceptualiser as the source of this particular trouble.

One final piece of evidence in favour of this general conclusion is
that many of Paul's intelligible utterances are oddly phrased. The conceptualiser seems to decide on an odd content for the message. The
following utterances repeated from above exemplify this:

b   I like [əL] (.) I like about the planets
d   [ʋaḥ] (..) I need to think (.) I (.) I need to think (.) I need to think
    before (.) before (.)before my party start
    [*Context: it is many days before the party is due to happen*]
f   the end of (.) the end of our school (.) is very little
g   no (.) it's lotsa (.) lots fields (.) another end of (.) school (.) is (.)
    being built (.) for school people work

All of these seem to be an 'odd way to put it', i.e. an oddly conceptualised message. The failure of the conceptualiser to download in
good time, as a result of a reduced ability while the formulator is operating, leads to the hesitant, repetitious, ungrammatical and poorly
flowing speech that he produces. Paul is a good deal closer to Levelt's
'game of chess' production described previously than is the speech of
those with normal language development.

Voice quality and phonation

One of the features that divides normal discontinuities of speech from
abnormal dysfluencies is that of effort or tension during production
(Starkweather, 1987). Paul's speech contains examples of extreme
effort leading to loss of control of phonation. In a significant number of
his utterances there are quite dramatic and sudden changes of voice
dynamics, many of which seem unconnected with other aspects of
utterance organisation. These manifest as jumps in loudness and pitch,
and in quality and type of phonation, often to the extent of being barely identifiable as the same speaker's voice. Future detailed analysis of a
larger sample of his speech may enable more of a pattern to be established in these apparently random excursions, but from the data available a few persistent tendencies can be identified:

1. After a pause phonation often shows evidence of excessive laryngeal tension, with phonologically voiced phonemes being realised with creak and/or some degree of harshness (Laver, 1980b). This typically lasts up to the first voiceless segment, for example:

[ʔˤaskɛːʋə]   *its scary*
{! !}

[ʔˤa ʔa βəˈskʋiːm]   *I –I will/would scream*
{!   !}

['nɒsˋtʰesəleɪts]   *?? tessellates*
{ˤ ˤ}

[lɒs ˈfɨɫz]   *lots of fields*
{!}

[ənəviˋɛnd ɒv] (.)   *and at the end of (pause)*
{!   !}

There are, however, one or two exceptions to this in our data, for example:

[biˈfɑ bɑˈbɜv̆d̥ę]   *before my birthday*
    {!   !}

2. Although pitch often descends to very low *F*0 values for no apparent linguistic reason, this does not seem to occur when the context requires a rising tone; similarly, unusually high pitch does not seem to occur where a falling tone is required. The incidence of these pitch extremes sometimes correlates with linguistically appropriate pitch movement, i.e. very high pitch, to realise the final part of a rise and very low pitch to realise the final part of a fall, but not always. These observations indicate that Paul may have an appreciation of the linguistic significance of intonational pitch movements despite his inability to control absolute pitch. Some examples follow:

[ha ˈfɪʃ wɜːk ɪn ðə ˈgaːʐə pleɪ]   *I finish work and then go out to play*
               {v.high}

['ʋɜːlɪ 'ʋɜːlɪ ˋnid]   *really really need*
{ v.high }

[jʊˋtʰʋɪkɪd]   *you talking*
   {v.low}

These pitch extremes sometimes seem to follow a pattern of declination (Cruttenden, 1986) from the beginning of a stretch of speech to the next pause, for example:

[fẽzɪz'nɒ `t̠s̠ɹaɪtsə ən 'mʊʔʃ feə˞ːn̥zɪ]   *??? ??? and much ???*
{v.high}{   low }{ v.low   }

In fact there are no examples of a very high pitch succeeding a very low one within a stretch. It should be emphasised that what we are calling very low and very high here are quite marked and abrupt discontinuities and involve jumps of as much as 300 Hz in some cases. Abrupt pitch changes have been found to occur in people who are dysfluent, often at the beginning of the dysfluent episode (which is likely to be at the beginning of a phrase). These are most likely in people who are maintaining a high level of laryngeal tension. 'Switching the voice on' seems to be particularly difficult for dysfluent speakers (Adams and Reis, 1971). Paul appears to have some difficulty initiating voicing which would explain high tension in the larynx as he begins a phrase and reduced tension as he proceeds.

Sudden contrasts in perceived loudness also occur and are seemingly more random and there is little we can usefully say except to point out that the main acoustic correlates of both pitch and loudness, i.e. fundamental frequency and amplitude, are each related to intensity in the same way. In physiological terms the energy in the airstream can be taken up by increasing vocal fold movement either through enlarging the glottal opening in the voicing cycle or forcing the glottis open at a faster rate. The quantity of energy in the airstream is determined by initiator power (Catford, 1977). These observed fluctuations in pitch and loudness are possible further evidence that control over speech initiation is impaired. It is possible that some of the early and persistent respiratory problems experienced by people with Down's syndrome and the anatomical differences in the heart and lungs (Hallidie-Smith, 1985) may be responsible for poor initiatory as well as phonatory control. Paul suffered from recurrent upper respiratory infections as a child and the one subsection of the dysarthria profile that he found difficult was that of sustaining exhalation both with and without voice. It is possible therefore that voice quality and phonation are directly influenced by structural and physiological aspects of the Down's syndrome.

Rhythm

One of the immediately obvious features of Paul's production is his inability to sustain a flow of speech. Dalton and Hardcastle (1989) define dysfluency as a difficulty in smooth transitions between segments, whereas Wingate (1985) focuses on the feature of linguistic stress in his discussions of dysfluency. Paul's problems of fluency may be seen as a difficulty on these dimensions. We have discussed pauses and repetitions in Paul's speech and now we will look closely at how he deals with rhythm groups. We are using the term 'rhythm group' in the traditional sense of the term 'foot', i.e. as a stressed syllable and any other syllables up to but not including the next stressed syllable (see Catford, 1977; Cruttenden, 1986).

Heselwood et al. (1995) classified the rhythm groups used by their subject, an adult with Down's syndrome, as either basic dynamic units (one- and two-syllable feet) or extended dynamic units (feet of three syllables or more). This classification appears to be applicable also to Paul's speech. The example below is his production of *24th of February*, his birthday. It seems that Paul is aiming for the three-syllable form /ˈfɛbjərɪ/:

[ˈtʰɛfd̥ ˈ fɛbɜːɪ̈]

compare the target form /ˈtwɛntɪ fɔθ əf ˈfɛbjərɪ/

As well as rhythmic simplification there is also cluster reduction of the pattern common in children's developing phonological systems (Grunwell, 1987) where the more sonorous member of the cluster is the one that is omitted (Buckingham, 1988); the final consonant deletion in *fourth* could also be interpreted as being governed by the sonority principle (Christman, 1992). However, the important factor here is his reduction of the more complex rhythms to simple disyllabic feet, i.e. basic dynamic units.

In rhythm groups that are followed by pause, Paul produces the segments relatively accurately but he has many errors in non-pausal contexts. Paul's pauses are often hesitations within a tone group rather than being properly utterance final. As discussed previously, pauses might well be essential for Paul's ability to process simultaneously. The following sequence illustrates this:

[ⁿdɛks (.) ˈdɛxs wənˈsdeɪ (.) nɜ ˈnɛʔsʷwɛnsẹ (.) ˈdɛswə̃nsəbífɑː (.) biˈfɑː ˈbabɜːv̌dẹː]
next –next Wednesday – ne-next Wednesday – next Wednesday
before – before my birthday

Of the four productions of *next*, the first is prepausal and is correct save for somewhat reduced nasality on /n/. The word can be seen to be more error prone in the three non-pausal positions, showing: lenition of /k/, glottal substitution for /k/ and complete omission of /k/ – a progression towards complete articulatory simplification. The prepausal *next* is a monosyllabic rhythm group and therefore would be expected to be more error free. This is also true of the two prepausal instances of *Wednesday*. These are both target trochaic feet, i.e. the variant /ˈwɛnzdɪ/, and are less phonetically distorted than the third production of the word, in which both vowels are reduced to schwa and the /d/ is omitted.

Another sequence of Paul's speech exemplifies these rhythmic and junctural effects at work:

[ʔɑ̈ maɪ ˈfʊɛnːᵈz̥ (..) ʔə (.) ʔö̈ maɪ ˈfʊɛnːᵈz̥ (..) ə ö̈ maɪ ˈfɛz̥ əʊəʔ ˈstaneɹɪmö̈ː]
(last four syllables delivered with strong impression of syllable timing)
all my friends – uh – all my friends – uh all my friends (?)don't understand (?me?) anymore(?)

In prepausal position *friends* is a monosyllabic rhythm group – a basic dynamic unit – and is produced intelligibly without segmental deletions. The third realisation, by contrast, manifests two segment deletions (both involving high sonority values) and is the first syllable of a three-syllable foot – the target is difficult to reconstruct here but seems most likely to be the paeonic *friends don't under–*. The syllable timing of the following rhythm group can be interpreted as a strategy for coping with a target paeon in prepausal position, i.e. by reducing the production to a sequence of monosyllabic feet. Consequently the phonetic planner can take its time over each syllable.

These observations sustain the hypothesis that in Paul's speech items are generally more intelligible in prepausal position and that, coupled with the evidence that he has difficulty with complex rhythm groups, this is essentially for rhythmic reasons.

It would appear that the superimposition of an articulatory plan on a rhythmic base (Chiat, 1989; Garman, 1990; Caplan, 1992), and the carrying out of that plan, is easier when the phonetic planner is not under pressure from the demands of an up-and-coming rhythm group and has time to do its job. This parallels Paul's need for an unfilled pause as a 'breathing space' for calling information from the conceptualiser to the formulator.

There is evidence to show that a good command over speech rhythm has a developmental path (Young, 1991) and children with Down's syndrome are known to plateau on a number of developmental paths (Carr, 1985). Young discusses the inherent rhythmicality of young babies and their responsiveness to speech rhythms through body and/or arm movements and Kravitz and Boehm (1971) show that babies with Down's syndrome are delayed in a wide range of rhythmic habit patterns. Henry (1990) presents results to indicate that other children with speech disorders perform relatively poorly in tests of non-linguistic rhythmic skills. In the light of these studies, it is hardly surprising that Paul finds it difficult to imitate rhythms in a number of linguistic and non-linguistic tasks (Table 6.1).

It appears from the above examples and discussion that rhythmic difficulties underlie much of Paul's misarticulated speech and that in contexts where rhythm is under greater control his speech is relatively error free. Given a scenario such as this it is not necessary to hypothesise phonological disorder to account for the observed speech behaviour, but neither is it adequate to ascribe the errors to a malfunctioning articulatory apparatus. Rather we hypothesise that a large part of the problem lies in the rhythmic organisation of articulatory gestures which may be compounded by poor respiratory support.

Table 6.1 Paul's performance on imitative linguistic and non-linguistic rhythm tasks

	Clapping			Nonsense syllables	Single words	Phrases
1. M:	\x	\x	\x	ˋmaːma	ˋhamə	ˋgɒt ɪt
P:	\x	\x	\	ˋmaːma	ˋhamə	ˋgɒʔ ˋtɪt
2. M:	x\	x\	x\	maˋmaː	əˋweɪ	gɛt ˋʌp
P:	\x\	xx\	xxx\	˳m̩ˋmaː	əˋʋeɪ	getˋʌp
3. M:	\xx	\xx	\xx	ˋmaːmama	ˋsɪnəmə	ˋgɪv ɪt ɪm
P:	\	\	\	maˋmaːmaʔa	θɪnəmə	ˋgɪvʔtɪ
4 M.	ʌ ʌ\	ʍ ʍ\	ʍ ʍ\	maməˋməˑ	lɛmənˋeɪd	fə ðə ˋs̩kul
P:	\x\	xx\x	\ xx	m̩amạˋmaːmaː	leβɪn̩ˋeɪd	fʊˈˀ skul
5. M:	x\x	x\x	x\x	maˋmaːma	bəˋnɑnə	əˋfaːmə
P:	\ xx	(no attempt)		waˋmaːma	pʰəˋnaːm̥ə̥	əˋfaː waːmə
6. M:				ꞌmamaˋmaː	ꞌundəˋstand	ꞌteɪk ɪt ˋɒf
P:				m̩amạˋmaːmaː	ꞌhundəˋstand	ꞌteɪk ɪt ˋɒf
					{ f }	
7. M:				ˋmaːmamama	ˋfɔtʃənətlɪ	ˋgɪv ɪt tʊ ɪm
P:				maˋmaːha	ˋfɔʃn̩lɪ	glɫ tə ˋhɪm
8. M:				maˋmaːmama	ɪm̩ˋpɒsəbl	əˋbɪt əv ɪt
P:				mamaˋmaːm̩ama	ɪm̩ˋpɒsbl	ˋbɪt əv ɪt

M = model provided by therapist; P = Paul.

Follow-up investigations

Before undertaking the linguistic analysis, we had started with a general hypothesis that Paul would have difficulty in developing language at all levels because of his syndrome, but that he would probably have most difficulty as length and complexity of utterance increased because of specific phonetic and/or grammatical deficits. This was confirmed by the information gathered from data collected over time and from tests and measures in current clinical use. But we still had little information about where the main difficulty actually lay and why Paul was often, but not always, unintelligible.

Through a closer look at more conversational data which had been carefully transcribed both orthographically and phonetically, it was possible to hypothesise further. We now suggest the following:

1. That Paul has great difficulty in simultaneous processing of language levels – he cannot formulate while he is conceptualising, articulate while he is formulating and so on.
2. That Paul has most difficulty at the conceptual level so that his language is disjointed and oddly phrased.
3. That Paul has little phonological difficulty but a major difficulty with rhythmic organisation of articulatory gestures.
4. That Paul is unable to initiate utterances easily and evidences poor control of pitch and vocal quality because of inadequate respiratory support.

It should now be possible to go on to test out some of these hypotheses and relate the information obtained to remedial strategies. As a result of limited time and contact, only some small experiments have been undertaken but more can be done in time. It is sufficient at present to get a feel for whether our ideas might be valid.

Conceptualising and formulating

It is difficult to design experiments to identify levels of processing for people with learning difficulties because such investigations often rely on reading and other learned skills. General clinical awareness leads us to suggest that, if conceptualising is difficult, well-known and rehearsed language should contain fewer pauses, be more fluent and have fewer odd word combinations than newly created utterances.

We asked Paul to tell his own made-up story. For comparison, Paul completed 'The Bus Story' (Renfrew, 1969) which consists of a series of pictures providing a framework for the story. The examiner tells this story and then invites the child to re-tell it. As there are nine pictures in the sequence, direct imitation of words is avoided, but the child is given a formula to follow and has the pictures for support, thus reducing the amount of conceptualising that is needed while still demanding formulation of clearly presented sentences.

Results. Paul offered the following short story:

> hello this is (.) hello this is (.) Paul
> I got Monica with me
> I tell a story about Spooky (XX) and Christmas
> chapter one
> one day he was long long time
> (.) but (.) christ(mas) tree came
> (.) then something (.) strange coming
> (.) then (.) (XX) coming (X) coming c\coming down corridor
> into lamps
> he fall down some steps
> (.) saw me (...) dead

As was expected there are many unfilled pauses and dysfluencies in this story. In terms of discourse structure, there is a lack of coherence resulting from Paul's mistaken assumption of shared knowledge without which the story cannot be interpreted. There is, however, some cohesion in the use of 'but' and 'then' to give the narrative sequential structure. Other features of cohesion are lacking, for example, anaphoric reference, and it is not clear to the listener the extent to which one sentence presupposes another (Brown and Yule, 1983).

Paul attended well to the Bus Story and the following is his attempt to reproduce it.

> one day was naughty bus
> (.) the\the bus went past the police
> the police say stop
> (noisy inhalation) (.) a bus keep (.) keep going and police (XXXX)
> (..) the bus race (.) up to (.) a train
> but train into (.) to tunnel
> bus say alright
> (.) bus into town (XX) whistled
> (.) (XXX) bus is oh I'm tired of road an (de)cided jump over fence
> met the cow
> so cow say no
> (.) an um bus race straight down into (XX)
> was (be)cause stop into a mum (.) muddle
> stuck in a mud
> driver saw him
> (.) mm crane came back a road again

X = unintelligible syllable.

Contrary to expectation, Paul is as dysfluent and hesitant in the re-telling of the Bus Story as he was in his own story. Nevertheless, coher-ence and cohesion are more evident. Our original hypothesis is not therefore confirmed, but the apparently greater control over discourse structure provides a new avenue for investigation and suggests that for-mulation may be affected by his attempts to conceptualise his own story.

Rhythmic ability

To investigate Paul's linguistic and non-linguistic rhythm skills further, he was given a number of tasks which involved imitating clapped rhythms, spoken words and phrases, and non-words (see Table 6.1). Paul was keen to attempt to reproduce both the clapping and the spo-ken rhythms and imitated the author as closely as he could. The model and Paul's imitation were recorded on audio-tape and transcribed later.

Results. Table 6.2 gives the number of correct responses on the rhythm tasks for Paul and for G, an 8-year-old boy with no speech or language difficulties.

Table 6.2 Number and percentage of Paul's and G's correct responses for the rhythm tasks

	Clapping	Nonsense syllables	Single words	Phrases
P	0/5 (0.0%)	3/8 (37.5%)	6/8 (75.0%)	2/8 (25.0%)
G	4/5 (80.0%)	8/8 (100.0%)	8/8 (100.0%)	8/8 (100.0%)

Error analysis. Clapping: the following errors were found in Paul's responses on at least one occasion:

1. Incorrect number of feet in a sequence
2. Appending of extra weak beats
3. Weak beats realised with too much force.

Single words: the following error was found at least once:

1. Post-tonic unstressed syllables omitted (7, 8).

Phrases: the following errors were found at least once:

1. Post-tonic unstressed syllables omitted (3)
2. Pre-tonic unstressed syllables omitted (4, 8)
3. Unstressed syllable realised with stress, resulting in an extra stress (1)

4. Stress shifted to an unstressed syllable (7)
5. Addition of extra unstressed syllable (5).

Nonsense syllables: the following errors were found at least once:

1. Additional unstressed syllables appended (3, 6, 8)
2. Post-tonic unstressed syllables omitted (7).

The same battery of tests administered to a normal child indicates the extent of Paul's rhythmic difficulties. G is 8;0 years and has no history of speech or language disorder. On the clapping task he scored four correct out of five. His error occurred where the strong beat was not initial in the group, showing a preference for the rhythmic structure of a traditional foot. He made no errors on any of the other tasks beyond a very quiet voiceless realisation of *a* in *a bit of it* – a normal under-articulation.

These results add further evidence to the suggestion that Paul has major difficulties in controlling both linguistic and non-linguistic rhythm. The relatively high score on the single word task, and the fewer error types, can be accounted for if words are stored in the mental lexicon with their stress patterns specified (Cutler, 1980). For phrases and nonsense syllables, on the other hand, the speaker has to generate a rhythmic schema over and above lexical specifications, i.e. it is a problem of real-time organisation, as is the clapping task.

Common 'set-piece' phrases may be lexical entries in their own right and thus be specified for rhythm. This would account for Paul's correct production of *take it off* which has the same stress pattern as the correctly produced *understand*. By contrast, the nonsense sequence with this pattern shows both types of errors listed above for this task. The other error-free phrase, *get up*, is almost certainly stored as a single lexical item.

The general conclusion from the tests is that Paul has great difficulty building the correct structure of elements with low perceptual prominence around a prominent element. Handling elements with low perceptual prominence is troublesome for young children acquiring phonology (Waterson, 1971) and weak syllable deletion is clearly to be seen in these terms. In Paul's case, however, the difficulty gives rise to a wider range of errors, and of more frequent occurrence, than would be expected in a normally developing child.

Implications

Remedial

The process of investigation that formed the basis of this chapter brought together linguists and speech and language therapists to explore and consider the language of one particular child with Down's syndrome. As with Stackhouse and Wells (1993), this was a needs-driven approach that started with a careful look at the child's production, moved on to some theorising based on psycholinguistic models and arrived at some tentative suggestions about remediation listed below.

It is vitally important in any plan of intervention to consider both the child and those to whom he or she will speak as being equally involved in the changes to be made. As Paul's syndrome limits the final levels of language competence, it is even more important that the aim of therapy is to make linguistic exchanges between him and his conversational partners as meaningful as possible.

Difficulties at the conceptual and formulation level

The following possibilities for helping Paul emerge from our investigations and discussions:

1. Pauses are essential for Paul's planning and should not be interrupted or hurried by his partner.
2. Repetitions need to be seen as attempts to 'hold the floor' and accepted as such.
3. In other words, Paul's dysfluencies should not be seen as 'stammering' and should not be treated as this disorder might be.
4. Paul needs to be more aware of shared and unshared information when telling a story or giving information. This requires requests from listeners for this information when it is lacking.
5. Specific help in recognising and using discourse features such as cohesion and coherence would seem to be of value.

Difficulties in rhythmic ability

Paul's inability to maintain rhythmic structure could be helped by the following:

1. General training in non-linguistic rhythm to heighten his awareness of rhythmic patterns, for example, by clapping or drumming such patterns via a simple written form or in imitation.
2. Use of rhythmic movement to underpin fluent, rhythmic speech. This was found to be of benefit to a young boy who stuttered in a study by Grube and Smith (1989). (See also Grube et al., 1986.)
3. Learning to 'sound out' or 'clap out' the syllabic structure of words.

Paul has already been working on this and it has proved very helpful for making intelligible those words and simple phrases that he was unable to produce, for example, *spaghetti bolognaise*. By aiming for a syllabic rhythm, one is working within Paul's competencies (his inclination to use mono- or disyllabic feet) rather than attempt to aim for a normalisation of the rhythmic structure at this stage. This approach is also providing him with a strategy for repair when this is requested by his listener. He has begun to use this strategy spontaneously and quite effectively, and will attempt words that he has not had any training on. He often claps the wrong number of syllables (the number concept being a particular problem for him) but he does produce a much clearer approximation to the word.

Monitoring

1. Paul has little awareness of his own output and the way in which it needs to be modified. It is important that, while listeners are prepared to give him time to conceptualise and formulate his message, they do not accept an unintelligible utterance. Paul needs to be asked regularly for repairs. He also needs to become aware of paralinguistic cues that indicate a lack of listener comprehension, e.g. facial and vocal indicators.
2. At present Paul's family are working on his awareness of the need to notice and correct unintelligible speech. The family are, at times, reducing their own speech to unintelligibility and waiting for Paul to demand a repair, and similarly demanding repairs from Paul when he is not understood (or is unclear). Positive results are gradually emerging with Paul occasionally spontaneously correcting himself and starting to monitor and correct peers as well!
3. Paul's metalinguistic awareness is very rudimentary. At a phonological level, he is aware of alliteration but has a poor concept of rhyme – he can offer a rhyming word when asked (e.g. 'what rhymes with "man"') but cannot agree if two words rhyme either when shown two pictures where he is called upon to use an internal representation or when he is given the auditory prompt ('do "man" and "pan" rhyme'). His teacher has been encouraged to try to develop his awareness of rhyming words. Further exploration of Paul's metalinguistic skills at grammatical, semantic and phonological levels is needed.

Conclusions related to remediation

The main aim of intervention for Paul is to make communication adequate enough so that he will be encouraged to continue to participate in exchanges with as wide a variety of others as possible. To do this, we first must build up a knowledge of Paul's linguistic system as a framework for planning the most useful approaches to adopt. We have investigated a number of hypotheses relating to specific areas of language ability and have so confirmed our original hypothesis that Paul's language cannot develop because he is unable to control simultaneously all the systems required for on-line speech production. This chapter has shown the evolution of thinking about Paul and his language difficulties from a test score view of deviations from norms to a profile of his own linguistic strengths and weaknesses (compare Stackhouse and Wells, 1993). A therapy plan must contain the seeds of further exploration so the process of theorising and hypothesis testing can continue.

The aims of therapy would therefore be the following:

1. To investigate further such areas as metalinguistic skills, discourse, rhythmic skills and exhalatory control.
2. To reinforce Paul's positive approach to communication and his growing knowledge and vocabulary as a way of enhancing his self-esteem.
3. To encourage others to understand Paul's communication needs better.
4. To help Paul learn to monitor his own output as much as is possible.
5. To offer Paul strategies by which he can make his message more intelligible.
6. To aim for 'good-enough' communication, not 'correct' or 'normal' output which can only put Paul's linguistic capacity under great pressure and lead to reduced competence.

Theoretical

Paul is a child with a complex language disorder and Down's syndrome. These two facts are related although not in a simple one-to-one fashion. People with Down's syndrome all have language that differs from the norm, but the nature and the complexity of the language problem vary from person to person. Difficulties in the development of grammar are paramount, so short utterances with little extension of morphology or syntax are common features of the language in Down's syndrome (Miller, 1988). A few adults have been found to have very competent grammatical skills although they still show failures of comprehension and semantic ability. Probably the most influential negative factor in the language development of children with Down's syndrome is cognitive development (Rondal, 1988), and for this reason it is vital that a realistic and encouraging approach is taken in remediation. The suggestion arising from our data, that much of Paul's unintelligibility may be the result of his inability to conceptualise, must mitigate against too much direct emphasis on grammatical drilling.

We have shown too that, although phonological development is slow, Paul does not show any specific phonological disorder. Nor did we find any particular articulatory difficulty. Rather, his problem lies in the rhythmical patterning of his speech. This calls for a radical re-think about remediation. Possibly work should focus on developing a meta-linguistic awareness of the overriding rhythms of words and phrases and of how words and sentences fit these rhythms.

One other suggestion that arose from the data, but remains to be further investigated, was that poor respiratory support may be influential in difficulties Paul had in initiating utterances. If this is the case, work on breath support for speech and controlled exhalation may bear fruit. Some years ago a suggestion that all children with Down's syndrome should wear supportive corsets to improve respiratory control was discredited. There was no experimental support for such an idea. Although we would not see a solution in such simple terms, we feel that further research in this area may be warranted as loss of phonatory control is not an uncommon feature in Down's syndrome.

Finally, the information derived from our investigation of Paul's language adds a little to the delay–deviance debate which has been argued since the 1970s when Yoder and Miller (1972) suggested that children with Down's syndrome were delayed, not deviant, in language development. We would argue that Paul's production of speech is different rather than delayed in both its rhythmic patterning and its 'oddly' constructed sentences.

Rhythmic simplification is of course a normal developmental feature of children's speech, commonly taking the form of what has been called weak syllable deletion (Grunwell, 1987). Grunwell states that this usually manifests as deletion of pre-tonic unstressed syllables. For Paul, syllable deletion is joined by addition of syllables and incorrect placement of the tonic syllable such that the pattern of difference is more complex than might be expected in normal but delayed speech.

Methodological implications and conclusion

If Paul is similar to other people with Down's syndrome, and clinical 'intuition' would suggest that he is, the implications of this study are that much more careful linguistic evaluation of the speech of developing children with Down's syndrome is needed, with an emphasis on how they are responding to and evolving non-linguistic and linguistic rhythms. Language must be seen as closely bound to cognition and encouragement of language development must take place within a framework of the growth of knowledge and meaning.

The task for the speech and language therapist is therefore to work alongside other professionals such as linguists and psychologists and develop a dialogue around the issues of Down's syndrome and language that unites skills and leads to a creative approach to remediation based on the launching and testing of hypotheses within an adequate theoretical framework.

Chapter 7
Conversational disability: assessment and remediation

AMANDA WILLCOX and KAY MOGFORD-BEVAN

The following chapter is based on a research project which was designed to examine the issues of assessment and intervention in children who present with difficulties in participating in conversation. The project involved a case study of one child, N, who presented with a conversational disability. The study took place over a 10-month period, and involved repeated assessment and analysis of N's conversational skills. The data presented here are drawn from the baseline assessment before therapy and from the assessment that followed two periods of intervention.

Background

Case history

N is the third child of English-speaking parents. His parents are both teachers, and his twin siblings are 4 years older than he is. There is no history of communication problems in the immediate family. N was born following a difficult pregnancy during which his mother was hospitalised twice with high blood pressure. He was 2 weeks pre-term, but there were no perinatal complications. His mother reported that his developmental milestones occurred later than those of his siblings, particularly in the area of speech and language development. His parents became concerned about him when he was approximately 18 months old. He was not using language to communicate, and he exhibited atypical behaviours, e.g. hand flapping and running around in circles. He was placed in a mainstream nursery from the chronological age of 3;4 years to 4;8 years. He then spent a year in a school for autistic children, before being transferred to a language unit in a mainstream school at 5;8 years. At this time, N was diagnosed as having semantic–

pragmatic disorder by the educational psychologist in charge of his case.

The problem

The term 'semantic–pragmatic syndrome' was first used by Rapin and Allen (1983) as part of a framework in which developmental language disorders were classified. Children with this syndrome are described as having fluent expressive language, with no grammatical or phonological deficits, but they are unable to use their language to engage in meaningful interaction. N's communication certainly matched this description, but such a diagnosis did not explain exactly what was disordered about his conversation, or indicate how he might best be helped.

McTear (1990) challenges the usefulness of the diagnosis of semantic–pragmatic syndrome, suggesting that it implies too great a range of problems. Semantics and pragmatics represent two distinct levels of language, the former relating to aspects of meaning that fall within language structure and the latter referring to the aspects of meaning that are dependent on context. A semantic–pragmatic disorder would thus subsume a vast range of problems from difficulties with word meanings to difficulties with language usage in context. McTear argues that it would perhaps be more helpful to identify different types of conversational disability. For example, problems in conversation may be a result of a linguistic impairment in which the child lacks the phonological and/or grammatical competence necessary to participate in conversation. Alternatively, difficulties in conversation may be the result of an autistic deficit, which prevents the child from making sense of what is happening around him, or of what other people intend or believe. McTear suggests that there is also a possibility that a child might present with a conversational disability in the absence of either of these impairments. Such a child might exhibit difficulties with specific conversational rules, such as turn allocation, attention getting and directing, using speech acts appropriately and repairing conversational breakdown.

In N's case, it was not possible to assume that he presented with a specific impairment of conversation, because his case history indicated that he exhibited characteristics of both a grammatical and an autistic impairment. Assessments of N's language before his arrival at the language unit suggested that N had both grammatical and phonological language difficulties. There is a considerable body of evidence to suggest that any disorder affecting a child's reception or production of language will necessarily have some pragmatic implications (Gallagher and Darnton, 1978; Donahue et al., 1980; Brinton and Fujiki, 1982; Conti-Ramsden and Friel-Patti, 1983; Fey and Leonard, 1983; Craig and Evans, 1989). N's difficulties in interaction could therefore have been attributed to a disorder of linguistic form. Similarly, although N was never diagnosed as either autistic or having Asperger's syndrome, he presented with some of the features that are recognised in the medical diagnosis of these disorders (Rutter, 1978; Wing, 1981, 1988). N exhibited all the characteristics outlined by Rutter as diagnostic of autism: his disorder was diagnosed before 30 months, and was manifested in the key clinical features of impaired social development out of keeping with intellectual skills, delayed and deviant language acquisition and use, and an insistence on sameness. The evidence of N's case history thus only seemed to highlight the difficulties of disentangling the nature of his conversational disability.

The problem was further compounded by the lack of material designed to assess conversational disability. N's difficulties with language did not show up in results from conventional assessments where he achieved average or just below average scores. To examine his problems with language use, it was necessary to design an assessment procedure based on linguistic principles to look at his conversational behaviours. The assessment adopted drew heavily on the frameworks of conversational analysis outlined by McTear (1985a) and Milroy (1988). They suggest that data should be collected in a range of different situations and with different conversational partners. These data should then be scanned for specific conversational strategies, and the dynamic interaction between conversational partners should be considered when trying to identify clinically significant features. It was hypothesised that the use of linguistic techniques to analyse language samples collected in a variety of different situations might provide empirical evidence that N's conversational difficulties existed independently of either a grammatical or an autistic impairment.

It was also proposed that such an analysis would lead to the selection of achievable intervention goals. There has been little work done on the remediation of pragmatic disabilities, irrespective of their cause. Some authors (Conti-Ramsden and Gunn, 1986; Jones et al., 1986; Hyde-Wright and Cray, 1990) outline approaches to the treatment of semantic–pragmatic disorder, but the efficacy of therapy has not been demonstrated. The remediation programmes are not based on detailed linguistic analysis of the children's conversations and do not take account of current knowledge about pragmatic development. In this study, goals for intervention were selected on the basis of the conversational analysis. Where possible, conversational skills that have been demonstrated to emerge earlier in normal pragmatic development were taught to N. Where N was observed to have some skill in the use of a conversational strategy, that strategy was selected as one that was relevant to him, and one that was therefore more likely to be acquired in therapy. It was hoped that it would be possible to demonstrate that

N's conversational disability would respond to intervention. Two distinct methods were compared as part of the study. Intervention I involved behavioural methods of modelling, prompting and reinforcement. Intervention II was based on a metalinguistic approach in which conversational behaviours were demonstrated, practised and evaluated.

Analysis

A multiple baseline, across-behaviour design was adopted to assess N's conversational behaviours. Baseline data were collected on several independent conversational behaviours. Two treatments were applied (intervention I and intervention II). Changes in N's conversational behaviour were reassessed following both treatment phases.

Data collection

Assessment data were collected in school. N was 6;10 years at the time of the first assessment and 7;9 years at the time of the final assessment. Data were drawn from two sources.

Observation assessment

N's communication behaviours were observed in a variety of different settings:

1. In the language unit classroom where N was very familiar with the children and adults.
2. In the mainstream classroom where N was integrated for one day a week with his mainstream peers.
3. In the yard during playtime.
4. In the dining hall.

The researcher sat as close to N as possible without being intrusive in each setting, and made paper and pencil notes relating to N's interactions. The notes detailed the identity of N's conversational partners, the topic of conversation, the forms used to initiate and respond, and the linguistic and extralinguistic context. Where possible the researcher transcribed exactly what was said. Observation periods lasted between 15 and 30 minutes.

Video assessment

N was video and audio recorded playing with three different partners:

1. With a familiar adult (referred to as 'A'). This was the nursery nurse from the language unit.

2. With a familiar child (referred to as 'FC1' and 'FC2'). These were two other children from the language unit who were in the same academic year as N. They had both presented with severe phonological disorders which had resolved. It was not possible to use FC1 in the final assessment as he was no longer in the language unit.
3. With an unfamiliar child (referred to as 'UC'). This was one of the children from the mainstream class where N was integrated. UC was also in the same academic year as N.

The video sessions lasted approximately 20 minutes. N and his partners played with a choice of toys (the Play People Camper, Spaceship and Fire Engine, and some Lego). No one else was present during these play sessions. Utterances were transcribed according to the conventions in the Appendix.

Analytical framework

The conversational behaviours examined in each assessment were as follows.

Initiations. It was noted whether N was more likely to approach adults or other children. The linguistic form of N's initiations was examined, and an evaluation was made as to whether his initiations weakly or strongly demanded a response from the addressee.

Directives. The linguistic form of N's directives was noted to see what forms he used to direct others. Whether his directives were appropriate to the addressee and to the situation was also considered.

Attention-getting devices. The type of attention-getting device N used to secure the attention of the addressee was considered. It was noted whether N used attention-getting devices effectively and whether he followed up the summons implication with a reason for the summons.

Social routines. N's use of greetings and partings and his use of politeness words were examined.

Responses. N's awareness of the obligations of conversation was assessed. It was noted whether he fulfilled his role in conversation by responding to the initiations of others. It was also noted whether N related his responses to the preceding utterance of his conversational partner, and whether he was able to maintain topic over several turns. Instances where N failed to respond were counted, and were considered as a percentage of the total number of occasions when another speaker attempted to initiate conversation with N.

Repair and clarification. It was noted whether N requested clarification or was able to revise his own utterances in response to a request for clarification from his conversational partner. N's strategies for renegotiating interaction when an addressee failed to respond were also considered.

Cohesion. Devices used by N to maintain and link discourse were studied.

Findings of the assessment before intervention

The assessment indicated that N was aware of some conversational rules, and put them into practice in some situations. However, there was also evidence that he lacked an appreciation of other rules, and that he used strategies that were atypical of a child of his age and linguistic maturity.

Initiations

In the observation assessment, it was found that N was more likely to initiate interaction with adults rather than with other children. When he did approach another child it tended to be a child from the language unit with whom he was more familiar.

Many of N's initiations were declarative in form and thus only weakly demanded a response from his partner. Usually N initiated interaction by commenting on or describing what he was doing or what was happening around him. For example, he commented that another child had knocked his crayons over:

1 N: Brian's spilled his crayons

In the following example, N stood in the middle of the classroom and announced that he had got more housepoints than anyone else:

2 N: I'm the only one that's got three badges

There was no verbal or non-verbal evidence to suggest that these remarks and others like them were directed at anyone in particular. No one responded to them and N did not take any steps to follow them up either by indicating to whom they were addressed or by attempting to elicit a response.

There were many examples where N initiated interaction by using an interrogative to ask for information which he already had. For example, he asked the class teacher after she had just explained to him what she wanted him to do:

3 N: what shall I do?

Similarly when he had just found the 'D' page in his dictionary, he asked:

4 N: where's 'dr', 'd' for driving?

Directives

N frequently used declarative forms to direct others. For example, when he finished a piece of work and he wanted the teacher to mark it for him, N said:

5 N: I done good work

When he wanted an adult to help him put his poppy in his jumper (Armistice Day) he stood in front of her, trying to do it himself and said:

6 N: I got a poppy

Often only the non-verbal context in which these utterances occurred indicated what N wanted. To take the latter example, N might well have been merely commenting that he had a poppy, in which case his statement would have been appropriate. Only his non-verbal behaviour (standing in front of the adult, trying to get the poppy in and then holding it out to the adult) suggested that he wanted help putting it in his jumper. A request ('Will you put my poppy in my jumper') or a command ('Put my poppy in my jumper') might have been more effective.

N's directives were usually more effective when directed towards adults than towards children. Adults interpreted N's needs and usually complied with his implicit requests. Other children, however, did not respond to N's implicit directives. For example, here N appeared to be asking FC1 for help, but the latter failed to read the request implicit in N's declarative:

```
 7 FC1:   wait for me brother = [FC1 plays with men on motorbikes]
 8        = get on brother
 9 N:     – want help to get on [N tries to get a man on a bike]
10        – I need help to get on this bike
11        – this bike turns corners all the time
12 FC1:   [symbolic noise] [FC1 drives his bikes around]
```

N did not seem to be able to mobilise a different form to make FC1 respond to his request.

There was only one example where N used a polar interrogative to direct another person. N wanted UC to put a man on a bike:

```
13 N:        – – – – – I can't get on [N hands man on bike to UC]
14           I can't get on
```

15		would you help?
16 UC:		yeah [UC takes the bike]
17		I'll help

It is interesting that UC immediately recognised the polar interrogative form as a request. This was also the only example where N altered the linguistic form of his utterance to make his directive more explicit.

Attention-getting devices

N rarely used attention-getting devices to secure the attention of an addressee before speaking to him or her. Typically N would look intently at the other person or stand nearby before speaking. Often the intended listener was not aware that N was addressing him or her, and therefore did not reply.

Occasionally N was observed to use a vocative: he sometimes called other children by name when he was playing near them. Typically he would repeat the name as if he were going to direct their play but was apparently unable to follow-up the 'summons' with a 'reason for summons'.

Social routines

There were no occasions where N was observed to initiate a greeting or parting sequence during the observation assessment. In the play situation that was videoed with FC1, N ignored greeting/parting routines:

18 FC1:	Hi mate [N drives the camper up and down ignoring the FC1]
19	– I'm on my motorbike =
20	= Bye
21	– I'm going back to the caravette
22 N:	this one's going on their holidays

N was apparently unable to cooperate in such exchanges.

N did not use politeness routines, e.g. he pushed past people who were in his way and did not say 'excuse me'. Nor did he use words such as 'please' and 'thank you'.

Responses

N showed some awareness of the necessity of turn-taking and usually contributed verbally following an utterance from his conversational partner. However, he did not always fulfil his part in the conversation. Sometimes he failed to respond when it was his turn, and his partner, who was evidently expecting a reply, had to repeat or rephrase his or her preceding utterance to give N another opportunity to fill the response slot that had been set up for him. Sometimes it appeared that N had not listened to what his conversational partners had said, and his replies did not mesh with theirs or share the same topic. It often appeared that N was not paying attention to his conversational partners, because he was engrossed in his own activities.

N's communication was more effective when he was interacting with adults. As experienced conversationalists, adults took account of N's conversational difficulties, and designed their conversations to meet his needs. Thus A accepted and responded to N's contributions even when they only weakly demanded a response. She used questioning moves to initiate new exchanges to keep the conversation going. Often these exchanges were closed, in that there was little linkage between them except that they related to the overall topic or to the play activities in which she and N were involved. A persisted until she received a satisfactory response to her questions by repeating them and rephrasing them until N responded satisfactorily. These strategies are illustrated in the following example, where N and A were putting play people in the camper:

23 A: has he got a passenger? [N puts men in back of camper]
24 N: – – you have to get them all in yours
25 A: all of them
26   it'll be a bit crowded
27   – won't it?
28   haven't you got anybody to put in your car?
29 N: put it there
30 A: have you got a passenger that could sit on the front seat?
31   – – that's it [A points to front seat, and N puts man in]
32   he sit there
33   who's that?
34 N: yes he will sit there
35 A: who is it?
36 N: the man
37 A: the man
38   is it this man's friend or is it his brother?
39 N: [sings]
40 A: who is it? =
41   = his friend or his brother
42 N: his brother
43 A: his brother

This example also demonstrates how A reinforced N's responses by repeating and extending them (lines 1.25, 1.37 and 1.43), thus guiding the conversation, yet following N's train of thought. It also shows how she set up N's response in question–answer sequences, by giving him forced alternative questions (l.38). Consequently there were comparatively fewer occasions where N failed to respond: N failed to respond to 41% of A's initiations.

Other children did not have the conversational skills to compensate for N's difficulties. FC1 and UC had some conversational strategies which they used to try and get N to respond. In the following example, UC repeated his question to solicit a response from N. He wanted to know what N watched on television:

```
44 UC:  – – – – do you watch Blue Peter?
45        – – do you?
46 N:   no
```

FC1 repeated N's name to try to get him to agree that the play people were on holiday, but he could not get N to acknowledge what had been said:

```
47 FC1: – we're on holiday, aren't we N?
48        – – right [N moves toys towards the camper]
49        N we're * on holiday now
50 N:   * and all the rest #
51        and all the rest can go in your car
52 FC1: a barbie [FC1 finds a barbecue]
53        – – right we on holiday now, aren't we * N?
54 N:   * no
55 FC1: N we on holiday
56 N:   – – mum's on holiday
57 FC1: I've got a motorbike –
58        = got a motorbike helmet
59        – – right N we on holiday now
60 N:   – [symbolic noise]
```

The other children were less likely to follow up N's weak initiations as topics of conversation and they did not structure the conversation in a way in which N could respond. They were more interested in developing their own topics of play and conversation than in maintaining the discourse. After a while, they gave up trying to engage N in conversation. Thus, the N–FC1 and the N–UC exchanges were unproductive and fleeting in comparison with the A–N exchanges. The number of times N failed to respond in the FC1 and the UC interactions was much higher than in the A interaction. N failed to respond to 61% of FC1's initiations and 70% of UC's initiations. With no shared topic, discourse did not develop. It seemed that, unless the interaction was specifically structured to accommodate N's conversational problems, communication became less a dialogue than two collective monologues.

The same pattern emerged in the observation data. The proportion of initiations to which N failed to respond was calculated as a percentage of the number of initiations directed towards him. N failed to respond to only 11% of adult initiations. He failed to respond to 50% of initiations directed to him by other children. Other children in fact rarely approached N. When other children did try to interact with him, N frequently rejected their overtures.

Repair and clarification

N was not observed to request clarification either verbally or non-verbally, even when it was evident that he had not understood what the speaker had said. For example, the teacher in the mainstream class had been speaking to the children in French, and had explained the meaning of 'asseyez-vous' to them in N's absence. N did not respond when the teacher gave this instruction to the class, and he did not try to find out what she meant.

When his conversational partners requested clarification, N usually repeated his utterance or used non-verbal means to repair the conversation. Here UC asked N to show him how to take the top off the car. N showed him inadequately and UC indicated that he had not understood. N showed him again, this time more adequately:

> 61 UC: – – – – how does this open to get the people in? [UC points
> to the car]
> 62 N: – – you take the top off
> 63 UC : – how do you get the top off though?
> 64 N: you have to do it like this (N lifts car by roof but roof stays
> on)
> 65 UC: pardon
> 66 N: you have to do it like that (N takes roof off car)
> 67 UC: oh
> 68   – I see

Such strategies for repairing conversation were not always effective. In this example, UC and N were looking in a doll's house. N pointed to an ordinary clock on the wall that said 4 o'clock. He then confused UC by talking about a television clock. It appeared that he was trying to tell UC how the hour was marked on a digital clock (i.e. the television clock). UC obviously did not understand, and N could not clarify himself:

> 69 N: – – – – that says four o'clock on there [N points to clock]
> 70 UC: where?=

71   = four o'clock on where?
72 N: there [N points to clock]
73   – that says oh oh
74 UC: – four o'clock
75 N: on the television clock
76   the two ohs mean o'clock
77 UC: pardon
78 N: the two ohs mean o'clock on the television clock
79 UC: how did you know?
80 N: because the two ohs mean o'clock
81 UC: mhm right
82   – very good N

UC's tone in l.81–82 implied that he still did not understand what N meant, even though he concluded the topic. It is clear from these examples that N recognised when he had not been understood, and that he knew he had to take steps to repair the conversational breakdown. However, if repetition or non-verbal means failed to clarify the situation, N was unable to mobilise other strategies.

N also used repetition as a means of demanding his partner's attention and soliciting a reply when his partner failed to respond to him. Here N had put a little girl on a bike, but got no response from FC1 when he tried to tell him:

83 N: I think it was my little girl's bike
84   – that she was on
85   she's on a two wheeler bike
86   – she can drive a two wheeler bike [FC1 plays with toys and does not look at N]
87   – she can drive a two wheeler bike
88   – she can drive a two wheeler bike
89   she can now drive a *
90 FC1: * she can drive a two wheeler bike
91 N: yes

As soon as FC1 responded N stopped his repetition. This suggests that N was using repetition as a strategy for soliciting a response.

Cohesion

Previous discussion has indicated that N's contributions to conversation were not always related to the preceding utterances of his conversational partner, and that N was not always able to fulfil his role in maintaining cohesive discourse. N did demonstrate some strategies for linking his utterances to those of his conversational partner. He often repeated all or part of his conversational partners' preceding utterances when agreeing with them or affirming what they had said. A yes–no response or an ellipted reply would be more usual. This was only noted to occur when he was interacting with A. For example, A asked N if a play person was too big to fit in the driving seat of the camper. N used a full response to reply with the nuclear stress on 'big':

92 A: – – is he too big?
93 N: he's too big

N also repeated A in l.34 above to agree with her.

The findings of the first assessment are summarised in Table 7.1.

Intervention

Following the baseline assessment, two distinct intervention methods were applied to teach N effective control of specific conversational behaviours.

Intervention I

Intervention I was designed to teach N to make his directives more explicit. Halliday (1975a, b) demonstrates that the instrumental and regulatory functions are the first to develop in the young child. N appeared to be unable to realise these functions in a linguistic form that unambiguously demonstrated his intentions. Typically N used declarative forms where a polar interrogative or an imperative form might have been more successful. N's addressees consequently did not recognise that he was making a request. From a developmental viewpoint, it was felt important to teach N to perform these functions effectively. N was taught to use a polar interrogative form when making a request. This form was felt to be sufficiently explicit to be recognised unambiguously as a directive, and polite enough to be acceptable in most situations and with most addressees whatever their status in relation to N. N had already demonstrated that he could use such forms in the course of the assessment (1.15).

N was taught to use the word 'please' when he made a request. This word was considered important not only because it would immediately mark N's utterance as a request, but also because it would make the request more polite and therefore more acceptable to the addressee.

The assessment had also demonstrated that N was consistently having difficulties with 'recipient design' (Sacks and Schegloff, 1974). Keenan and Schieffelin (1976) specify that the need to secure the attention of the addressee and to make explicit who is being addressed is vital if successful interaction is to take place. N was consistently failing

Table 7.1 Summary of findings of the initial assessment before therapy

Initiations	N was more likely to approach familiar adults than other children. N's initiations only weakly demanded a response from the addressee
Directives	N frequently used declaratives to direct others even though he could use more explicit forms to command and request. N's implicit directives were effective with adult conversational partners who interpreted what he wanted. They were not effective with other children
Attention-getting devices	N rarely used attention getting devices to secure the attention of the addressee. When he did address others by name he often did not follow-up the summons implication of his attention-getting device
Social outines	N did not initiate or respond to greeting/parting sequences. N did not use politeness words or sequences
Responses	N showed some awareness of the obligations of conversation, but frequently failed to fulfil these. He did not always respond to the initiations of others, or he did not relate his response to their preceding utterance
Repair and clarification	N did not request clarification. N responded to requests for clarification. He used repetition or non-verbal means to repair conversational breakdown. N used repetition to solicit a response from an addressee, if the addressee did not immediately respond to N's initiation
Cohesion	N often repeated the utterance of his conversational partner to maintain conversation

to design his utterances so that the recipient knew that he or she was being addressed. It was therefore decided to teach N to use the name of the addressee as part of his directive.

Activities were set up where N was unable to complete a task unless he made a request. For example, N was asked to complete a colouring task, but was given pens of the wrong colour. N had to ask for the right coloured pens. The target structure, a request couched in a polar interrogative form, was modelled for N to imitate:

94 T: If you want a pen, N, you could ask. You could say Please
         Miss W can I have a red pen

When N imitated the request, his response was reinforced by
rewarding him with whatever it was that he had asked for, and by
telling him that he had done 'good asking'. If he failed to imitate a
request it was modelled again until he imitated it correctly. N was not
rewarded until he responded with the modelled request form.

Once N became adept at imitating the request forms, a prompt was
used to elicit N's request:

95 T: If you want a red pen N, you will have to ask

Again N's response was reinforced by complying with his request, and
by telling him that he had done 'good asking'. If N failed to produce a
request following a prompt, a request was modelled by the therapist
and N was required to imitate it.

Prompts were then faded, so that N was gradually required to identify for himself the situations where he needed to make a request.
Whenever N made a request spontaneously it was reinforced by complying with the request and by telling N that he had done 'good asking'. The same procedure was then used to establish requests in more
natural situations in school.

The therapist identified situations in the classroom where N could
be encouraged to make requests of the teacher or other children. The
staff in the language unit and N's parents were encouraged to model,
prompt and reward 'good asking'.

(For a summary of intervention I see Table 7.2.)

Intervention II

Intervention II was designed to encourage N to react to the verbal and
non-verbal initiations of others. It was noted in a reassessment after
intervention I that the number of initiations to which N failed to
respond had decreased. It seemed that N had learned something of the
obligations of discourse, and now understood that he was expected to
reply. The skills of listening and of responding to his conversational
partner were therefore selected as target areas when setting up intervention II.

Intervention II took place in the language unit classroom. N participated in a group with nine other children. The other children had a
variety of communication disorders, and although none of them had a
conversational disorder per se, they all experienced interaction difficulties as a result of their disorders. It was thus beneficial for them to participate in the group as well. It also provided N with the opportunity to
observe their mistakes, and led to useful discussion and evaluation.

Table 7.2 Summary of the goals and activities of intervention I

No. of sessions	Goals of intervention	Activities
5	(a) To teach N to imitate requests in the form of polar interrogatives (b) To teach N to produce requests in the form of polar interrogatives following a prompt (c) To teach N to produce requests in the form of polar interrogatives spontaneously	Activities were set up in the speech therapy room where N could not complete a task unless he requested an action. Models and prompts were given by the therapist, and N's requests were directed to the therapist
4	As above	Activities were set up in the language unit classroom where N could not complete a task unless he requested an action. Models and prompts were given by the therapist, and N's requests were directed to other children and to other members of staff
7	As above	Naturally occurring situations were identified where N could not complete a task unless he requested an action. Models and prompts were given by the therapist and by other members of staff, and were directed to other members of staff and to other children

The group observed the therapist and the class teacher demonstrating target communication behaviours, and the children took turns to practise these within the group. The children also observed role-plays of poor communication, and were encouraged to discuss why communication broke down in these sequences. The children monitored and commented on one another's performance, and were encouraged to evaluate their own communication skills within the group. They were also asked to think of ways in which unsuccessful communication sequences could be improved so that successful interaction took place (see Table 7.3 for a summary of intervention II).

N was occasionally withdrawn for individual sessions with the therapist, to practise the skills he had learned in the group in a one-to-one setting. N was also encouraged to use the skills discussed in relevant communication situations. His family were informed of his progress, and

Table 7.3 Summary of the goals and activities of intervention II

No.of sessions	Goals of intervention	Activities
10	To identify situations in which a greeting/parting sequence should be initiated and/or responded to	N made aware of various greeting/parting words and rehearsed using them out of context in the group. N encouraged to identify situations in which such words would be appropriately used
10	To identify when a greeting/parting sequence had not been responded to and to take steps to re-negotiate the sequence	N made aware of various methods of attracting the attention of the addressee and encouraged to practise these in situations where his greeting/parting sequence had been ignored
8	To identify and react to smiles and to respond by smiling back	N made aware of different facial expressions and encouraged to recognise and produce them out of context. N encouraged to identify situations where he should smile at others, and to watch the faces of others and react to their expressions
7	To identify, label and demonstrate key non-verbal behaviours associatedwith listening (Dollaghan andKaston, 1986)	N taught to distinguish successful and unsuccessful performance of listening behaviours (e.g. looking at speaker, not fidgeting, etc.) Situations where 'good listening' was imperative in order to achieve a goal were identified
2	To identify situations where as a result of not listening, the addressee needed to initiate a repair sequence to ensure that communication could continue successfully	N made aware of various words and phrases that he could use to ask the speaker to repeat him-/herself
16	To identify, label and demonstrate key verbal behaviours associated with listening to and acknowledging what the speaker had said (e.g. back-channel responses and topic maintenance skills)	N made aware of backchannel responses and rehearsed them in the role of listener in conversation with an adult N encouraged to incorporate the topic of his conversational partner's initiation by requesting or giving further information on that topic

were invited to prompt him to practise his newly acquired conversation skills at home.

Findings of assessment following intervention

The assessment procedure was repeated following intervention. The findings are presented here.

Initiations

The observation assessment indicated that N had started to initiate interaction more frequently with other children than with adults. Analysis of N's initiations indicated that N was using a wider range of initiation types than had previously been observed. Although he continued to use declarative forms, he also used interrogative and imperative forms to ask questions and to give commands. These forms demand a response more strongly than declaratives.

N used interrogative forms in a more meaningful way to ask for information. There was no evidence that N knew the answer to his own questions, as he had done in the first assessment. Thus, for example, when he found the lid for the spaceship in the fire engine box, he asked A directly where it had come from:

96 N: where does that come from? [N picks up lid]
97 A: I don't know
98   – I haven't come across all this before [A rummages in the box]
99   I don't know where any of the bits go
100   I think that must be something from the spaceship
101   I think things * have got muddled up
102 N: * where's the spaceship?
103 A: is it behind you?

On another occasion N used interrogative forms to make suggestions about the construction of the rocket that he was sharing with UC:

104 N: shall we stick a bunch of flowers on top?
105 UC: [laughs] no
106 N: shall we stick this thing on top to make it look nice? [N picks up a piece of Lego]
107 UC: no

N used imperative forms to initiate and to tell his partner what he wanted. His imperative forms demanded a response. For example, N organised A to tidy the fire engine back into its box because he wanted the spaceship instead:

108 A: well what will we have to do [A gets fire engine box]
109 N: tidy it up
110   – – – put the biggest things in first =
        [N passes fire engine to A]
111   = because they're the heaviest
112 A: right

The most striking change in N's initiations was his awareness that he was now able to control both the conversation and the play. He knew that he could get a response from his partner. This was indicated in a conversation with A, who was reluctant to reply to N's question about which planet she would like to visit. N insisted on a reply:

113 N: which one would you like to visit?
114 A: none
115 N: – – which #
116   come on
117   which one: Mercury Venus Mars Jupiter Saturn Uranus
          Neptune or Pluto?
118 A: I like #
119   I quite like the name Saturn
120   I think that might be nice

Directives

N's directives were more forceful and effective in the second assessment. It was noted that N changed the form that he used to communicate what he wanted depending on the addressee. This goes beyond what he was taught in intervention and indicates a sensitivity to the familiarity and status of the addressee.

He generally made polite requests using a polar interrogative, when he was addressing adults or less familiar children. For example, when struggling to carry a chair across the language unit classroom, N asked a nearby adult for help:

121 N: it's heavy
122   please would you carry it for me?

When needing some paper to perform a maths exercise in the mainstream classroom, N asked the teacher for it:

123 N: Miss D, please can I have some paper?

N also used polar interrogatives when interacting with children in the mainstream classroom. Here N wanted to borrow another child's rubber:

124 N: please can I borrow your rubber?
125 L: yes [L hands rubber to N]
126   there you are

When addressing the more familiar children from the language unit, N tended to use imperative forms. For example, at playtime, N was pretending with some other children that they were in a car. N directed Sally to get in the car:

127 N: get in the back Sally please

and he continued to organise the others once they were in the car:

128 N: you sit down there
129   Daniel sit down there

Following such explicit directives, the other children usually complied.

Attention-getting devices

There were still occasions where N called another person's name, but did not follow up the summons with a further communication, but this occurred infrequently. More often, N used the name of the addressee in conjunction with a command, request or statement. When the other person knew that they were being addressed, they were more likely to respond (see l.123, 1.127 and 1.129).

N also started to use other attention-getting devices such as 'look', 'excuse me' and 'do you know what . . .' to alert potential addressees that they were being spoken to. For example, N wanted FC2, who was busy trying to put a man on a bike, to put a helmet on the man first. N called FC2's attention away from the man to the helmet:

130 N: look [FC2 tries to put man on bike]
131   look at this [N shows FC2 helmet]
132   – – this is a helmet [FC2 takes helmet from N]
133   has to have a helmet first

N's use of an attention-getting device here was important, because FC2 was occupied with the toys. On other occasions, N used non-verbal means, such as tapping the addressee, to get their attention.

Social routines

N was frequently noted to use greeting and parting words and gestures. He was observed to greet another child in the queue for lunch. He regularly greeted the staff in the unit. Sometimes N used non-verbal means to greet others. For example, he was much more aware of the therapist when she was observing him, and would greet her by smiling and waving.

N appeared to be much more aware of social routines. When N made a request, he tended to use the word 'please' as he had been taught (1.122, 1.123, 1.124 and 1.127). He was noted to use 'please' on other occasions as well. He responded to the dinner nanny who was serving his lunch:

134 DN:would you like bacon N?
135 N: yes please

Responses

Although there were still occasions where N's conversational partner
initiated an interaction and N failed to respond, such occasions had
decreased significantly. N was observed to take a much more active role
in participating in conversation, and he was prepared to respond to
and follow-up the topics of conversation introduced by his partners.

The change in N's response behaviour was more obvious when N
was conversing with other children. In the following example N and
UC were playing with Lego. They were both making their own rockets.
UC requested N's help, and N stopped what he was doing to look for
Lego pieces for UC:

136 UC:could you find some fourers?
137 N: what's fourers like?
138 UC:like – these [UC picks up a fourer and shows N]
139   one two three four
140 N: – no [N picks up a piece of Lego and holds it out to UC]
141   that #
142   [unintelligible] not that can't be #
143 UC:that is the kind but I don't want that on [UC takes Lego
        piece then discards it]
144   it has to be red [N starts to look through Lego]
145 N: and it has to be red
146   I wonder [unintelligible]
147   I found sixers [N finds a sixer and gives it to UC. UC
        discards it]
148 UC:sixers?
149   – that's a threer
150 N: that's a three
151   [sings] [N continues to look through Lego]
152 UC:found some more
153   [unintelligible]
154 N: there's # [N finds two red fourers]
155   I've found two fourers that are red
156 UC:lets see yours [N gives them to UC who puts them on his
        rocket)
157   oh good
158   – – thank you very much

This conversation indicates that N appreciated what UC was saying and
doing, and that he was able to participate in the shared goal of building
the rocket.

N also demonstrated that he was able to contribute more information to the conversation when he was talking to another child. Here, for example, UC and N were talking about some of the other children in the language unit. UC suggested that N was wrong about the age of the twins. N assured him that the twins were 8, and argued that they had just had their birthday, 4 days previously:

159 N: Roger's the oldest in our class
160   he's eight
161 UC: how old are the twins?
162 N: eight
163   and their birthday is a bit later next year than Roger's
164 UC: the twins cannot be eight
165   – they're so small, man
166 N: – they are
167   they've had their birthday on the sixteenth
168 UC: oh
169 N: – – oh they've had their birthday on the sixteenth of
         September

It seems that N had grasped the principles of conversation and understood that he needed not only to fill the response slots allocated to him but also to relate the topic of his response to that of his partner's previous utterance. N no longer required his conversational partner to structure the conversation in such a way that he could respond, and thus exchanges with his peers were as successful as exchanges with adults. This was reflected in the decrease in the percentage of FC2's and UC's initiations to which N failed to respond (14% and 16% respectively). The percentage of A's initiations to which N failed to respond remained relatively constant (31%).

Again the same pattern emerged in the observation data. There was an increase in the number of occasions where other children initiated interaction with N. There was a corresponding decrease in the number of initiations from other children to which N failed to respond. N failed to respond to only 14% of other child initiations. N did not reject other children when they approached him to initiate interaction as he had done previously. In contrast he took an active interest in their initiations, and joined in their conversations.

Repair and clarification

In the final assessment, N requested clarification to indicate when he did not understand. Here, N was trying to put a man in a spaceship, and A indicated that perhaps, if he took the helmet off, the man would fit in. A used the deictic term 'this' together with a non verbal gesture

to indicate what she meant. N let her know that he had not understood, and A clarified what she meant:

170 A: does he need this [A points to man's helmet]
171 N: what?
172 A: does he need his hat off do you think?
173   when he's going in there
174 N: yeah [N takes helmet off]

N also demonstrated that he could be more explicit in his clarification request when he asked UC to clarify a specific word ('fourer' 1.137).

N used strategies other than repetition to respond to requests for
clarification in the second assessment. N rephrased utterances to make
it more evident to the addressee what he meant. In the following example, N had made a rocket out of Lego and he tried to explain to UC that
when the rocket took off, it left the wheels behind. UC indicated that
he did not understand:

175 N: and when you take the wheels off it just flies #
176   it just flies away
177 UC: what?
178 N: because when you take the wheels off
179   and you tell #
180   and you say five four three two one it #
181   and * you drive it
182 UC: * [unintelligible]
183 N: it blasts off
184 UC: – – I see what you mean

Often N rephrased his utterances without being prompted by the
addressee. Here, N asked A if he could change the fire engine, which
was in an orange box, for the spaceship, which was in a green one. N
seemed to feel that his use of the deictic terms 'it' and 'this' was not
sufficient for A to understand what he wanted. N spontaneously gave
more information:

185 N: please can I change it?
186 A: please can you change it
187   what would you like to change it for?
188 N: this
189   this the green one

N now had more sophisticated strategies for re-negotiating an initiation when the addressee failed to respond. Rather than relying on repetition to demand his partner's attention and to solicit a reply, he now
made use of attention-getting devices or he changed the structure of
his initiation. In this example, N had gone to the lavatory while the
teacher in the language unit was giving the children instructions about

what they had to do. On returning, N alerted the teacher that he was back and ready for his instructions:

190 N: Mrs C I'm back
191 CT: did you wash your hands?
192 N: yes

The class teacher did not go on to give N instructions but returned to helping another child with the work. N persisted:

193 N: what can I do now Mrs C

The teacher then told him what he had to do. This example demonstrates that N was now more flexible in his communication patterns. When his initial statement to the class teacher did not get him the response he wanted, N altered his initiation to make his needs more explicit.

Cohesion
As in the first assessment, N often repeated all or part of his partner's preceding utterance when agreeing with them or affirming what they had said. For example, here, A and N had just discussed whether they would rather be hot or cold. N thought he would not like to be on Mercury, because it would be too hot. He repeated back A's conversational contribution:

194 N.   Mercury's too hot
195 A.   oh of course
196   you don't like too much heat do you?
197 N: I don't like too much heat

This use of repetition to acknowledge his partner's utterance was again only observed when N was interacting with A.

The findings of the final assessment are summarised in Table 7.4.

Implications

Theoretical

The assessment and intervention demonstrated that, although N initially had exhibited some of the characteristics of a grammatical impairment, these were not significant in relation to his specific difficulties in conversation. One of the most striking features of N's communication difficulties in the first assessment was his inability to use the linguistic forms within his grammatical system in a conventional way. Thus although N frequently used non-verbal means to communicate, and he

Table 7.4 Summary of findings of the final assessment after therapy

Initiations	N initiated interaction with his peers more frequently than with adults
	N's initiations more strongly demanded a response and related to topics shared with the addressee
Directives	N used polar interrogatives to direct adults and less familiar children. He used imperatives to direct familiar children. His directives were much more effective
Attention-getting devices	N used attention-getting devices in conjunction with commands, requests and statements to secure the addressee's attention
	N used a variety of attention-getting devices, e.g. vocatives, notice verbs and non-verbal signals
Social routines	N initiated and responded to verbal and non-verbal greeting/parting sequences
	N continued to use 'please' as part of his requests and on other occasions
Responses	N was more likely to respond to the initiations of others and to follow up their topics of conversation over several turns
Repair and clarification	N requested clarification either by asking for repetition or by asking for more specific information
	N revised his own utterances spontaneously to clarify them for the addressee. When an addressee failed to respond to an initiation, N used attention-getting devices, or he changed his initiation in order to solicit a reply
Cohesion	N continued to repeat all or part of his conversational partner's utterance to acknowledge it

relied on declarative forms to express himself, there were examples in the data where he used imperative and interrogative structures effectively to command, question and request. It was not that N lacked the adequate formal linguistic competence to produce the grammatical structures. He evidently did not know the rules governing the circumstances in which such structures should be used. This evidence is corroborated by N's response to intervention. Had he experienced grammatical problems, N would presumably have had considerable difficulties in acquiring polar interrogative forms to make requests. N began to use these forms with a flexibility and a creativity that was not typical of a child with a grammatical impairment. He did not need to be taught different forms for different situations, but generated his own new utterances with different auxiliaries spontaneously. Similarly, N learned to alter the grammatical form of his utterances to make them more salient to the addressee and to elicit a response. These features indicate strongly that N did not have a grammatical impairment.

In the course of the study, it also became clear that N did not exhibit the communicative symptoms of autism, even though the details of N's case history were inconclusive regarding this diagnosis. Recent research suggests that the features of autism are best explained by the child's inability to infer the mental states of others (Baron-Cohen et al., 1985; Frith, 1989a). It is argued that autistic children cannot 'mentalise', and are unable to think or reason about the content of their own or other people's minds. The final assessment demonstrated on the contrary that N was interested in what other people were thinking and was using language purposefully to achieve interactive ends. He started to share topics of conversation introduced by his partners, and to use language creatively in imaginative play. He adapted his requests according to the status of the addressee. He anticipated when listeners might have had difficulty in understanding him, and could clarify himself before he was asked. These features suggest N could 'mentalise'. It is also significant that N had acquired a far wider range of communicative functions during the intervention period than he had been explicitly taught. Prizant and Schuler (1987) suggest that autism is characterised by generalised cognitive deficits which affect in particular the individual's ability to learn. Prizant and Schuler argue that autistic children tend to have an inflexible means of processing information such that they memorise ideas and patterns as a whole. Autistic children are unable to use a more analytical style of learning, where material is processed in sequence, and the specific meanings of component parts are decoded in relation to one another. This has obvious implications in language acquisition, and more specifically in learning the skills necessary to participate in conversation. Were the child to rely on a 'gestalt' method of learning language, his or her learning would be situation specific. He or she would not be able to select among the communication forms at his or her disposal to chose the one that would be most effective in any given communication situation. The data suggested that N was capable of analysing what he was learning, both in terms of its meaning and of its effect on the addressee. N was taught to use requests in a limited number of situations. Yet on the basis of this, he started to use requests in a variety of different situations as the need arose. He began to change the requests according to the situation and the status of the addressee. These changes in N's conversational behaviour have to be explained in terms of N being able to extract the meaning behind the use of requests, and being able to relate the information about the current situation to previous experiences. Similarly, in intervention II, N was invited to discuss and practise conversational behaviours out of context. N extended the use of these conversational behaviours from the group to the situations where they would occur naturally. Had N been autistic, he presumably would not have extended his use of the conversational strategies beyond the specific circumstances in which they had been taught. The way in which N was able to apply what he had learned in therapy clearly precludes a diagnosis of autism.

Research on the development of conversational skills in children who are developing language normally suggests that many of the conversational behaviours that N demonstrated are typical of children at a much earlier stage of language development. It is in fact possible to take each aspect of N's conversational development and to draw parallels with the conversational behaviours documented in studies of preverbal and early verbal behaviour of children who are acquiring language normally. It could be argued that, although N had mastered the grammatical and phonological structures appropriate to his age, his conversational development was significantly delayed. This might also be true of other children described as having a conversational disability. For example, data on other children described as having semantic–pragmatic disorder suggest that they, like N, had difficulties using requests (Conti-Ramsden and Gunn, 1986) or used declaratives with directive force (Greenlee, 1981). However, research on the development of requests in children who are acquiring language normally indicates that the earliest form of directive to develop is the 'need statement' where the child states what he wants, and relies on nurturant adults to interpret the declarative as a request and respond accordingly (Ervin-Tripp, 1977). Frequently, the child needs only to gesture or vocalise for the adult to respond (Bates et al., 1979). N's declaratives in the first assessment could be described as need statements, and were certainly more likely to be complied with when N was addressing an adult. Ervin-Tripp suggests that in the third year of normal language development, as the repertoire of grammatical forms increases, so children typically begin to use different forms, and to show appreciation of the situation and the addressee when selecting among such forms. Following intervention I, this appeared to occur in N's conversation. Not only did he use polar interrogatives as he had been taught, but he also began to use other grammatical forms and to differentiate among addressees when selecting which grammatical form to use. These developments, as in children with normal language, occurred spontaneously.

The development of N's ability to secure the attention of the addressee can be described in a similar way. Again, problems with soliciting the addressee's attention have been noted in other children described as exhibiting a conversational disorder (Blank et al., 1979; Greenlee, 1981; Bishop and Adams, 1989). As with N, they have been noted to rely on gaze to signal that an utterance was designed for a particular addressee, or to repeat a vocative frequently without following up the implication that they had something further to say. Alternatively, they asked questions to which they already knew the answer. These features again can be compared with developments in children who are developing language normally. The use of gaze, the repetition of vocatives and even the use of questions to solicit attention have all been noted to occur in very young children who are developing language normally (Keenan and Schieffelin, 1976; Atkinson, 1979). Atkinson argues that children who are developing language normally use their single word utterances both to secure the attention of the addressee and to establish a referent or topic of conversation. The adult addressee will typically take up this topic, and expand upon it. This reliance on conversational partners to respond on topic apparently continues even as the child learns more sophisticated grammatical forms. For example, Craig and Gallagher (1979) found that 71% of the dialogue utterances of 2–3 year olds were declarative in form. This is paralleled in N's attempts to secure attention and to initiate conversation in assessment 1. N used declaratives to initiate conversation in much the same way as a younger child might use a single word utterance. The conversational responsibility of responding on topic fell to N's conversational partner. Only when N began to use attention-getting devices as part of his initiations, and to use grammatical forms that were more obviously the first part of an adjacency pair and that therefore more strongly demanded a response from the addressee, did his communication improve. These are changes that occur in children who are developing language normally. In N, they occurred at a later stage, and at a stage when his grammatical and phonological development was more advanced.

Another striking feature of N's conversation was his difficulty in sharing in the responsibility of maintaining cohesive discourse. Again this has been noted in other children described as having a conversational disability. Like N, these children were noted to find it difficult to respond on topic and to maintain topic over several turns. In some instances, they did not offer a reply, or their reply was unrelated to the preceding utterance of their conversational partner (Blank et al., 1979; Greenlee, 1981). When they did respond on topic, such children frequently repeated all or part of their conversational partner's preceding utterance (Greenlee, 1981; McTear, 1985b; Conti-Ramsden and Gunn, 1986; Jones et al., 1986; Bishop and Adams, 1989). However, such features are not considered atypical in very young children who are developing language normally. Young children are often so absorbed in their own activities that they do not attend to their conversational partner's utterances (Piaget, 1926; Keenan and Schieffelin, 1976). It is left to the child's conversational partner to make the child's contribution relevant in the conversation. There is also evidence to suggest that in early mother–child and child–child interactions, maintenance of topic is achieved by repetition (Keenan, 1974; Ochs-Keenan, 1977). Repetitions are used to agree, to answer questions, to query and to self-inform. Subsequently, children improve in their ability to contribute new information to a topic (Chapman, 1981) in much the same way as N did. N's strategies for maintaining conversation correspond to those observed in younger children who are developing language normally.

The changes that took place in N's ability to initiate conversational repair also show a similarity to those of children who are developing language normally. The inability to deal with misunderstandings in conversation has been observed in other children with a conversational disability. Like N, they are unable to provide adequate responses to clarification requests (Greenlee, 1981) and often repeat their utterances to try to re-negotiate failed initiations (Blank et al., 1979). However, young children who are developing language normally tend to repeat their preceding utterance if asked for clarification. With developing grammatical competence, other strategies (e.g. phonetic revisions, constituent elaboration, reduction or substitution) become available to them when they perceive that they have not been understood (Gallagher, 1977; Brinton et al., 1986). There was evidence in the data that N's ability to respond to clarification requests developed from repetition to elaboration in this way. N also apparently developed the skill of initiating conversational repair by asking for clarification himself. N started to use non-specific requests for repetition, but he was also able to specify exactly which part of an utterance he had not understood. This parallels the development of clarification requests in children who are developing language normally (Johnson, 1979). N's strategies for re-negotiating failed interactions were also similar to those used by younger children. Young children frequently repeat their utterances when they receive no response (Keenan, 1974; Keenan and Schieffelin, 1976; Atkinson, 1979) as N did. Children later develop other strategies of using attention-getting devices or rephrasing their utterances to elicit a response from their partner (Garvey and Berninger, 1981; McTear, 1985a). N's ability to rephrase his utterances in order to reinitiate was observed particularly in his request sequences, where he frequently changed declaratives to polar interrogatives.

The findings of this study suggest that N presented with a cluster of conversational behaviours that usually occur in the very early stages of language development. The combination of these immature conversational behaviours with linguistic forms that were grammatically and phonologically mature appears to go some way in accounting for N's deviant patterns of communication. Unlike the child with a grammatical or phonological impairment, N had the linguistic forms with which to express himself. Unlike the autistic child, N was also obviously motivated to communicate. N typified the difficulties of a child with conversational problems, and needed help to be able to use the language forms at his disposal to be able to communicate with others.

Remedial

The evidence from this study suggests that intervention targeted at goals identified from the application of conversational analysis was effective. N's communication improved significantly following intervention, and both the intervention methods successful. The implications of this for the remediation of other children who present with a conversational disability need to be considered.

It could be argued that N was an ideal candidate for treatment. N's educational attainments suggested that he was of average intelligence. N was anxious to please adults, and was highly motivated in intervention. His attention control was felt to be age appropriate, and he had a good memory. N had sufficient grammatical and phonological competence to be able to cope with the linguistic forms taught to him and to generate new forms where necessary. N did not have an autistic disorder. As a result, N was able to capitalise on the input that was provided. This suggests that perhaps the therapist working with children with conversational difficulties needs to establish a certain level of cognitive and communicative competence before therapy can be effective.

There is strong evidence to suggest that the conversational behaviours that were assessed cannot be treated as if they were independent of one another. The first assessment highlighted a range of N's communication behaviours that were atypical or immature. Of these, only a specific number were selected as targets for intervention. Following intervention, improvements were noted not only in those aspects of conversation targeted in therapy, but also in other areas. This was illustrated by the results of intervention I, where therapy focusing on requesting resulted in N being more likely to respond to the initiations of others. Having learned to use interrogatives to make requests, and having learned to expect a response, N also learned that he was obliged to respond himself in conversation. Conversational behaviours are clearly interrelated, and working on one conversational skill may well have effects on other aspects of communication.

The context in which intervention took place was also felt to be important. Where possible, intervention took place in the environments where N would be required to use the communication behaviours he was learning. Where N was withdrawn for treatment on his own, teaching took place within a communicative context. For example, N was not required to make a request as an end in itself, but he needed to request in order to complete an activity (e.g. colouring a picture). Similarly, N did not use back-channel responses or topic-related questions in isolated sequences, but as part of ongoing conversation. Intervention also took place with a variety of conversational partners, both adults and children. It is interesting that N's communication difficulties were most obvious with other children in the first assessment, and that this was also the area in which he showed most improvement. During intervention, N learned to use strategies which helped him interact with his peers. N was encouraged to make requests of his peers in situations where an adult was present and where his addressee was therefore unlikely to refuse to comply. N practised conversational behaviours with other children in a group, and when anyone demonstrated good conversational behaviours, reinforcement was supplied by other members of the group, who applauded that behaviour. N was thus receiving reinforcement from his peers. Comb and Slaby (1977) suggest that there is a potential positive cycle in which increased interaction with peers leads to the development of social skills and to increased peer acceptance. The reinforcement N received when he used requests or when he participated in role-play in the intervention group must have been a powerful factor in his using the behaviours in other situations where they would also have been rewarded. Following intervention, N was caught in a more positive cycle where communication had become intrinsically rewarding both for him and for his peers. The situations in which conversational skills are taught, and the conversational partners chosen to participate in the intervention procedure are evidently significant. Conversational behaviours should be taught in the context in which they are to be used.

There are also implications for the way in which adults interact with children who are experiencing difficulties in conversation. N used many of the conversational strategies that adults typically use with young children or with children who have a language impairment. For example, adults frequently use questions to initiate and sustain dialogue with children (Conti-Ramsden and Friel-Patti, 1983; Stubbs, 1986; Conti-Ramsden, 1990). Such questions are often asked in situations where it is evident that both the child and the adult know the answer. N was noted to ask questions to which he knew the answer. Adults also typically repeat all or part of the child's utterances to let the child know that they have understood (Demetras et al., 1986). N's failure to use ellipsis may reflect a similar strategy for acknowledging his partner's utterance. It is interesting that N was only noted to repeat all or part of his partner's utterances when he was interacting with A. It is argued that adults who are working with children who have conversational difficulties should be particularly sensitive to their own conversational strategies. It is possible that otherwise such adults are modelling and reinforcing conversational behaviours that will be considered atypical or inappropriate in the child.

Methodological

The study demonstrates clearly that the standardised assessments of language used routinely by professionals working with speech and language impaired children are of little or no use in the assessment of children with conversational difficulties. Formal assessments are in fact designed to strip away the variation of context, topic and conversational partner that appear to be precisely the features that the child with a conversational disability finds difficult. It makes little sense therefore to use them for any other purpose than to exclude the diagnoses of semantic, grammatical or phonological impairment. On the other hand, samples of natural conversational data will highlight much more effectively where the child's difficulties lie.

The information gleaned from sampling natural conversation in this study illustrates how important it is to collect data in a variety of different contexts. It is unrealistic to assume that a true picture of a child's conversational abilities will be obtained from just one sample of conversation with one partner, particularly if that partner is an adult. N's interactions were considerably more successful and productive when he was talking to an adult, largely because of the ways in which adults compensated for his poor conversational skills. N's poor conversational skills precluded him from conversations with other children, who did not have the skills to structure conversation for N, or to interpret his intentions. This finding only emerged because N was observed with more than one conversational partner in more than one situation. Moreover, it is only by varying the partner and the situation that the researcher can begin to identify abnormal or atypical conversational behaviours. Conversation has to be seen as the product of at least two communicators, who work together to maintain interaction. Under normal circumstances, all conversations are susceptible to breakdown, and need to be repaired. For example, conversational partners may fail to fulfil their obligations in conversation. Frequently a speaker assumes shared knowledge which in fact the other person does not have, and the addressee has to take steps to let the speaker know that he does not share that knowledge. Often an addressee fails to fill a response slot, and the speaker has to make other moves to elicit a reply. Sometimes conversational partners violate turn-taking rules, and start to speak at the same time or interrupt each other. Competent conversationalists have a variety of strategies to deal with such problems. What made N stand out as different was his apparent obliviousness of his obligations in conversation, and of the strategies that are usually used to repair failed interactions. This lack of awareness of conversational rules emerged in whatever situation N was observed, and with all of the partners who interacted with him. It was only the skill and motivation of his conversational partners that determined whether or not conversation was successfully sustained.

Whether it would be appropriate to describe N's conversation as pathological remains, however, a moot point. As conversationalists are so skilled at resolving problems, conversational failure is difficult to identify. Given that the analyst cannot make judgements about the appropriacy or otherwise of any contribution in a conversation in which he or she did not participate, breakdown in conversation can only surely be identified when one participant signals it. Although there are many examples of N's conversational partners initiating repair, either by repeating or rephrasing initiations to which N did not reply, by using attention-getting devices to secure his attention or by asking for clarification, none of these things is abnormal in conversation. Had there been examples of explicit feedback, where N's conversational partners criticised or corrected his contributions, this might have been considered as empirical evidence of disorder. Feedback of this nature, however, occurred rarely. Furthermore it has already been noted how similar N's conversational behaviours are to those observed in very young children who are developing language normally. Although such features are atypical in adult conversation, they cannot be described as pathological. Perhaps it is only the frequency of conversational problems that marks N out as different. It remains very difficult to give an accurate and unambiguous characterisation of disordered conversation.

Nevertheless, the framework provided by conversation analysis proved invaluable in highlighting specific and recurring problems in N's conversations. A diagnosis of autism, or of grammatical impairment, or indeed of semantic–pragmatic disorder, seemed irrelevant once it was possible to pinpoint such problems. This study demonstrates unequivocally that by using a linguistic framework to analyse conversation data, it is possible to identify intervention goals, and to treat conversational behaviours directly and successfully.

Appendix: transcription conventions

1. Pauses are marked by – or a sequence of – . Each – is equivalent to a pulse of the speaker's rhythm.
2. An overlap is marked by * at the point of overlap.
3. Non-verbal responses and other remarks which put the utterance into context and were relevant to it's interpretation are written in brackets next to the utterances with which they co-occurred.
4. Utterances that were considered to be incomplete are marked by # at the point where the speaker stopped talking.
5. Where there was no gap between utterances, the two latched utterances are linked by =.
6. Utterances are numbered serially in the text. Where there are instances of several utterances which illustrate the same conversational behaviours, the line number of those utterances is cited in the text.

Part III
Acquired Communication
Disorders

Chapter 8
Acquired dysarthria: a segmental phonological, prosodic and electropalatographic investigation of intelligibility

ROSEMARIE MORGANBARRY

Introduction

This chapter discusses how segmental phonological, prosodic and electropalatographic analyses may help our understanding of some of the factors that contribute to the unintelligibility of dysarthric speech. The subject, George H, was one of a number of subjects included in a larger study which carried out in-depth analyses of the speech of patients with neurological disorders, and compared them across developmental and acquired conditions and types of neurological impairment (Hardcastle et al, 1985; MorganBarry, 1990a, 1994). The aims of the study were the following:

1. To analyse the speech of six subjects in depth, using instrumental techniques to provide additional information on lingual activity.
2. To compare the phonological, prosodic and instrumental profiles of the subjects so as to gain insight into the nature and complexity of their disorder.

This report presents new, and hitherto unpublished, aspects of the analyses undertaken, and aims to show how clinical linguistics can be used not only to gain insight into aspects of unintelligibility, but also to help formulate a therapy programme.

Background

Case history

It must be remembered that subjects selected for study are real people,

181

whose problems are the result of complex interactions of their physical, physiological and medical conditions with their personality, intelligence, education, life experience and social behaviours. A brief background history of George will therefore be given, comprising details of his medical condition, speech and language diagnosis and presentation, general intellectual abilities and educational history.

George had been retired from his job with a local dairy for some years before suffering a left cerebrovascular accident (CVA), but had continued active and well. He was married, with a son and daughter-in-law living nearby. Both he and his wife had adapted well to his condition after the stroke which had occurred 17 months before the beginning of the project. He had made a good recovery and they were both involved in social and family activities. A summary of the features of his medical, educational and speech–language presentations is given in Table 8.1.

The Frenchay Dysarthria Assessment (Enderby, 1983a) was carried out immediately before acceptance on to the research project. Results are given in Appendix I at the end of the chapter.

Initial assessments

A number of assessments were carried out where appropriate at the

Table 8.1 Summary of George's background data

Age	68 years
Medical aetiology	Left CVA
Communication diagnosis	Moderately severe dysarthria
Language comprehension	Within normal limits
Language expression	Acceptable vocabulary and syntax
Speech production:	
Acceptable components	Vowels
Observed abnormalities	Weak, imprecise consonants; frication of stops
General impression	Slurred, some dysphonia
Intelligibility	Poor
Educational background	Left school at 14
Intelligence	Good, average
Additional factors	Mild right hemiplegia; no dysphagia
Therapy	Intensive during hospitalisation; regular weekly at outpatients.

start of the study in which George took part, to establish a baseline of ability from which to formulate speech assessment. These included the following:

- A speech musculature movement examination
- An oral stereognosis test
- An assessment of diadochokinesis.

Speech musculature movement examination

This was adapted from the Dysarthria Assessment Profile (Robertson, 1982). The profile uses a quantitative method of scoring based on the tester's clinical judgement which rates the patient's performance on a scale of five points: 0 (unable, nil), 1 (severe, very poor), 2 (moderate, fair), 3 (slight difficulty but adequate attempt), 4 (normal, no difficulty). This qualitative score is described as a means of rating muscular movement in terms of features which, in the absence of instrumentation such as electromyographic (EMG) recording, cannot be quantified. It nevertheless provides important information for the clinician for both diagnosis and therapy (Robertson and Thomson, 1986). George performed all movements slowly, but remained nevertheless within normal limits (Table 8.2).

Table 8.2 Speech musculature movement examination

	Test movement	Result
Lips	Protrusion	4
	Lateral movement	4
	/b/	4
	/m/	4
Jaw	Open/close	4
	Lateral right	3
	Lateral left	3
Tongue	Protrusion	4
	Lateral right	4
	Lateral left	4
	Around lips	4
	Lateral in mouth right	4
	Lateral in mouth left	4
	Upward	3
	Downward	4
	/lɑː/ repeat	3
Palate	/ɑː/	4
	/ɑːm/	4

Rating scale: 4 = normal; 3 = slight difficulty.

Oral stereognosis

There have been a number of investigations of oral form discrimination and perception with normal subjects (Bosma, 1967; Ringel et al., 1968), with apraxic and aphasic subjects (Rosenbek et al., 1973; Lum and Russell, 1978), and with dysarthric patients (Creech et al., 1973). These investigations used two forms of assessment involving plastic three-dimensional shapes: one method required intersensory matching between the oral sensory ability (the feel of the shape in the mouth) and its visual appearance; the other required the subject to manipulate pairs of objects in the mouth one at a time and to decide whether they were the same or different. The latter also presupposes normal motor coordination and manipulative movement, which, particularly in the case of dysarthric subjects, cannot be assumed, and this may well have an effect on the results. In fact both experimental designs have disadvantages: the first because it requires tactile-to-visual matching, the second because it necessitates both memory for tactile sensation and the concept of 'same/different'.

George was given an adaptation of the above procedures. Sugar-free peppermint sweets of different shapes were used instead of plastic forms; the shapes were: large round, large square and small square. Each of these was paired with each other, and he was given three trials of each pair and asked both to name and to identify by visual matching the three shapes when placed in the mouth. This he could do without difficulty or error, although he reported diminished sensation for touch on the right side of the face and mouth.

Assessment of diadochokinesis (DDK)

Data pertaining to this skill for normal speaking subjects have been elicited from children by Canning and Rose (1974) and from children and young adults by Oliver et al. (1985). The studies differ in their presentation of test criteria and results. It was decided in this study to use data from the production of /pə, tə, kə/. Ten repetitions of these syllables were timed, and rated as follows: very slow – below the 10th percentile of the Canning and Rose (1974) study; slow – on the 10th percentile. George's results fell in the very slow range; he found this task difficult.

Assessments of the kinds discussed above are included in a number of diagnostic procedures for neurological disorders: Darley et al. (1975), Dabul (1978), Enderby (1983a) and Robertson and Thomson (1986). However, the tests were chosen to provide an indication of George's abilities in the given areas, and to note whether these related to the expected performances of patients presenting with aspects of dysarthria. He presented with acceptable performance on assessments related to general fine muscular coordination of the articulators in non-speech movement activities, but very poor DDK abilities. His speech was, however, rated very poor in intelligibility for most tasks (reading, sentence repetition and spontaneous conversation), and it was felt that in-depth analysis of segmental phonology and prosodic characteristics could help to explain the discrepancy between his performance on non-speech movement activities and his poor level of intelligibility.

Theoretical background

Dysarthria comprises a group of speech disorders resulting from disturbances in muscular control. Because there has been damage to the central or peripheral nervous system, some degree of weakness, slowness, inco-ordination, or altered muscle tone characterises the activity of the speech mechanism.

Darley et al. (1975, p. 2)

The aetiology of acquired dysarthrias is well documented (Berry, 1983; McNeil et al.,1984; Rosenbek and La Pointe, 1985; Wertz, 1985) and descriptions from these authors suggest the following points to note:

- They are a group of disorders whose symptomatology, although possessing recognisable similarities, varies according to type of aetiology and site and extent of neural damage.
- The speech disruption covers all subsystems of production: respiration, phonation, resonance and articulation; therefore it affects suprasegmental as well as segmental aspects.

Traumatic events such as brain injury and CVA may result in a dysarthria, but the condition also results from progressive disorders, such as infection, degeneration, palsy and chorea. The last present a clinical picture that varies over time: gradual increases in severity with, in some instances, periods of remission. Total recovery is, however, extremely rare and treatment needs to aim for compensatory means of achieving intelligibility (Yorkston and Beukelman, 1981; Robertson and Thomson, 1986).

Classification of the dysarthrias according to both symptomatology and neuropathology has been carried out by a number of authors (Canter, 1967, cited in Rosenbek and La Pointe, 1985), but probably the most well known remains that of the Mayo Clinic Study (Darley et al., 1975) which combines clinical presentation with neural damage in an aetiological and diagnostic relationship. Espir and Rose (1983) and Edwards (1984) also provide summaries of causative and disorder factors.

Netsell (1986) takes a neurobiological view of the dysarthrias, and relates them to phylogenetic development, ontogeny through neural maturation and spatiotemporal organisation, motor equivalence and the development of feedback/feedforward systems. He raises the important point of shared and specialised neuronal mechanisms in that both speech and oral feeding movements share musculature and, inevitably, some peripheral and central neural involvement, although, in the fully functioning system, different action and inhibition networks may be involved. Speech mechanisms are not merely neuronally over-laid on the vegetative mechanisms, and damage to cranial nerves and nuclei, brain-stem pathways and integrative structures cause disruption of all oromotor functions. In a further paper (Netsell, 1986), he relates representative forms of dysarthria to aspects of motor control, with the following (tentative) conclusions:

- Peripheral (lower motor neuron) dysarthrias show reduced ampli-tude EMG patterns, and it is presumed that the nerve lesion results in a pathological 'low-pass filter' causing the typical muscular hypo-tonicity.
- Cerebellar dysarthrias – here Netsell's data appear to define what the cerebellum does *not* do – show problems of phasic timing of muscular contractions in that all these are long and slow, and the ability to make rapid short movements (for example, for unstressed syllables) is lost.
- Parkinsonian (extrapyramidal) dysarthria is characterised by fluctua-tions in intelligibility, pace, loudness, voice quality, etc., and this may result from an inability to adjust motor neuron facilitation from one level to another.

The role of the cerebellum as a 'velocity adjuster' was made by Bowman (1971) when considering the function and neural connec-tions of the muscle spindle (compare Hardcastle, 1976, and his discus-sion of proprioceptive feedback). Citing evidence from the effects of cerebellar lesions on speech, Bowman (1971) considers the resulting problems to constitute timing disorders. The cerebellum receives audi-tory and tactile information via these input channels; it also receives neural projections from the muscle spindles of the limbs, but *not* from those of the tongue. Thus, of the two forms of feedback from lingual movement, only one – tactile information – is conveyed direct to the cerebellum. These afferent data vary as a function of articulatory dynamics, i.e. spindle and tactile feedback processes vary in relative amounts according to whether the tongue is moving from one position to another, or whether it is making contact with the teeth or palate. According to Bowman (1971) the observation of cerebellar dysarthria reveals that the latter – the relatively static, 'target contact' or 'steady-state' – function of the tongue appears more impaired than the move-ment towards 'steady states'. He observes (p. 92):

The dysfunction, then, appears to be one in which the movement cannot be terminated motorically, that is, via a set of precisely timed, discrete motor commands delivered to the functional antagonists of the muscles maintaining the contact.

Considering this in terms of neural information being forwarded through the cerebellum, tactile feedback is functionally greatest at both the moment and the point of contact. Cerebellar dysfunction is correlated with this period which must (presumably) be significant in the cerebellar mediation of lingual activity. This is not, however, in accordance with the perceived characteristics of imprecise and *prolonged* consonants (Darley et al., 1975; Kent et al., 1979) and the build-up of EMG activity with subsequent failure to reduce, resulting in prolongation of activity (Netsell, 1986) unless it is hypothesised that tactile information is necessary for the cessation of movement and change from the dynamic to static muscular control. It is, however, in accordance with the generalised 'undershoot' aspect of dysarthric speech (Abbs et al., 1983). Bowman (1971) does not consider other aspects of dysarthric speech relating to cerebellar lesions – those of respiration, phonation and resonance – and it would be interesting to note how spindle and tactile projections from musculature relating to these functions are represented in the cerebellum. Nor does he consider the implications of the fact that proprioceptive feedback information reaches the cerebellum only via the motor cortex and the cerebrocerebellar link, thus reinforcing the view that its function would appear to be linked to generating corrective signals (i.e. monitoring) from cerebellum to neuromuscular command system back to motor cortex (see motor schema programmes – Laver, 1980b; Abbs and Cole, 1982; Evarts, 1982).

Netsell and Abbs (1976) and Netsell (1986) considered diagnostic aspects of cortical lesions relating to dysarthria, and generally agreed that the condition may coexist with dyspraxia and/or aphasia to varying degrees. Netsell and Abbs (1976) went so far as to hypothesise unique roles for cortical and subcortical mechanisms for the motor control of speech, motor–sensory cortical involvement being necessary for phasic movement, and subcortical structures for posture and tone circuits. Brodal's (1973) self-observation of the effects of (what he considered to be) a right hemisphere lesion included (among other linguistic symptoms) a 'marked dysarthria' which receded over time but continued to be obvious with fatigue even after 6 months. He comments (p. 684):

. . . the marked dysarthria could not be due to the left-sided facial paresis alone . . . It appears that articulation is not governed from one hemisphere only. Thus dysarthria occurs after left as well as right hemisphere lesions. The peripheral motor neurone groups concerned in speech are supplied bilaterally by direct corticofugal fibres.

Lesser (1978) comments on right hemisphere lesion dysarthria in her discussion on laterality and cerebral dominance. It would appear that a dysarthria resulting from a cortical lesion is much more vague in definitional symptomatology than that resulting from a subcortical disturbance.

The clinical presentation varies with the different types of dysarthria (Enderby, 1983b; Netsell, 1986), and therefore it constitutes a group of disorders (Wertz, 1985). Studies of the clinical presentation of the dysarthrias fall into two main groups: the mainly perceptual studies (descriptions and assessments) and research using instrumental techniques. Rosenbek and LaPointe (1985, p. 268) provide evaluative comments on the two methods:

> Probably the greatest hazard of perceptual data . . . is that similar perceptual symptoms can result from very different abnormal conditions . . . even the most careful history and perceptual evaluation may not satisfactorily expose the neuro-muscular abnormalities.

However (p. 268):

> Alone, instrumental evaluation is far from a panacea. A history and clinical acumen are as mandatory in instrumental as in perceptual evaluation.

Therefore (p. 269):

> . . . instruments confirm what the clinician hears . . . the diagnostician would do well to learn both forms of evaluation . . .

(These adages were followed in the present study!)

As noted above, the classic perceptual description of the speech pathology of this group of disorders is that of the Mayo Clinic study of Darley et al. (1975). Their classification follows neurological lines, and is a sixfold system, according to neuromuscular conditions, around which the 38 speech dimensions organised under seven groupings are differentially clustered. The value of the Mayo study lies in its emphasis on definition and description based on careful perceptual research and evaluation (Rosenbek and LaPointe, 1985). From this study arose the view – still held – of the dysarthrias as a group of clinically distinct disorders resulting from disruption of motor control and which involve all the basic motor processes of speech (Wertz, 1985; Netsell, 1986). Subsequent neurophysiological studies have confirmed and extended this work (Netsell, 1986; Ziegler and von Cramon, 1986).

Grunwell and Huskins (1979, p. 9) also present:

> a descriptive framework of phonetic parameters for the assessment of dysarthric speech

using the four basic physiological mechanisms that operate in speech production: respiratory, phonatory, resonatory and articulatory. These subsystems integrate and coordinate, such that a disruption in any one system has a 'knock-on' effect on other systems. Thus, for example, inadequate breath control (respiratory mechanism) may result in slow rate of articulatory movements and inadequate or incoordinated vocal fold closure (phonatory mechanism) with disruption of sequenced organisation of the utterance into prosodic and informational units. The authors also point out that describing the dysarthrias in phonetic terms involves relating these aspects to the activities of the speech musculature, and to the disorders of movement and muscle tone relating to the different neurological pathologies.

If Grunwell and Huskins (1979) appear to favour a 'top-down' approach to the clinical description of the dysarthrias, Enderby (1983a, b) and Robertson (1982) adopt a more 'bottom-up' approach in their assessments and descriptions. The Frenchay Dysarthria Assessment (Enderby, 1983a) tests motor movement and control in seven areas: reflex, respiration, lips, jaw, palate, laryngeal and tongue, and provides sections for the assessment of intelligibility, rate, sensation and associated factors. The Robertson Dysarthria Profile (Robertson, 1982) consists of subtests which relate to respiration, phonation, facial musculature, DDK, reflexes, articulation, intelligibility and prosody.

Wertz (1985) provides a theoretical clinical profile of dysarthria indicating:

- No language problems
- No speech programming problems
- No intellectual deficits of orientation problems, but
- An impairment of neuromuscular conditions for motor speech.

(He does, however, point out that all of the above conditions can, and frequently do, coexist.) Evaluation of dysarthric speech should, according to Wertz, include traditional word and sentence articulation tests for analysing error type, frequency and distribution: for example, the Assessment of Intelligibility of Dysarthric Speech (Yorkston and Beukelman, 1978).

The dysarthric patient discussed in this study was described (on the basis of initial assessments) as presenting with the following:

- imprecise consonants and distorted vowels;
- monopitch and monoloudness;
- breathy voice quality, tending to harshness when he was being emphatic in conversation;
- slowed speaking rate;
- occasional hypernasality (again when speaking under emotional stress);
- short phrases; attempts to lengthen phrases resulting in strained–strangled voice quality.

He thus fitted the Mayo clinic dimensions related to spastic dysarthria, but, as observed earlier, the severity of his non-speech movement abilities was not compatible with the severity of his unintelligibility.

Approach to analysis

In any one subject, the combination of a number of variables – assessment results, general intellectual ability, motivation and personality–behaviour factors – results in a complex picture that has implications for both type and severity of a disorder. It is therefore difficult to distinguish cause and effect or to decide whether a particular factor contributes to the disorder or manifests as an intrinsic part, or as a result of it. Motivation, attention and response to intrinsic rewards are all factors affecting speech–language learning and reaction to disability, as are the more diffuse personality factors such as attitude to and acceptance of limitations. For adult subjects, there is also the consideration that they have to pay attention to, and make an effort over, a skill that for many years they had taken for granted. Feelings of resentment, depression and annoyance may contribute to their difficulties, as well as fluctuating performance resulting from tiredness, anxieties, stress and minor ailments.

Attempts to take all these variables into account throughout the operation of the study were impossible, but steps were taken to ensure that during the data collection the subject was performing to the best of his ability. Testing was halted, and resumed on a subsequent occasion if there were signs of ill health, tiredness, lapse of attention or any other debilitating factor.

Analyses

The investigations undertaken combined perceptual analysis of both segmental and prosodic aspects of George's speech with electropalatographic examination of the lingual–palatal contact patterns contributing to the auditory perceptual effect of George's speech production. This combination of perceptual and instrumental approaches was carried out on the grounds that the limitations of using either approach in isolation may be overcome on a cancel-out basis by using both (Rosenbek and LaPointe, 1985).

Analytical frameworks: segmental phonological considerations

In the application of phonological principles to adult acquired disorders, dysarthric speech can be seen as resulting from problems affecting the accuracy, precision and timing of articulatory movements, rather than as a phonological problem per se, which would imply some cognitive or linguistic deficit. The articulatory difficulties experienced by dysarthric speakers affect speech production both at the segmental level and at the prosodic level, which includes parameters such as stress, rhythm and rate (Grunwell and Huskins, 1979).

Edwards (1983) lists a number of issues that she considers of potential importance in phonological assessments which can be related specifically to the dysarthrias. These include:

- size and type of language sample;
- spontaneous or imitated production;
- isolated words, phrases or continuous speech;
- syntactic, pragmatic, prosodic variables;
- phonetic context;
- word length, complexity, familiarity;
- specific stimuli or 'free conversation';
- number of attempts at each sound and attempts to apply processes;
- number of renditions of each lexical item.

To take account of these factors, a phonological analysis has to meet certain criteria, and it was felt that an adaptation of the PACS procedure (Phonological Analysis of Children's Speech – Grunwell, 1985b) would be the most useful procedure. It was designed to be a clinical assessment tool and as such was compatible with the clinical focus of this study.

The adaptation of the procedure for the purposes of this study involved two extended usages of PACS. The first arises from the fact that the PACS unit of analysis is the syllable, and that therefore a certain amount of information on co-articulation at word boundaries is lost. This is perhaps inevitable, but bearing in mind the findings from the literature on the interrelationship of phonology and syntactic complexity (see Crystal, 1987b, on the interaction between linguistic levels), it was felt that for speech-disordered subjects, examination should be made of operations that occur across syllable, morpheme and word boundaries in connected spontaneous speech. (See Hewlett, 1987, for a critical review of PACS, which elaborates on these points and raises a number of issues related to communicative adequacy.)

The second extension concerns the use of a procedure designed (as its name states) for the analysis of *children's* speech for *adult* disorders. The main reason was that the data reported here were part of a study looking at the differences and similarities between child and adult speech disorders, and therefore needed one system that would enable such a comparison to be meaningful (MorganBarry, 1990a, 1994).

Two main types of speech sample were collected for the subject, and both were used in the analysis. These included the following.

- A spontaneous speech sample, in conversation with the clinician.
- A naming task of five repetitions of lists of single words.

These word lists were designed to elicit obstruents both as singletons, and as clusters in two forms: within a single morpheme and across morpheme boundaries. The wordlists are presented in Table 8.3.

Transcriptions were made from notes taken at the time of recording, and from good quality audio recordings which, for the spontaneous speech, were made in a soundproof room. Where uncertainties over the transcriptions arose, an experienced phonetician was asked to transcribe these data: differences between the two transcriptions were resolved by discussion. The conventions used were those of the International Phonetics Association, with diacritics and additional symbols as recommended (PRDS, 1980; Duckworth et al., 1990).

Phonological analysis

The spontaneous conversation speech sample consisted of approximately half an hour's discourse, but about 10% of this was unintelligible and unglossable. However, 127 word types with 222 tokens were analysed. It was assumed that, within the physiological constraints of his speech disorder, George would aim to preserve as much as possible all the contrasts of English. This was found to be the case. A south-east British English accent was also assumed and features differing accept-

Table 8.3 Wordlists used as test items

List A	List B	List C	List D
a dart	a sun	the salt	a Kitkat
a lamb	a mouse	a clock	a headlight
a cot	a zoo	a tractor	a catkin
a deer	a sheep	the Welsh	a milking
a leg	a brush	a star	a weekday
a chain	a seed	a box	a tickling
a key	a shark	a slide	a deckchair
the dolls	a shop	the hats	a bookshop
a leaf	a bush	a skirt	a crashlanding
a book	a shoe		a bikeshop
a well	a racer		a fishcake
a car			a squashkit
a girl			the fish soup
a beak			
a knot			

These words were also used for the EPG analyses, which have been reported in Hardcastle et al. (1985) and MorganBarry (1990, 1994).

ably from standard southern British English as a result of regional accent were noted. As reported elsewhere (MorganBarry, 1990a, 1994), the main systemic features noted from the singleton obstruent data were the following:

* allophonic variants [β, x, ɣ] for /b, k, g/;
* some loss of voiced/voiceless distinction;
* glottal replacement (over and above that which would be expected as a result of regional accent);
* affrication of fricatives;
* spirantisation of plosives and affricates.

Structurally disordered aspects of George's speech noted were the following:

* weak syllable deletion;
* final consonant deletion;
* omission of approximants;
* consonant harmony;
* cluster reduction by consonant omission or coalescence.

The repetitions of the wordlists supplied a number of tokens for each word and produced significant information about phoneme realisations: oral and nasal stops and approximants remained perceptually within normal limits, but there were many more variant realisations for the fricatives and affricates:

/s/ — [ç, t͡s, j̥, ɬ]
/z/ — [dj, d͡ʒ, ʒ]
/ʃ/ — [tç, dʒ, j̥, ʧ, sj, s, j, z, ʒ|
/ʧ/ — [ʨj, dj, t͡ç]

and for the clusters:

/tr/ — [t, d͡ʒ]
/kl/ — [k, k͡x]
/st/ — [s, ʃ, sɣ]
/sl/ — [t͡s, s, ç]
/skw/— [sw, zw, zg, sː g]
/ks/ — [xs, ʔs]

This raises a number of interesting questions relating to lexical choice, word/sound avoidance strategies, increasing difficulty when repeating words, the nature of the task (i.e. the wordlists were seen as a specific speech assessment from which performance was to be judged) and the semantic importance of the words themselves. To achieve a 'true' picture of the subject's speech articulation ability, it may be necessary to assess the performance in tasks that take him or her to the limits of such ability, regardless of whether the subject would choose to use words and phrases of such linguistic complexity in everyday conversational interchange.

As stated earlier, it was felt that phonological information on units larger than the syllable would provide insight into aspects of George's unintelligibility. Therefore analysis of abutting consonants (i.e. those that cross syllable boundaries as in wordlist D – Table 8.3) was carried out. Table 8.4 provides evidence that George has difficulty with these within-word clusters, and produces them in variable ways.

Table 8.4 Consonant cluster production: abutting consonants across syllable boundaries

- /tk/ -	kitkat	[k͡xɪdiːgæt]
		[ɣɪtɪwəɣæt]
	catkin	[kækɪŋ]
		[k͡xæʔxɪn]
- /kt/ -	tractor	[tæʔtə]
		[ʤæktə]
- /kd/ -	weekday	[wiːɣgeɪ]
		[wiːɣeɪ]
- /kʧ/ -	deckchair	[dɛksjea]
		[dɛkjea]
		[ʤɛkʤea]
- /kʃ/ -	bikeshop	[bəujɒp]
		[baɪʔʃɒp]
	bookshop	[bʊɣʒɒp]
		[bʊgʒɒp]
- /ʃk/ -	fishcake	[fɪʃgeɪk]
		[fɪʃːː . . keɪk]
	squashkit	[zgɒʒː . kɪt]
		[zwɒːː ʒgɪt]
- /kl/ -	tickling	[t͡sɪk͡xɪn]
		[tiːxjɪn]
- /dl/ -	headlight	[ejaɪt]
		[heʔlaɪt]

Further examples of abutting consonant cluster reduction were taken from George's spontaneous conversation, and this, frequently combined with his difficulties in signalling word stress patterns, contributed further to loss of intelligibility:

[ɛzˈpɛnzɪz]   expenses

['lʌviː]   lovely
['pʌbɪ]   public

The conversational data also provided information on morpheme boundaries, and it was found, significantly, that George usually signalled semantically and grammatically important endings such as plurals and the verb copula -s even, if necessary, at the expense of preserving target consonant clusters; compare for example:

[ɪt], [ɪʔ]   it
[ɪz], [ɪs]   it's
[wɒz], [wɒʔz]   what's
[lɔz]   lords

A significant problem affecting the transcription of the conversational data was concerned with speech production over word boundaries and with deciding how best to interpret and transcribe word boundaries where intersegmental transitional phenomena, including co-articulation, durational distortions such as consonant lengthening and vowel shortening, the deletion of segments or even of whole syllables and abnormal stress patterns, made the identification of clear segment and word boundaries difficult (see also Chapter 9 for a discussion of similar methodological problems.) The following data illustrate some of these problems:

['buf ɪz . z . z . . neɪn]
Bouf is his name

[nəʊ 'lɔz n̩ leɪz aʊ 'ɛə]
no lords and ladies out there

[iː 'jusɪ ɪv ɪneː]
he used (to) live in there

[ɪf ə 'ɹʌŋ]
if you're young

Analytical frameworks: prosodic considerations

Definitions of prosody may seek to distinguish between segmental and prosodic features of speech production, but they inevitably overlap and interrelate, so that prosodic elements may be seen as sequential considerations of speech segments (Couper-Kuhlen, 1986). Thus every sound segment has its intrinsic intensity and duration, which are its segmental features and which vary according to the nature and relative position of the segment in an utterance. Combined and extended over several segments, these segmental prosodic aspects give rise to perceivable modulations of pitch, relative loudness and duration of syllables, and therefore to overall speech rhythm (Kent and Rosenbek ,1982).

The prosodic difficulties evident in dysarthric speech would be seen by Crystal (1981) as examples of dysprosody, i.e. articulatory difficulties in realising prosodic variables such as pitch, loudness, rhythm, duration and silence, rather than as phonological prosodic disabilities signalling the speaker's failure to use the linguistics parameters of intonation, stress, tempo, rhythmicality and pause appropriately. Brewster (1989) further suggests that dysarthric speakers may evidence what he calls prosodic deviation or 'functional shift', whereby prosodic variables are manipulated in unusual or unexpected ways as positive compensatory strategies aimed at improving intelligibility which has been impaired by, for example, difficulties in segmental production.

Prosodic bizarreness of various kinds has been cited as diagnostically significant for parkinsonian speech, cerebellar ataxia and right hemisphere dysarthria (Kent and Rosenbek, 1982). In this study, the prosodic dimensions of George's speech will be described with reference to a prosodic profile (Prosody Profile or PROP – Crystal, 1992; see Appendix II) and, as PROP is mainly restricted to analysis of intonation, impressionistic descriptions will be given relating to overall rate, rhythm, stress and pausing, etc.

The conversational speech sample used for the prosodic assessment was the same as that used for segmental phonological analysis.

Prosodic analysis

The general impression of George's speech was that of an overall low, monotonous pitch, with evidence of dysphonia and erratic pausing. The tone unit section of PROP (see Appendix II) shows that in a relatively short data sample of 92 units, 10 were incomplete, six indeterminate (these frequently contained sections of unglossable utterance) and 26 were clause minus. However, the remainder of the data were appropriate – the word and phrase tone units were grammatically acceptable and the remaining prosodic units coincided with acceptable grammatical clause structures.

Most of the tones used were fairly low, narrow and falling. There were no complex tones and only a few rising tones. The rising tones which did occur were used to signal continuation or incompleteness of utterance, usually appropriately:

then he 'went – / 'into – / 'market 'gardening / but 'he – /
Cl–   W   Cl–   Cl–

never 'had to – / 'make a 'profit /
Cl–   Cl–

There were no examples of questions in the sample, and only one instance of uncertainty, appropriately signalled by rising tone.

The Tonicity section of PROP shows that generally the placement of the nuclear tone within a tone unit was appropriate both finally and non-finally and for lexical and grammatical items, with most nuclear tones falling on final lexical items. There were, however, a few examples where the nuclear tone was inappropriately placed on a grammatical item.

his wife is the – um / cook I think /

George's erratic use of pauses, the high number of hesitations, conversational fillers and pause markers ('um', 'er', etc.) and his segment and syllable elisions increased the general impression of dysprosody. Added to this, his speech rate was slowed overall, the intensity reduced and his voice had dysphonic elements of both hoarseness and creakiness.

As some significant aspects of George's dysprosody can be related to difficulties in segmental timing which are revealed by instrumental analysis, these are discussed further in the section on electropalatographic analysis below.

Analytical frameworks: instrumental considerations

There has been extensive discussion of the use of electropalatography (EPG) in the field of speech pathology (Hardcastle et al., 1989a; MorganBarry, 1989; see also Chapters 3, 4 and 9) and some of George's data have been reported elsewhere (Hardcastle et al., 1985; MorganBarry, 1989, 1990a, b, 1993, 1994). The aim here is to provide a brief and general overview of the results of the initial study and to examine these in relation to the perceptual segmental phonological and prosodic analyses of George's speech to elucidate his poor levels of intelligibility further.

There are two aspects of the EPG data that will be presented and discussed: specific lingual–palatal contact patterns and the timing of these articulatory movements with specific reference to the approach and release phases of segments.

Speech can be described as both static and dynamic (Borden and Harris, 1980; Daniloff et al., 1980). It is organised across space and time, with the space dimension being measured in millimetres within the oral cavity and the temporal dimension in milliseconds. EPG can provide simultaneous information on both of these aspects of the speech signal (albeit restricted to segments involving lingual–palatal contact). Characteristic quasistatic lingual–palatal contact patterns can be linked to the perception of specific sound segments (phonemes) and EPG data are available on the contact patterns produced by normal speakers for a range of European languages, including standard southern British English (Marchal et al., 1991; Marchal and Hardcastle, 1993). Stylised representations of normal speakers' patterns for each of the target segments investigated are given in Figure 8.1. (Stylised representations of the EPG printout patterns are provided throughout this chapter, for reasons of economy of space; the legends relating to each figure explain how these stylisations were achieved.)

Discussion of the use of EPG analysis for the examination of dynamic timing aspects of speech can be found in MorganBarry (1993). In the present study George's data is examined for the segmental timing aspects which appear to link specifically with a dysarthric condition and which have a significant effect on his intelligibility. These can be related to three phases of obstruent segment production:

1. The approach phase, where the tongue contact is seen to increase steadily towards the maximum amount required for successful articulation of the segment.
2. The hold phase (known as 'closure' for stops and 'maximum constriction' for fricatives), where the maximum contact is held with no systemic change
3. The release phase, where the amount of contact steadily diminishes or changes towards the configuration of the next segment (Butcher, 1989).

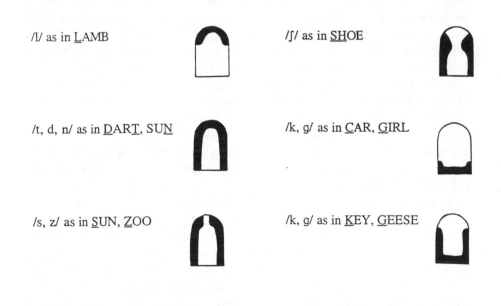

/l/ as in LAMB

/ʃ/ as in SHOE

/t, d, n/ as in DART, SUN

/k, g/ as in CAR, GIRL

/s, z/ as in SUN, ZOO

/k, g/ as in KEY, GEESE

Figure 8.1 Normal speaker's stylised EPG patterns for target obstruent segments. The patterns represent the point of maximum contact or constriction.

These three phases can be clearly seen in normal speakers' data when preceded and followed by open vowels. In close vowel environments, next to other consonants or word finally, the beginning and end points of approach and release phases are not so easy to identify. Data from pathological speakers, especially those with types of dysarthria, are even more difficult to analyse; nevertheless, selected measurements were made of a number of tokens in George's data, and these were compared with data from normal speakers (MorganBarry, 1993). A summary of these measurements, together with further, new analysis is presented here.

As noted in the section on prosodic considerations, the durations of the individual segments within an utterance, which have their own intrinsic values relative to the overall prosodic pattern of the phrase or sentence, are of paramount importance to the perception of the rhythm of speech. Awareness of a disorder of prosody is intrinsically linked in one aspect to perception of disordered segmental timing. Although a listener may be unable to pinpoint the precise location of the error, perceptions of altered rate and the use of such descriptions as 'slurring' and 'imprecise consonants' (Darley et al., 1975; Ziegler and von Cramon, 1986) may denote errors of accurate timing, particularly of the approach and release phases in proportion to the hold phase.

The word lists shown in Table 8.3, which were used for the phonological analysis, were also used for the EPG analysis. George was fitted with the requisite artificial palate set with 62 electrodes and, after a period of practice and adjustment, produced four repetitions of each of the words. For EPG analysis, the words were arranged according to target phonemes at different places of articulation, as shown in Tables 8.5 and 8.6.

Electropalatographic analysis 1: articulatory placement

Alveolar stops
As discussed in Hardcastle et al. (1985), /t, d, n/ were seen to be within normal limits for articulatory placement in word-initial position. In word-final position, there was incomplete closure for some tokens.

Velar stops
The word lists were constructed so that /k, g, ŋ/ were produced in both front and back vowel contexts, to establish whether the pathological speakers followed normal patterns of co-articulation. Normal speakers' configurations are shown in the stylised patterns of Figure 8.1. George, however, did not appear to signal normal co-articulatory effects. The velar zone lingual–palatal contacts for the target word 'key', for example, were in all repetitions less anterior than expected when compared with normal patterns and, indeed, less anterior than for the target

Table 8.5 Wordlists organised according to place of articulation of singleton consonant targets

---

Alveolar stops /t, d, n/

Word initial	Word final	Within word
dart	dart	kitkat
deer	cot	catkin
dolls	knot	kitkat
knot	seed	tractor
tickling	sun	
deckchair	slide	
	skirt	

Velar stops /k, g, ŋ/

cot	leg	kitkat
key	book	catkin
car	beak	milking
kitkat	shark	tickling
catkin	milking	fishcake
	fishcake	weekday
		deckchair

Alveolar fricative /s, z/

sun	mouse	racer
zoo		
seed		
salt		

Postalveolar fricative /ʃ/

sheep	fish	
shop	brush	
shoe	bush	

Lateral approximant /l/

leg	well	
lamb	girl	
leaf		

Postalveolar affricate /ʧ/

chain	deckchair	

---

word 'girl'. In 'key', the contact along the sides of the palate for the /iː/ vowel did not appear until *after* the release of the /k/ in three of the four repetitions. Similarly, in word-final positions, the amount and place of contact for the /k/ in the target word 'beak' was essentially the same as that for /k/ in the target 'book'; a stylised representation of this can be seen in Figure 8.2.

Alveolar fricatives

The perceptual analysis of these segments had provided subjective evidence of the affrication of some of the fricative tokens. This was corrob-

Table 8.6 Wordlists organised according to cluster target segments

---

Stop + stop clusters /tk, kt, kd/

Within-word clusters, abutting consonants across syllable boundaries
    ki<u>tk</u>at
    ca<u>tk</u>in
    tra<u>ct</u>or
    wee<u>kd</u>ay

Stop + affricate /ktʃ/

Within-word cluster, abutting consonants across syllable boundary
    de<u>ckch</u>air

Stop + lateral approximant /kl, dl/

Word initial
    <u>cl</u>ock

Within-word clusters, abutting consonants across syllable boundaries
    ti<u>ckl</u>ing
    hea<u>dl</u>ight

Lateral approximant + stop /lt, lk/

Within-word clusters, abutting consonants across syllable boundaries
    mi<u>lk</u>ing

Word final
    hu<u>lk</u>
    sa<u>lt</u>

---

orated by EPG patterns revealing strictures of complete closure in the alveolar zone, followed by a slow release into a constriction phase, which was held for a variable length of time (see Figure 8.2 and see also timing data in Tables 8.9 and 8.10). Some examples were also seen of constriction in the palatal zone of the palate, as in the target word 'zoo', which had been transcribed as [ʒu].

Postalveolar fricative

/ʃ/ was subject to considerable variability, with inappropriate anterior contact in some repetitions of the target words, some examples of strictures of complete closure (perceived auditorily as affricates) and some patterns within normal limits. The variability of place of constriction seemed unrelated to vowel environment, in that close front vowels were no more or less likely to produce anterior zone/alveolar contact. These results are summarised in Table 8.7, where the realisation of /ʃ/ is given descriptively for each target word.

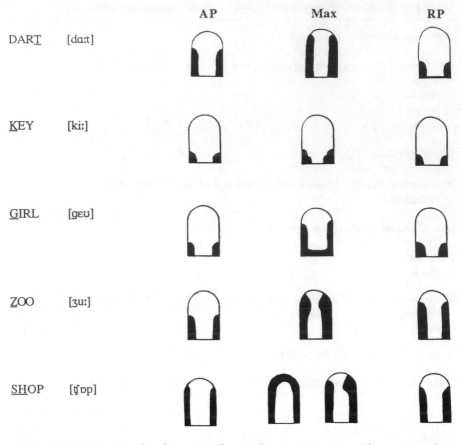

Figure 8.2 George's stylised patterns for singleton consonants. The patterns have been taken from the centre point of each phase: AP, approach phase; Max, maximum closure or constriction; RP, release phase. Where two patterns occur in the Max phase, an affricate was noted.

Alveolar lateral approximant

All realisations of target /l/ word initially were seen to be within normal limits. Word finally there was no evidence of lingual–palatal contacts and this was ascribed to the vocalisation of the lateral to [ʊ] typical of George's accent.

Postalveolar affricate

/tʃ/ was realised in three repetitions of the target word 'chain' as a stricture of complete closure in the alveolar zone, followed by variable alveolar or palatal constriction. The fourth repetition of the word showed velar zone closure for the stop element of the affricate.

Table 8.7 George's realisations of /ʃ/ within different vowel environments

Target word	Contact patterns		
	Within normal limits	Alveolar constriction	Alveolar closure
shop	0	2	2
shoe	4	0	0
shark	1	0	3
sheep	1	0	3
brush	4	0	0
bush	4	0	0
fish	1	3	0

Numbers refer to the number of repetitions realised as a given contact pattern.

Consonant clusters

As noted in the phonological analysis, consonant clusters were seen to be difficult for George and there was considerable variation across the four repetitions of the wordlists. Examples of some of his attempts are given in Figure 8.3.

Word initial clusters (see Table 8.6)

The cluster /kl/ was, in three repetitions out of four, reduced to the first element, which was realised as either a closure or a constriction in the velar zone. The fourth attempt at the cluster was within normal limits. The group of /s/ plus plosive (plus approximant) – /sk/, /skw/, /st/ – was also variably realised and nearly always reduced to one element, either the fricative or the plosive. The target word 'star' presented some interesting examples of metathesis and sound searching (Figure 8.3). The fricative plus lateral cluster, /sl/, was seen and heard as either an affricated stop or as an alveolar or palatal fricative.

Within-word clusters (abutting syllables)

Table 8.4 summarised the phonological analysis of the words containing these target structures; Figure 8.4 provides schematic representations of some examples of their EPG characteristics. Comparing the two analyses, it can be seen that, in most instances, the visual data from the EPG recordings confirms the perceptual impressions. Reduction to one segment of the cluster was seen in some instances where glottal substitutions were heard. Frication of stop elements, backing of alveolar targets, and pausing and prolongation of segments were noted from both sets of data.

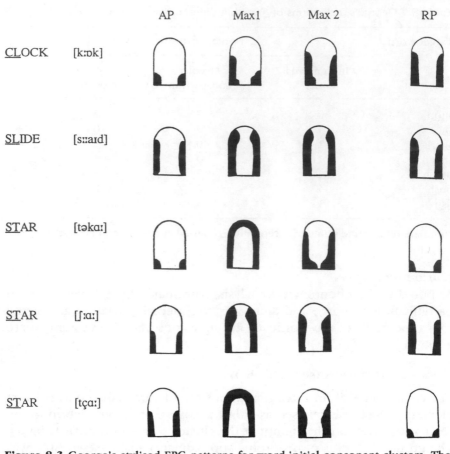

Figure 8.3 George's stylised EPG patterns for word-initial consonant clusters. The patterns have been taken from the centre points of the phases: AP, approach phase; Max 1, maximum closure/constriction of first segment; Max 2, maximum closure/constriction of second segment; RP, release phase.

Electropalatographic analysis 2: articulatory timing

As described in MorganBarry (1993), a selection of the target words were taken from the test word lists of Table 3 (shown in Table 8.8) and the duration times of the initial segments were measured across four repetitions for normal speakers.

The means and standard deviations of the pooled normal data were compared with the means and range of four repetitions of George's data for the selected words. The results are presented in Table 8.9.

It was noted from these and from earlier literature (Butcher and Weiher, 1976; Butcher, 1989) that for normal speakers, fricatives are generally longer than stops, with /ʃ/ being of the longest duration; alveolar stops are shorter than velar stops; the lateral approximant, /l/, has the shortest duration and is least subject to variability across repetitions and target words. George's data compared well with the norms

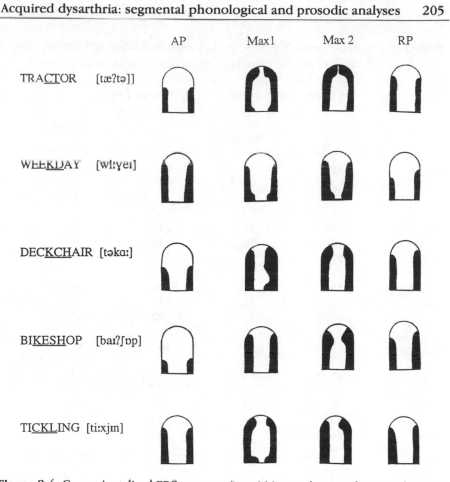

Figure 8.4 George's stylised EPG patterns for within-word target clusters (abutting syllables). The patterns were selected as described for Figure 8.3.

on these measurements, with some notable exceptions. The target word 'dolls' was extremely variable; the alveolar fricatives – /s, z/ – were shorter than for normal speakers, and the lateral approximant – /l/ – showed greater variation. The postalveolar fricative – /ʃ/ – was noted in the phonological analysis as being problematic and variably realised as an affricate – [t͡s, t͡ʃ]. Both closure and constriction phases were included in the segmental timing measurements and, rather surprisingly, also found to be shorter than normal speakers' realisations, but with a range within normal limits.

Table 8.8 Items selected from the text wordlists for the timing analysis

deer	key	seed	sheep	leaf
dart	car	sun	shop	lamb
dolls	cot	zoo	shoe	leg

Table 8.9 Duration times of the hold phase of selected word-initial consonants: a comparison of George's data with pooled normal data (four normal speakers)

Word	Normal speakers (ms)		George (ms)	
	x	Standard deviation	x	Range
a deer	135.6	38	100	50
a dart	105	30	97.5	20
the dolls	114.2	23	113	190
a key	158	35	110	70
a car	123	30	85	10
a cot	120	31	117.5	30
a seed	183.3	25	95	60
a sun	165.3	42	115	50
a zoo	187.5	27	97.5	20
a sheep	201.3	35	160	60
a shop	211.3	40	125	30
a shoe	172.5	60	137.5	60
a leaf	113.4	11	87.5	50
a lamb	116.3	17	150	50
a leg	109.4	34	120	40

The approach phase of each segment was, for the normal speakers, typically 10–50% shorter than the duration of the hold phase for all stop consonants. For the normal speakers' fricative durations, however, approach and hold phases were sometimes found to be of almost equal duration. The release phase could seldom be accurately measured, and only when followed by an open vowel: in these cases normal speakers had a segment release phase between 25% and 60% shorter than the hold phase. Data of approach compared with hold phases are summarised in Table 8.10 for one normal speaker matched to George for age. The means and range of variation of these durations are given.

Measurement of these phases for George's dysarthric speech show some differences from normal data. The approach phase for stop consonants was seen in some repetitions to be equal to or longer than the hold phase by as much as 30 milliseconds. For the fricative data there is less difference from the norm, although for the alveolar fricative in the target word 'seed' a greater range of variation was noted.

It was difficult to know what to measure for the release phases of many of the target sounds, particularly where affrication of stops occurred. Indeed, it could be argued that the perceived affrication,

Table 8.10 Means (x) and range of variation (R) of duration times of the approach phase (AP) and hold phases (HP) of selected word-initial consonants: a comparison of one normal age-matched speaker and George

Word		Normal speaker		George	
		AP	HP	AP	HP
DART	x (ms)	15	87.5	67.5	97.5
	R (ms)	10	30	100	30
COT	x (ms)	45	90	42.5	117.5
	R (ms)	20	30	30	30
CAR	x (ms)	45	92.5	50	85
	R (ms)	10	30	50	10
ZOO	x (ms)	47.5	145	72.5	97.5
	R (ms)	10	10	20	20
SEED	x (ms)	67.5	92.5	35	95
	R (ms)	40	20	80	60
SHOP	x (ms)	62.5	127.5	62.5	137.5
	R (ms)	20	10	30	40
LEG	x (ms)	10	85	20	120
	R (ms)	0	10	30	40

shown on EPG as the release of a stricture of complete closure into a definite phase of fricative constriction, was a manifestation of prolonged movement away from a target posture. For the stop consonants therefore, measurement of a release phase should begin at the point where full closure is seen to end. In George's data, the release time was sometimes more than double the hold phase.

Discussion of the analyses

Summarising the data from all of these analyses given above, it can be seen that the initial impressionistic description of George's speech can be extended and exemplified. Thus the following can be seen to be directly related to the disorders of both articulatory placement and timing as revealed in the EPG analyses:

• Imprecise consonants and distorted vowels.

The following were noted in the prosodic analysis as part of his difficulty in realising tone units appropriately:

- Slowed speaking rate.
- Short utterances.

Similarly the following were all analysed as part of his general dysprosody and can be related to problems of general incoordination of respiration, resonance and phonation:

- Monopitch and monoloudness.
- Breathy voice quality, tending to harshness when being emphatic in conversation.
- Occasional hypernasality (again when speaking under emotional stress).
- Short utterances; attempts to lengthen utterances resulting in strained–strangled voice quality.

The articulatory imprecisions noted both within and across syllables can, in turn, be linked to incoordination of the respiratory and articulatory functions.

The EPG timing data exemplify a number of important issues raised in the literature concerning cortical and cerebellar control of extent, duration and cessation of muscular activity and the problems of smooth coordination of articulatory activity.

As stated earlier, one of the problems in understanding and transcribing George's speech was concerned with his inability to mark word boundaries. In normal conversational speech, these are not signalled except at phrase and clause boundaries, but listeners are able to use their knowledge of linguistic parameters within the context of the conversation to compensate for this. In George's speech, the deletion of phonemes, lengthening of consonants and shortening of vowels, together with the elements of disordered prosody noted above, contributed to his unintelligibility and made it difficult to perceive his overall meaning, especially when he initiated a conversational shift.

A further pragmatic aspect of George's dysprosody was the fact that he was unable to signal humour, attitude or conversational importance prosodically, and this was at variance with the perceived content of his speech and non-verbal signals such as gesture, facial expression, and a twinkle in his eye when he was recounting some of his more risqué stories. Thus the conversational roles ascribed to prosody (such as the informational, illocutionary and attitudinal roles – Couper-Kuhlen, 1986; Crystal, 1992) could not be fulfilled.

Clinical implications

Detailed assessment, although intrinsically interesting for the researcher, is useful for the busy clinician only as a means of establishing aspects of diagnosis and therapy. In planning remediation, all aspects of the disordered speech must be considered, and while the overall aspects of dysarthric speech are always assessed, specific segmental phonological and prosodic analyses have not always received attention. However, the present study shows how close phonetic and phonological analysis can reveal clinically significant features of speech production in dysarthria which are not revealed by the use of the typical formal assessment alone. It is also important to note whether the patient has devised compensatory strategies and to take these into account when planning therapy (Brewster, 1989; Vance, 1994).

Results of the analyses reported here permitted the creation of a therapy programme which was finely tuned to George's needs.The programme of six 1-hour therapy sessions, spread over 4 weeks, began with a discussion with him of the results of all the analyses carried out.

It was then decided to target the segmental aspects of his speech production first, particularly those of phoneme and syllable elision. Consonant clusters were identified by George as being particularly difficult and he selected a number of much-used words and phrases for daily between-sessions 'target practice'. Using his own tape-recorder for self-analysis, and his wife as a 'useful listener' (his own phrase!), he set himself a specific number of practice repetitions a day. By trial and error, he found an optimum number of repetitions (too many *decreased* improvement as fatigue set in) for any one daily session, and an optimum number of sessions in any one day As he became marginally more proficient, we extended the target list to multisyllabic words (particularly those with clusters within-word as in wordlists C and D) and phrases containing complex phoneme combinations, even though these were not necessarily words he would frequently use.

It was agreed that it was more useful to practise consonant clusters than single phonemes. Precision of articulation of the stop consonants was less important except in word-initial and syllable-initial, within-word places in structure, and these latter were included in the target word lists. Fricatives were not specifically targeted.

As always, carry-over into conversational speech was difficult; reading aloud was not considered useful, as George reported difficulty in focusing on the written word. However, 'banner' headlines were devised for fun, and large newsprint was sometimes used.

It was more difficult to target prosody in therapy. George was unable to vary his already slowed rate, but he did work at increasing his range of intonation and to aim for rising tones for questions. Converting statements into questions, using intonational changes only, led to some interesting exchanges between George and his family. Complex fall–rise and rise–fall tones were also practised. It was significant that in these sessions, when he tried for a slightly higher and more varied pitch, his segmental phonological errors increased, but his speech was deemed to be more intelligible (MorganBarry, 1987, 1990b).

The aim throughout the therapy sessions was to preserve as much as possible the naturalness of speech. Yorkston et al. (1984, also cited in Vance, 1994) discuss therapy strategies that may be effective in some aspects of overall speech production, but which actually increase the perceived bizarreness of dysarthric speech. George, his friends and family had accepted many of the aspects of his speech, and the aim and focus of therapy was, for all of us involved with him, an overall increase in intelligibility rather than complete accuracy of articulation of particular sound segments.

Appendix I: Results of the Frenchay Dysarthria Assessment

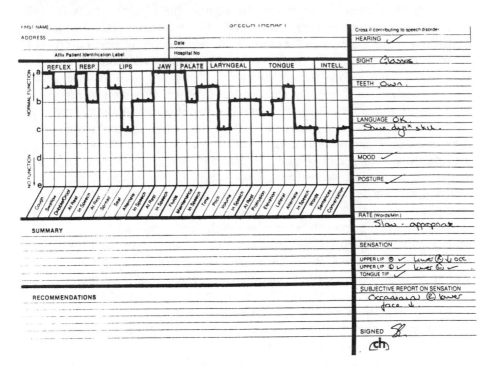

Appendix II: PROP (Prosody Profile)

Prosody Profile (PROP)

Name	Mr H		Duration	92 Tone Units
Age	68	Sample date	Type	Conversation

Tone Unit (0; 9 +)   Total   Average words

Structures

Incomplete	10	Indeterminate	6	Stereotyped	Imitation
Clause	26			**Functions**	
Phrase	10				
Word	11				
Other Cl+	3				
Cl−	26				

Tone (0; 9 +)

Data   Variants   ꜀꜀꜀"꜀"꜀ ꜀꜀꜀꜀꜀'꜀'꜀ ꜀꜀꜀꜀꜀'꜀꜀'꜀ ꜀꜀꜀‾꜀꜀꜀꜀꜀꜀‾‾‾‾‾‾‾꜀‾‾'꜀꜀꜀_N

Deviant

Summary:

		Other	N	W	↓	?↑	↑	॥		∅
0; 9+	−									
	﹨			1		5	2	24		
1: 0+	╱							8		
1: 3 1	∧									
	∨									
1: 6+	C									
	?									

Tonicity (1; 6 +)

Indeterminate	1	Stereotyped	Imitation

	Non Final		Final	
	✓	×	✓	×
Simple				
Lexical	16		38	
Grammatical	3	3	6	2
Complex	NF+NF		NF+F	

Other

Tone unit pitch	low overall, monopitch	Prosodic features (TU +)	
Tone unit other	erratic pausing, slow rate.	Paraling features	Dysphonia (creaky or hoarse)

© David Crystal 1981

Chapter 9
Acquired speech disorder: differential diagnosis using perceptual and instrumental analysis

SARA HOWARD and ROSEMARY VARLEY

Background

Case history

AD is a 47-year-old man who, 2 years before this investigation, was admitted to hospital after the sudden onset of aphasia. He was diagnosed as having a subdural empyema in the left sylvian fissure and meningitis. An empyema is a collection of pus and infection can spread from this locus into the subarachnoid space, causing a diffuse infection of the membranes surrounding the brain. A left frontotemporal craniotomy was performed and the empyema removed. He was premorbidly right-handed.

One month after surgery he was discharged home. At this point he had fluctuating levels of understanding of speech and profound expressive problems. The output problems consisted of a severe motor speech disorder and aphasic difficulties. His speech was markedly hypernasal, monotonal and with the phonatory characteristics of spastic dysphonia. Articulatory problems were also present. Evidence of some degree of underlying linguistic competence was indicated by AD's ability to write single words, although not always correctly. There was considerable evidence that intellectual–cognitive functioning was relatively intact. AD was alert, attentive and very motivated to improve. He used the linguistic and other communicative resources available to him to the maximum. He communicated through a mixture of drawing (at which he was very competent), writing of word fragments and gesture. AD had no significant motor deficits but did experience some sensory impairments on the right side of his body. This affected fine hand movements – for example, control of the pen in writing – and also oral sensation and perception.

212

The focus of this investigation concerns AD's speech production difficulties, with relative neglect of his language processing performances. Before we move to this more narrow focus, we will summarise his linguistic processing abilities.

Input processing

AD has reduced auditory verbal memory capacity. Digit span is restricted to three to four items. He also has some auditory attention problems. AD's family noted very early on that if a message was preceded by alerting signals (e.g. a verbal alerter of 'Listen' or a non-verbal alerter such as touching his arm), his comprehension improved. This impression was subsequently confirmed in clinical testing. AD's lexical comprehension varies across word classes: it is good on nouns and adjectives, but he has greater difficulty in accessing verb semantics. Performance is influenced by frequency and imageability effects. AD is able to decode morphological information (e.g. number, gender), but he does have difficulties assigning thematic roles to elements (e.g. which noun phrase in the sentence is acting as subject).

AD made errors on the Test for Reception of Grammar (TROG: Bishop, 1983) in understanding active and passive sentences with reversible word order, comparatives, those encoding a spatial relationship (e.g. X is on Y) and embedded sentences. There appeared to be two deficits underlying performance. The first was misunderstanding of predicators (accounting for errors on comparatives and spatial sentences) which, in turn, might relate to AD's difficulties with the verb category in lexical comprehension. The second difficulty was in establishing the role of elements in the sentence where no semantic or heuristic constraints operate to guide performance. The PALPA sentence–picture matching test (Kay et al., 1992) showed a clear influence of reversibility on performance. The comprehension of active and passive sentences was of equal accuracy, whereas reversible sentences of all types (active and passive) were successfully decoded on 40% of trials and non-reversible sentences were understood correctly on 75% of trials (chance = 33%). All errors on reversible sentences were the result of reversals as opposed to lexical errors. This would argue against a non-grammatical factor such as auditory memory or overload of input processing mechanisms as being the source of the deficit.

In spite of these deficits, AD makes full use of contextual support for messages. He is adept at using schema knowledge, contextual information and prosody to support damaged linguistic processing systems.

AD's processing of written language is generally more accurate than of speech. Spoken messages that have not been understood can be successfully conveyed by writing them down (e.g. in an informal lexical test, accuracy via an auditory route was 35/48 and via a written one, 44/48). Visual memory is stronger than auditory, with a digit span of five to six items. There were, however, some areas of similarity between performances across the two routes – particularly in the area of assigning thematic roles and the difficulty with access to verb semantics.

Language output

The most striking characteristic evident in any interaction with AD is the severity of his speech difficulties. Unless the interlocutor is aware of the target of his utterance, his output is unintelligible. AD normally communicates through a combination of writing single words, drawing and gesture. In many ways AD is a good communicator because of his flexible use of these representational systems.

In addition to AD's speech production difficulties, there was evidence of underlying language processing deficits. Fine-grained analyses of these deficits in speech data were difficult because of the speech production difficulties. On the phonological output route there were, however, indications of lexical access difficulties using tests of silent phonology (e.g. Psycholinguistic Assessments of Language Processing in Aphasia or PALPA word–rhyme judgement test: Kay et al., 1992), whereas in orthographic processing there again seemed to be a problem with verb access. This is illustrated in AD's attempt to write a sentence to describe an action picture. The stimulus picture showed a Chinese man, with greying hair, brushing his hair. AD's response was:

    Asia (Honk Kong)
    Black hair
    Silver hair
    Young man
    Black jumper
    Moustache
    A brush hair

There is clear evidence of ability to construct noun phrases with premodification of the head, but an inability to construct predicate–argument structure. The only form that might qualify for verb status ('brush') seems more likely to be a nominal form.

The problem

The most prominent of AD's communicative difficulties is the unintelligibility of his speech. All utterances are distorted by a tendency to marked hypernasality. Consonant production is severely limited, and vowels are subject to distortion. Prosodically speech is monotonal, with disrupted stress patterns and the phonatory characteristics of spastic dysphonia. Performance is consistent across a range of tasks (e.g. automatic and propositional speech). The hypernasality and the phonatory disorder led to an initial diagnosis on an auditory–perceptual basis of a dysarthria. Such a diagnosis, however, was to some degree incongruous with AD's brain pathology. A focal, left cortical lesion is unlikely to cause a dysarthria which is both severe and chronic. Bilateral innervation of the speech musculature means that the dysarthria resulting from unilateral cortical lesion is often mild, and resolves rapidly.

The diagnosis of dysarthria was subsequently questioned in the light of behavioural data. Muscle tone was normal. Investigation of AD's non-speech oral movements indicated a good range, speed and power of movement. This was true of lip, tongue and palatal movements in isolation and in rapid alternating movement. The disparity between non-speech and speech movements was marked and led to a tentative diagnosis of apraxia. This was also supported by the observation of difficulties in initiating tongue movement. Ancillary forcing movements were also noted; facial grimacing and increase in tone in upper thoracic and neck muscles accompanied attempts at speech. Both oral and articulatory apraxia were noted. Non-speech complex oral movements requiring sequencing of component movements (e.g. puffing out of cheeks) were impossible.

There was considerable uncertainty about this diagnosis, however, as apraxia is more usually described as affecting the articulatory characteristics of speech to a far greater extent than the resonatory or phonatory ones. Darley et al. (1975, p. 251) write that:

> . . . in apraxia of speech the continuing impairment is specifically articulatory . . . At onset of the problem the patient may experience difficulty initiating phonation at will, once this difficulty passes . . . phonation and resonance are normal.

Other investigators, however, have reported apraxic difficulties beyond the articulatory level. Itoh et al. (1979) describe the instrumental investigation of an apraxic subject in whom velic movements were disturbed.

A second reason for uncertainty in diagnosis was that AD reported some swallowing difficulties – suggesting that the motor deficit was not restricted to volitional speech activities, but also extended into involuntary oral–pharyngeal movements. However, AD did have a coexisting oral sensory deficit. On an oral stereognosis test (AD was required to match a geometric shape placed in his mouth to one presented visually) his accuracy was good (9/10) but response latencies were very slow (mean response time 30 seconds, range 5 seconds to 2 minutes). On a further test of oral sensation, AD was required to discriminate between one- and two-point touch on the tongue and palate. Tongue sensation/perception was relatively good, but performance on stimuli applied to the palate showed more difficulty, with responses being slow and with a trend towards interpreting two-point stimuli as a single touch. Discussion with AD revealed that the swallowing difficulty occurred with liquids and certain food types – in particular, rice – all of which fail to form a solid bolus and provide strong intraoral tactile feedback. Therefore the swallowing difficulties might not result from muscular weakness but primarily from a sensory deficit.

The major question in the present investigation was therefore one of differential diagnosis: could a combination of perceptual and instrumental analysis shed light on whether AD is suffering from an apraxic deficit or a dysarthric one?

Theoretical background

Apraxia

The term 'apraxia' describes a disorder of volitional movement which cannot be attributed to weakness or incoordination in effector systems. The classically described characteristic of apraxia is a disparity between volitional and non-volitional movement. In apraxia, volitional movement is disrupted (e.g. speech), whereas automatic movement (e.g. swallowing) is spared. This contrasts apraxia with dysarthria. In the latter, both volitional and automatic movements are impaired as a result of a lesion of the motor pathway at any point between the primary motor cortex and the effector system. The inconsistency between performances in apraxia suggests a disorder at a higher level of movement control than that of the effector system. The system involved is usually conceptualised as that of a motor programmer or a repository of blueprints for learned movements. Luria (1966) suggests that lesions causing apraxia lie in the secondary (or association) motor cortex, resulting in efferent apraxia, or the secondary (association) sensory cortex, causing afferent apraxia. These views were supported by Rosenbek and Wertz (1973) who were able to differentiate two groups within an apraxic population on the basis of presence or absence of coexisting sensory–perceptual deficits. These investigators also found that apraxic subjects with an afferent component to their disorder had more severe speech disorders.

Luria's conceptualisation of apraxia emphasises the need for sensory information in the programming of complex movements, and this would match more contemporary theories on movement control. This sensory information is likely to be of different types. Just as learned movements are likely to have a motor programme, or schema, stored in memory, there is likely also to be a sensory schema associated with this. This schema builds up from previous experience of the movement and then can be used to evaluate subsequent instances of a movement – to examine whether the incoming sensory information from an executed movement matches up to existing sensory schemata for that movement (Schmidt, 1975). Second, in implementing a motor schema, the programming mechanism needs information about where the effector systems currently are, and other facts such as the load under which they are operating, and the current velocities of movement. Only with such information can the complex and finely controlled movements of speech be accurately programmed. An afferent component in AD's speech disorder is indicated both by his performance on an oral stereognosis and a two-point discrimination test, and also by his report of abnormalities of oral and facial sensation since his illness. A further characteristic of note is that AD often requested visual information before attempting a production of a word, suggesting an attempt to supplement kinaesthetic information with visual.

Phonetic and phonological features of acquired apraxia

In the past considerable controversy has existed over whether apraxia of speech should be considered a disorder of language or of speech. Darley and his co-workers (e.g. Darley et al., 1975) have argued that apraxia is a phonetic disorder, whereas Martin (1974) has argued that it represents an aphasic phonological disorder within language encoding. Martin argued that the phonetic performance of apraxic individuals was influenced by linguistic variables, such as word class, which would suggest that the notion of a motor programmer as an independent cognitive module outside of linguistic encoding was not viable. Other authors point to the importance of placing the phonetic–phonological performance of the apraxic in the context of characteristic non-linguistic behaviours, particularly struggle and searching behaviours, which are suggestive of a motoric impairment (Wertz et al., 1984). If apraxia of speech is viewed as a language disorder at the level of phonology, the suggestion is that the patient has problems selecting the appropriate phoneme for production, whereas if it is thought of as an articulatory disorder, the patient is presumed to experience problems in the actual articulation of sound segments. This classificatory problem can perhaps be resolved if one sees it as the consequence of imposing a three-way distinction of disorder on to a two-way classificatory system. Most investigators would accept that it is possible to differentiate dysarthria, apraxia and an aphasic disorder of phonological encoding (which often results in fluent speech containing many phonemic paraphasias and neologisms). If one attempts to impose this three-way differentiation of disorder upon a traditional phonetic–phonological distinction, it might permit dysarthria to be unambiguously classified as a phonetic disorder and the numerous phonemic errors found in certain aphasias as constituting a disorder of phonology, but classification of apraxia is not clear. Hewlett (1985) instead suggests a three-way classificatory system in which phonological disorder describes those cases where the problem is indeed with the organisation of and selection from the sound system; articulatory disorder describes disruptions that result from physical problems in respiration, phonation, resonance and/or articulation which hamper the successful realisation of speech sounds, and finally phonetic disorder, which would include apraxia as a speech motor problem. Use of Hewlett's system avoids a simple either/or decision as to whether apraxia is a phonetic or a phonological disorder and captures the notion that the disorder lies at the interface between phonology and articulation.

Traditional accounts comment on the effortful nature of apraxic speech production where the speaker visibly 'gropes' for sounds or 'sound–searches' and the resultant speech is highly variable and unpredictable. This variability and inconsistency is usually seen as a key factor in distinguishing apraxic speech from dysarthric speech. Dysarthric speakers will tend to show a much more consistent pattern of breakdown with performance being similar both within and across different contexts. Thus their speech problems will manifest in similar ways and to a similar degree whether they are producing spontaneous speech or imitations and repetitions of modelled utterances, and whether those productions are of meaningful or nonsense items. Apraxic inidividuals, on the other hand, perform variably across different contexts and within contexts.

Whereas the neurophysiogical problems underlying dysarthric speech can be seen to produce primary problems in each of the three critical and interlinked areas of articulation, phonation and resonance as a result of restricted range and speed of movements, in apraxic speech the articulatory difficulties the speaker manifests in actually attaining target postures and gestures are usually seen as the primary problem. These, in turn, cause secondary problems in the areas of phonation and resonance mainly resulting from compensatory strategies to aid intelligibility and accuracy of articulation. Thus the various prosodic disturbances of apraxic speech, which include slow rate, pauses between segments, abnormal stress patterns and abnormal speech rhythms (Kent and Rosenbek, 1983), are seen as byproducts of the central problem of articulation rather than as primary areas of difficulty in their own right.

One of the main problems of traditional attempts to characterise apraxic speech is their reliance on auditory perception and transcription. Apraxic speech is notoriously difficult to transcribe phonetically and, although there is undoubted value in attempting close phonetic transcription of the disorder, it has become clear over recent years that the auditory impressions of apraxic speech may sometimes constitute an inaccurate reflection of what is actually happening in articulatory terms (Hardcastle, 1987; Hardcastle and Edwards, 1992). As a result of this it now appears important to augment our auditory perceptions of apraxic speech with evidence from instrumental investigations, and over the last 20 years a significant body of work has emerged using a range of instrumental techniques to this end. A fundamental observation from these studies has been that apraxic speech is best viewed as the product of difficulties in initiating and coordinating movements of the subsystems of articulation, phonation and resonance and that errors, which were traditionally classified as substitutions of one segment for another, on closer examination emerge as phonetic distortions of the target segment caused by these timing problems. This reanalysis of apraxic speech as the result of phonetic distortion rather than phonological selection also fits more comfortably with the observed variability of the apraxic individual's productions. Different attempts at the same target phoneme may approximate more or less successfully to the target, and as a result of categorical hearing we will hear those that cross language-specific categorical boundaries as different phonemes or segments whereas those that remain within categorical boundaries will be judged as the 'same' phoneme. Thus successive attempts at /t/ may consist of [tʰ] [d] [t⁼] [d̥] [k] and [ts], where [tʰ] and [t⁼] will be judged acceptable, whereas [d] and [d̥] will not, because they fall at the other side of the categorical boundary for voicing in English, even though in reality there may be as little difference between [d̥] and [t⁼] as between [t⁼] and [tʰ] on the voicing continuum. Likewise [k] may be judged unacceptable as it transgresses another phonemic boundary, whereas [ts] may be tolerated even though it clearly differs from a standard realisation of the voiceless alveolar plosive. To complicate matters further, it has been observed that our auditory judgements of apraxic speech production may sometimes fail to identify abnormal productions and judge as perceptually satisfactory productions whose articulation is in fact quite abnormal (Hardcastle and Edwards, 1992).

In response to the limitations in characterising apraxia of speech using auditory perceptions, a number of different instrumental approaches have been used to examine each of the subsystems of speech production (articulation, phonation and resonance), both individually and in combination to identify more accurately the breakdowns in performance and coordination which characterise apraxic speech production. Early electromyographic (EMG) studies (Shankweiler et al., 1968; Huffman, 1978) revealed great variability in the muscular activity involved in speech production, including difficulties in initiating movement and in sequencing and timing movements, suggesting that apraxic subjects have a lack of sensory feedback regarding their muscular movements for speech. Itoh et al. (1979) used a flexible fibrescope inserted into the nasal cavity to investigate velic movement in an apraxic subject's speech and suggested that the velum tended towards a neutral position for both nasal and non nasal targets (thus affecting resonance across all of the speaker's utterances), but that overall considerable variability could be seen in velic activity which sometimes led to segmental production that transgressed phonemic boundaries (e.g. /d/ being heard as [n]). Itoh and Sasanuma (1984) also used X-ray microbeam techniques to observe articulatory activity in apraxic speech production, and identified variability and discoordination of articulatory movements which resulted in phonetic distortions of target phonemes.

By far the greatest amount of instrumental research into apraxic speech, however, has been carried out using two techniques: sound spectrography to provide acoustic information and electropalatography (EPG) to identify patterns of lingual activity.

Spectrographic analysis has been able to provide insights into the problems apraxic speakers appear to have in signalling voiced and voiceless segments, and also into the marked durational differences in the segments produced by apraxic speakers in comparison with normal speech. A number of studies have investigated voice-onset time (VOT) in target voiced and voiceless consonant targets. In general it would seem that, although they have clear problems with the coordination of voicing with articulatory activity, apraxic subjects do have the intention of preserving the phonological distinctions expressed by voicing differences (Blumstein et al., 1980; Kent and Rosenbek 1983; Hardcastle et al., 1985).

Another area of spectrographic analysis which throws light on the phonological intentions of apraxic speakers is that of vowel length. In normal English, vowels are generally longer before voiced segments than voiceless segments and thus, even if voicing problems mask voiced–voiceless distinctions, the intended consonantal contrasts may still be indicated by the preservation of vowel length differences. Code and Ball (1982), Duffy and Gawle (1984) and Hardcastle et al. (1985) all report cases where relative vowel differences were preserved in this way preceding voiced and voiceless consonants, although the last group note that there was less differentiation between values than is found in normal speech. Although Duffy and Gawle reported that vowels overall tended to be of shorter than normal duration, Kent and Rosenbek (1983) showed a strong tendency for *all* segmental articulations to be significantly prolonged, linking this to the observation that normally unstressed vowels gave the impression of being stressed. Indeed they noted that all sound segments, both vocalic and consonantal, had increased durations, an observation that is backed up by Code and Ball (1982) whose analyses indicate a lengthening of fricative segments in the subject they studied.

Electropalatography is a technique that provides information about the contacts made by the tongue with the palate across the alveolar-to-velar regions. As such, it can capture aspects of lingual movement in both speech and non-speech activities. EPG studies have provided information on the spatial and temporal organisation of lingual movements which has proved useful in the differential diagnosis of apraxia and dysarthria. Hardcastle et al. (1985) give a clear account of the differences revealed by EPG, and Hardcastle and Edwards (1992) describe six types of lingual production error present in apraxia of speech. These are summarised in Table 9.1.

Table 9.1 Lingual production errors in aquired apraxia

Lingual production error	Description	Sources
Misdirected articulatory gestures	Normal lingual patterns produced in the wrong context (e.g. /t/ being realised as a normal-looking [k])	Hardcastle and Edwards (1992); Sugishita et al. (1987)
Distorted spatial patterns (may be more typical of dysarthria)	Differ spatially from the contact patterns typical of normal speech	Hardcastle et al. (1985); Hardcastle and Edwards (1992); Washino et al. (1981)
Omission of target gestures	A contact pattern which would be expected in a given context but is not actually present	Hardcastle and Edwards (1992)
Seriation problems	Refers to difficulties in achieving normal transitions between successive segments or gestures	Washino et al. (1981); Hardcastle (1987); Hardcastle and Edwards (1992)
Repetitions	Soundless arching or groping to achieve particular articulatory postures	Washino et al. (1981); Edwards and Miller (1989)
Abnormal spatial and temporal variability	Inconsistent performance across repetitions of a target utterance	Hardcastle (1987); Washino et al. (1981); Hardcastle and Edwards (1992); MorganBarry (1993)

Analysis

Our approach arose from the desire to test out the scope of narrow phonetic transcription based on auditory and visual perceptions in the task of differential diagnosis of a complex acquired speech disorder. We were interested in establishing whether phonetic transcription alone could reliably capture the nature of AD's speech problems and, further, to see how far our auditory and visual perceptions matched information provided by subsequent instrumental analysis of the data.

In recent years many authors have questioned the reliability and value of phonetic transcription (see Chapter 2), suggesting that it provides a limited and potentially misleading representation of the physical events of speech, which can be more accurately captured by instrumental techniques. This has particularly been suggested to be the case in the analysis of apraxic speech (Hardcastle,1987; Hardcastle and Edwards,1992). In reality, however, speech and language therapists generally have limited access to speech instrumentation and rely, for clinical analysis, on transcription of live or recorded data. It is thus important to assess the usefulness and limitations of this method of working.

As each case of disordered speech is potentially unique in its phonetic and phonological features and cannot be assumed to correspond in a close or simple way with normal speech production or target phonological systems, we adopt the position of Kelly and Local (1989, p. 5), who observe:

> If we wish to work on, say, an unwritten, and so far unstudied language, we know of no other means of doing this than taking it down at first hand in all its detail.

Our analysis of AD's speech thus took the form of an initial narrow phonetic transcription of the data, followed by further analysis by instrumental techniques to evaluate the accuracy of our perceptual observations.

Auditory phonetic analysis

The starting point of our analysis of AD's speech production was a narrow phonetic transcription of his production of approximately 150 glossable single word items taken from the Sheffield Computerised Articulation Test (SCAT: Eastwood, 1981), together with a short sample of spontaneous conversational speech. The transcription was based on the symbols provided by the International Phonetic Alphabet (IPA, revised to 1993) and ExtIPA (Extensions to the IPA: Duckworth et al., 1990), augmented by notes where appropriate. The single word items comprised a combination of spontaneous picture naming and imitations of modelled utterances. Although in an ideal situation we would have wished for more data and, in particular, for a larger sample of spontaneous speech, in reality the severity of AD's speech production problems prevented this.

The data sample was recorded one month before the onset of a programme of EPG therapy. Six months before this, a recording of AD's speech had revealed an extremely limited sound system, which was largely confined to the production of CV syllables realised with some variability as [njɑ] or [ɲɑ]. This is interesting in the light of the observation by Sugishita et al. (1987) that the best preserved consonant phoneme for their two Japanese apraxic speakers was the palatal nasal [ɲ]. For AD, of course, no similar claim can be made that his productions are preserving a segment with phonemic status. Rather [nj] and [ɲ] appear to result from inappropriate velic setting and activity, together with a tendency observed throughout the data to favour the tip and blade of the tongue in consonant articulations. (It is interesting at this point, however, to note that in non-linear phonological representations coronals, i.e. tip and blade articulations, are said to be unmarked forms (Paradis and Prunet, 1991) and the segments with minimal specifications are /t/ and /j/ (Bernhardt and Stoel-Gammon, 1994).) By the time of our full auditory analysis, AD's speech production had changed but there was still strong evidence of these articulatory tendencies. The immediate auditory impression of AD's speech at the point of analysis was that it contained dysarthric features such as hypernasality, dysphonia, abnormally articulated consonantal segments and prosodic disturbances including a noticeably slow rate of speech and problems in maintaining stress patterns appropriately across utterances.

In embarking on a narrow phonetic transcription of AD's speech, we were quickly reminded that apraxic speech is notoriously difficult to transcribe. Given that phonetic transcription generally attempts to impose some sort of linear segmental organisation on the data, the main problem posed for us, in attempting a segmental transcription, was how to decide on what constituted a segment. Although the concept of the segment is currently receiving a great deal of criticism (e.g. Local, 1992), it nevertheless remains the starting point for most attempts at the perceptual phonetic analysis of speech data and arguably underpins most phonetic and phonological frameworks at some level (Kohler, 1992). As Laver (1994, p. 568) remarks:

> . . . the concept of the segment is neither natural nor (in some ultimate analysis) necessary. It is merely one rather convenient way of organising our initial analytic thinking about speech.

If the division of speech into a linear sequence of segments is difficult and contentious for normal speech, it is compounded in speech disorders such as AD's which feature abnormally slow rates of speech, because the transitions between segments are subject to distortion and prolongation. At times their perceptual salience is increased to an extent that may suggest the presence of another auditorily distinct 'steady-state' segment. At other times the transitions of different subsystems occur in such an uncoordinated manner as to obfuscate perceptual boundaries between segments to an abnormal degree. Any divergence from normal transitional and co-articulatory coordination of speech gestures poses a particular challenge to accurate phonetic transcription and this was to prove the case with AD's speech.

This ongoing dilemma proved particularly difficult, for example, in moving from phonetic to phonological analysis and attempting to establish the segmental phonotactic structure underlying AD's productions. We were, however, aware that it actually illuminated significant aspects of his speech production problems and helped to explain some of the variability typical of apraxic speech which was present in the data. What emerged as we progressed was a picture of severe problems with the timing and coordination of the movements of the speech production subsystems of articulation, phonation and resonance. Thus, for example, the following transcriptions illustrate our attempts to capture the perceptual impressions of what appear to be inappropriately timed and coordinated movements of the lips, tongue, vocal folds and velum:

measure	/ˈmɛʒə/	[ˈ̩ɓɛ̆ŋjə˞]
spoon	/spun/	[əm̥ˈɓɔ̃uː]
budgie	/ˈbʊʤɪ/	[m̥ˈbjɔːədjiː]

The apparent incoordination of independent speech gestures cause many problems for AD and lead to the variability and unpredictability evidenced in his speech production. This is not, however, to suggest that his speech production and resultant phonological system are without a number of consistent patterns and tendencies which were auditorily perceptible and identifiable by narrow phonetic transcription and subsequent analysis, and which we will now discuss in relation to the subsystems of articulation, phonation and resonance.

Resonance and the oral–nasal contrast

The immediate impression of hypernasality in AD's speech had initially suggested a provisional diagnosis of dysarthria and was presumed to be the product of an inability to achieve velic closure and of a permanently lowered velic setting. We were also mindful, given the slow rate of his speech, of the observation that normal speakers tend to appear more nasalised if they slow down their speech rate significantly (Colton and Cooker, 1968). However, our transcriptions indicated that although AD might be generally adopting a neutral velic setting which was neither fully raised nor fully lowered, and thus reminiscent of the apraxic subject of the study by Itoh et al. (1979), he *was* also capable of raising and lowering the velum to direct airflow appropriately through the nasal and oral cavities. His problem lay in the fact that velic movement was not successfully coordinated with other articulatory activity. Acceptable oral–nasal resonances were occasionally achieved for target oral and nasal segments but this was variable and unreliable. As English does not have a phonological contrast that is expressed phonetically by the difference between nasalised and fully oral vowels, the inappropriate nasalisation of vowels that occurred variably in AD's speech had less implications for his general intelligibility than the inappropriate nasalisation and denasalisation of consonant segments which threatens the maintenance of the oral–nasal contrast in the English phonological system.

Problems with the inappropriate timing of velic movements produced various and variable auditory effects. Where the velum appeared to have lowered inappropriately early in anticipation of a nasal target segment, nasalisation of preceding segments occurred. The auditory effects of this ranged from nasal resonance superimposed on a perceptibly oral segment to the apparent complete substitution of a nasal segment for an oral target, for example:

| tent | /tent/ | [ɟjẽə] |
| oven | /ʊvən/ | ['ɑ̃ə̃mə̃n] |

There were also instances that indicated a very slow transition from an inappropriately lowered velum to an appropriately raised velum for the production of a target oral segment, but where the transitional phase was so slow that it gave the auditory impression not of transient prenasalisation, but of an interpolated nasal segment, for example:

| ladder | /'ladə/ | ['ɹãndə] |

Conversely, where the lowering of the velum to permit an appropriate ratio of air to escape via the nasal cavity was slow in taking place, partial or complete denasalisation of nasal targets occurred, for example:

thumbs	/'θʊmz/	[əy'p̬=ũɓ]
mouth	/'maʊθ/	[ə̃m'ɓɒːʊ]
milk	/mɪlk/	[bɛɣ̟]

In the next example, we see how the discoordination of velic activity results in both inappropriate nasalisation *and* inappropriate denasalisation:

| penny | /'penɪ/ | ['p̬ãɪ'de] |

Our data also contained examples of friction occurring in the nasal cavity. Instances of velopharyngeal friction suggested an audible phase of close approximation of the velum with the rear pharyngeal wall before velic closure was achieved, for example:

| van | /van/ | ['ŋpɸaə] |
| sky | /skaɪ/ | ['ŋpjaɪ] |

Nareal friction was also occasionally evident in the production of some target oral fricatives (although this is not, of course, directly related to velic movement), for example:

five   /faɪv/   [b̥βãh̃m̥]

It becomes clear from our attempts to capture the timing of velic movements in relation to target segments that we are not witnessing wholesale hypernasalisation of AD's speech, or simple phonological substitutions of nasal segments for oral targets or vice versa. Rather the auditory impression of AD's speech productions across different targets and across different tokens of the same target is created by the variability of the timing of velic movement in relation to other speech activities, with a possible default setting of a neutral position, neither fully raised nor lowered (compare Itoh et al., 1979). All of these phenomena have a detrimental effect on the preservation of oral/nasal phonological contrasts.

Phonation and the voiced–voiceless contrast

Just as the contrast between nasal and oral segments is of fundamental importance in the English phonological system, so obviously is the contrast between the many pairs of consonant segments which are differentiated by the voiced–voiceless (or fortis–lenis) distinction. Although context-conditioned variability permits the occurrence of partially and even fully devoiced 'voiced' segments, an unambiguous contrast is usually preserved as a result of the fortis–lenis distinction and also because even devoiced 'voiced' segments will have VOT values that remain distant from the VOT values for voiceless targets. This is, of course, also still the case for speakers of a northern British English accent such as AD's who tend to realise initial voiceless plosives without aspiration. AD's speech gave the auditory impression of a partial blurring of the voiced–voiceless contrast. Although some target segments were realised appropriately, many others revealed problems regarding the timing of vocal fold vibration in relation to articulatory gestures. In general the pattern revealed was that of the voicing of target voiceless segments, but such was the variability of the data that many examples were also noted of other types of phonatory incoordination. Instances were recorded of the prevoicing of both voiced and voiceless segments. At times this was of such considerable duration perceptually that we chose to transcribe it with shortened schwa, [ə̆], rather than the conventional diacritic for prevoicing, [ᵥ]. This distinguished these transitional phenomena from AD's realisations of the determiner 'a' in pre-nominal position as [ə], because these segments were of significantly longer duration, (indeed abnormally long compared with normal speech), for example:

chair	/ʧɛə/	[ˌd̃d̃ə]
toffee	/ˈtɒfɪ/	[ʃvˈbauˈɓvɛ̌]
ball	/bɔl/	[ˌɓõʊ]

Voiced targets were also sometimes devoiced, although this was a rarer occurrence, suggesting either the late onset of vocal fold vibration or the cessation of vibration inappropriately either before or during the articulation of a segment. Devoicing is applied to vowels as well as consonants, although this, of course, does not result in the collapse of phonological contrasts in the way that inappropriate phonatory activity obscures contrasts between consonant segments, for example:

van	/van/	[m̩pɸ̃aə]
sausages	/ˈsɒsɪʤɪz/	[ˈʤəʊˈdɪndʒ̊ə]

Concomitant with this variability in the timing and coordination of vocal fold activity was a variably harsh voice quality which was particularly evident during moments of articulatory struggle and groping and which had the effect of further obscuring the voiced–voiceless contrast.

Consonants: place and manner of articulation

We have seen that both resonatory and phonatory aspects of AD's speech are abnormal and now turn to the area of articulation. It is here that the literature suggests that apraxic speakers' predominant problems lie and our initial auditory impression had suggested significant problems for AD in this area. We were interested to establish whether the problems revealed by narrow phonetic transcription were more suggestive of apraxic or of dysarthric difficulties.

Place of articulation. In spite of a good deal of variability across words and across tokens of the same word, a significant pattern which emerged from the data was of the restricted utilisation by AD of different places of articulation. A striking aspect of AD's speech was the relative rarity of obstruent segments produced in the postalveolar-to-velar region. Palatal nasals and approximants were noted relatively frequently in the data and there were a limited number of velar nasals, but otherwise there were only a few instances of speech segments produced by lingual–palatal approximation posterior to the alveolar region. The data showed that for AD's lingual consonant articulations, tip/blade articulations predominated and that the body of the tongue was less active or successful as a primary articulator. This brings to mind Hardcastle and Edwards' (1992) argument that there are strong grounds for regarding the tongue as comprising two independently controllable systems: the tip/blade of the tongue and the tongue body.

For AD the former system appeared to be operate more effectively than the latter in speech production. Indeed, in spite of the variability of the data, AD appeared to have only one fairly consistent contrast of place of articulation: labial versus lingual, where lingual targets across the locations from alveolar to velar were predominantly realised anteriorly in the oral cavity, whereas labial, labiodental and also dental targets were produced bilabially. Both types of segment may be variably accompanied by a palatal approximant release phase, for example:

bee	/biː/	[b̥i]
fish	/fɪʃ/	[vb̥βɜː]
throw	/θɹəʊ/	[ə̃mˈboʊ]
watch	/wɒtʃ/	[b̥wɔːə]
oven	/ˈʊvən/	[aə̃mə̃n]
tap	/tap/	[djæ]
doll	/dɒl/	[djɑ]
zoo	/zuː/	[əždəʊ]
chair	/tʃɛə/	[ˌd̃ãə̌]
jelly	/ˈdʒelɪ/	[dʒelɪ]
grass	/grɑs/	[dæə̌]

Although this broad contrast of place of articulation was fairly well preserved in the data, there was still evidence of variability and of co-articulation of labial and lingual segments, although not of co-articulation of different places of lingual articulation, for example:

pram	/pram/	[djãmd̃ə]
paper	/ˈpeɪpə/	[baɫt̃ə]
toffee	/ˈtɒfɪ/	[ˌvˈbɑʊˈb̥vɛ]
sock	/sɒk/	[m̥ṽɑˑ]
shop	/ʃɒp/	[pjo̞ə̌]
car	/kɑ/	[ẵˈbjŏ]

Manner of articulation. Although there was evidence in the data of each of the manners of articulation represented in the phonological system of English (nasal, plosive, affricate, fricative, and median and lateral approximants), the distribution of the different manners was uneven and was not related in a straightforward way with the manner of articulation of target segments.

A striking feature of AD's speech production was his marked tendency to realise a range of target initial consonant segments (both singly and in clusters) as an oral or nasal stop followed by a palatal approximant: thus [mj] [bj] [dj] [tj] [nj], etc. This suggested a tendency for the body of the tongue to be habitually raised towards the hard palate as the tip or blade of the tongue (or the lips) produced the primary articulatory stricture. Stop articulations (oral, nasal and nasalised) and the palatal approximant, /j/, predominated in AD's speech and there were significantly fewer instances of fricative segments. Affricates were represented in the data at bilabial and alveolar places of articulation, but did not appear to have any contrastive phonological function. Of those fricatives that did occur, many were not members of the target phonological system – [j̊, ɬ, ɦ, hn̩, m̥] – and seemed to be the product of various incoordinations of articulatory, phonatory and resonatory activities. Other than /j/, there was very little evidence of approximant articulations.

Vowels

Although acknowledging that the auditory perception and transcription of vowels is itself problematical (see the classic experiment by Ladefoged, 1967), it was clear from our data that AD's vowel productions were a source of difficulty. Perhaps because there is more latitude in terms of phonological space for realisational variability in vowel production, traditionally little attention has been paid to problems with vowels, although recently there has been a growing recognition of such problems. AD's vowels were quite variable and contributed in no insignificant way to his high levels of unintelligibility. His tendency in the early period post-trauma to neutralise many vocalic contrasts to the open back realisation /ʊ/ had lessened somewhat by the time of our analysis, but his vowel system was still subject to significant distortion with a resultant collapse of phonological contrasts. Our transcriptions showed that for each vowel target AD produced a number of variant realisations, for example.

/ɪ/ – [ɪ, ɜ(ː), əʊ, aɪ, e, ɛə, i(ː), eɪ, eaɪ]
/u/ – [u, ŭ, əʊ, ŭu, ou, oː, ou]
/aɪ/ – [aɪ, ɑ̝, eː]

However, the phonetic relationship of AD's productions to the target segments was not random and analysis of our transcriptions revealed a number of clear patterns. For each vowel target segment AD produced a range of realisations which, although sometimes articulatorily and auditorily distant from the target, clustered in a definable space if mapped onto a traditional vowel quadrilateral. Thus, for example, almost all realisations of front targets were located in the front half of the vowel space, although variations of vowel height, a tendency towards centralisation of some realisations and the variable production of monophthong targets as diphthongs all contributed to the inconsistency of realisations. Equally, realisations of back targets remained for the most part in the posterior area of the vowel space, though similar realisational problems contributed to the variability of productions. Long vowels in particular were prone to realisation as diphthongs which had an inappropriate starting point but which generally developed towards an appropriate steady-state articulatory posture. Diphthongs also displayed the general tendency to achieve a posture appropriate to the final part of the diphthong but had quite variable starting points and were occasionally realised as long monophthongs. A number of high vowel targets (e.g. /ɪ/, /ʊ/, /u/, /i/) were realised either as more open vowels or as diphthongs with an open starting point.

Phonotactic structure

We noted earlier that one of the difficulties in attempting a linear segmental transcription of AD's speech production was that of deciding what constituted a segment. This problem has implications for our analysis of AD's preservation of the phonotactic structure of target utterances. Some intersegmental transitions, as we have noted, were so long as to give the auditory impression of an independent segment. Taking a listener-oriented perspective, we could argue that this, of course, changes the phonotactic structure of AD's production in relation to the target. A speaker-oriented perspective, however (Hewlett, 1985), would propose that AD has the intention of preserving and producing the appropriate phonotactic structure which is obscured for the listener by his production problems in the transitional phases between segments. In general, our transcriptions show that AD does preserve the phonotactic structure of target utterances. There are, however, two particular exceptions to this observation. First, AD variably reduces consonant clusters. Some clusters preserve the appropriate number of target segments, albeit phonetically distorted, but others reduce the cluster to a single consonantal element. Final clusters, other than those containing a nasal target segment, are almost invariably deleted. This is consistent with our second observation, that from a perceptual perspective AD appears to delete word-final consonants quite consistently. The most robust consonants in final position are nasals but even these are only variably signalled.

Indeed, it might be argued that AD's canonical syllable structure in terms of speech production is CV. The C element is realised typically either as a labial segment or as a segment involving a tip/blade rather than tongue body stricture, whereas the V element is produced mainly by a tongue body gesture.

Prosody

At a suprasegmental level the auditory impression of AD's speech displayed a disturbance in the production of a number of prosodic variables. A very noticable feature of AD's speech was a slow rate which was linked to the audible prolongation of both consonant and vowel segments and of transitional phases between segments. The prolongation of both short and particularly unstressed vowel targets perceptually created abnormalities both of rhythm and of stress. In particular there was an equalisation of stress (Kent and Rosenbek, 1983) across syllables which had a detrimental effect on intelligibility. Segmental durations and the durations of audible transitions between segments were generally longer than normal but there was evidence of variability. Some segments sounded particularly long, even relative to the general tendency to prolongation, whereas there were also some examples of perceptually relatively short segments.

This prosodic impairment can be categorised according to Crystal (1981) as dysprosody rather than as a prosodic disability, i.e. as the result of phonetic impairment in the ability to produce and control variables such as volume, pitch, rhythm and speed of speech rather than as a phonological impairment in the functional organisation and use of these variables. Brewster (1989) in a further subcategorisation of prosodic impairments suggests the term 'prosodic deviation' to describe cases where a speaker uses prosodic variables in abnormal ways as strategies to compensate for impaired performance at other levels. In the apraxic literature it has been suggested that the unusual prosodic behaviour of speakers is in fact an attempt at maximising intelligibility in the face of segmental articulatory constraints and this may also be a factor in some of AD's prosodically abnormal productions.

Instrumental analysis

The analysis of AD's speech based on auditory perceptions and narrow phonetic transcription suggested that his problems were predominantly of an apraxic nature, albeit a very severe one, characterised by particular articulatory difficulties combined with a marked lack of coordination of the subsystems of articulation, phonation and resonance, resulting in a level of variability of output which has extremely detrimental effects on his intelligibility. However, given the established difficulties of capturing an accurate record of apraxic speech production using auditory evidence alone, we wished to make a number of instrumental investigations of AD's speech. Evidence from instrumental analysis could confirm or disconfirm our perceptual judgements and could provide additional information which could not be extracted from auditory transcription. We used two methods of analysis, both independently and in combination: EPG, to capture aspects of lingual contact with the palatal region from immediately behind the upper incisors to the margin of the hard and soft palates, and spectrography, to provide information on acoustic events during speech production. Single word data were collected using two wordlists: list A which was designed to obtain a sample of both lingual and non-lingual consonantal targets in syllable-initial and syllable-final positions in monosyllables containing a range of vowels and list B which comprised a short selection of word initial voiced and voiceless plosive contrasts (see the Appendix).

Neither list claimed to be exhaustive and the words chosen were constrained by the requirement that they were all nouns, so as not to introduce the further problems that AD displayed with, for example, verb targets. Simultaneous high quality acoustic and EPG recordings were made of each list and the data was transcribed before further analysis.

Results

Analysis of the EPG data confirmed our perceptual observation that AD's consonantal lingual gestures during speech production were primarily the result of activity of the tip/blade system rather than of the tongue body system, (Hardcastle and Edwards, 1992). In general, alveolar through to velar targets were realised lingually, whereas bilabial, labiodental and also dental targets were realised labially, although there were some instances of bilabial–alveolar co-articulation and some inconsistencies and overlap. For AD the tip/blade system was an active primary articulator, whereas the body of the tongue took a secondary role in articulatory gestures for consonant production. Although the EPG data confirmed our auditory perceptions of inconsistent, unpredictable fragments of articulatory activity in the palatal-to-velar regions, generally the tongue body cannot be said to be an active articulating system in its own right. Rather the tongue body variably accompanied tip/blade gestures by secondary strictures of differing degrees of approximation. For example, AD produced a number of perceptible phonetic variants – [n, nj, ɲ] – for what appeared to be a broad phonemic contrast – /n/. From EPG recordings it was apparent that this variation related significantly to the variable width of a lingual closure which was focused in the alveolar region.

Thus, as can be seen in Figure 9.1, sometimes AD produced a closure which was appropriately confined to the alveolar region. Sometimes, however, a much broader closure extended back across the region of the hard palate, even very occasionally as far as the margin of the soft palate. According to the EPG data, however, there was little evidence of consonant strictures produced by the tongue body independently of tip/blade activity during speech production activity. Thus those segments that we might transcribe according to auditory perceptions as palatal or even velar, implying a discrete stricture in the region

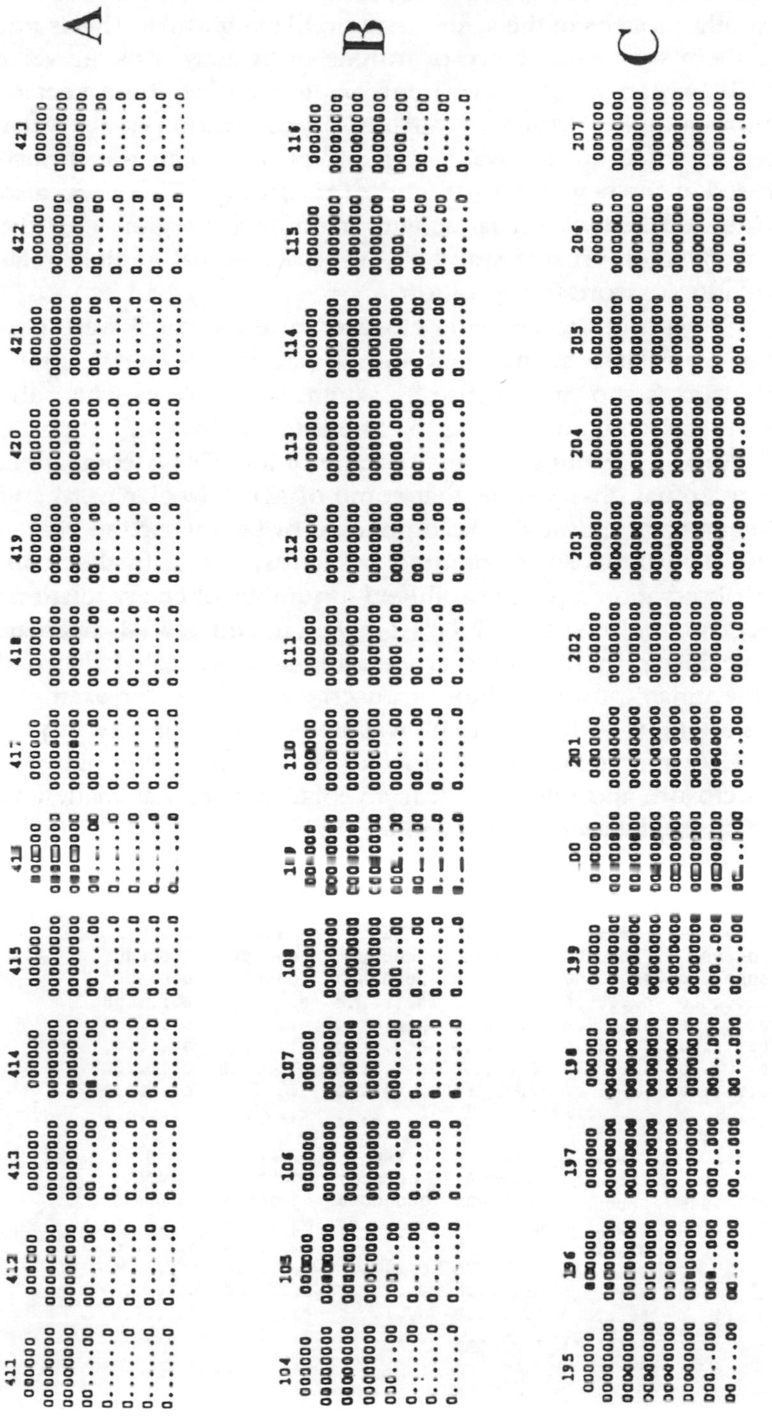

Figure 9.1 Three different lingual–palatal contact patterns for AD's realisations of /n/.

of the hard or soft palate, were revealed as variants of the pervasive tip/blade gesture which happen to extend further back across the palate than other tokens of the same basic tip/blade gesture. This is not to say that there was no evidence of tongue body activity in the velar region at all, which would have been suggestive of some sort of dysarthric limitation. Strictures of various approximation in the velar region were recorded during swallowing and also in some at rest positions captured at the beginning and end of recordings. There was also limited evidence of silent lingual activity in the velar region after the articulation of target structures and the very occasional audible velar nasal articulation in word-final position.

A further variant of the tip/blade closure patterns which were predominant in AD's data was that of abnormal patterns of lateral lingual closure. Thus, as is shown in Figure 9.2, there were tokens where the lateral closure is incomplete, failing to extend to the back of the palate and thus failing to prevent the lateral escape of air. This is compatible with our perceptual observations that some of AD's alveolar nasal and oral stop segments were variably accompanied by lateral friction.

The EPG recordings supplemented by acoustic data further confirmed our observation that AD produced a number of co-articulations (or double articulations) both bilabial–alveolar and glottal–alveolar. Indeed some instances of double articulation were revealed that had not been identifiable using auditory transcription. Thus, for example, one of AD's attempts at the target JAW was transcribed [bɑː], but inspection of the EPG and acoustic data showed that in the period between the bilabial closure and release a clear alveolar closure was made and maintained, as can be seen in Figure 9.3.

```
   ■37        ■38        ■39        ■40        ■41        ■42
  000000     000000     000000     000000     000000     000000
 0000..00   0000..00   0000.000   0000.00q   q0000000   00000000
 0......0   0......0   0......0   0......0   0......0   0.....00
 0......0   0......0   0......0   0......0   0......0   0......0
 0......0   0......0   0......0   0......0   0......0   0......0
 0......0   0......0   0......0   0......0   0......0   0......0
 ......0    ......0    ......0    ......0    ......0    0......0
 ........   ........   ........   ........   ........   ........

   ■43        ■44        ■45        ■46        ■47        ■48
  000000     000000     000000     000000     000000     000000
 00000000   00000000   00000000   00000000   00000000   00000000
 0.....00   0.....00   0.....00   0.....00   0.....00   0.....00
 0......0   0......0   0......0   0......0   0......0   0......0
 0......0   0......0   0......0   0......0   0......0   0......0
 0......0   0......0   0......0   0......0   0......0   0......0
 0......0   0......0   0......0   0......0   0......0   0......0
 ........   ........   ........   ........   ........   ........
```

Figure 9.2 Incomplete lateral lingual–palatal closure for /n/ causing lateral friction.

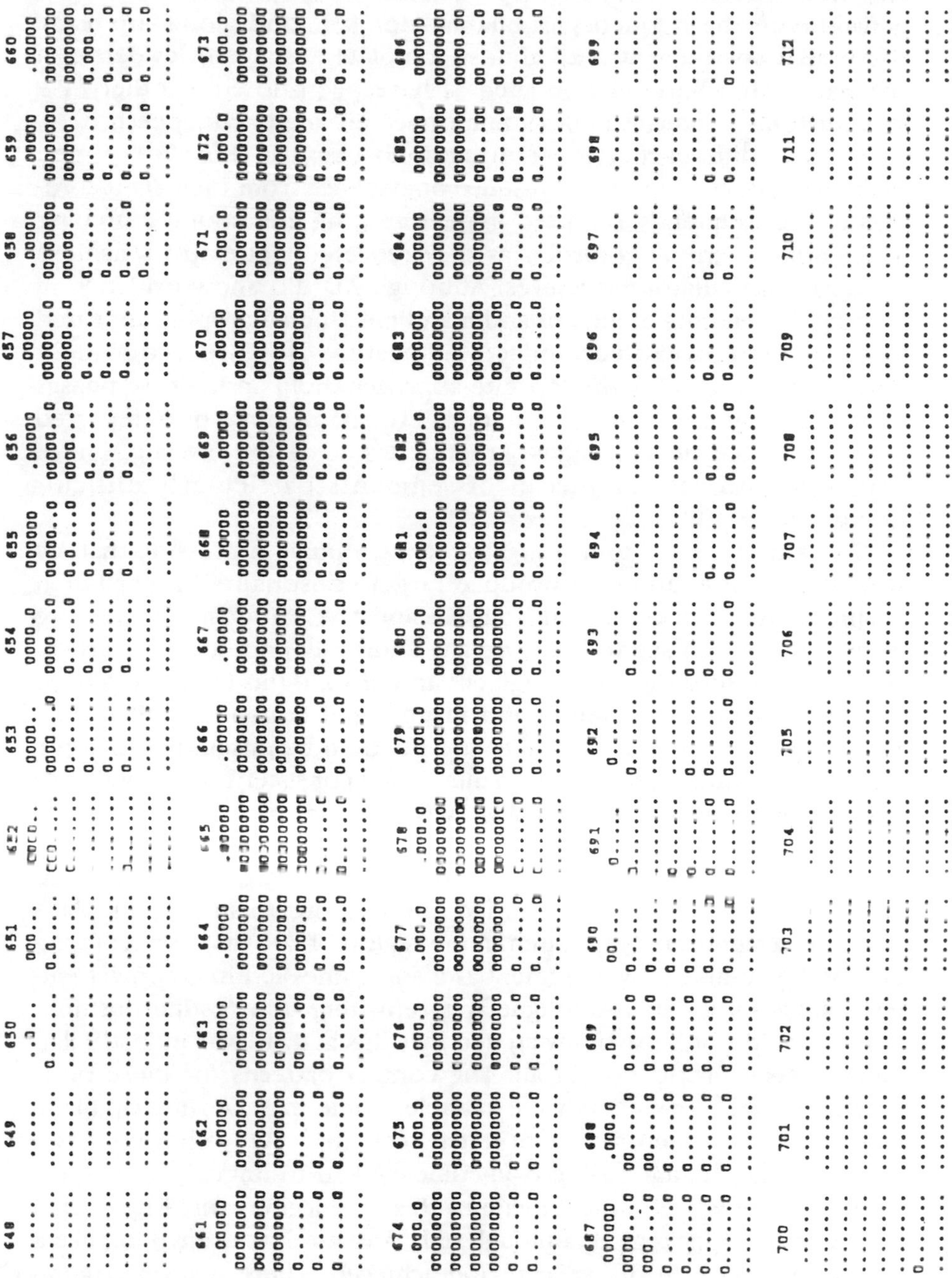

Figure 9.3 Co-articulated alveolar lingual–palatal closure during bilabial closure: transcribed as [b].

However, it was significant in relation to the difference in articulatory activity noted between the tip/blade and body systems, that in comparison with the frequency of bilabial–tip/blade and glottal–tip/blade co-articulations there was an almost complete absence of evidence of alveolar–velar co-articulation such as have been noted in other EPG investigations as constituting a common feature of apraxic speech.

A further difference between AD and most apraxic subjects reported in the EPG literature was the absence of evidence from the EPG recordings of the frequently reported lingual groping and sound searching which apraxic speakers display as they repeatedly attempt to achieve successful articulatory strictures. Although AD did show evidence of groping movements of the lips and mandible, lingual groping appeared to be almost non-existent. Indeed this feature of his speech made it much easier to identify the separate approach, hold and release phases of his consonantal articulations in our EPG data than has been reported by other sources where lingual groping has made the investigation of approach and release phases of segments particularly difficult (MorganBarry, 1993).

EPG was also used to investigate the perceptual impression that AD was consistently failing to produce target consonants in word-final position. Our data contained both CV and CVC monosyllables so we were interested to see if there was any auditorily imperceptible articulatory activity after the vowel segment and, if so, if this could be related to the presence or absence of a target final consonant. The data revealed a good deal of variability and it would be misguided to argue that AD was marking final consonants in any consistent way. There was indeed often some silent lingual activity after completion of the vowel segment but this happened frequently for CV targets, and equally there was not always postvocalic lingual activity for CVC targets. Furthermore such lingual activity as was recorded in this context usually took place only after a significant gap, often in the region of 200 ms, from completion of the audible vowel segment and sometimes led into contact patterns suggesting that the tongue was returning to a resting position. Thus it could not be strongly argued that this activity was indeed related to speech production at all. The contact patterns for these postvocalic lingual movements were variable. Some matched the tip/blade closure patterns seen for target initial segments. Many showed a pattern of lateral lingual raising (sometimes linked to lingual patterns for the preceding vowel) and sometimes this was accompanied by lingual raising in the velar region, although only very rarely was anything like a complete closure in the velar region achieved. There was one significant exception to these observations. For the target structures containing final nasal consonants, AD variably gave the auditory impression of producing the appropriate target segments. For the targets THING and HANG this could be seen to include appropriate lingual closure patterns in the velar region. However, looking at a combination of EPG and spectrographic data, we were able to observe that some of these velar closures occurred after acoustic activity had ceased and indeed that for some tokens where our auditory perceptions had indicated the presence of a final nasal consonant no lingual closure pattern has occurred. Thus it seemed to be the case that our perceptions were the product of the abnormal prolongation and increasing nasalisation of the vowel element of the target structure.

We also combined EPG and acoustic data to examine the durational aspects of AD's speech and to try to establish the relationship of the timing of vocal fold vibration with other articulatory activity. Spectrographic analysis immediately reinforced our auditory impression of the gross incoordination of AD's speech movements. If it is difficult to attempt a linear segmentation of the acoustic signal in normal speech production; this was even more the case with AD's data, where the lack of coordination of vocal fold vibration with any other discrete points in the signal made measurements such as VOT generally unrealistic. We were, however, able to confirm AD's tendency to voice target voiceless segments in the data and to identify instances of inappropriate prevoicing and devoicing.

The problems of segmentation of the speech signal also to a lesser extent affected our attempts to make durational measures of AD's speech, but we were able to make some significant observations from the instrumental evidence. To illustrate AD's marked tendency to prolong most utterances, we can compare his production of the target utterance A CAR with that of two normal speakers, using a combination of acoustic and EPG data. For this utterance the normal speakers had very similar inter- and intraspeaker durations and these, in turn, were very different from AD's. If we compare the durations for the whole utterance, we see that the mean duration for the normal speakers was 0.45 s whereas the mean duration for AD's realisations was 1.36 s. If we then look at the durations of the component segments, we see the following measures:

	AD	Normals
/ə/	0.42 s	0.045 s
/k/ (closure/silence phase)	0.41 s	0.09 s
/ɑ/	0.53 s	0.31 s

Although the target stressed vowel /ɑ/ *is* longer for AD than for the normal speakers, we can see that the perceptual impression of longer utterance duration is mainly the result of the extremely protracted /ə/ and /k/ elements of the utterance. Comparisons of the EPG and acoustic data suggest that for the normal speakers the silent intervocalic phase coincides with the period of lingual–palatal closure for the plosive, but that this is not the case for AD. For AD this intervocalic silence corresponds to a period of zero acoustic activity which is only accompanied in its latter half by lingual closure patterns. Thus AD's lingual closure for the target plosive is, at approximately 0.2 s, over twice as long as the comparable phase for normals, but it does not correspond to the whole intervocalic period. What is strongly suggested by these data is that AD is programming and producing speech in terms of discrete syllables which may be bounded on either side by silence and a brief period of absence of articulatory activity.

Summary

Our detailed phonetic investigation of AD's speech proved interesting in that it, to some extent, confirmed the diagnostic quandary that the clinicians dealing with AD faced. Analyses gave some support to the initial auditory–perceptual diagnosis of dysarthria. For example, EPG analysis revealed some distorted spatial patterns in lingual movements, which have sometimes been regarded as typical of a dysarthric problem. However, detailed analyses also revealed the inconsistencies and variability typical of the speech of the apraxic subject. An important point here is that the clinical phonetic investigation does not stand alone, but has to be integrated with evidence from other components of clinical assessment. One key feature of AD's performance during the assessment process was a disparity between speech and non-speech oral movements. This was evident in EPG 'warm-up' activities, where AD was as fast and sometimes faster than clinicians in producing lingual alveolar–velar alternating movements. This behaviour was strikingly different from lingual activity in speech. Furthermore, the struggle and forcing behaviours seen before and during speech also suggested the initiation problems of an apraxic disorder.

Implications

Theoretical

Much of the theoretical basis of aphasiology has developed from single case studies, most obviously in the work of Pierre Broca and Carl Wernicke in the latter half of the last century. The insights derived from these case studies are then applied to the broader population of patients. Occasionally further case studies are reported which refine and develop, and sometimes demand a reformulation of, the theory of a disorder. The insights we have gained by close examination of AD's articulatory and phonological abilities have a number of implications for traditional views of acquired apraxia of speech.

Our study of AD's speech difficulties indicates that he differs from classically described apraxic subjects on two main dimensions: first, the severity of his condition is such that he shows difficulties in phonation and resonance in addition to the more usually described difficulties in articulation; second, AD's speech production difficulties are more consistent than those usually described in apraxia. He does not show great disparities between his propositional and non-propositional speech performances, and although our analysis showed variability in performance characteristic of apraxic subjects, the extent of this variability was not as great as is often described in apraxia.

Our data have implications for both production and perception of apraxic speech. One of the central issues for us, mirroring a central issue currently in the fields of linguistics and psychology, is the size of the sublexical units used in encoding and decoding speech. Currently there is a great deal of controversy about this among phoneticians, phonologists and psycholinguists. As Cutler (1992) points out, different specialists have different aims and perspectives. In the phonetic and phonological literature, for example, Local (1992) argues that there is neither need nor justification for positing segment-sized units corresponding to traditional phonemes at either the phonetic or phonological levels of representation. O'Hala (1992), on the other hand, suggests that the speech segment is necessary both for the production and perception of speech. In the psycholinguistic literature sublexical 'building blocks' of various sizes have been suggested, the two most popular being the segment and the syllable. The growing recognition of the importance of the syllable as a processing unit can be linked to the importance of prosodic variables such as stress and rhythm in speech production and perception. This, in turn, relates to approaches to speech motor control such as action theory and task dynamics, proponents of which emphasise the importance of the coordination of speech movements in integrated gestures which may span stretches of speech significantly longer than a traditional segment (Wilson and Morton, 1990; Gracco, 1994;). However, Cutler (1992, p. 290) observes that at some level:

> . . . something very like the segment must be involved in the mental operations by which human language users speak and understand.

For AD, our data suggest that the syllable is indeed an important sublexical unit in speech production. There is very strong evidence, as we have mentioned previously, of a canonical syllable structure of the form CV, where the initial consonant is realised either bilabially or as some sort of tip/blade articulation, followed by a vowel element mainly involving tongue body adjustments. The rare occasions where an audible final consonant might be posited involve articulations using the back of the tongue. Thus we might suggest a syllable-sized unit which involves a gradual progression of articulatory activity from front to back across the oral cavity. Our instrumental analyses suggest that individual syllables are usually separated by periods of little or no articulatory or acoustic activity.

However, if we also accept that at some level phonetic specification of the individual segments of the speech message is necessary, we may speculate on the mechanisms involved in speech production at the segmental level. Once language-processing mechanisms have selected and arranged appropriate lexical forms into well-structured sentences, mechanisms involved in the phonetic realisation of the message scan the planned output for the sublexical units involved. At the segmental level motor and sensory schemata are retrieved from memory for each segment and are assembled in a working memory buffer before production. The segmental schema should contain a multilayered description or command plan of what is required for the gesture in terms of the interlinked movement tasks governing the subsystems of phonation, resonance and articulation. Coordination of these movements with controlled respiratory activity will also be necessary. Although we will assume that the respiratory level is not specified in the segmental plan because, in a language such as English, the whole of the speech signal is produced on a pulmonic egressive airstream, it is important to note the suggestion that 'respiratory apraxia' (Mitchell and Berger, 1975; Keatley and Pike, 1976) is possible, where there would be difficulties in the control of non-automatic breathing for speech. At all other levels the segment plan will be specified for state of the glottis, position of the velum and type of stricture made by the articulators. The coordination of the different movements necessary for the segmental gesture will be particularly important, otherwise incoordination of different subsystems, as is often characteristic of apraxia, will occur. We might note in passing that the articulatory specification is likely to be particularly complex, requiring specification of the active articulator(s) (e.g. tongue tip, tongue body, lips, jaw), the destination of the movement, and the type and duration of stricture, and may represent a more complex level of movement specification.

Traditional approaches to apraxia (e.g. Darley et al., 1975) suggest that the disorder is predominantly a disruption to the articulatory specification of speech movements and that phonation and resonance are largely unaffected. A theory which suggests that the articulatory plan is particularly complex would be able to account for this observation. However, there is no theoretical reason why all levels of the movement plan cannot be disrupted in apraxia. In severe cases of apraxia, it may well be that the difficulties in initiating phonation do not resolve rapidly as Darley et al. claim, and that the severe apraxic may have difficulties in controlling all levels of the speech production system and in coordinating the movements of different subsystems. This certainly appears to characterise AD's speech production difficulties and the analysis we have presented of AD's speech output reveals the extent of his phonatory and resonatory difficulties; if we accept that AD is apraxic, our conceptualisation of apraxia should be extended to include disturbances of phonation and resonance.

We claim that AD has a severe apraxic disorder and the severity of disorder may, in turn, link to the comparative lack of variability in AD's speech output. The detailed phonetic analysis revealed that, from a speaker perspective (Hewlett, 1985), AD was attempting to maintain phonological contrasts to some degree, but his phonetic resources are so limited that massive collapse of phonological contrasts from listener perspective occurred, with resultant poor intelligibility. AD's canonical output is likely to consist of a CV syllable structure, where the initial consonant is likely to be a bilabial or tip/blade articulation with some degree of voicing and probable nasalisation, the following vowel is likely to be nasalised and voice quality is likely to be harsh. We would like to suggest that, in the absence of a fully functioning speech programmer in AD's case, what governs his output is a series of 'default options' – where the movement is not fully specified, a set of pre-existing baseline settings of the articulatory system operate. Some of these defaults can be explained by phonetic or phonological naturalness. It is interesting to compare AD's canonical output of open syllables and a preference for coronal consonants and [j] with current hypotheses about unmarked phonological forms in the phonological component of a Universal Grammar (Paradis and Prunet, 1991). The phonatory setting – vocal fold adduction and harsh quality – might be a default setting of a different order. This may be attributed to AD's struggle to initiate speech, and would link to observations of hyperfunction of thoracic and neck musculature (e.g. the platsyma muscle) during speech. These default positions first result in a greater degree of consistency in errors than is often reported in apraxia and, second, as some of these defaults involve neutral settings of the vocal tract, cause AD to sound on initial impression like a dysarthric speaker.

Our arguments are leading to the suggestion that there is a need to accept heterogeneity in apraxic disorders. This view is identical to that espoused by many investigators of aphasia (e.g. Caramazza, 1985), who suggest that syndrome labels such as 'Broca's aphasia', 'Wernicke's aphasia' and the like, are rather abstract terms which have little that is meaningful to say about the individual aphasic. 'Apraxia of speech' may be a similar umbrella term which covers a considerable degree of variability. The message of apraxic heterogeneity is apparent in Wertz et al.'s (1984) major review of the disorder where they suggest that a number of the maxims of apraxia (e.g. apraxic subjects make more errors on initial sounds than medials or finals) are not absolute and that inconsistencies in findings can be found between studies and, where studies report individual performances, inconsistencies abound between individual subjects. In the investigation of

AD's difficulties, we have suggested that severity is the factor that differentiates him from the 'typical' apraxic, whatever that might be. However, other factors may also operate to result in heterogeneity in the apraxic syndrome: possible candidates might include the efferent/afferent factor; movement organisation disorders resulting from sequencing deficits, versus those resulting from spatial deformations.

A further issue we would like to address in considering the theoretical implications of our case study is to develop an old, but often neglected, theme in the apraxia literature that this disorder needs to be viewed not solely as one of movement, and to re-emphasise the need for consideration of sensory–perceptual abilities in at least some cases of apraxia. AD showed evidence of sensory–perceptual deficits on a number of tests, and also through self-report. Many investigators (e.g. Luria, 1966; Rosenbek and Wertz, 1973) have emphasised that apraxia cannot be considered to be purely a motor output disorder. Similarly theories of motor control stress the importance of sensory information in the organisation and control of movement. However, in spite of this, there is a trend within speech pathology to focus predominantly on the efferent aspects of apraxia. This trend is evident in research work, where the articulatory aspects of apraxia are finely described, and in clinical assessment and treatment procedures. We will discuss the clinical implications of this issue below.

From a perceptual point of view, it is interesting to consider AD's speech production in terms of O'Hala's suggestions about the nature and importance of the speech segment for the listener. O'Hala argues that the segment is a significant unit in speech perception and that the perceptually important points in the stream of speech are not what he calls the 'dead' intervals corresponding to something like segmental steady states, but the transitional points between these dead intervals where there is maximum change in the acoustic signal caused by the coordinated adjustments of the articulatory, phonatory and resonatory subsystems. If, as he suggests, it is these transitional points that aid the listener in making sense of the continuous steam of speech, it is not surprising that we should find AD's speech so unintelligible because the discoordination of the subsystems of speech in his output are so extreme that we have noted difficulties both perceptually and instrumentally in identifying or characterising transitions between target segments. Indeed, such is the lack of coordination in AD's speech that it may be more illuminating to take a parametric rather than linear approach to its phonetic representation, whereas Laver (1994, p. 101) explains:

> . . . each component of vocal performance is treated as a parameter whose value is in a state of constant potential change.

Parametric representations of speech production permit graphic illustrations of the relative timing of the various components of speech gestures and thus we could compare AD's production of a particular utterance with a parametric representation of the performance of a normal speaker and in this way capture the striking abnormalities which result in such severe unintelligibility.

Clinical implications

In the case of AD, a combination of detailed perceptual and instrumental analysis of his speech output provided important evidence to support a diagnosis of an unusual and severe apraxia. Although the perceptual analysis was rich in information contributing to our diagnosis, instrumental analysis revealed further important features of AD's speech production which had not been available from perceptual analysis alone. Such analyses are time-consuming and require either a clinician skilled in phonetic transcription and analysis who has access to appropriate instrumentation or the involvement of a tame clinical linguist! However, an important point here is that the clinical phonetic analysis could not stand alone, but needed to be integrated with evidence from other components of clinical assessment by a speech and language therapist. The availability and commitment of time and resources are important issues for the management of speech and language pathology services. Working practices that measure the efficiency of a service in terms of the number of patients attending a clinic will not make allowance for the time-consuming nature of clinical linguistic analyses. Similarly, the idea of a 'generic therapist' – one who deals with all aspects of the rehabilitation of the neurologically impaired – which is gaining some popularity in the field of health planning and provision, would lead to clinicians who were unlikely to be equipped with the skills to perform such analyses. Our concern is that in the absence of service management practices which permit detailed assessment of a patient, clinical linguistic and indeed other in-depth behavioural analyses will become confined to a very small number of specialist treatment facilities. This, of course, would be clearly detrimental to the diagnosis and treatment of a significant proportion of those individuals with disorders of communication. In the case of AD, without the analysis undertaken he may well have been deemed dysarthric and there may have been surprise at his failure to respond positively to therapy designed for the management of dysarthria, when in fact our analyses show that this would be quite inappropriate.

The provision of appropriate therapy links to the final issue which we would like to address concerning the need for evaluation of the apraxic patient's sensory–perceptual abilities. There has been controversy surrounding Luria's notion of afferent apraxia, and it may well be that two populations of apraxic individuals exist: one with sensory impairment and the second with minimal impairment. Our investigations of AD suggest that evaluation of the apraxic patient's sensory–perceptual skills should be part of routine evaluation. Standard apraxia tests, such as the Apraxia Battery for Adults (Dabul, 1979), include no sensory–perceptual evaluation. Similarly, usual treatment procedures rely upon tasks such as production drills, and also presenting the patient with multisensory feedback on speech movements. The latter task is directed towards rebuilding movement schemata, but can be viewed as very non-specific (just as before cognitive–neuropsychological models deepened our understanding of lexical processing disorders, a patient with word-finding difficulties would be given tasks which practised the deficient skill rather than intervention which targeted deficient subskills within lexical processing). A clear implication of the notion of afferent apraxia is the need for treatment to be targeted at sensory–perceptual skills. Forms of therapy that increase a patient's afferent feedback from speech movements, such as EPG, may have an important role in the treatment of apraxia.

Appendix: Wordlists for instrumental analysis

List A

a car	a cheep	a zoo	a horse
a cat	a chore	a jaw	paws
a key	a sheep	a jeep	thing
a sea	a shore	ark	hang
a saw	a go	art	porch
a tea	a knee	arm	barge
a no	arch	porch	

List B

a paw	a door	a coat	a do
a doe	a toe	a bee	a coal
a two	a goal	a girl	a curl
a pea	a tor	a goat	a bore

Chapter 10
Aphasia: assessment and remediation of a speech discrimination deficit

JULIE MORRIS and SUE FRANKLIN

This chapter presents details of a single case study with an aphasic patient, JS. His language deficits were investigated in considerable detail and, based on these findings, a therapy programme was designed and carried out. Following therapy, JS's language abilities were reassessed to evaluate the effectiveness of the therapy. Long-term follow-up assessment (7 months post-therapy) was also carried out to examine the maintenance of the improvements seen.

Background

Case history

JS left school at 14 and began work in a clothes factory, cutting patterns. He continued to work there until he retired. He is married and enjoys an independent lifestyle, living at home with his wife. They are well supported by close family who live nearby.

JS suffered a cerebrovascular accident (CVA) in March 1992 at the age of 72. A computed tomographic (CT) scan shortly afterwards revealed multiple large areas of low attenuation throughout the white matter of both cerebral hemispheres, with several well-described areas of very low attenuation in the region of the left basal ganglia. These were consistent with some infarcts and extensive areas of ischaemia. The language deficits of the patient described here were assessed in detail between 6 months and 1 year following his stroke. Leading up to this assessment, JS had been in once-weekly therapy at his local hospital. JS was 1 year post-onset when the actual therapy began.

JS presented with difficulties understanding spoken language. This was particularly marked if the topic of conversation was rapidly changed or if the subject of conversation was not obvious. JS's responses to questions often showed some vague awareness of the topic of conversation. He reported difficulties with newspaper reading, although he continued to enjoy looking at his daily paper. Functionally JS's own communication was good. JS used single words and short phrases combined with gesture, facial expression and reliance on context to express his message. He was also adept at using the listener to ask him questions about his intended message, and informed them if they had misinterpreted his attempt. Communication with people other than family members was usually restricted to social greetings etc., which JS had no difficulty with. It will be JS's problems with spoken word comprehension that are the main focus of the discussion here.

Comprehension deficits

It is suggested that the processing of a heard word involves several stages (Patterson and Shewell, 1987; Franklin, 1989). Information processing approaches often use models such as that in Figure 10.1 which attempts to describe the processing stages involved when a word is heard or seen. In this discussion it will be the comprehension of spoken words that is considered in detail. The initial stimulus is an auditory presentation of the word which then undergoes some kind of acoustic analysis. Many researchers consider that this analysis results in a breakdown of the spoken input in terms of units of phonemes and/or their distinctive features (see Caplan and Utman, 1994), but this issue remains controversial, with some researchers favouring syllables or

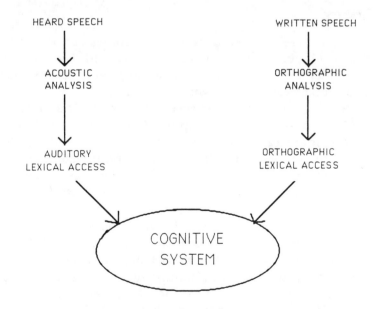

Figure 10.1 A model of spoken (and written) single word comprehension.

even whole words as the unit of analysis (Pisoni and Luce, 1987). Following this coding of the original input, lexical access occurs. Finally, the word meaning is accessed in some central store of semantic information in the cognitive system. Reading of single words is achieved partially by separate systems, involving orthographic analysis followed by access to an orthographic word form which then accesses meaning in the common cognitive system.

Franklin (1989) presented data from nine aphasic patients who showed dissociations in their performance on a range of tasks. These patterns of performance provide evidence for the existence of different stages of processing of a heard word, as she demonstrated that each stage can be selectively impaired. Of course in any assessment of patients' difficulties understanding spoken language, problems such as cortical deafness need to be considered. In some of the earlier descriptions of patients with word deafness they were mistakenly assumed to have some peripheral difficulty with hearing (e.g. Shoumaker et al., 1977).

Such a model of single word processing predicts four levels at which impairment of comprehension of a spoken word could occur. These predictions are born out by the patient data reported by Franklin. She describes three forms of word deafness. In all forms, comprehension of spoken words is impaired, whereas in pure cases of word deafness comprehension of written words remains intact so that the deficit is modality specific. Word *sound* deafness is one of the subtypes described in the literature though often termed 'pure word deafness'. Although occasionally seen in a pure form, it more commonly occurs in combination with other aphasic problems. The underlying problem is at the stage of acoustic analysis of the speech input and so the patient has problems discriminating between similar sounding words. In contrast to this, patients with word *form* deafness have a problem accessing the lexical form of the word (in the auditory input lexicon), and so have difficulty with tasks in which they have to distinguish words from non-words (lexical decision). Patients with word form deafness would have no difficulty with phoneme discrimination tasks. The third form of word deafness is word *meaning* deafness, where the problem lies in access to the cognitive system itself. Patients with word meaning deafness have intact ability to make fine discriminations based on the sound of the word (e.g. in minimal pairs discrimination tasks), and can access the lexical form, so that lexical decision is unimpaired, but in spite of this they cannot access the word meanings from spoken input. This would be revealed by difficulties with a test that involved accessing word meanings, but only when items were presented auditorily. Comprehension of the same items presented in written form should be unimpaired, or at least superior.

The fourth type of deficit the model would predict is an actual problem with the semantic representations themselves, and this Franklin terms a 'general semantic deficit'. The problem lies within the cognitive system, and so the patient has difficulty accessing the meanings of words from *both* spoken *and* written input.

Results from assessment of the patient presented here, JS, suggest that he has difficulties with sound discrimination (word sound deafness), but that he also shows difficulty at the level of central semantic representations, so has a mild general semantic deficit in addition. His pattern of word sound deafness will be the focus of the discussion here.

Word sound deafness

Word sound deafness in its pure form is characterised by an inability to discriminate speech sounds, so that patients with word sound deafness will have difficulty with tasks such as minimal pairs discrimination where the decision is based on fine sound changes. Presumably as a result of the auditory discrimination deficit patients usually have difficulties with auditory lexical decision and with auditorily presented semantic tasks. Franklin points out that for patients with word sound deafness their repetition will be as impaired as their auditory discrimination, because analysis of the input is necessary for repetition. However, it is the discrimination deficit that is the defining symptom of word sound deafness.

Auerbach et al. (1982) suggest from their findings and a review of the literature that 'pure word deafness' (word sound deafness) occurs in two forms and that this has led to some of the confusion found in the literature. One form they describe as a disorder of 'prephonemic auditory acuity' and provide results from a patient who they feel demonstrates this type of word sound deafness. The patient was impaired at prespeech tests which aim to examine temporal auditory skills. He had additional difficulties in a consonant–vowel (CV) identification task, having only mild difficulty when distracter items were two distinctive features removed from the target, with error rate increasing if items were only one distinctive feature different. The second type of word sound deafness they describe is a disorder in 'phonemic discrimination' not attributable to a difficulty in temporal auditory acuity. The case reported by Denes and Semenza (1975) is put forward as an example of this second type of word sound deafness. Denes and Semenza report that the patient showed great difficulty with phoneme discrimination and identification in the presence of good non-verbal sound discrimination. Although the patient was not assessed on the temporal prespeech tasks, other prespeech processing tasks (e.g. pitch discrimination) showed no impairment. The patient's word sound deafness is therefore considered to be 'phonemic' in nature.

This distinction between types of word sound deafness is not universally accepted. The results from their study of a patient with word sound deafness led Praamstra et al. (1991) to suggest that word sound deafness is caused by both phonetic deficits and more general non-linguistic processing deficits.

Best and Howard (1994) summarise word sound deafness as 'impaired speech perception in the context of good speech production, reading and writing'. They report a patient, BCR, who they describe as having word sound deafness. However, the results show, and Best and Howard point out, that BCR was less impaired than most patients reported in the literature. They note that BCR initially presented as a fairly classic case of word sound deafness but that the deficits showed rapid improvement, before formal testing began. BCR had difficulty with discrimination tasks when distracters differed from the target by one distinctive feature, and also showed impaired performance on a prespeech (temporal) task.

Lip reading

There are many references in the literature to the fact that patients with word sound deafness are assisted in auditory tasks if lip-reading information is available to them. Franklin (1989) discusses a patient with word sound deafness, ES, in her study, who benefits from lip-reading cues. Shindo et al. (1991) reported a patient with word deafness whose performance on tests involving both three-syllable words and short sentences was assisted by allowing lip-reading information to be used. Buchman et al. (1986) reported that two of their three cases of word sound deafness were assisted on auditory comprehension tasks if the speaker's face remained in view. Buchman et al.'s review of the literature revealed that 19 out of the 34 studies of word deafness/auditory agnosia they reviewed referred to lip reading assisting comprehension. Best and Howard also reported that their patient, BCR, was assisted by lip-reading information. This was shown by improved performance on a repetition task when lip reading was allowed and also by BCR's self-report. Best and Howard suggest that lip reading assists performance because the visual information it provides supplements the auditory information, which in some way is deteriorated for these patients with word sound deafness.

The use of assessment in planning therapy

The assessment and remediation of JS was considered within a cognitive–neuropsychological approach. Disorders of auditory comprehension have previously been considered in various other frameworks. Authors have attempted to group patients in terms of the clusters of symptoms they exhibit following brain damage. For example,

Goodglass and Kaplan (1983) use profiles of performance to describe patients. However, there is evidence showing that these attempts at grouping a very heterogeneous population are inadequate (e.g. Marshall, 1982; Schwartz, 1984) because the results are difficult to interpret given the diversity of language deficits that may be classified into one 'group'. It therefore becomes difficult to apply findings to any one particular patient. More recent work has focused on describing individual patient performance in greater detail. Within this type of approach, tests have been designed to examine patient performance on a variety of tasks, in an attempt to locate the underlying language breakdown. The aim is then to use this detailed information to plan or target therapy, with the assumption that different types of deficit will require different types of remediation. Therapy then becomes theory driven, and so it becomes possible to test hypotheses regarding the nature of the deficit and appropriate remediation. According to Byng et al. (1990, p. 67):

> . . . first and foremost, a clinical aphasia therapist requires an aphasia test to elucidate the nature of the language impairment and to indicate what aspects of language performance are most appropriate for treatment.

Kay et al. (1992, p. 3) point out that:

> . . . the assessments should be tailored to those that are appropriate to the hypothesis under investigation. Once a hypothesis about which modules are dysfunctioning is set up, the clinician can then plan a treatment programme which would be appropriate to restoring, reorganising, or compensating for the impaired processes.

A cognitive–neuropsychological approach provides detail regarding the underlying impairment, and assists in subsequent assessment-driven therapy, targeting the root of the problem (e.g. a general semantic deficit) rather than its surface manifestation (e.g. word-finding difficulties). Byng et al. describe it as 'reaching a hypothesis' about the language impairment from a variety of task measures, the types of errors made, and information about how the patient performs the task. However, such an approach does not prescribe therapy itself. Kay et al. (1992) also emphasise that tests such as those within the PALPA battery of amendments are not designed to specify what treatment programme should be used, but rather aim to provide an in-depth understanding of the disorder upon which treatment is then based. Kertesz (1990) suggests that this is a criticism of this type of approach, because it does not give information regarding 'how' to treat the identified deficit. As yet it would seem no theory does. Weniger (1990) also makes the point that regardless of assessment type used 'the task of working out a therapeutic scheme remains'. Wilson and Patterson (1990) suggest that even within published therapy studies choice of therapy is often not explicitly driven by theory. However, they point out that in many of these cases, *post-hoc* analysis suggests that theory could have *informed* the choice of therapy. Use of a cognitive–neuropsychological approach does not necessarily entail the use of new therapeutic tasks. It is rather that the rationale for choosing them is much more explicit. As a result of this lack of prescriptiveness, it is probable that techniques and therapy methods used, such as those described here, will be those that are already in use. This approach should assist in targeting them appropriately and evaluating their efficacy with particular patients.

Previous therapy studies

Therapy methods that focus on auditory discrimination skills are frequently used in the clinical situation, and are often reported as a possible therapeutic tool. However, in spite of the fact that this type of therapeutic intervention is often employed, a review of the relevant literature reveals no in-depth studies of its efficacy. Most relevant articles are similar to that of Shewan and Bandur (1986), giving only a general description of the types of auditory deficits which may occur, and possible approaches to their treatment. They provide no case studies, either descriptive or with data, and are therefore unhelpful in terms of guiding further study. At best, they contain some information on patients' performance before and after therapy, but these tend to be largely descriptive and impressionistic.

One of the most thorough descriptions of therapy for auditory discrimination problems is that given by Gielewski (1989), although this only contains brief subjective descriptions of patients' patterns of impairment and the improvement they made. Gielewski discusses a therapeutic rationale she used with patients described as having 'sensory aphasia', which is a term used by Luria (1973) to describe patients who have difficulty distinguishing between the sounds of speech. Gielewski's therapy begins by using articulograms (mouth drawings) to assist the patients' discrimination; for example, contrasting plosives with fricatives. The degree of difficulty is gradually increased by making the sounds more similar, and reliance on watching the therapist's mouth is reduced over time. The rationale used appears logical; unfortunately Gielewski presents no results of pre- and post-therapy performance, so it is not possible to evaluate the effectiveness of therapy.

Burger et al. (1983) treated a patient who had difficulty responding to auditorily presented stimuli and who was aided in assessment by lip-reading information, which they describe as 'speech reading cues'. Within therapy they presented items similar to those in the Revised Token Test (McNeil and Prescott, 1978). Initially the patient heard the command. If he was unsuccessful this was repeated with lip reading, and if again he was unsuccessful the item was presented in written form. However, baseline results from before therapy were somewhat variable and restricted in their scope, making interpretation of their findings difficult. There did seem to be improvement on performance on the test items and also on the actual Token Test (Spreen and Benton, 1969). Improvement was not seen in any other language measure used. Their conclusion was that the patient was able to use the redundant sentence context in the therapy and test items to compensate for poor auditory discrimination skills. One possible explanation of the effect found was that the patient was trained on the items he was exposed to. It would have been interesting to look at effects of the therapy on treated versus untreated items, and on performance in other tasks involving redundant sentence contexts.

This difficulty interpreting reports of therapeutic effectiveness is of course not restricted to this area of therapy. As Byng and Coltheart (1986, p. 195) point out:

> . . . there are very few published studies in which positive outcomes of treatment can confidently be interpreted as specific treatment effects and not as general treatment effects or consequences of spontaneous recovery.

The data presented here demonstrate that, for JS, the improvements seen following therapy are specific to the area of language processing targeted, and so are not simply part of a general improvement.

Assessment and intervention

JS's assessment

A range of language assessments was used to examine JS's language problems. Hearing was tested to eliminate this as a cause of any of his difficulties with auditory tasks. His performance on a range of phoneme discrimination tests was measured to look at his auditory discrimination skills. Effects of the availability of lip-reading information on his performance on these tests were also considered. His ability to access the lexical forms of words was examined for both spoken and written items. Access to semantic knowledge was assessed with a range of tests: synonym judgement, word–picture matching and a test of picture semantics. His ability to repeat both words and non-words was tested, as was reading of single words and non-words. Ability to name pictures was also assessed. In addition to this, performance on a range of prespeech tasks was tested. These examined contrasts relevant to the speech signal such as ability to hear pitch change or to detect gaps in signals. However, these are beyond the scope of this article (see Morris et al., 1995, for details).

JS's hearing was tested with pure-tone audiometry. His mean hearing level averaged across the speech frequencies was 20 dB, and so was within the range of normal hearing.

Auditory discrimination tests

JS's ability to hear fine differences between speech sounds was assessed using three versions of a minimal pairs task. These were all taken from the ADA Comprehension Battery (Franklin et al., 1992). In this test battery, all heard items are presented on audio-tape to minimise extraneous clues given inadvertently in the testing situation. The tasks were presented to JS over headphones, on digital audio-tape (DAT). These tests consist of pairs of CVC items and the task is to decide if the two items are the same or different. The manipulation of the different items is in terms of the number of distinctive features by which one of the consonants has been altered. However, the range of change is small: the consonants are only altered by one, or at most two, distinctive features. The response required for JS was simply to point to the written words 'same' or 'different' which were accompanied by a tick or cross.

The ADA CVC non-word test, which again involves a same–different judgement (e.g. /sʌg/, /kʌg/) was given to JS, and he scored 23 out of a possible 40, which does not differ significantly from a chance level of performance (binomial test; score required to exceed chance significantly = 26). The ADA CVC word test (e.g. dug, duck) was also administered, and he scored 25/40, again showing a very impaired level of performance. A third version again involving non-word items was also given. In this test the same items as in the first non-word test were used and an extra manipulation is introduced: the items in each pair are spoken by different voices, one in a female voice, the other in a male voice. JS showed a similar level of difficulty, scoring 23/40.

At the beginning of each of these tests, JS had a practice block of 12 items, which were repeated with feedback until it appeared he had understood what was required in the task. However, it was impossible to be sure he had understood the task, as none of his scores differed significantly from a chance performance. To establish that JS was actually having a problem discriminating between items, rather than with understanding the task itself, a further auditory discrimination task was devised. This used an identical format of deciding if two CVC items (in this case non-words) were the same or different. However, the manipulation of the different items was extended to include a range of difficulty. This test of maximal pairs is available in full (Morris et al., 1995), and examples of the range of conditions are given in Table 10.1. Test items include the one or two distinctive feature changes seen in tests such as the ADA minimal pairs tests described previously, but this is carefully extended through increasing the number of distinctive

Table 10.1 Description of the maximal pairs test, with examples, and detailing JS's errors on taped presentation

Differences	Examples		Errors (maximum = 4)
Three DFs changed, both consonants +vowel change	/sæs/	/bʌb/	0
Two DFs, both consonants + vowel change	/dʌt/	/pæg/	0
One DF, both consonants + vowel change	/tæd/	/keb/	1
Three DFs, both consonants only	/bʌb/	/sʌs/	1
Two DFs, both consonants	/tʌs/	/gʌp/	2
One DF, both consonants	/tet/	/des/	4
Three DFs, either consonant	/seg/	/geg/	4
Two DFs, either consonant	/pʌd/	/gʌd/	4
One DF, either consonant	/gæt/	/gæk/	4
Same	/kig/	/kig/	0

DF, distinctive features.
Taken from Morris et al. (1995).

features changed, changing both phonemes in the pair, and also involving a vowel change in some items. In this way the test involves a range of difficulty, from minimally different items (one distinctive feature change, one consonant) to maximally different items (three distinctive feature change, both consonants and a change of vowel).

On this test JS scored 28/48 which again demonstrates significant difficulty. Consideration of the error pattern (as shown in Table 10.1) clearly demonstrates that JS's difficulty with the task is related to the similarity of the two items. JS had no difficulty, providing the items were sufficiently distinct. However, as the items in the pair became closer, he began to find the task harder, and if the differences were small then JS failed completely. This test of maximal pairs clearly demonstrates that JS was not simply responding at chance performance levels in the discrimination tasks, but was able to complete the task successfully providing the items in a pair are sufficiently different from each other.

As discussed, it is well documented that many patients with word sound deafness are able to benefit from using lip-reading information to process spoken language. To examine whether this assisted JS, several auditorily presented tests were later readministered manipulating the availability of lip-reading information. As all heard tests were presented on audio tape, JS had previously been prevented from having access to information at this level. To consider this issue, two further testing conditions were employed. The first, which will be referred to as a 'free voice' condition, involved the tester saying the words, but JS having to look down or away so that he was unable to see the tester's face. In the second condition JS was encouraged to focus on the tester's face. Before each item was presented, if not already looking at the tester, JS was asked to do so. This will be described as the lip-reading condition.

The non-word version of the minimal pairs task was repeated in these two additional conditions. With a free voice presentation JS scored 23/40 which was an identical score to that obtained from taped presentation. When lip reading was allowed, JS scored 28/40 which suggests that lip reading improves performance, but this trend of improvement does not reach statistical significance. The word version of the minimal pairs task was also repeated, but only in the lip-reading condition. JS scored only 25/40 which did not differ from performance when the items had been presented on tape.

When the maximal pairs test was repeated in the free voice condition JS scored 30/48 which does not significantly differ from his score when the items were presented on tape (28/48). However, when the maximal pairs test was given with lip reading allowed, JS only makes four errors, scoring 44/48 which is a significant increase from performance when the items were presented in the free voice condition (McNemar: $p < 0.01$), or on tape. It is also important to note that the small number of errors made when lip reading was allowed, all occurred for minimally different items, where only one consonant was changed by one or two distinctive features. This confirms the notion that JS is able to discriminate between phonemes providing the contrast is sufficiently large. It seems therefore that allowing JS to use lip-reading information improves his performance if he can already succeed at the task to some extent. The fact that lip reading does not assist him in the minimal pairs tasks may be the result of the fact that the discriminations involved are simply too difficult for him.

Lexical decision tests

JS's ability to access the lexical form of the word was assessed using the ADA lexical decision test. This was presented in both a spoken and a written form, with the spoken items again presented on tape over headphones. In this test a list of real words is heard interspersed with non-word items which only differ from real words in one phoneme, for example, /gɒlt/ (gault), /ˈkæsbərt/ (kaspberry), and the task is to identify the items as real words or non-words. In the auditory presentation JS scored 108/160 which is clearly an impaired performance. When JS read the same items, he scored 133/160, which again is impaired (older normal subjects score 150–160). However, his performance on the written version is superior to that for auditory presentation, and this result is highly significant (McNemar: $p < 0.001$).

Word–picture matching tests

Several tasks were employed to look at JS's ability to access semantics. The ADA word–picture matching task was given. In this the subject sees four pictures and has to select the target from them. The target is either written in the centre of the display, or is heard via audio-tape. One of the distracters bears a semantic and/or phonological relationship to the target. The remaining distracters are unrelated to the target but are related to each other. For example, the target picture 'toast' has a phonological distracter in the picture 'ghost'; the two remaining distracters 'rain' and chain' are phonologically related to each other, but unrelated to the target and its distracter. An example of a semantic distracter would be 'blackboard' with the target 'chalk'.

JS scored 47/66 when the target word was presented auditorily (via headphones). When the target was written, he scored 53/66. Both these scores represent impaired performance compared with that of control subjects (range = 60–66 for the auditory version). The apparent difference between modes of presentation does not reach significance here. Most errors were selection of a semantically related distracter but other error types also occurred.

Synonym judgement tests

Both the auditory and written versions of the ADA synonym judgement task were administered. In this task a pair of words are either heard or read, and a decision is made as to whether the items have similar meanings or not. Pairs of items differ in the frequency with which they occur in the language, and also in how imageable the items are. When the items were presented auditorily, again via DAT and over headphones, JS scored 100/160. His performance is just above chance (binomial test; score required to exceed chance significantly = 96), but significantly impaired. Scores of older control subjects ranged from 146 to 159. His performance when the items were presented in written form was similarly poor, with a score of 109/160 (control subjects range = 148–160).

The PALPA (Kay et al., 1992) written synonym judgement task was also given, and on this JS scored 41/60.

Picture semantics test

The Pyramids and Palm Trees test (Howard and Patterson, 1992) is a test that examines semantic knowledge. The three-picture version was used in an attempt to obtain a measure of semantic ability independent of verbal modalities. In this test one main picture is presented, and the task is to choose from two other pictures which one is related to the main picture. The two possible response pictures always have a fairly close semantic relationship. For example, the main picture 'ink' has related item 'pen', and the distracter item is 'pencil'. JS made seven errors on this task, with the range for normals being 0–3 errors (Howard and Patterson, 1992). Although this difference is small it does give some suggestion that JS has difficulty with semantic tasks, irrespective of modality, i.e. the 'general semantic deficit' as described by Franklin (1989).

Sentence comprehension test

Ability to comprehend spoken sentences was assessed using the Test for Reception of Grammar (TROG: Bishop, 1983). This uses a variety of grammatical constructions organised into 'blocks' of four examples of each type. To pass a block, the subject must be successful at all four items. JS completed 5/20 blocks correctly (normal mean score = 18; Bishop, 1983), with an overall score of 45/80.

Repetition tests

JS's ability to repeat items was assessed using two repetition tasks. The first was the ADA test of word repetition. Items were presented over headphones so that lip-reading information was not available. JS had great difficulty with this task, managing to repeat only one out of the 80 words correctly. Similarly, in a repetition task which involved words and non-words, he correctly repeated only 5/60 words and 1/100 of the non-words. JS's incorrect attempts tended to be fairly distant from the target, and were usually single word neologisms, e.g. 'rent' → /'nekjul/.

Reading tests

Single word reading was assessed using the ADA test of word reading and the ADA non-word reading test. JS was unable to read any item correctly in either of these tests, and again his errors tended to be neologistic, and rarely related to the target item, e.g. beat → /'mɒstɔ/. JS also tended to perseverate these incorrect responses, with minor changes which again were unrelated to the target.

Naming tests

A subset of target pictures from the ADA word-picture matching test which have good naming agreement were given to JS to name. He was able to name 1/16 of these correctly. His errors on the naming task were of a slightly different nature to errors made on reading and repetition tasks. In the naming task they consisted of single word neologisms (as in the reading and repetition tests), but also of multi-item neologistic responses, for example, a picture of a 'horse' produced the attempt – /smɒl ... smɒl ... kɔn/.

Diagnosis of underlying impairments

It was clear from assessment that JS's language difficulties were not of a 'pure' nature. Assessment revealed that he had a specific difficulty with auditory discrimination and was therefore unsuccessful at minimal pairs discrimination tasks. Performance on a test of maximal pairs demonstrated that JS's difficulties were related to how easy it was to discriminate the items. If items were sufficiently distinct from each other, then he was able to perform the task. He had considerable difficulty with other auditorily presented tasks. JS's performance was impaired on lexical decision, word–picture matching and synonym judgement. His performance on the written version of the lexical decision task was superior to performance for the same items when presented in auditory form. However, it was clear that performance was not intact for written stimuli. Access to semantics from the written word, as evidenced by synonym judgement, also showed impairment. The slightly impaired performance on the three-picture version of Pyramids and Palm Trees suggested that this problem with semantics occurs irrespective of modality. It also appeared that JS has an additional problem involving output. His inability to produce even single words in the test situation or in his everyday language suggested that there must be an output level difficulty. To conclude, the assessment findings revealed JS has at least three discrete difficulties with language; an auditory discrimination deficit, a central semantic deficit and a speech production problem.

Therapeutic intervention

Baseline assessments

To ensure that any changes observed following the therapeutic intervention were caused by specific effects of therapy and not by other factors such as spontaneous recovery, JS was reassessed on a subset of the assessments before therapy began. This allowed comparison of the results to ascertain that performance was stable before the therapy began. These tests were repeated 2–4 months after their initial presentation.

JS's performance on the ADA non-word minimal pairs task was assessed at a second point before therapy began. JS scored 23/40 initially compared with 25/40 at the second pre-therapy assessment, demonstrating a stable performance. The ADA test of auditory synonym judgements was also readministered. JS had scored 100/160 when first tested and on subsequent pre-therapy testing he scored 102/160. Thus for both tests JS's performance was stable, and so any improvement seen following therapy could be attributed to the therapy itself.

JS's performance did show some change on the ADA auditory word–picture matching tests. He scored 47/66 on the initial testing and this increased to 56/66 on the second pre-therapy assessment. This difference, though suggestive, does not reach significance (McNemar: $\chi^2 = 3.76, p < 0.1$).

Therapy

Following this detailed assessment a short period of therapy was undertaken with JS. It was decided that initially work would focus on the auditory discrimination deficit. It was felt that working on the output problem was not a possibility as his output skills were so limited. Auditory discrimination was chosen as the initial focus, in preference to the semantic problem, because in terms of order of levels of processing this was an earlier stage, and would be presumed to affect subsequent levels of processing, including access to semantics from the auditory modality. It was also evident from the assessment data that there was a clear starting point for therapy if working on auditory discrimination. Results from the maximal pairs test showed that JS was not simply making his decision based on a chance decision (a guess), but that, if the difference between items was sufficiently large, then he was able to succeed at the task.

An auditory discrimination therapy programme was planned, using phoneme-based contrasts. Tasks involved either discrimination or identification of CV, VC or CVC stimuli, and these were manipulated according to the information obtained during assessment. Therapy tasks began using distracter items which were relatively different from the target. To start with items were chosen that JS had shown some ability to discriminate in assessment. Work moved forward gradually, to involve more similar items. This was closely based on the conditions or levels described in the test of maximal pairs, i.e. in terms of the numbers of distinctive features (voice, place and manner of articulation) that distracter items differed by.

Assessment data had also shown that, providing the task was not too difficult, JS was able to make use of lip-reading information to assist his performance. Tasks were therefore introduced with lip reading encouraged. JS was asked to look at the experimenter before each item was given. This meant that JS had a maximum amount of information initially. As he became successful, then items of the same difficulty were given in the free voice condition, i.e. with JS requested to look away/down. Finally taped stimuli were used.

A variety of tasks was employed in therapy to ensure that JS remained motivated by what was fairly repetitive work. From the selection described four were used per session. This gave the sessions some variety, but also allowed previous success on a task to be built upon. Tasks used can be grouped into those involving consonants (+ schwa), those involving CV and VC combinations, and tasks involving real CVC words. It became evident very early in the therapy sessions that JS did not find the different tasks of equivalent difficulty. This meant that it was not possible to manipulate distracter items in the same way across tasks within a session as JS was successful at some tasks while continuing to find other tasks difficult. This was in spite of the fact that the distracter items differed by the same number of distinctive features. The complexity involved in each task was therefore varied according to JS's success on that particular task. Once he reached around 80% correct on a task, the task complexity was increased either by moving the distracter items closer to the target, or by changing the mode of presentation.

Consonantal-based tasks

Consonant identification. JS was presented with two written letters, and then one of these was presented auditorily (i.e. consonant + schwa), e.g. /pə/ and he had to point to which one he had heard. The distracter item was carefully controlled so that in early sessions it differed by two distinctive features and in later sessions by only one. Task complexity was also manipulated by allowing JS to use lip-reading information initially and then moving to free voice presentation.

Consonant discrimination. Pairs of consonants (+ schwa) were presented auditorily and JS had to decide if they were the same or different. His response was to point to the written word 'same' or 'different'. As in the previous task complexity was increased by both making the distracter items closer to the target and moving from lip reading to free voice presentation.

CV/VC based tasks

CV discrimination. Pairs of consonant–vowel (CV) items were presented and JS had to decide if the pairs sounded the same or different. The vowel used was always /ɑ/ so that JS had to focus only on the consonant phoneme, e.g. /gɑ bɑ/. As before, and as in all discrimination tasks, he was simply required to point to the written word 'same' or 'different'. This task was introduced some way into therapy (session 5) and so distracter items only ever differed by one distinctive feature. Lip-reading information was withdrawn once JS was successful at the task and finally taped presentation was used.

VC discrimination. This task was identical in format to that described above, except the items were vowel–consonant (VC) units, e.g. /ɑʃ ɑf/.

Real word tasks

Auditory word–picture matching. This was considered a core task as it allowed for inclusion of more distracter items than was possible in other tasks and also maintained attention. It was therefore the only task that was used across all sessions. All items were CVC real words. Initially JS was given two pictures and then the target was presented auditorily for him to identify. Once the task concept was clear, three pictures were used on each trial so that two distracter items were present. Initially both phonemes differed by two distinctive features in the distracter items, e.g. bat–can, and this was reduced over sessions to only one distinctive feature changed on one of the consonants, e.g. bowl–mole–pole. Lip reading was allowed at each stage until JS was successful; free voice presentation was then used and finally items were presented on tape over headphones.

Auditory word–written word matching. Two written words were presented and then JS heard one of the items and had to decide which of the written items matched the auditory item. Manipulations were similar to those above, although these proceeded at slightly different rates as JS did not find tasks equivalently difficult.

Auditory–written word judgement. In this task JS was given a *written* CVC word and then *heard* a CVC word. The task was to decide if the item presented auditorily was a correct match or not. Similar manipulations were used as in the word–picture matching task but again the introduction of increased complexity varied across the tasks.

It is important to note that the core assessment tasks (i.e. CVC minimal/maximal pairs) were never used in the therapy period.

To illustrate the tasks and how the degree of complexity was manipulated, examples will be given of a session which occurred close to the start of therapy, and of one from near to the end.

Session 2 consisted of the following:

1. Consonant identification. The distracter item was two distinctive features removed from the target.
2. Consonant discrimination. Where items differed this was by one distinctive feature only.
3. Auditory word–picture matching. Both consonants in the distracter items were changed by one distinctive feature only.
4. Auditory–written word judgement. As with the auditory word–picture task, both consonants in the distracter items differed by one distinctive feature.

Presentation throughout the session was with lip reading allowed, except in the consonant identification task, where for the second half of the items JS was requested to look down to introduce the idea of free voice presentation to him.

Session 12 (i.e. the final session) consisted of the following:

1. Auditory–written word judgement. In this the incorrect items differed by only one distinctive feature in the initial consonant only.
2. Auditory word–written word matching. Again, distracter items differed by only one distinctive feature on the initial consonant.
3. VC discrimination. Where items differed this was by one distinctive feature only.
4. Auditory word–picture matching. Two distracter items were used with the final consonant changed by only one or two distinctive features from the target.

Presentation throughout the session was via tape, over headphones, except for the consonant identification. The single consonant tasks were never presented on tape as this made the tasks almost impossible.

Whereas in the assessment phase JS had been given no feedback (other than on practice items) within the therapy sessions JS was given immediate and accurate feedback on every attempt. If he was incorrect, then the item was repeated. The degree of difficulty was reduced in the repetition so that, for example, if the item had been presented on tape, then on repetition the item was presented in the free voice condition. If after repetition JS was still incorrect or expressed some uncertainty the item was repeated by the therapist with attention being drawn to the changed phoneme by the use of 'cued articulation' (Passy, 1990). This is a system of hand signs which represent phonemes and allows demonstration of the voice, place and manner of articulation. The use of cues was never overtly introduced or discussed with JS. They were merely used as a way of highlighting the relevant part of the item he should focus on and to avoid a simple repetition of an item he was clearly having difficulty with. On occasions JS's attention was also drawn to the relevant contrast verbally, e.g. by discussing noisy versus quiet sounds to highlight a voiced/voiceless distinction. As no measure was taken of the effectiveness of the cues it is difficult to know if JS was making any use of this metaphonological knowledge.

When JS was corrected he often attempted to repeat the item, particularly in the real word tasks. Repetition was never requested but if he did repeat and was incorrect in his attempt (as was often the case) then he was corrected.

JS was seen in his own home for 12 sessions of therapy, on a twice-weekly basis. Sessions lasted around 40 minutes, but this depended on JS's level of concentration on a particular day.

Post-therapy results

Directly following this 6-week period of therapy, JS's performance was reassessed on a number of the tests which had been administered before therapy started. Baseline measurements had been taken, and no significant change in his performance was seen across a 4-month period. Therefore, any difference seen in these pre- and post-therapy measures must be attributable to the therapeutic intervention, and not to spontaneous recovery.

There is a problem that improved scores on re-test could just reflect fluctuating performance (e.g. attention, motivation) rather than actual improvement, a point made by Weniger (1990). However, this would not apply across the whole series of tests. In reality, assessment yields a collection of results, and it is within this pattern or context that any one score is considered.

Auditory discrimination tests

Performance on both minimal and maximal pairs discrimination tasks was reassessed following therapy. JS's performance on the non-word minimal pairs tests was readministered in both the free voice and lip-reading conditions. In the free voice condition, pre-therapy JS had scored 23/40. Post-therapy his score increased to 32/40. This improvement is statistically significant (McNemar: $p < 0.05$). When lip reading was allowed, there was a trend of improvement with his score increasing from 28/40 to 36/40, although in this instance statistical significance is not reached (McNemar: $p < 0.1$). The ADA word minimal pairs test (taped version) was also readministered. JS scored 25/40 pre-therapy compared with 36/40 following the therapy period which is a significant improvement (McNemar: $p < 0.01$). Table 10.2 gives a summary of the results for the auditory discrimination tests in percentage correct form.

Table 10.2 Percentage of correct responses before and after therapy and at the 7-month follow-up for the discrimination tasks

	Assessment		
	Before therapy	After therapy	Maintenance
Non-word minimal pairs	58 (FV)	80 (FV)	70 (FV)
	70 (LR)	90 (LR)	87 (LR)
Word minimal pairs (taped presentation)	62	90	80
Maximal pairs	58 (tape)	94 (tape)	81 (tape)
	62 (FV)	79 (FV)	81 (FV)
	92 (LR)	90 (LR)	92 (LR)

FV = free voice presentation; LR = lip-reading presentation.

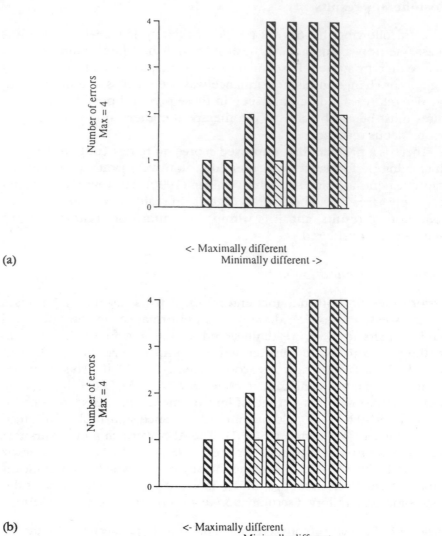

(a)

<- Maximally different
Minimally different ->

(b)

<- Maximally different
Minimally different ->

Figure 10.2 Comparison of JS's errors on the maximal pairs test ▨ before and ▨ after therapy: (a) tape; (b) free voice.

Comparable improvement was also seen in the maximal pairs test. When the items were presented on tape, JS scored 45/48 post-therapy, compared with 28/48 pre-therapy, which is highly significant (McNemar: $p < 0.001$). In the free voice presentation his score increases from 30 to 38/48, again reaching significance (McNemar: $p < 0.05$). As his performance on this test when lip reading was allowed was so close to ceiling before therapy, there was little possibility of improvement. In fact, JS scored very similarly pre- and post-therapy on the lip-reading version, scoring 44 and 43/48 respectively.

Consideration of the error pattern on the maximal pairs test reveals that there is not only a general reduction in the number of errors being made. Figure 10.2 shows the distribution of errors for (a) taped presentation and (b) free voice presentation. It can be seen that following therapy JS made few errors on the maximally different conditions. JS's ability to discriminate had improved in relation to how distinct the items were.

Lexical decision tests

The auditory version of the ADA lexical decision test was readministered as it was feasible that some improvement might be seen following therapy in this auditorily presented task. Before therapy JS scored 108/160 compared with 120/160 following the therapy period. A trend toward improvement is seen but this does not reach significance (McNemar: $\chi^2 = 2.24$).

Word–picture matching tests

The ADA auditory word–picture matching test was repeated following the therapy period. This was the only test where a suggestion of increased score (non-significant) had been seen across the baseline period. JS scored 61/66 following therapy compared with baselines of 47 and 56 respectively. Although there is a trend towards improved score in the pre- to post-therapy measures, the fact that the score was not completely stable pre-therapy makes it difficult to interpret.

Synonym judgement tests

At the two baseline (pre-therapy) measures JS had scored 100 and 102/160 on the ADA auditory synonym judgement task. As with the auditory lexical decision it was possible that the improvement in discrimination tasks might result in some improvement in other auditorily presented tasks, such as auditory synonym judgement. Post-therapy JS was correct for 116/160 of the items, showing a similar trend of improvement as for the auditory lexical decision. Again this trend does not reach statistical significance.

The PALPA written synonym judgement task was also readministered following therapy. No improvement was expected on this test as therapy was purely auditory and did not involve semantics. Pre-therapy JS scored 41/60 and obtained a similar score post-therapy of 38/40. No change was therefore seen in the pre- and post-therapy scores, although his poor performance allows sufficient room for any improvement to be seen. Table 10.3 provides a summary of the pre- and post-therapy results across the range of lexical tests.

Table 10.3 Correct responses pre–hyp and post-therapy for the lexical tests

	Pre-therapy assessment	Post-therapy assessment
ADA Auditory Lexical Decision (160 items)	67%	75%
ADA Auditory Synonyms (160 items)	62% (baseline 1) 64% (baseline 2)	72%
PALPA Written Synonyms (60 items)	68%	63%
ADA Auditory word–picture matching (66 items)	71% (baseline 1) 85% (baseline 2)	92%
TROG (free voice presentation) (80 items)	57%	66%
ADA Word Repetition (80 items)	1%	12%
ADA Naming Test (score out of 16)	1	2

Sentence comprehension test

The Test for Reception of Grammar was readministered with free voice presentation; JS passed five blocks both before and after. His total score increased from 45/80 to 55/80 but this trend towards improvement does not reach significance. This is a similar pattern to the other auditorily presented tasks where a suggestion of improvement is seen that does not achieve significance.

Repetition tests

Pre-therapy JS only managed correctly to repeat 1/80 of the items from the ADA word repetition test. Following the therapy period JS was correct for 10/80 of the items, which is a significantly different score (McNemar: $p < 0.02$). Of course, any interpretation of such a result must be made with caution as a result of the very small number of correct items in both instances.

Naming tests

It was important to look at performance following therapy on another task involving output. The improvement seen in the word repetition test may have been the result of a concurrent improvement in speech production which was not the focus of therapy. JS was therefore again asked to name the items that he had named before the therapy period. JS correctly named 1/16 items pre-therapy compared with 2/16 post-therapy. Performance on the naming test therefore showed no change in contrast to the improvement in repetition skills.

Following the therapy period both JS's wife and daughter commented on the fact that they felt JS was more able to concentrate on what was being said to him. JS appeared to focus more consistently on the speaker than he had previously done. His expressive language did not seem to have shown any change in the everyday communication setting.

Summary of therapy results

Results from post-therapy assessment show a clear improvement in auditory discrimination which was the area of language processing targeted during therapy. JS's performance on both minimal and maximal pairs discrimination tasks showed significant change when reassessed following the therapy period. Improvement generalised across the processing level being worked upon (i.e. auditory discrimination). This was shown by the fact that improvement was not item-specific. Items used in assessment did not form part of the therapy materials.

We hoped that this improvement in auditory discrimination would have led to improvement in other auditorily presented tasks, so showing generalisation to other associated tasks. Every auditory test that was presented post-therapy showed an improved score: auditory lexical decision, auditory synonym judgements and the TROG. Unfortunately, the improvement did not reach statistical significance for any of the tests. However, the general trend of improvement in these tests is in contrast to the clear lack of any change pre- to post-therapy seen in the written synonym judgement task.

The other task which showed statistically significant improvement was word repetition. This is presumably a result of the improved discrimination skills, allowing JS to analyse somewhat more efficiently the auditory input to be repeated. If the improvement in repetition was the result of a change in his speech production, then the other task involving speech production (i.e. naming) would also be expected to have improved, and this showed no change.

The possibility that effects seen following therapy were caused by spontaneous recovery was eliminated by the baseline assessment data presented earlier. Another possible explanation of why significant improvement occurred is that there was a general response to treatment or contact with the therapist. Byng and Coltheart (1986) point out that therapy studies need to demonstrate that improvement seen is specifically as a result of the treatment given. This is clearly demonstrated for JS because improvement is only seen on a subset of tests and these are the ones that would have been predicted to improve given the therapeutic procedures involved.

Maintenance of improvement

More than 7 months after this initial stage of therapy JS was reassessed on some of the tests previously administered. Only the results of the retesting on the auditory discrimination tests will be considered here because, following the period of therapy reported here, JS was involved in a second period of written semantic therapy. Any consideration of semantic level tasks at this follow-up would therefore be affected by this intervening period of semantic therapy.

Mixed results were obtained for the various versions of the ADA minimal pairs test. On free voice presentation of the ADA test of non-word minimal pairs JS had scored 23/40 pre-therapy. This had shown significant change when reassessed post-therapy (post-therapy score = 32/40). However, at this 7-month post-therapy interval JS's score dropped to 28/40. Although this still suggests an improved score, the difference between the scores pre-therapy and at 7 months' follow-up is not significantly different. On lip-reading presentation JS scored 28/40 pre-therapy and at the 7-month follow-up scored 35/40 which is a significant change (McNemar: $p < 0.05$).

The ADA word minimal pairs test was also repeated. JS had scored 25/40 pre-therapy. At the 7-month follow-up the score was 32/40 (compared with 36/40 immediately following therapy). Again the same trend of an increased score post-therapy remains, but does not reach significance. Table 10.3 shows details of the three sets of results.

The picture for the maximal pairs test is clearer. JS's score for the test presented with lip reading allowed shows no change from pre-therapy to the 7-month follow-up, which is expected given the high pre-therapy score of 44/48. When the items were presented on tape JS scored 28/48 pre-therapy compared with 39/48 at the 7-month follow-up assessment, and so the improvement in performance remains significant (McNemar: $p < 0.01$). Similarly when free voice presentation was used JS scored 30/48 pre-therapy and 39/48 at the 7-month reassessment, again maintaining a significant improvement (McNemar: $p < 0.01$). Table 10.2 provides a summary of JS's performance at this 7-month follow-up compared with pre- and post-therapy scores.

Although the picture is mixed for the minimal pairs tests, all scores appear to have remained elevated, although significance is not always reached. However, for both versions of the maximal pairs test (tape and free voice) the improvement seen immediately following the therapy period was maintained at the 7-month follow-up. It can be seen that the improvement in tests of auditory discrimination in the immediate post-therapy assessment appears to have been maintained over a period of over 7 months (over 8 months since the actual end of the therapeutic intervention). In this interval JS received no further therapy which focused at this level, but was involved in a short period of therapy which focused on written semantics.

Discussion

JS's language abilities were assessed in detail using a cognitive–neuropsychological approach. This allowed the identification of three areas of deficit: auditory discrimination, semantics and a speech production problem. It was felt appropriate to focus on the auditory discrimination deficit (the word sound deafness) initially during therapy. Further pre-therapy assessment showed that he was able to make discriminations providing items were sufficiently distinct. The effect of lip-reading information on his performance was examined and it was found that JS's ability to discriminate sounds was improved if he was encouraged to look at the tester's face.

Following a short period of therapy JS's performance on a subset of the tests was measured. Improvement was seen across the range of auditory discrimination tests, though not all reached statistical significance. This improvement was not item-specific. The items and test format were never used in the therapy situation. Improvement had therefore generalised across the level of processing that therapy had focused on, i.e. auditory discrimination. In any future study it would be advantageous to look at item-specific effects. This can be achieved by splitting test items into two groups, one that is treated and the other not. Although not always functionally useful to treat a patient on a specific set of items, it is often informative regarding what is occurring in therapy (Howard et al., 1985; Byng and Coltheart, 1989).

The improvement seen in JS's language was specific to his auditory discrimination, which was the area of focus of therapy. There was possibly some generalisation to other auditorily presented tasks, but this was not part of some general improvement unrelated to therapy; written synonym judgements and naming showed no trace of any change. The improvement was the result of a fairly short period of therapy (12 sessions) and demonstrates that it is essential to pinpoint the underlying deficit(s) in detail during the assessment phase, allowing therapy to be targeted specifically.

It should be noted that all scores at the 7-month follow-up assessment were consistently lower than when JS was assessed immediately following therapy. The implications of this are that perhaps this patient would have benefited from more than a single period of therapy. Performance may well have been aided by a subsequent therapy interval which allowed 'revision' of the work done earlier.

JS shows that a specific treatment programme such as this is not only useful for patients who have a pure, isolated deficit. JS presented with severe multilevel aphasia and thorough assessment allowed identification of three (presumably separate) underlying deficits. As Wilson and Patterson (1990) state it is only necessary that 'the specificity of the treatment should match the specificity of the deficit' (p. 248).

The therapeutic procedure outlined in this chapter could be of use with any patient identified (by assessment) as having difficulties with auditory discrimination tasks. This is likely to occur in the context of additional language deficits. The speed of progression through therapy will depend, as is always the case, on the individual patients' responses to treatment. The degree of difficulty should be built up gradually, and increased as the patient becomes successful at the task.

Whether this type of therapy will be of use to other patients who have difficulties with auditory material (but not necessarily difficulties with auditory discrimination tests) must be the subject of further study. For example, it would be interesting to examine if the improvement seen was a specific effect of the phoneme-based therapy or was the result of more general attentional factors. It will be important to attempt to replicate the findings of this therapy study with other patients. It is necessary to examine which therapeutic procedures are appropriate to which patients and replication studies offer a possibility to explore this. It would be of interest in a replication study to look particularly at issues of generalisation to other related areas of processing, such as performance on auditory semantic tasks, as the results for JS are somewhat ambiguous.

Performance of the patient, BCR, presented by Best and Howard (1994) was reassessed to look at change in her language status irrespective of any intervention. Changes seen reflect spontaneous recovery. Assessment of BCR's language deficit had started very early post-onset, at around 1 month. BCR showed improvement in both a test of word–picture matching with phonological distracters, and on the TROG. BCR's performance on naming did not change and Best and Howard suggest therefore that BCR's recovery was confined to a specific deficit: her word sound deafness.

In conclusion, using a cognitive–neuropsychological approach to assess this patient with multilevel problems allowed identification of the separate components of his language difficulties. This is in direct contrast to Kertesz's (1990) claim that cognitive–psychological methods applied to single cases 'almost always involves recovered or moderate to mildly affected patients . . .'. Although this may have been true at the time of Kertesz's paper (1990, p. 98), there seems to be no basis to his suggestion that:

> . . . this methodology is often not applicable to the majority of severely affected patients with poor output and little comprehension for whom diagnosis, prognosis, and therapy are even more important than the mild 'testable' subject.

The data presented here show that detailed assessment which allows a hypothesis to be formed regarding the underlying deficit(s) can subsequently be used to plan specific therapeutic intervention. The use of baseline and post-therapy measurements allows us to demonstrate that any specific effects seen are the result of the therapy, and allow the necessary evaluation of the efficacy of therapy. The results show that JS's auditory discrimination difficulties improved as a result of a relatively short period of assessment-motivated therapy.

Chapter 11
Aphasia: conversation analysis of a non-fluent aphasic person

RAY WILKINSON

Background

Introduction

The patient's language abilities in conversation are obviously of central importance for the aphasiologist; although in theory it is possible that some patients could find making a speech or giving a lecture their main problem, in practice difficulties in talking with others will be the most distressing aspect of aphasic communication problems for most patients and their families.

Recently the methodology and empirical findings of a body of work known as conversation analysis (CA) have begun to be applied in aphasiology (e.g. Milroy and Perkins, 1992; Lesser and Milroy, 1993; Ferguson, 1994). This chapter presents a case study of how CA was of use in the assessment of a particular patient's language abilities in conversation and includes some discussion of its relation to other assessment approaches and some implications for therapy.

Case history

At the time of assessment the patient (P) was a 44-year-old man who had suffered a cerebrovascular accident (CVA) in the region of the left cerebral artery 5 years previously. There were no hearing or vision problems. P had a right hemiparesis and walked with the aid of a stick. He lived independently.

P was attending speech and language therapy for assessment by a therapist ('T') with a view to starting a new period of therapy after a break of several months. He agreed to have the session videoed. The session consisted of a 15-minute conversation between the therapist and patient followed by a number of assessments such as picture description and comprehension tests.

The conversation was analysed as part of a project looking at aphasic language in interaction. In the second half of the conversation, T initiated the subject of flower arranging (one of P's hobbies). This led to an attempt by P to tell T about something that had happened to him. It was obvious from the video that the telling proved problematic, both for P in telling it and for the therapist in understanding it, and both commented on these difficulties at the end of the conversation. However, even on repeated viewings of the video it was difficult to grasp exactly 'what was going on' here.

It was therefore decided to transcribe this 5-minute section and use some concepts from conversation analysis to examine this fragment of talk (Schegloff, 1987a) to be able to get more insight into the problems that aphasia was causing in this interaction.

Conversation analysis

There is no space here to present either an overview of CA's methodology and findings (see, for example, Atkinson and Heritage, 1984; Heritage, 1989) or to explore in any detail its significance for aphasiology. Discussion will be limited to those points that will be of use in the analysis of the aphasic data and to the methodological implications that arise from the analysis.

CA emerged as part of the wider sociological movement of ethnomethodology which investigates how social order and social interaction are constituted through the common sets of procedures used by society's members. CA has given attention to the procedures used by participants in constituting talk-in-interaction (this term is used in preference to conversation because CA is not only interested in casual conversations: Schegloff, 1987a).

Interest in this method of studying spoken language in its natural environment (i.e. interaction) has been shown by both linguists and subsequently aphasiologists. Levinson (1983), for example, has used CA as an empirical method to examine questions of linguistic pragmatics which were previously analysed by philosophers such as Grice and Searle. More recently linguists have adopted a CA approach in other areas as well as pragmatics. Ford (1993), for example, has used it as a framework for the study of aspects of grammar and Taylor (1992) has discussed CA in relation to theories of language understanding.

Sequential context

One obvious difference between CA and other approaches in aphasiology is CA's view of the relationship between language and context (Goodwin and Duranti, 1992). Rather than starting from the decontextualised word or sentence and then trying to generalise these findings to some situated context of language use, CA starts with recordings of real-life talk-in-interaction and analyses the procedures that the participants are using to make sense of this talk. The primary unit of analysis is the turn and the turn within the sequence (Atkinson and Heritage, 1984) and turns can be made up of one or more utterances or 'turn constructional units' (Sacks et al., 1974).

From a CA perspective, context is not primarily something external to the talk (such as the attributes of the participants or the spatial location of the talk); what is most important is the sequential organisation of the talk itself (Atkinson and Heritage, 1984; Schiffrin, 1994). Whatever is said will be said within some sequential context of preceding talk and action.

Each utterance is thus constitutive of context and it is primarily by orienting to the utterance's context, its sequential location, that participants make sense of it (Schegloff and Sacks, 1973). Each utterance is both 'context shaped' and 'context renewing' (Heritage, 1989). It is context shaped because it will be understood in relation to the preceding talk (particularly the immediately preceding utterance). It is context renewing because it constitutes the immediate context for the following utterance; indeed it projects what may appropriately follow it. A question, for example, projects or 'sequentially implicates' an answer as the appropriate next utterance.

This relationship between an utterance and its sequential context provides a resource for the recipient to make sense of it; recipients analyse an utterance in terms of 'why that now?' (Schegloff and Sacks, 1973). Speakers are therefore accountable to construct their utterances with this in mind if they are to be understood. Some of the ways in which this is problematic for an aphasic speaker will be explored in the analysis section below.

Trouble sources and repairs

A basic building block of talk's sequential organisation is a series of two turns, a current turn and a next turn, with each next turn becoming a current turn as it is started (Schegloff, 1979a). After each current turn there is the possibility that the next turn by the other interactant will take the form of a repair, most commonly a repair initiation. 'Other-initiated repairs', otherwise termed 'next turn repair initiations' (NTRIs), can take several forms such as 'what?' or various forms of repetition (Schegloff et al., 1977). Next turns which do not initiate repair are therefore treated by interactants as displaying that the previous turn has been understood at least adequately for present purposes (Schegloff, 1982).

NTRI turns carry out two functions simultaneously. First, they display that this speaker is having difficulty in dealing with something the other interactant has said. The trouble source is often in the immediately preceding turn, although it can be something said earlier. Second, they leave it to the speaker of the trouble source to carry out the repair. An example is the following (from Schegloff et al., 1977 – simplified; see Appendix for transcription conventions).

Example 1
B: well I'm working through the Amfat Corporation.
A: the who?
B: Amfah Corporation. it's a holding company.

Here B's turn is followed by a turn by A which locates a part of B's turn as a trouble source and initiates repair on it. B completes the repair in the following turn.

This three-way relationship of the trouble source, the repair initiation and the repair completion has several permutations which have been described in the CA literature. The relationship between a trouble source and its repair is obviously of interest in the analysis of aphasic data where there are so many potential trouble sources. Three sorts of trouble source–repair relationships which will be referred to in the analysis of the aphasic data will be described here.

First, in non-aphasic interaction there is a preference for speakers to initiate and complete repair themselves on any potential trouble source in their turn (Schegloff et al., 1977). This means in effect that, in talk-in-interaction, troubles are sorted out in the current turn, leaving the next turn free to carry on with the topic of discussion rather than deal with repair. The following is an example (from Schegloff et al., 1977).

Example 2
N: she was givin' me a:ll the people that were go:ne this yea:r I mean
    this quarter y' [know
J: [yeah

In this example N displays that he did not mean 'this year' and self repairs to 'this quarter'. The following turn is taken up not with a repair of the previous turn but with J's contribution to the conversation.

Another pattern is where the speaker initiates repair on a trouble source in his own turn but has trouble completing the repair and it is left to the other interactant to make a candidate repair (as in the following from Schegloff, 1979a).

Example 3
B: she bought a chest of drawers from uhm (4.0) what's the gal's name?

just went back to Michigan (2.0) Helen uhm
A: oh I know who you mean, (1.0) Brady– Brady
B: yeah! Helen Brady.

Word-finding difficulties are a common form of this pattern of repair and this pattern is therefore common in aphasic talk.

A third pattern is where a speaker (interactant A) realises that the other interactant (B) has misunderstood a previous turn of A's. A then initiates repair on the trouble source in his earlier turn. This is termed 'third position repair' (Schegloff, 1987b, 1992). The following is an example (from Schegloff, 1987b).

Example 4
A: which ones are closed, an' which ones are open.
B: (pointing to map) most of 'em. This, this, [this, this
A: [I don't mean on the
                                             shelters, I mean on
                                             the roads.
B: oh!

Here A realises that B has misunderstood what 'ones' is referring to and initiates and carries out repair in the following turn.

The notion of repair is different from that of 'correction'. Utterances that contain what could be seen as errors or omissions are frequently not treated as sources of trouble and repair is not initiated in the following turn. Rather it seems that in non aphasic talk recipients are commonly able to make sense of these sorts of utterances as in the following example from Schegloff et al. (1977).

Example 5.
Avon Lady: and for ninety-nine cents uh especially in, Rapture, and the Au Coeur which is the newest fragrances, uh that is a very good value.
Customer: uh huh

The application of these insights to one piece of aphasic data will be the subject of the next section. Other CA findings will be brought into the analysis as necessary.

Analysis

Data collection

Before the session T was instructed not to make any particular changes to the usual pattern of the session for the benefit of the recording. The

conversation was to have no preconceived format or topics but rather
was to be the sort of 'social chat' that speech and language therapists
generally have with patients at the start of a session. The video recorder
was set up in a corner of the room and left to run during the session.

Transcription

[for transcription notation see Appendix]

```
1   T   how about your flower arranging?
2       (.) °is [that uh°
3   P           [uh actually: (.) still: (.) only now and then,
4   T   [mm hm
5   P   [but uh:m uh:m (0.5) I think me and more more:, (1.8)
6       uh:m >I mean< no. only now and then
7       but maybe (.) °ah: right!° maybe (.) not plain
8       but uh speckled and (.) much (.) better
9   T   [mm.
10  P   [and also (.) uh flowers much (0.2) pretty or something
11      [>you know?< but uh:          ]
12  T   [oh right! sounds interesting.]
13  P   >I mean< maybe maybe not. I [don't know] you know.
14  T                               [right     ]
15      so the speckled flowers is that uhm something [you'd ( ) ]
16  P                                                 [n–no      ]
17      but no uh:m (0.3) vase.
18  T   oh::!=
19  P   =but not uh (.) uh:m (.) uh: (1.6) just ordinary
20      but uh: speckled [also in–] ins [ide ( )   ]
21  T                    [mm      ]     [you used] to paint them
22      didn't you (.) the– [the] vases any [way so that]
23  P                       [yes]           [right right ]
24      yes.
25  T   y [es        an–] an extension of that.
26  P     [>yeah right<]
27      yes
28  T   righ: [t.
29  P         [right.
30  T   sounds good.
31  P   °mm°
32  T   so do you still go (.) and get flowers from a market on
33      a, (.)
34  P   [yes] uh but uh: uh actually Christmas last l–uh last
35  T   [( )]
36  P   time.=
```

37 T   =mm [hm,
38 P   [so
39 T   right.
40 P   so uh:m, (0.5) uh >but maybe< uh:m
41   right. (0.5) uhm very soon right?
42   uh:m I think uh:m (1.0) >three weeks<
43   then (.) one more time, (.) uh:m
44 T   ((nods))
45 P   because me (.) after stroke,(.) and uh no car
46 T   ri:ght
47 P   okay right?
48 T   yes.
49 P   and uh:m uh:m last (0.3) m– uh year
50   (.) and uhm: >very famous< uh::m, (1.8) uh:m
51   not England but (2.0) °hm° (0.8) °terrible° (0.8)
52   uh:m (4.0) I think (4.0) uh:m (3.0)
53   °not England° but (2.0) °not Scotland° but (.)
54   Wales right?
55 T   °right°
56 P   and uh one:,(1.5) °oh God almighty° (0.8) one (1.0)
57   uh:m (3.0) ↓town.
58 T   ((nods))
59 P   uh:m (.) and >obviously< uh:m people (0.5) uh
60   every (.) part of the (.) country.
61 T   mm hm=
62 P   =uh:m and >sorry< and uh:m (2.0)
63   an- and (3.0) car or van or something (.)
64   what the word? >I mean< what the (1.0) uh:m (1.0)
65   very famous or very, (3.5)
66 T   are these this people round the country go to somewhere
67   in Wales, with (.) are they=
68 P   =or [yes   ]
69 T   [what] –what do they go there for?
70 P   hh [right   ]
71 T   [is that] to [something] to do with driving?
72 P   [uh:m   ]
73   yes [right right]
74 T   [for people] who (.) dis [abled?   ]
75 P   [no >no] no no.<
76 T   no?
77 P   no ↓ordinary that,
78 T   right
79 P   uhm:,
80 T   for some kind of car racing. (.) ()
81 P   >no no no< (.) >no no no no no no<

82   this uh:m very ordinary.
83 T   ((nods))
84 P   uh::m (0.8) uh:m (0.8) °God almighty° (0.5)
85 T   °somewhere in° (.)
86   is it [round] Cardiff
87 P   [Wales]
88   ye [s
89 T   [Wales?
90 P   yes uhm:: (2.0) n:o (1.2) uh:m hh
91   anyway that uh last (.) year.
92 T   mm hm
93 P   in that uh place and me right?
94 T   >you went< [there right]
95 P   [right right]
96   but uh that time actually no and me ↓failed.right?
97 T   was this you failed,
98   you tried to take a dr- a te- a [test, a driving test,or]
99 P   [yes right right yes yes]
100 T   [right]
101 P   [but] I think either (.) uh:m:,(.) high up >you know<
102   and finally ↓no
103   because me, uh after stroke and uh (1.5) three or four
104   different times and fainting ri [ght?]
105 T   [right]
106 P   and uh: (.) uhm: (0.3) basically I think uh: (0.5)
107   high up and sorry, f↓no.
108 T   ri: [ght]
109 P   [but] maybe this time.
110 T   [( )   ]
111 P   [but now] also me uh different now uh London instead.
112   and sp- this time, uh special:
113   not ordinary people but strokes or something=
114 T   =mm hm. so this is where they adapt cars
115   [so that you can drive them]
116 P   [( ) right right right   ]
117 T   [right right right   ]
118 P   [right right   ]
119 T   yes
120 P   right
121 T   oh right [( )]
122 P   [so] maybe this time you know.=
123 T   =so you'll have a set of wheels and be a lot more mobile
124   then [t– t–] to drive around.
125 P   [yes yes]
126   yes

127 T   [right]
128 P   [right] right
129 T   well I'll keep my fingers crossed for you.
130 P   right.
131 T   so is that coming up fairly soon
132   that [(you're going to)]
133 P   [uh three weeks   ]
134 T   three weeks right right

Analysis of aphasic talk

Introduction

Although various kinds of analysis could be useful for this piece of talk, examination here will be limited to an analysis applying insights from CA. There are two reasons for this: first, this approach appears to offer a way in to the analysis of aphasic language as it actually occurs in interactive talk. Although this area is of central concern to aphasiologists, most of the current tools of linguistic and psycholinguistic analysis available have emerged from the study of idealised and decontextualised individual words and sentences (Heritage, 1984a), and are often difficult to apply to an actual piece of data. Second, this sequential analysis is useful for discovering the order that underlies even apparently disorderly bits of talk and seems particularly appropriate in examining this piece of data which appears rather messy on the first approach.

The analysis will proceed in the following way. There will be examination of three points in the talk where it becomes clear that the talk has become problematic for the participants. These are termed 'trouble A', 'trouble B' and 'trouble C' respectively. 'Trouble B' and 'trouble C' are treated together because they become entwined in the interaction. The analysis will concentrate on the question of why these problems have occurred in the talk here, i.e. what aspects of P's talk have been the source of the trouble that has necessitated repair. This has implications for therapy because if the trouble sources can be identified, this information can be used in planning a therapy programme. The methods used to initiate repair and the success of the repairs will also be examined. The analysis is summarised at the end of the section.

Some of the implications of a CA approach for assessment and planning of therapy are discussed in the final section.

Trouble A. At lines 16 and 17 it becomes clear that T has misunderstood P's talk:

```
15 T   so the speckled flowers is that uhm something [you'd ( ) ]
16 P                                                [n–no       ]
17       but no uh:m (0.3) vase.
18 T   oh::!=
```

P, realising during line 15 that he has been misunderstood, initiates a third position repair by interrupting T's turn with 'no'. He then is able to use his linguistic resources to complete the repair. First, he provides the word 'vase' which, by contrasting with 'flowers', locates and addresses the problematic understanding. Second, at lines 19 and 20 P 're-says' the misunderstood utterance of lines 7 and 8 making the sense clearer by adding to 'speckled' the location 'inside' which in this context distinguishes 'vase' from 'flowers'.

The repair is successful in that T shows understanding of it in two ways. First, by the use of 'oh!' in line 18 T displays that whereas she was previously misinformed, she is now informed (see Heritage, 1984b and Example 4). Second, T constructs her turn at lines 21–22 so as to display this new understanding:

```
21 T   you used to paint them
22       didn't you (.) the– the vases anyway
```

The source of T's initial misunderstanding is evident earlier in the talk. In lines 7 and 8 P has described something using the terms 'not plain but uh speckled'. T uses the common procedure for making sense of utterances in talk which is to analyse the utterance in terms of 'why that now?'. The obvious noun or noun phrase which these adjectives belong with is 'flowers' understood from T's initiation of the topic 'flower arranging' in line 1 (they also do not appear to refer to anything in the topic preceding this one which had concerned learning English at night class).

The problem here appears to be one of 'recipient design' (Sacks et al.,1974). P does not appear to realise that the way in which he is designing his turn is likely to make him misunderstood. Although one way to characterise the problem here would be in terms of a 'missing word', it is worth distinguishing this problem from a word-finding difficulty. First, there is no sign in lines 7–8 either that P is searching for a word or that he feels the need to do so. Second, it can be seen that when P realises his utterance was misunderstood, he is able to access the word 'vase' (line 17).

Troubles B and C. Troubles B and C both occur in the extended 'telling sequence' which begins at line 41 and ends at lines 125–126 and both become temporarily entwined at lines 69 and following. These two troubles and their relationship to the overall structure of this piece of talk will be analysed in the order in which they appear in the talk.

Trouble B is the long word-finding difficulty that starts in line 50. At this point in P's telling he has begun to tell about something which occurred in the past:

```
49  P    and uh:m uh:m last (0.3) m– uh year
50       (.) and uhm: >very famous<
```

Following line 49 a description of what happened last year is due. In line 50, however, P initiates a repair and it is clear from this repair that the description is the source of trouble. Although the description projected in line 49 does not appear where it is due, in its place P is able to give some information about what it involves; not only does it involve something that is very famous (i.e. something T may well know and therefore something that she may be able to help P search for) but also it is a specific name, presumably either a person or place. In line 51 P is able to be more specific:

```
51  P    not England but . . .
```

P has thus been able to display that the word search is for a place name. The method involved in the search is indirect; P at this stage is unable to access not only the name of the specific place, but also the name of the country it is in. The method employed therefore is to name a country which is not the desired name and then to work towards the target. Thus P is able to display in line 54 that it is in Wales and in line 57 that it is a specific town in Wales. Other pieces of information about the place are given in lines 59–60 and 63.

Although P has been able to give a good deal of information about the word that is being searched for, at this stage T does not try to guess to complete the repair. There are obvious reasons for this. As was noted above, there is a preference in talk for speakers to self-repair if they are able to do so. Thus while P is showing progress towards the target, T may be giving him a chance of successfully completing the repair. As Lesser and Milroy (1993) note, therapists often appear to encourage patients to self-repair even if it takes some time.

In this case, however, an extra factor is involved in that it becomes clear that T is unable to help. At lines 64 and 65 P displays that he may need help from T to complete the repair. The use of a question here such as 'what the word?' in line 64 is commonly heard by other interactants as an indication that it is relevant for them to intervene in the search (see Example 3 above). When T does intervene at line 66, however, she displays that she is having difficulty in supplying suggestions for the word search:

66 T   are these this people round the country go to somewhere
67   in Wales, with (.) are they=
68 P   =or [yes]
69 T   [what] –what do they go there for?
70 P   hh right

In line 69 T displays that she is unable to help to complete the current word search because she has another problem in understanding
P's talk which will have to be resolved first: she has not understood the
previous part of P's telling sequence in which this problematic report
of the past event is embedded. The insinuation is that this second trouble (trouble C) will have to be resolved before T will have enough
information to help complete the repair of the first trouble (trouble B).
    T's questions at lines 69, 71, 74 and 80 locate the source of her
understanding difficulty to be P's utterances at lines 41–48. To analyse
what it is that has made these utterances problematic, it is necessary to
discuss the construction of extended turns in general before specifically analysing the extended turn in this talk.
    The structure of extended turns (i.e. turns of more than one utter-
ance) has been analysed in several CA studies. Schegloff (1982), for
example, points out that extended turns are an interactional accom-
plishment in that they require the other interactant to allow them to
progress. One method for this is the other interactant's use of 'continuers' such as 'mm hm', 'yeah' or head nods. In this way, the speaker
can build up an extended turn on an utterance-by-utterance basis.
    Jefferson (1978) has examined one particular type of extended turn,
stories told in conversation, and analysed how they fit into the surrounding talk. As with other turns, recipients make sense of these
extended turns by asking 'why that now?'. As Jefferson notes, one particular aspect of extended turns such as stories is that they are often
potentially more difficult than shorter turns for recipients to understand, at least in their first utterances, because the reason for their
telling at this point in the conversation is not displayed until after a
number of utterances into the sequence. An example of this is the following story in a conversation between three American teenagers. In
the first two turns Al and Ken are teasing Roger about sniffing glue.
Roger then relates a story about how at New Year when they were
arranging to buy drinks for a party one person ordered Ripple (cheap
alcohol) and another person ordered glue [Jefferson, 1978: simplified
transcription]:

1 Al: ((To Roger)) probably poured glue over it .
2   if I know you:,
3   (0.4)
4 Ken: °hhhh no:, you got to be careful every so often he

```
5          takes that cup and he takes a deep whiff he's got a
6          tube of glue in it.
7             (0.7)
8   Roger: New Years we:: split up the dues so we each had a
9          buck fifty to buy booze with for the New Years
10         party?
11 Al:    mm hm,
12 Roger: so we went around the room they were taking orders.
13         so Lance k- so:, one guy bought a, dollar fifty
14         worth of Ripple, hh next guy b(hh)ought a dollar
15         fifty worth of glue:, uhh!
16 (    ): °hhh=
17 Ken:   =heh huh [huh
18 Al:             [he-eh hehh hehh
```

The relationship between Roger's story and the preceding talk is not displayed until the end of the story at line 15 when the last word 'glue' links the story to Al and Ken's turns preceding it. This is a common procedure in the structure of extended turns such as stories and in Roger's turn, constructed as a funny story, it functions as a punchline.

It can be seen that, although Roger's utterances in the story preceding its end at line 15 are therefore potentially problematic for the recipients to understand in terms of the 'why that now?' question, in practice there is no sign that they have any difficulty with these utterances; at line 11, for example, Al's turn (mm hm) is not an attempt to initiate repair but rather functions as a continuer. One reason why Roger's utterance at lines 8–10 is not problematic for the participants is that it is recognised as the first utterance of a multi-utterance turn; the use of a 'temporal locator', such as in this case 'New Years' in line 8, is a sign that this utterance is likely to be followed by others in the turn. Recipients in extended turns can therefore delay initiating repair on something in the early utterances of the turn which is not clear in the knowledge that there are more utterances to follow and that these latter utterances will be able to be used as a resource to understand the earlier ones.

As Schegloff (1982) therefore notes, recipients' responses such as 'mm hm', 'yeah', head nods and so on are fulfilling two functions: first, they can be 'continuers', i.e. a display by the recipient that he or she is willing to allow the other speaker to carry on and construct a multi-utterance turn. Second, they can be 'understanding claims' in that the recipient has declined an opportunity to initiate repair on the turn. This second function is equivocal, however, because the claim of understanding can turn out to be incorrect and the turn recipient may initiate repair later.

It is now possible to examine P's extended turn (lines 41–126) to analyse why the beginning of the turn proves to be a source of trouble for T and why this trouble only emerges later in the talk.

Figure 11.1 shows in schematic form the structure of the extended turn. As was noted above, when T's help is invoked for trouble B, T displays that she is unable to help because an earlier part of the extended turn is problematic for her. Her questions at lines 69, 71, 74 and 80

A.   Ongoing exchange of turns
32   T   you still..get flowers from a market..
34   P   yes..but..actually Christmas last
35   time
40   so..but maybe

B. Telling Sequence
la. Future Event
41   P   rightvery soon
42   ..three weeks
43   then.one more time
45   because me after stroke and no car
46   T   right
47   P   okay right?
48   T   yes

2a. Past Event
49   P   and..last..year

Repair sequence
50   P   ..very famous..
51   not England
64   what the word?..
66   T   ..people round the country go to somewhere
67   in Wales
69   ..what do they go there for?
71   is that..something to do with driving?
74   for peoplewho disabled?
80   for some kind of car racing?
86   is it round Cardiff

2b Past Event
91   P   anyway that ..last year
96   that time actually no and me failed
98   T   you tried to take a...driving test
99   P   yesright..

lb Future Event
109   P   but maybe this time
114   T   ..so this is where they adapt cars
115   so that you can drive them

C.   Re -engagement of exchange of turns
123   T   so you'll have a set of wheels and be a lot more mobile
124   ..to drive around
125   P   yes yes

Figure 11.1 The structure of P's telling sequence.

display that the source of the trouble concerns several lines at the beginning of the turn.

T's questions reveal that she knows P's telling concerns cars but she is unable to work out the exact nature of the event. The part of P's talk which appears to be causing the problem is line 43 and line 45's relation to it. It is not only the vagueness of the description which causes the difficulty but its sequential occurrence at the beginning of the extended turn:

```
40 P    so uh:m, (0.5) uh >but maybe< uh:m
41      right. (0.5) uhm very soon right?
42      uh:m I think uh:m (1.0) >three weeks<
43      then (.) one more time, (.) uh:m
44 T    ((nods))
45 P    because me (.) after stroke,(.) and uh no car
46 T    ri:ght
47 P    okay right?
48 T    yes.
```

One effect of the sequential position of these utterances is that T has very little sequential context to use as a resource in understanding them. The beginning of P's extended turn, like Roger's story in Jefferson's example, displays no obvious relationship to the immediately preceding turns. In P and T's conversation, for example, the preceding utterances have referred to getting flowers from the market (an on-going event) and the fact that the last time P went was Christmas (a past event). At line 41, however, the talk takes an obviously different direction; P abandons his on-going utterance and begins a new one with 'right' delivered louder than the preceding utterance. At the same time he raises his hand in a 'stop' gesture. This combination displays that the immediately forthcoming talk will not be directly related to the preceding utterances. The new sequence of talk concerns something that is going to happen in the future. It's relation to the preceding talk about getting flowers from the market is at this stage unclear.

As a result, T has less access to the resource that is often available for understanding an utterance, the resource of analysing the utterance in its sequential context and making sense of it by thinking in terms of 'why that now?'.

A second problem for T is that P does not try to clarify the utterances in lines 43–45 before moving on in the sequence to talk about a past event. Part of the problem here, however, may be a difficulty between P and T about how problematic these utterances have been to understand. 'Right' in lines 46 and 47 has a potential dual function as both continuer and understanding claim at this point in an extended turn as was noted above in Schegloff's (1982) analyses. P, after checking in line 47 ('okay right?'), appears to take T's utterances at lines 46 and 48 as indications that T has an adequate understanding of the telling so far and he moves on in line 49 to talking about a past event. T's questions later in the talk at lines 69 and following, however, indicate that she has indeed had difficulty in understanding the beginning of the telling sequence.

From line 69, therefore, troubles B and C become temporarily treated simultaneously. T's questions at lines 69, 71, 74 and 80 are attempts to elucidate the nature of the event. At lines 85–86, with this problem still unresolved, she tries a different approach and attempts to find the problematic place name. At line 91, P initiates the end of the repair sequence with 'anyway' and returns to the description of the past event. The repairs on troubles B and C are left uncompleted.

The nature of the event becomes elucidated later at lines 98–99; P uses the verb 'failed' while continuing the telling and T is able to use this to make a guess that the event is a driving test. With this confirmed, P returns to the original subject of the telling, the future event now clarified as a driving test. At lines 123–124 T displays her understanding of the overall sequence by summing up its point. P accepts this and the conversation moves towards its close.

Summary of the analysis

Five minutes of a conversation between a patient and therapist was transcribed and analysed using a CA approach. Two concepts from CA were applied: the notion of sequential context and the relationship between trouble sources and repairs.

Three parts of the conversation were analysed where a repair was initiated on a trouble source in P's talk. This repair initiation was used as a starting point both for the analysis of the trouble source that had made the repair initiation necessary and also the methods used by the interactants to try and achieve successful repair completion. In two of the troubles analysed (trouble A and trouble C), the sequential placement of the utterance(s) played a significant role in causing these utterances subsequently to become trouble sources for the interactants.

In trouble A, T misunderstood an utterance of P's (lines 7–8) because its design at this point in an ongoing series of utterances made it vulnerable to misunderstanding if analysed in terms of the 'why that now?' principle (Schegloff and Sacks, 1973).

In trouble C, the occurrence of the utterances at the beginning of an extended turn contributed to their subsequent development into sources of trouble for the interactants. In trouble B, the sequential placement created difficulties in terms of achieving successful repair completion. The occurrence of a word-finding difficulty at this point in the extended turn meant that when P was unable to self-repair, T was unable to help because she had not understood the context of the word search.

Implications

The application of CA research to aphasic talk is still in the early stages and care is needed in applying CA in new ways while still paying due respect to its method and aims (Drew, 1990). At the same time, this approach does appear to offer substantial benefits to any applied science such as aphasiology which is ultimately trying to describe and explain the functioning of real life language and its breakdown. The implications of applying CA in aphasiology cannot be fully analysed here and discussion will be limited to some implications for assessment and therapy that emerge out of the preceding analysis of P's talk.

First, CA is of interest to aphasiology in that it has developed methods of analysis that are sensitive to the contextual nature of language in talk. Utterances are analysed both as being within the context of turns and sequences of turns and simultaneously adding to that context. It has been noted in non-aphasic talk, for example, that a hearable error in an utterance does not invariably cause difficulty in the talk. In assessing aphasic talk, therefore, a starting point for analysis is the examination of points in the talk where the interactants themselves display that there is a problem. In the assessment of P's talk, for example, analysis was made of how each of three problems arose in the talk, how repair was initiated and pursued, and whether it was successfully completed.

It was noted that sequential factors (e.g. the place of an utterance within a series of utterances) played a significant role in how problems arose in P's talk and whether they were resolved. In attempting to describe and explain aphasic language, most analyses have concentrated on language removed from its sequential context. Detailed investigation of aphasic speakers in conversation, however, suggests that analysing aphasic language within its sequential context may be a useful additional tool in explaining how troubles arise and are dealt with.

As a method of assessing language in the natural context of interactive talk, CA therefore offers an ecologically valid approach which complements more 'decontextualised' methods of sampling language such as picture description tasks. An example of the complementary nature of these two approaches can be seen by comparing P's language in the conversation and on an SVO picture description task carried out immediately after the conversation. The picture description task below has been transcribed using a CA transcription procedure in order to allow comparison with the conversation.

Picture description task

1 The woman is carrying books

(1.0) hhh (0.8) the books either uhm (0.5) girl and *carr-y-ing or or uhm or library. I don't know.

2 The woman is eating a bun/cake

(3.0) uhm (0.3) the girl (1.0) °oh God° (0.8) *<u>ea</u>-ting? yes eating (.) uh bun.

3 The man is pouring orange juice

(0.8) the (0.8) oh God (5.0) the jug *pour the (0.5) uhm (3.0) <u>some</u>-thing on the <u>s(h)ome</u>thing hh God almighty! uh <u>app</u>le no >I don't know< (0.3) <u>that</u> uh sorry gone away

4 The woman is breaking eggs into a bowl

(3.0) hhh (3.5) uhm: (0.8) the <u>egg</u> *break-ing uh bowl and whisk >well almost< somewhere whisk.

5 The girl is pointing

(2.0) the girl (.) *<u>point</u> the <u>finger</u>

6 The man is ironing trousers

P (10.0) the man (.) uhm (8.0) °hot° (3.5) hot (2.5) uhm paint? hot
   uhm: (5.0) °hot° (9.0) ( ) uhm sm- not smoke- not uhm (3.5) this
   thing >I don't know<
T iron
P iron (.) uhm and different clothes. thank you.

7 The woman is knitting a jumper

(2.0) the uh <u>old</u> <u>dear</u> uh (.) *<u>knitting</u> <u>on</u> <u>the</u> table.

8 The man is writing on the envelope

(1.5) the man uhm (.) *was writing (2.0) <u>different</u> <u>things</u>.

There is no space here to compare in detail P's performance in the talk and on the picture description task and discussion here will be limited to a couple of points.

It can be seen that in all the picture descriptions but one (no. 6) P is able to access the target verb to describe the action (these verbs/verb phrases have been marked with an asterisk to aid retrieval from the text).

Second, several of the verbs appear to be functioning as part of the sentence structure; in numbers 2, 5 and 8, for example, P constructs an SVO sentence, in number 7 an SVA sentence and in number 3 there appears to be an attempt to use the construction SVOA.

P's ability to use verbs in this task appears much better than in the conversation. The utterances in the conversation which contain verbs are the following (again the verbs are marked with asterisks to aid retrieval):

5   but uh:m uh:m (0.5) I think <u>me</u> and more more:, (1.8)
6   uh:m >I mean< <u>no</u>. only now and then

10   and also (.) uh flowers much (0.2) <u>pre</u>tty or something.
11   >you know?< but uh:]

13   >I mean< <u>may</u>be maybe not. I don't know you know.

41   <u>right</u>. (0.5) uhm very soon right?
42   uh:m I think uh:m (1.0) >three weeks<
43   then (.) <u>one more time</u>, (.) uh:m

51   not England but (2.0) °hm° (0.8) °terrible° (0.8)
52   uh:m (4.0) I think (4.0) uh:m (3.0)
53   °not England° but (2.0) °not Scotland° but (.)
54   <u>Wales</u> right?

64   what the word? >I mean< what the (1.0) uh:m (1.0)
65   very famous or very, (3.5)

96   but uh that time actually <u>no</u> and me ↓<u>failed</u>.right?

101 P but I think either (.) uh:m:,(.) high up >you know<
102   and finally ↓<u>no</u>

106 P and uh: (.) uhm: (0.3) basically I think uh: (0.5)
107   high up and <u>sorry</u>, ↓<u>no</u>.

Apart from 'failed', all the verbs used have low semantic content. They appear to recur as set phrases which often display no integration as part of the sentence structure; 'I think', for example, occurs five times here, 'I mean' and 'you know' three times and 'I don't know' once.

As Lesser and Milroy (1993) note, part of the reason why some patients' language on tasks such as picture description may be noticeably superior to their language in conversation is that the patient may be helped by the structure of the task. The use of pictures as stimuli, the extra time involved and the repetitive nature of the structures elicited may all be among the factors involved in making processing easier for a particular patient.

Although there appears to have been little detailed research into the relationship between aphasic speakers' ability to access certain linguistic structures on tasks such as picture description and in conversation it may be the case that this relationship varies among patients. In the project from which the data presented here were taken, for example, another patient displaying problems with verbs showed a far less dramatic difference between picture description and conversation (Wilkinson, 1995).

It may be useful, therefore, to combine the results of the two assessment approaches when making judgements about further investigations and initiating a therapy programme. For P, for example, the conversation data highlight the difficulties P has with verbs; not only can almost all of the few verbs present be seen to be functioning in recurring set phrases, but also the communicational effect of this lack of verbs can be seen in the fact that when P accesses the verb 'failed' in line 96, T is able to work out the nature of the event which P has been unable to communicate by other means over a number of utterances. At the same time, P shows ability in the constrained environment of the picture description task to access verbs and use them in SVO and SVA structures. This suggests that further investigation into P's sentence processing (Jones 1986; Byng 1988; Marshall et al.,1993) would be useful in terms of devising a direct therapy programme aimed at using P's ability to access certain verbs in decontextualised tasks and attempting to generalise this ability into interactive talk.

Another complementary therapy approach suggested by the conversation data would be to develop P's metalinguistic awareness of how problems arise in his talk. An advantage of applying a CA approach to aphasic data is that it allows a means of investigating why psycholinguistic impairments cause problems for the interactants at certain points in the talk.

From the analysis of the data presented here, an obvious starting point for P would be awareness of the ways in which extended turns, which are relatively common in P's talk, are particularly vulnerable to becoming trouble sources. As with Holland's (1991) programme of 'conversational coaching', the patient would watch himself talking on video and this would be used as a starting point for discussion of how particular trouble sources arose. One of the patient's everyday interactants could also be involved in this discussion.

A final implication of a CA approach in aphasiology is in terms of measuring change and examining the efficacy of therapy (Wilkinson, 1995). It has long been argued that ultimately the efficacy of therapy for spoken language should be shown in terms of change in spontaneous speech (Sarno, 1980; Jones, 1986). Little work has been done in this area so far using CA but the insights this approach provides into the construction of talk make this an area of obvious interest for the future.

Appendix: transcript notation

The symbols used in this study are as follows (a fuller version of the CA transcript notation is available in Atkinson and Heritage, 1984, and Button and Lee, 1987):

[a single left-hand bracket links an ongoing utterance with an overlapping utterance at the point where the overlap begins

]   a single right-hand bracket marks where overlapping utterances stop overlapping

=   an equals sign marks where there is no interval between adjacent utterances

( )   intervals in the stream of talk marked in tenths of a second

(.)   an interval of tenth of a second or less in the stream of talk

:   a colon indicates an extension of the sound or syllable it follows (more colons prolong the stretch)

.   a full stop indicates a stopping fall in tone, not necessarily the end of a sentence

,   a comma indicates a continuing intonation, not necessarily between clauses

↑↓   a question mark indicates a rising inflection, not necessarily a question

!   an exclamation mark indicates an animated tone, not necessarily an exclamation

–   a single dash indicates a halting, abrupt cut-off

⌃⌄   marked rising and falling shifts in intonation are indicated by upward and downward pointing arrows immediately before the rise or fall

__   underlining indicates emphasis

° °   degree signs indicate a passage of talk which is quieter than surrounding talk hh   discernible exhalation (the more hs the longer the exhalation)

(h)   discernible exhalation within a component in an utterance

°hh   discernible inhalation (the more hs the longer the inhalation)

><   lesser than/greater than signs indicate sections of an utterance
        delivered at a greater pace than the surrounding talk

(( ))   double brackets indicate descriptions of the talk or activity

( )   single brackets with nothing between them mark where an
        item is in doubt

Chapter 12
Closed head injury: assessment and remediation of topic bias and repetitiveness

MICHAEL PERKINS, RICHARD BODY and MARK PARKER

Background

Case history

Colin, a bricklayer in his late 40s, suffered a severe head injury in a fall from a roof in December 1991. He was unconscious on admission to casualty and was ventilated for 3 weeks. Computed tomography (CT) showed extensive fractures over the vault of the skull, an acute subdural collection on the right side and marked oedema. No neurosurgical intervention was performed. Computed tomograpy 3 months later at time of discharge showed a small low density area in the posterior lobe consistent with previous ischaemia or haemorrhage.

Before the injury Colin was in full time employment. Outside work he was involved in football coaching and other pastimes included gardening, model building and drawing. He has not returned to employment since the injury.

Initial assessment of communicative ability

In June 1992 Colin was referred to a Head Injury Rehabilitation Centre where a multidisciplinary team carried out a wide range of assessments. The following observations were made relating to his communicative ability.

Colin's speech rate was rapid, though this was felt to reflect his psychological state rather than a motor speech disorder. There was no evidence of dysphasia, as demonstrated on tests of auditory comprehension of syntax or verbal naming.

In conversation, however, a number of communicative difficulties were apparent. Colin was repetitive in questioning, interrupted inappropriately, changed topic frequently and apologised excessively.

Within a conversational turn, there appeared to be a general lack of coherent narrative structure typified by redundant and inaccurate information, topic shifts and bias, and situational inappropriateness. It was also noted that Colin's non-verbal communication was similarly inappropriate (e.g. excessive eye contact) and produced what some described as 'a negative effect' on his interlocutor. According to Colin's family, none of these abnormal conversational behaviours had been in evidence premorbidly.

Formal assessment of reading skills using the National Adult Reading Test (NART: Nelson, 1991) and the Reading Comprehension Battery for Aphasia (RCBA: LaPointe and Horner, 1979) showed low ability. It was established by talking to his wife that Colin's formal education had been patchy and premorbid literacy level was not high, but that he had been able to read tabloid newspapers without problem before injury.

Psychometric testing using the Wechsler Adult Intelligence Scale (WAIS: Wechsler, 1981) revealed deficits in a range of cognitive skills, particularly with regard to attention, memory and executive function, with obvious implications for communicative performance. On the Rivermead Behavioural Memory Test (RBMT: Wilson et al., 1991). Colin performed very poorly both on verbal and non-verbal recall. His performance was poor both for free recall of information such as a short story and on a verbal learning task. Recognition memory for both verbal and non-verbal information was at chance level.

Colin had severe difficulties in all areas of executive functioning. His ability to formulate goals was limited by poor insight into his current problems and by cognitive deficits in memory and reasoning. Planning of activities was similarly affected, and the problems were exacerbated by a lack of initiation. Execution of activities was impaired by Colin's inability to concentrate on tasks without prompting. There were also difficulties in monitoring errors in performance and developing strategies to compensate for errors.

Within the head-injured population, the combination of problems outlined above is by no means unique to Colin. Numerous studies over the last 30 years have identified a frequently occurring pattern of cognitive deficits involving attention, memory and the higher integrative functions. Similarly, although documented only relatively recently, it is now widely accepted that the communicative patterns seen in many head-injured people may be a reflection of deficits in other cognitive processes. Although it is also accepted that the neuroanatomical damage sustained in traumatic head injury tends to be diffuse, cognitive deficits that may produce particular patterns of communication have their anatomical basis in areas of most frequently occurring focal damage, namely the frontal and temporal lobes (McDonald, 1993).

The idea that cognition and communication are inextricably linked in head injury first became popular in the early 1980s. Hagen (1981) described the link in the following terms: 'The majority of the patient's language impairment is a symptom of the dysfunction of those cognitive processes that support language processing.' The idea was developed further by a number of authors to the stage where (particularly in the American literature) the term 'cognitive–communicative' (or sometimes 'cognitive–linguistic') came to be used of communication after head injury (Milton, 1988; Sbordone, 1988; Cherney, 1991).

In spite of the widespread acceptance of this idea, it is by no means clear what mechanisms are involved, whether the causal link is only in one direction, which aspects of cognition lead to communication disorders, and thus what patterns of communication can be expected in the presence of specific deficits in cognition. It is on these questions – in particular the last one – that this chapter is focused.

The problem

Although Colin's initial assessment had succeeded in narrowing down his communicative problems to areas such as conversational disability and topic maintenance, these terms are not very specific and it was not immediately obvious how to proceed to be able to devise an appropriate remedial strategy. At the same time, it was clear that Colin's communication problems were putting his wife and family under great strain and that if at all possible some means of enabling them to cope with his problems was needed.

It was felt that, to proceed further, a more detailed linguistic analysis of Colin's communication might prove helpful in characterising more precisely the nature of his communication problem and in establishing its relationship to his cognitive problems.

Preliminary investigations and hypotheses

A video recording was made of Colin in a story re-telling task, describing a picture and in free conversation with one of the authors. This was transcribed and studied in some detail in a preliminary attempt to ascertain the type of linguistic abnormalities present and to focus on any particular features that might merit further exploration. This initial scan yielded the following observations.

Linguistic ability

Colin's phonology and syntax appeared normal in both production and comprehension, and there was no apparent impairment to his range of vocabulary and his ability to access it. However, a number of phrases and sentences such as *sound as a pound* and *I look on every day as a bonus* were overused to the point at which they could be considered as stereotypes, and there appeared to be a lot of linguistic repetitiveness generally, although it was not immediately clear whether this was simply a result of his tendency to focus in his conversation on a restricted range of topics (see below).

A further, rather unusual feature of Colin's conversation was the occasional reference to himself in the third person. Sometimes his own name would be used in conjunction with a third person pronoun, as in the following sample.

Sample 1.
and did you 'know then what's 'happened to 'Colin ˇnow
fallen off a ˋroof and fractured <u>his</u> ´skull

Sometimes, more oddly, his name would be used in conjunction with a first person pronoun, as in the following sample.

Sample 2.
they can 'bump into ´Colin and <u>I</u>'ll 'just say – ˋwatch it

<u>I</u> 'don't like ˋanyone who tells ´lies es`pecially to ˇColin

<u>my</u> 'attitude changed to'ward other ˋpeople and – the 'people what's

up'set ˇColin

changing a lightbulb <u>to Colin . to me</u> . is very simple

Pragmatic ability

Colin's most obvious pragmatic problem was with conversational topic. He would invariably bring the conversation round to one of a restricted range of topics such as swearing, lying, people he disliked, religion, the building trade and football coaching. In other words, he had a definite topic 'bias'. In addition, his topic 'maintenance' was poor in that he would frequently shift topic without an appropriate signal to the hearer, and drift apparently aimlessly from topic to topic. Colin's family referred to this as 'not keeping to the point' such that they had difficulty 'following what he was on about'. For example, see the following sample.

Sample 3.
and did you 'know then what's 'happened to 'Colin ˇnow
fallen off a ˋroof and fractured his ´skull you ˉknow that
I look on life as a ˋbonus
and just en'joy 'every ˋday as it ˋcomes

but . I would ˇsay . a 'bad fault of ˇmine
and I would ˉsay s it's 'happening over t 'last – 'couple of ˇmonth
I 'call a spade a ´spade a 'trump a ´trump
and – I 'just said to ˋSarah
because I 'do go to ˋchurch a ´lot
and I 'said she says 'what people do I ˋlove
and I says I only ˋlove ´four

Colin's problems with topic appeared to be part of a more general pragmatic difficulty with taking proper account of his interlocutor's perspective and conversational needs. This was also apparent in his tendency to hold on to his conversational turn.

A related pragmatically relevant feature is Colin's occasional odd use of prosody. He would at times produce utterances with a low, narrow pitch range, low intensity and sometimes rapid tempo to such an extent as to render them virtually inaudible and unintelligible. On occasions this could be regarded as in keeping with a 'conspiratorial' manner that he would sometimes adopt, together with appropriate semantic content and paralinguistic behaviour, but quite often there would be no obvious reason for it and it would feel pragmatically inappropriate. This, combined with a tendency to maintain fixed eye contact during his conversational turn, to move close to his interlocutor sometimes during conversation and to bring up topics of an inappropriately personal nature appeared to underlie the 'negative effect' sometimes experienced by Colin's conversational partner.

Conceptual confusion

Finally, mention should be made of occasional conceptual confusions in the content of Colin's language, as in instances such as the following sample.

Sample 4.
and don't ˋswear see
because 'someone ˇdeaf would like be able to ˋhear that
– or someone ˋblind
which I (mean?) to say if you're 'blind or ˇdeaf
you 'look on ´that as a ˋbonus

This preliminary analysis raised a number of issues which seemed to merit further investigation:

1. Is the repetitive and stereotyped nature of Colin's language simply a result of his topic bias, or are there other factors involved?
2. Is there any underlying pattern to Colin's handling of topic?

3. Do the topics that Colin continually reverts to have anything in common, or are they arbitrary?
4. Are Colin's repetitiveness and topic bias distinguishable from the kinds of obsessive behaviour sometimes found in conditions such as autism, Asperger's syndrome and general learning disability?
5. To what extent can Colin's abnormal communicative behaviour be regarded as resulting from other cognitive impairment such as poor memory and poor executive function?

To address these issues, a further set of investigations was carried out. Audio and video recordings were made of interactions between Colin and several different conversational partners including the three authors and members of his immediate family, and these were subsequently transcribed and analysed. In addition, one of the authors interviewed Colin's wife to obtain information about his communicative behaviour and other activities in his home setting. The results of the investigations are reported in the next section.

Further analyses

Stereotyped and repetitive language

Stereotyped language is a common feature of language disability and ranges from the holistic rote learned 'chunks' typical of children with autism noted by Prizant (1983) and others, to the 'non-propositional' speech that often survives in cases of aphasia where there is virtually no productive language left (Van Lancker, 1987). Unfortunately, however, the terms 'stereotype', 'stereotypy' and 'stereotyped' are not always used consistently. Some choose to emphasise the repetitiveness of stereotypes whereas others emphasise their 'sameness'. Frith and Done (1990, p. 233), for example, define stereotyped behaviour generally as 'any purposeless movement or act that occurs repeatedly', and Lebrun (1986) uses the term 'stereotypy' very narrowly to refer to recurring speech automatisms. Linguists, on the other hand, tend to be more interested in the lack of structural variability of stereotypes, i.e. their 'sameness', than in their tendency to recur. Crystal (1991, p. 326), for example, defines a stereotype as 'a sequence of words which resembles a productive grammatical structure but which in fact has been learned as a single unit and has little or no productivity'. This works well enough for idioms, proverbs, song lyrics and clichés which are easily recognisable, but if one is trying to identify such a non-productive sequence in a sample of disordered language, often the only clue one has to its status as an invariant structure is the frequency with which the form is repeated (see Perkins, 1994).

Colin's language can be described as stereotyped to the extent that it includes a range of expressions which appear to be used with greater than normal frequency. It was suggested above that it might be possible to regard this as a consequence of his topic bias. So, for example, expressions like 'a bad fault of mine; I have got my faults; my biggest fault' is related to the topic of Colin's own faults.

Not all of Colin's stereotyped expressions, however, can be easily linked to one of his stereotyped topics. Expressions such as 'sound as a pound' and 'I look on every day as a bonus', for example, occur frequently no matter what Colin happens to be talking about and are not always contextually appropriate. In the following sample, for example.

Sample 5.
and she says `no I'm just `talking to you
and – I didn't ˇswear I 'just told her to get `knotted
<u>I 'look on every day I 'look on every day as a `bonus</u>
and I just 'put the phone down from ˇher
and I said to `Sarah
I shall 'never see my sister a´gain

The underlined section appears to be quite unrelated to what is being talked about and is also, incidentally, prosodically differentiated from the surrounding language by being spoken very rapidly. Examples like this are more akin to the the kind of 'speech automatisms' found in some severely impaired aphasic individuals.

There are also grounds for suggesting a third type of stereotyped expression in Colin's language which does not fall comfortably into either of the categories just mentioned but appears to lie somewhere in between. This includes frequently used adverbial expressions such as *basically* which are not related to a specific topic, but which are not used entirely inappropriately. For example:

Sample 6.
but I don't tell `lies and I – ˇ<u>basically</u> – I don't ´swear

I've ('nowt but) res'pect for my mother and ´father and my ˇsister
and `<u>basically</u> ´sir I've only come to this conˇclusion this 'last two
`month

I just feel 'very ´sorry for my `father who worked 'hard all his ´life
and ˇ<u>basically</u> I've just . my ˇmother – – she just `swears a lot

'that's the way I `feel
and ˇ<u>basically</u> it's falling off a `roof and . 'fracturing my `skull

Frequent use of adverbials such as *basically* is, admittedly, not uncommon in the normal population, although we shall see later that the discourse function they perform is a particularly significant one for understanding Colin's conversational behaviour.

A further source of repetitiveness in Colin's language arises from an occasional tendency to perseverate on a word or expression that cannot always be attributed to topic bias. Sometimes, in fact, this can actually trigger a topic change, as in the following sample.

Sample 7.
and the digs that I've stopped are farms or hostels with a big <u>garden</u>
and <u>I do actually</u> like <u>gardening</u>
<u>I do actually</u> get on with people at work

The second utterance picks up on the word *garden* in the first, causing a shift in topic, and the third utterance similarly picks up on *I do actually* in the second utterance producing yet another topic change. This type of repetitiveness, which has been referred to by Sandson and Albert (1984) as 'recurrent' perseveration, is also common in dementia (see, for example, Bayles et al., 1985). The contrast and interplay between recurrent perseveration and topic bias can be clearly seen in the following sample where Colin was asked to describe in detail how he would write a letter.

Sample 8.
basically I write a letter to whom it is
either for a job or to the wife or to some friends
it's not abusive
I get straight to the point and I write it
I've seen some letters that people get
and they go on forever and a day instead of just getting to the point
I get to the point speak it or write it

One of his preferred topics, abusive language, is brought in almost immediately. He then perseverates on the phrase 'get to the point'. These two factors both divert him from directly answering the question, and in fact from getting to the point!

Instances of repetitiveness in Colin's language appear, therefore, to range along a continuum of which one extreme consists of non-productive stereotypes and the other of productive but topic-restricted utterances. The middle ground is covered by sets of expressions which range from those that are similar in semantic content and similar (although not identical) in form, as in the following – one of which is almost invariably used by Colin when referring to his accident:

fall<u>en</u> off a roof and fractur<u>ed</u> <u>my</u> skull
fall<u>ing</u> off a roof and fractur<u>ing</u> <u>my</u> skull
fall<u>en</u> off a roof and fractur<u>ed</u> <u>his</u> skull

to those that are similar in semantic content but formally dissimilar, as in *I will never see X again; X doesn't exist; X swears; X tells lies* — which Colin frequently uses when he is talking about people he dislikes.*

Overall, though, the repetitiveness and stereotypy in Colin's language is probably most striking at the level of topic. We will now move on to consider the handling of topic in more detail.

Topic management

So far, the term 'topic' has been used with little supporting explanation. It is, however, notoriously difficult to define. As Atkinson and Heritage (1984, p. 165) note in an introduction to topic organisation: '. . . 'topic' may well prove to be among the most complex conversational phenomena to be investigated and, correspondingly, the most recalcitrant to systematic analysis.' The term is used in linguistics in two separate senses. At the level of grammatical structure, it may be used to refer to 'who or what the sentence is about' (i.e. 'grammatical topic') and frequently coincides with the grammatical subject. In conversation analysis, on the other hand, it is used more generally and loosely to refer to 'what is talked about' in conversational interaction (Schegloff, 1979b), i.e. 'conversational' or 'discourse' topic. This second sense is obviously a lot broader than the first and may refer to a feature shared by a set of sentences rather than being restricted to just one. Both senses are linked in that they are both concerned with what Levinson (1983) refers to as 'aboutness', but differ in terms of their scope.

Colin's problem appears to be with topic in its broader conversational sense, but there is no real agreement on how to define this version of the term 'topic'. Some definitions are based on the notion of 'proposition' such as the following by Keenan and Schieffelin (1976, p. 342 *et seq.*): 'a proposition (or set of propositions) expressing a concern (or set of concerns) the speaker is addressing'. Such definitions, however, are severely limited, as Brown and Yule (1983) have pointed out, by the fact that there exists no formal algorithm for converting surface utterances into underlying propositions and each investigator may identify a different (though probably similar) set of propositions for a given stretch of text. Even approaches such as that of Maynard (1980) which focus on formal features used to signal topic boundaries still presuppose some implicit notion of what a topic is. However, in spite of the elusiveness of a tight formal definition of 'topic', and the use by many researchers of a loose general definition such as that of Schegloff by way of default, the notion remains a central one, particularly in the description of conversational disability. It may be that the problem lies

---

*For a comparison of Colin's repetitiveness profile with that of three other non-head injured patients, see Perkins (1994).

in the attempt to achieve a formal definition of topic as a discrete entity, rather than regarding it, as Lesser and Milroy (1993) do, as simply a byproduct of conversational coherence, and some even go as far as to suggest jettisoning 'topic' as a technical term altogether (Schlobinski and Schütze-Coburn, 1992). In spite of this, there still seem to be sound practical (and especially clinical) reasons for retaining the notion of topic as a category of analysis because of its clear intuitive links to descriptions such as 'It is not clear what X is talking about' and 'X has gone off the point' which are frequently used in informal accounts of disordered conversation.

The only detailed analysis of topic in a head-injured individual to date is that of Mentis and Prutting (1991) who noted a higher than normal incidence of (1) non-coherent topic changes, (2) ambiguous, unrelated and incomplete 'ideational' units (i.e. propositional language) and (3) 'unrelated issues' (i.e. introduction of material unrelated to the current topic in monologues). The main aim of their study was, however, to test the effectiveness of an analytical framework they had devised for describing topic management differences between a closed head-injured individual and a normal subject, rather than to explore in detail the actual areas of difference. Although Colin's communicative behaviour resembles that of Mentis and Prutting's subject as regards (1) and (3), there are important differences in the area of (2). For example, as far as one can judge from the two short samples provided, the language of Mentis and Prutting's subject appears generally far less specific and more vague in terms of reference assignment than is the case with Colin. In addition, Mentis and Prutting's subject appears highly dependent on his conversational partner in structuring his conversation, whereas Colin was quite the opposite.[†]

Although Mentis and Prutting's system appears to differentiate the topic management strategies of the two individuals in their study, the lack of a generally accepted method of analysis means that there is no body of normative data which can encompass the (probably) broad range of topic management styles in the 'normal' population. In other words, the various methods of formal topic analysis can offer different ways of modelling topic use but are as yet completely unable to establish whether a particular style is 'disordered' or even merely unusual. The approach we have adopted here, which draws on the analytical techniques and notions of conversational analysis (see also Chapters 7 and 11), tries to avoid imposing preconceived categories and norms as far as possible, and instead seeks to characterise the nature of Colin's communicative behaviour by examining fairly large samples of tran-

---

[†]It may well be the case, nevertheless, that Colin's independence of his communicative partner is just as disrupted (and disruptive) because it may signal an inability to take the partner into account at all.

scribed conversational data for recurring patterns. The analysis of Colin's conversation was informed by discussion among the authors and feedback from Colin's most frequent communicative partners as to what they found most disruptive.

Here, we will first consider a number of formal aspects of Colin's failure to manage topic successfully, and then we will go on to consider the significance of his topic content and the way it relates to his use of prosody.

Formal topic handling strategies

One skill necessary for the successful manipulation of topic is the ability to introduce a topic in such a way that the listener knows who and what are being discussed. Keenan and Schieffelin (1976) outline four prerequisites for successfully establishing a topic, namely (1) securing the speaker's attention, (2) articulating clearly, (3) providing sufficient information for the listener to identify objects etc., and (4) providing sufficient information for the listener to reconstruct the semantic relations obtaining between referents in the discourse topic. The following sample (recorded 15 months post-injury) illustrates Colin's successful use of (3) and (4) (C = Colin).

Sample 9.
C I've 'never actually 'pulled work `down for being `rough
  and I've 'worked all `over the place
R ´right
C so . and `basically
  I would 'say one of the most `interesting places I've ´worked on
R m´hm
C and you 'see it on `T´´V
  and 'that's Caer'narvon ' Castle
R m´hm

When one also adds that Colin fulfilled conditions (1) and (2) we may conclude that Colin is able – at least on this occasion and in fact on many others – to introduce a topic successfully. In this sample Colin also demonstrates the ability to link elements within a text to form a 'cohesive chain' (Halliday and Hasan, 1985), i.e. 'place → (interesting) places → it → Caernarvon Castle' and 'work → worked' in such a way that it is quite clear what he is talking about.

In spite of this ability to introduce topics effectively (such that listeners did not generally find themselves thinking 'What is he talking about?'), it was frequently much more difficult to establish exactly why Colin was talking about a particular topic at a given point in the conversation. This is illustrated in the following sample, recorded 14 months post-injury:

Sample 10.

[Colin has been talking about Trades Unions]

C I ad'mit this 'government we've 'got is 'not doing a good ˇjob
    but the 'unions are 'trying to 'make them sound 'worse than 'what
they `are

M `mm

C they . they . – cos I'm a `Tory ´actually
    but I I 'do vote . if there's a . er . a `communist ´bloke there
    I 'will vote `communist
    but . it 'all de'pends what his `principles are
    but I `don't a´gree. with the `Chinese ´communism –
    and the `Russian 'communism

M `right

C but I believe ˇevery . should be `equal
    but . I'm 'not ˇknocking the 'royal `family
    because y . you `need them

M `mm

C and they they they 'bring people in to ´see
    take ´photos (`–)

Here, Colin appears to be relying on what Maynard (1980) terms
'co-class membership' to develop his train of thought. Co-class membership refers to the linking of two or more items (concepts, objects,
actions, etc.) as belonging in some way to the 'same class of things'.
Thus Colin links Trade Unions – government, government – Tory, Tory
– communist, communism – Chinese/Russian communism, communism – equality, equality – Royal Family, Royal Family – tourist attrac-
tion. (There is clearly no definitive way of representing this train of
thought – this is one of a number of options.) This particular sample,
however, also demonstrates that although co-class membership may be
a necessary condition for coherence, it is certainly not a sufficient one.
It is essentially a linear device, whereas what is lacking here is a sense
of how each topic is related hierarchically.

The notion of hierarchy in topic is generally accepted, albeit in different forms, by different authors. Thus Stech (1982) discusses the concept of topic sequence structures in which topics incorporate
subtopics. Brinton and Fujuki (1984) and Mentis and Prutting (1991)
both develop this theme. The difficulty of reliably labelling topics at different levels in a putative hierarchy has not prevented the acceptance
of the central idea. The linear development of topic in the last sample
would perhaps have been felt to have a more appropriate hierarchical
resolution if Colin had rounded it off in some way with an utterance
such as 'so Trade Unions in general are good/bad'.

In spite of the issues just outlined, the last sample does at least
appear to be an improvement on Colin's earlier conversational style,

exemplified in the following sample, recorded 3 months post-injury.

Sample 11
because – I actually ˋdo – – I . I ˈhave got ´faults
and – my biggest ´fault is –
I ˈdo enjoy ´sport
it's ˈsomething that I've ˈalways ˋdone
I've ˈdone it ˈall my ˋlife
I've (ˈnowt but) resˈpect for my mother and ´father and
my ˇsister
and ˋbasically ´sir
I've only come to this concˇlusion this ˈlast two ˋmonth
and – as far as ˋI'm con´cerned
my ˈsister ˈdoesn't eˋxist

It would be extremely difficult in this sample to construct even a linear link between sport and Colin's opinions of his family without (and quite possibly even with) a large amount of knowledge external to the conversation itself (which in this instance was not available to the listener).

In later conversations, however, there is evidence that such links are at least sometimes apparent to Colin but that he is unable to express them in a way that takes account of the needs of his conversational partner. Consider the following sample for example, recorded 14 months post-injury.

Sample 12
    C   I ˈthink the nicest place I've ˇbeen
        I ˈcan't remember t' adˋdress .
        but it were a ˋfarm
        and . I ˈused to play . table ˋtennis for a ˋpub
5 M   ´yeah
    C   these ˋbirds beat me at . ˋwell . ˋwomen . ˈbeat me at ˈten pin
        ˋbowling
        and t' ˋbowls are ˇheavy .
        they ˋbeat me at ˇthat
        and I ˈplayed at ˈtable ˇtennis
10   I ˋwon ˇthen
        and they were . one of them were ˈchampion of t' ˇpub
        ˈthat means (you're ˈplaying for ˋthem?) . at ˇhome
        at ˈtable ˋtennis

The mention of ten pin bowling in line 6 initially appears to clash with the topic of 'table tennis'. However, this is soon resolved retrospectively in lines 9–10 when it becomes clear that the bowling episode is intended as background information which merely has a bearing on the foregrounded table tennis episode.

In summary, then, many of Colin's incoherent topic changes may be characterised in one of the following two ways:

1. Links between a series of topic pairs are legitimised by their co-class membership, but the overall sequence lacks an appropriate hierarchical structure (samples 9 and 10).
2. Insufficient information is provided for the listener to establish co-class membership between topics. (This makes the assumption–which may on occasions be false – that Colin is actually aware of the link: samples 11 and 12.)

We will now consider the significance of semantic content in Colin's topic management.

Topic content

A very obvious feature of Colin's discourse is the frequency with which he returns to the same limited set of subjects, i.e. what we have referred to above as his 'topic bias'.* Sometimes the transition between topics is managed successfully and sometimes not – there are examples of both in the samples above – but it seems clear that Colin's topic bias must put considerable strain on his resources for effecting smooth topic changes. We will look first at whether Colin's favourite topics share any common features, and then at how he manages the transition into a favourite topic.

Colin's favourite topics seem to divide into two broad classes. First there are topics such as religion, politics, abusive language and people he likes and dislikes. When he moves on to such topics Colin adopts a rather moralising tone and expresses very strong, clear opinions. In fact, the defining feature of this category of topic could be described as the 'expression of opinion'. There is nothing wrong with the expression of opinion in itself, but it was felt by Colin's family and by staff at the Rehabilitation Centre that Colin did this excessively and often inappropriately. In the words of his wife he 'gets on to strong opinions and won't let go'. Opinions are often given where they are neither required nor appropriate.[†] In the following sample, for example, Colin has been

---

*As with the previous analysis of topic management, any discussion of Colin's topic bias is forced to make judgements as to what constitutes a topic. This again was based to a large extent on discussions with his family, who often made comments such as 'He's always talking about X'.

[†]It is interesting to note that a similar phenomenon has also been observed in individuals with Alzheimer's disease. In a comparative study of normal, aphasic, Alzheimer's and depressed subjects reported in Maxim et al. (1991) it was found that only the Alzheimer's subjects expressed inappropriate 'value judgements' during the description of a picture.

asked to re-tell a story that he has just read involving a dolphin but soon shifts from the story to the expression of general opinions (note the underlined sections).

Sample 13
`well – it were a'bout a `dolphin
I think it were `David or something like `that
and it had got ('killed) doing some `damage 'somewhere
I don't know (what `emanated)
but I think it sur`vived I'm not quite `sure
but 'that's 'life
and the 'story – was a bit hap`hazard
and they were 'taking . 'taking `short 'cuts to 'make 'life `easy for theirselves
`basically I 'think – 'such as `dolphins and `sea 'frish – `sea 'fish . and 'animals in `general . have a 'life to lead and 'us `humans

A similar instance occurs in the following sample where Colin has been asked to describe in detail how he would fill up a car with petrol (again note underlined sections).

Sample 14
right . you basically . it's just filling up a car with petrol
but there's quite a few things I would say .
not a motorist . well . most motorists I would say aren't too bad
but people . I would say learners . who've just passed their test
or getting overconfident or a lax(?) attitude in putting petrol into the car
a lot of drivers male or female actually seem to don't give two monkeys about where the petrol goes

His introduction of opinion topics is also often socially inappropriate. For example, he will sometimes give his views on extremely personal issues to people he has not met before.

Colin's second category of favourite topics consists of a fairly small set of autobiographical episodes which he continually recounts, sometimes repeating the same episode twice in the space of a few minutes, using very similar words without being aware that he has done so. These include working away from home (in particular doing some rebuilding work on Caernarvon Castle), his apprenticeship and work as a builder, football coaching, gardening and fights he has been involved in (or avoided being involved in). Sometimes episodes are run together, and often incorporate the expression of opinion as well.

There is no obvious common conceptual ground between the two topic categories apart from the fact that both appear to be of considerable personal significance to Colin, for whatever reason. However, either or both can trigger a shift in topic which has the effect of disrupting Colin's conversational coherence. In fact, much of Colin's difficulty with topic management as described in the previous section can be attributed to the intrusion of topic bias into his ordinary conversational behaviour. The following example, which is the full text of Colin's response to a written request to 'describe in detail how you would write and post a letter (it is important that you keep to the point)', shows this clearly. (In this sample, Colin was speaking into a tape recorder with no one else present in the room.)

Sample 15

    basically . I write a letter to whom it is
    either for a job or to the wife or to some friends
    then I write a letter
    it's not abusive
5 I get straight to the point and I write it
    I've seen some letters that people get
    and they go on forever and a day instead of just getting to the point
    I get to the point . speak it or write it
    what I do . well basically the only letters I wrote is to the wife
10 obviously the wife I write to very rarely by letter
    so I just write at work
    and I've worked all over the country
    she's been as sound as a pound
    and basically . I write the address on it . then write whatever I put
15 and basically if the job's O.K. which normally it will be
    and what I do write about is the digs that I've stopped in
    and the digs that I've stopped in have farms or hostels with a big
        garden
    and I do actually like gardening
    I do actually get on with people at work because they've been
        smashing
20 the best digs I've had has been Caernarvon Castle
    I redid it . rebuilt that (for ?) for the Prince of Wales
    and then I were only there for two or three month
    or four month or something like that
    and I just stayed in guest houses
25 the owner were smashing
    the wife thought we were Sheffield lads just going out for a beer
        session
    I don't work away
    I do the job . I work the hours and I'm alright
    when I write letters I get straight to the point about what I'm writing
30 and then basically that's it

then . what I don't do . I don't write abusive words
because I think it's out of bounds
basically all I do is to the wife
rarely do I write to the two girls
35 that's something I haven't done
I will say . is this O.K. . everyone following
and when I work away I lived in a place on a farm a full four miles
     from a pub
I built five blocks of houses . pairs . two blocks of flats . er . bungalows
they were smashing . very useful
40 I went out to t' pub . well not every night
in a week . in five days I'd go two nights
(unintelligible) they beat me at bowls and were quite nice
and after I said to my wife . I says let's have a week's holiday down
     there
it were a nice place
45 that's basically all I've got to say
I just write what I'm gonna do in a letter
get straight to the point and write off
I just put an address on and it's no trouble
and I think that's about it
50 thank you . that's all I've got to say
I certainly don't want to offend anybody

In this sample there are instances of Colin being nearly led into 'favourite territory' (e.g. line 4) but managing to avoid an intrusive topic while he still has relatively easy access to something to say about the subject in question. There is a potential crisis point at line 12 but Colin returns immediately to the subject of writing letters. However, at line 16 the mention of digs (as written about in letters) sets him off on a chain of favourite topics similar in style to that in sample 10 (trade unions–communism etc.). Interestingly in the light of the comments on sample 10 above (i.e. that there might have been a greater sense of hierarchical organisation if Colin had rounded it off with a mention of the original subject), in sample 15 he does return to letter writing in line 29.* Here, however, there is a sense that Colin has either strayed too far from the original point, covered too many areas in the intervening period or made too abrupt a return to the original for it to be acceptable.

*This may be the result of the presence of the visual reminder to 'describe in detail how you would write and post a letter'. Similarly, the presence of the additional visual prompt to 'keep to the point' appears to be responsible for the inappropriate introduction of a topic of 'keeping to the point' at lines 5 and 48. See also discussion of sample 16 below.

We have looked at the manifestation of repetitiveness in Colin's language, and the way that his topic bias disrupts his management of topic generally. In the next section we will consider these factors together with several other aspects of Colin's communicative and non-communicative behaviour, and will suggest a holistic explanation for why his pragmatic difficulties manifest themselves in the particular way they do.

Integration and attempted holistic explanation

The effect of impaired memory and executive function

We have already mentioned Colin's poor memory as demonstrated in a number of psychometric tests and the fact that he appears to be unaware of how repetitive his language is. His awareness of time generally is also poor. In a conversation recorded 2 months after his accident he was unable to reply accurately to questions asking how old he and his daughters were, or how long he had been married. In spite of some improvement, 10 months later he was still referring to his accident as having occurred 2 months previously. In a conversation recorded 15 months post-injury he attempts to recount his Caernarvon Castle episode three times within a quarter of an hour using virtually the same words, yet under direct questioning seems unable to recall having mentioned it before in the current conversation. When Colin is responding to written stimuli his topic management is a great deal better because the written words are a constant visual reminder of the topic in hand. This is apparent in sample 15 above, and in the following sample where he is asked to provide a written response to 'describe in detail how you would make baked beans on toast' although he does finish off with an opinion which includes one of his stereotyped phrases.

Sample 16†
OPEN A CAN OF BEAN'S PUT INTO SOURSPAN. MAKE TOAT. WHEN iS DONE & BEAN'S OR COOKT . BUTTER TOAT CAN DO TWO THINGS HAVE THE TOAT HOLE OR CUT INTO SOLDER'S THEN TAKE YOUR BEAN OFF THE CUKER WHEN ALL THiS iS DONE PUT ON PLATE iT iS A NiCE BREAKFAST & SOUND AS A POUND

In addition to his memory difficulties, Colin's poor executive functioning and ability to monitor his behaviour are also evident in the following conversation where he has just covered the topics of Caernarvon, farming/gardening and religion.

†Readers should not be misled by the poor spelling and punctuation which merely reflect Colin's premorbid low literacy level.

Sample 17

R `right – – –
    can you re'member what the original `question was
    the . the `subject I 'asked you to `talk about
C `no (– –) – for`gotten [spoken very softly]
5 R have a `think
C – – – – – I don't `know . it's `gone [spoken very softly]
R 'what em . as you've 'just been `talking 'there
    'what 'what do you 'think you've been `talking about
    what what `subjects have you 'covered –
10 'what have you just been `telling me about
C – – – about re`ligion
R 'that was . `one of 'them
C – – – I `like `gardening
    I 'wanted to be a `farmer . but .
15 I 'don't `know 'now
R 'right . you `did say you 'wanted to be a `farmer
    'how did you get 'on to `farming
C cos I 'like `gardening
R – – – 'could be
20 C – – and – –
R 'what . 'what possible . er – –
    `no . well 'let me tell you that `wasn't how you got onto
    'farming about 'gardening
    it was a it was a`nother way
25 'what other . what other `links might be.
    what `else might you have been `talking about
C `oh
R to 'get onto `farming
C I 'wanted to be a 'farmer when I left `school
30 and I 'wanted my a`pprenticeship . so *(– – –)
R *`yeah . but 'why did you . 'why did you `tell me
    . that you 'wanted to be a 'farmer
    'what brought the i'dea of `farming into your 'head
C `well . that's . I `like to be out`side
35 and I 'like to 'see things `growing –
    and it 'is `nice . that 'when d you 'do enough `food for 'people
    you either `eat them 'straight a'way or 'put them in the `freezer
R 'O'K I'm 'going to 'give you 'one of the 'subjects that you
    'talked about
    be`fore you got 'onto 'farming
40 and I 'want you to 'see if you can 'tell me how you 'then got
    onto `farming
    . you 'told me a 'bit about Caer'narvon `Castle
    'how did you get from `there to farming

        C   – – – – Caer'narvon `Castle . and `farming
        R   `yeah
   45   C   `well it 'might be
            `oh I 'think it were `digs
            I had some `lodging allowance
            there were 'people who . 'woman put me ´up
            I 'did t' 'job on Caer'narvon ˇCastle . then she says
   50   do you . 'stop here and 'do these 'three `jobs
            and . I 'got digs for `nowt
        R   m´hm
        C   ˇbasically

Colin proceeds to go over the Caernarvon episode again, and related issues. When asked again how he got on to the topic of Caernarvon Castle, he proceeds to get involved in the episode again and goes off on a different tangent.

Colin has little awareness of what topics have already been covered. When he is asked directly about how he got on to a particular topic he either attempts to improvise an answer as in lines 34 *et seq.* and 45 *et seq.*, or else moves directly back into the topic he is being asked about, as in lines 13 *et seq.* and 29 *et seq.* He is unable to monitor where the discourse has come from or where it is going to and gets totally caught up in the topic of the moment. He is nearly always either in 'opinion mode' or 'episode narrative mode', but his lack of metapragmatic awareness makes him unable to discuss either.*

Topic shift as a repair strategy

In spite of Colin's inability to respond appropriately to conversational repair requests as a result of his lack of metapragmatic ability, there is nevertheless considerable evidence that he is sometimes aware that 'something has gone wrong' with his conversational performance. There are at least three ways in which Colin indicates this. The first is by means of an explicit apology, as in the following examples.

Sample 18
C   and I'm (a bit) dis'pleased that I'm not ´working
    because I've `always ´worked
    then
    `<u>sorry</u> [acknowledges he's gone off topic]
M   `no it's `alright

---

*This lack of metapragmatic awareness may well be a result of poor memory, but it is not possible to be entirely certain.

C *I 'don't I 'don't like
M *don't – `no . we'll come back to that in a bit [takes picture away]
C * <u>I do a`pologise</u>
M * `no – a bit `later

Sample 19
C 'that's the way I `feel
   and ˇbasically it's falling off a `roof and . 'fracturing my `skull
   'cos I 'don't think I've been (– – –) ever `since
   <u>and I do a`pologise I'm `sorry</u>
M `no
C <u>`no I 'am `sorry I really `am</u>

Sample 20
[Describing story from comic strip pictures.]
C they con'tinue playing ˉcricket
   t' 'ball goes through ´window .
   and t' 'fellow sends him `off
   – 'shouldn't have been 'playing in t' `first place
   in 'front of `window
M `yeah
C he de`serves to have a 'broken window 'broken
   – – `<u>sorry about ´that</u>
M ^no . no that's `fine
C cos I I [nt] 'that's how what 'that's what I `feel

The second way in which Colin indicates that he has lost the
thread is to make a joking admission of it, as in the following example.

Sample 21
C they were . 'old enough to be my ˇmother
   and they were `smashing
M `right – er
C but I 'talk to `everybody `don't I
   [laughs]
   <u>I'd 'better give `up `hadn't I</u>
C and M [both laugh]

Sample 22
C `that's ´me
   I just 'like to do 'people `favours
M `mm
C if I 'can't do them a ´favour I say 'hard `lines – –
   <u>I'd 'better give `up `hadn't I</u>

      [laughs]
      `sorry
M `no `that's al´right

Sample 23
C but . I 'don't bear 'malice to 'anybody who 'swears or `smokes
      cos well I 'do believe in ´Jesus (there I'm `right?)
R m´hm
C or be'lieve in ˇsomething `anyway
R `mm
C and ˇhopefully it's `Jesus [breathes in]
      I'd better 'not say no `more `had I [laughs]

Apologising or making a joking admission of the fact are both
explicit means that Colin uses to acknowledge openly that he has lost
his way in the conversation. The third device that Colin uses is a shift in
prosody. This may occur by itself or in conjunction with either of the
first two devices, but it differs from them in that it is not clearly an
open acknowledgement of conversational breakdown, and Colin may
even be unconscious of it. Mention was made in an earlier section of
Colin's occasional production of utterances with a low, narrow pitch
range, low intensity and sometimes rapid tempo which occurred inappropriately and apparently randomly. Analysis of the entire data sample
shows, however, that such prosodic 'shifts' nearly always occur at topic
boundaries and precede either an inappropriate shift to one of his
favourite topics, an apology or a joking admission, or some combination of the three. The following are some examples.

Sample 24
C ˇobviously I swear at ˇwork
      to 'keep face with t' `blokes
      but – it's 'summat I don't `like
R m´hm
C but I . I'm a practising [low pitched, nearly inaudible]
      I'm a practising `catholic

Sample 25
[C is describing a picture]
C she's either wàving for ˇhelp
      or 'waving to that 'bloke in 't `boat
M [nods]
C I would ex . I'm just ac´cepting [low, narrow pitch range, very
      quiet]
      I just feel 'sorry for 'people who's `caught out there
      and . I must ad ˇmit

I've 'done `fund ´raising and saw a lot of things like `this for 'floods

Sample 26
C   I don't think you `will ´have
    because I 'don't think 'people `are like that in `general
    I'm just talking about '**** `****   [almost inaudible]
    and – that's `twice I've 'mentioned it
    and I 'shan't mention it 'ever a`gain
    and I `do a`pologise

To the extent that such prosodic behaviour is a concomitant of other communicative features, it may be seen as an instance of what Brewster (1989, p. 178 *et seq.*) calls 'prosodic disturbance', i.e. abnormal prosody 'resulting from problems on another linguistic level' as opposed to primary dysprosody or prosodic disability *per se*.

A further feature which often accompanies a change of Colin's topic – usually to an expression of opinion – is the use of subjective adverbial expressions such as *basically*, *I must admit* and *I would say* (see in particular samples 3, 6, 9, 11, 13, 14, 15, 19 and 25). Their frequency in Colin's language is hardly surprising given their function as a means of inserting an opinion into a conversation.

What all of this adds up to is that a shift to one of Colin's favourite topics appears to be a conversational repair strategy on a par with apology and joking admission. When faced with the realisation that he has lost his conversational thread, Colin is unable to remember the original topic unless he has, for example, a written reminder of it. He may either apologise, make a joke of it or else try to carry on. If he cannot recall how the conversation reached the current point (i.e. its hierarchical structure is lost), one possible safe option is to use as a default a topic whose conversational import relies on its subjective significance to Colin rather than on an objective link to a previous topic – namely, an opinion or an autobiographical episode. While deciding on a topic, and to avoid too abrupt a transition, he may use as 'fillers' discourse adverbials such as *basically* to indicate a change to a subjective topic. In addition, poor memory makes it difficult to estimate how much his interlocutor already knows about what is currently being talked about, which means that he may sometimes repeat information that has already been given and at other times not give enough information to enable the interlocutor to follow what is being talked about.

What we are proposing, then, is that Colin's linguistic repetitiveness, topic bias, topic handling and occasionally odd prosody are not primary deficits in themselves, but are at least partially explicable as direct consequences of a communication strategy which attempts to compensate for impaired memory and executive function.

Outcome

Remediation

The ultimate purpose of the type of analysis outlined in this chapter is to apply it in some way that benefits the client. Potentially, this may involve a number of different approaches, e.g. working directly with the client in facilitatory 'exercises', explanation to the client, structuring of the client's communicative environment, explanation and advice to the closest communicative partners, etc. Moreover, each of these approaches may have a different aim, such as improving a linguistic ability, decreasing an inappropriate behaviour, reducing psychological distress, facilitating adjustment to the social effects of the disorder. Below is a brief description of the approaches taken with Colin and his family over the course of his rehabilitation.

Broadly speaking, the therapeutic work with Colin fell into three areas. The intervention was based on wide assessment of Colin's cognitive and psychosocial styles, and in particular on the linguistic analysis outlined above. It is important to note that although detailed assessment can provide a description of someone's communication, and may in particular highlight structural patterns that guide the clinician towards the most fundamental aspects of a disorder, decisions on methods of remediation have to be based on a number of additional sources. In other words, assessment may tell us what needs to be worked on, but not how to go about it. There is little material in the literature on methods of remediation of topic bias/management in neurological disorders. Alderman and Ward (1991) describe therapy techniques used with a woman following herpes simplex encephalitis but the speech pattern in that case revolved around repetition of extremely limited ideas rather than broad topics.

Much of the detailed ongoing assessment ran concurrently with therapeutic intervention, with the results of one feeding back into the other. The first stage was based on attempts to raise Colin's awareness of the patterns of communication that he was using and give him structured opportunities to alter these patterns, together with overt feedback on his performance. It was recognised that this would require Colin to process (at some level) complex theoretical issues and to use them 'on-line' during conversation and thus might be a little ambitious. In spite of this, it was perhaps a necessary first step, because success could have precluded the need for further work. Colin was introduced to the idea of topic, particularly in the form of keeping to the point. He was asked to describe procedures and narratives (structured in terms of complexity and levels of prompts, preparation, etc.) while 'keeping to the point' and was given an opportunity to reflect on his performance via video and audio feedback and the therapist's opinion. It rapidly became clear that Colin was unable to recognise any but the most blatant shifts of topic in his own or others' output after the event and completely unable to use these notions 'on-line'. Further explanation led inevitably up a cul-de-sac of misinterpretations on both sides.

Following this, the focus of therapy moved to structuring Colin's communication without requiring him to monitor the process. Given the links between Colin's topic management and his topic bias (and the corresponding assumption that improvement in one would lead to improvement in the other) it was felt that the easiest area to target via external direction was his topic bias. At the time, Colin was being introduced to using a memory aid in the form of a 'personal organiser' by which he could access information retrospectively and help himself to remember prospective information such as appointments. Within this was added a list of topics which it was agreed (with Colin's family) that he should not talk about. These were very broad, and included religion, football and people he disliked. Each time Colin introduced one of these topics within the Rehabilitation Centre he was referred to the list of 'prohibited' subjects in his book.

The first stage of this work met with some success in that Colin came to start a topic and would say 'I'm not supposed to talk about that, am I?' (see, for example, sample 23). However, it soon became clear that the breadth of the subjects made it difficult to pin down exactly what Colin should and should not talk about. For example, as football was a major interest (and Colin had taken an active role in the training of professional youth teams) it seemed reasonable for Colin to discuss a match he had seen the day before but less appropriate for him to express for the umpteenth time his dissatisfaction with the local team's youth policies. This tied in with the analysis of his topic handling, which identified that when faced with a difficulty in maintaining a topic or shifting appropriately to a new one, Colin frequently resorted to the expression of a pet opinion. It was recognised that the on-line processing of awareness necessary for Colin to control this aspect of topic maintenance placed too great a cognitive burden on him. It therefore seemed appropriate to make use of his immediate communicative partners as the external controlling factors. They were clearly going to be the people most affected by Colin's communicative behaviour, so therapeutic intervention moved into the family sphere.

Although Colin's family (particularly his wife and two daughters) had been involved in the discussions from the beginning of therapy, at this point they were asked to take a more active role. This coincided with his wife's increasing embarrassment at Colin's tendency to veer towards the subject of people he disliked at the most inopportune moments. Following explanation that this tendency seemed to be the result of 'topic crisis management' rather than an obsessive thought pattern in itself, Colin's family agreed to a procedure whereby at the first mention of the topic in question, the listener would say to Colin

'You've agreed not to talk about that' and would leave the room for 2 minutes. It should be noted here that this is an extremely difficult thing for relatives to do, and especially to do consistently. Fortunately, Colin's family were amenable to this type of behaviour management, and as a result the behaviour decreased rapidly. This type of approach was subsequently applied to a number of similar conversational patterns, especially the expression of violent feelings of retribution at what Colin considered unjust news stories. In addition, Colin was given some 'safe' questions he could ask new visitors to the house, when his conversational skills appeared to be at their most vulnerable.

The process of intervention was informed throughout by the continuing analysis of Colin's verbal output. In this way the mass of complex information was broken down into a manageable framework, both for the therapists responsible for devising a programme for Colin, and for the team at the Rehabilitation Centre who had to incorporate it into other areas of work.

From the clinical point of view, a particularly useful aspect of having a theoretical framework was in being able to deal productively with the variety of issues raised by Colin's family, along the lines of 'Why does he keep saying that?' or 'He's like a dog with a bone that won't let go'. Furthermore, the fact that they could be given a framework by which to understand Colin's conversational style legitimised for them the adoption of a seemingly peculiar pattern of interaction, in which they were required to interrupt verbally, to reflect overtly on the content of Colin's conversation, to supply Colin with appropriate phrases and to terminate conversations that were getting out of hand.

There is no doubt that Colin remains to some extent verbally inappropriate, characterised by milder forms of the behaviour described above. However, his family now describe him as 'manageable'. For them this 'manageability' consists of reduced incidence of socially inappropriate and embarrassing behaviours, a system for understanding why Colin is reacting in certain ways and having a means of dealing with the behaviour if it does arise.

Methodological and theoretical implications

It would clearly have been useful if there had been a standard assessment of conversational or pragmatic disability which had been able to characterise Colin's problem accurately, but although numerous pragmatic profiles do exist – a few specifically aimed at the closed head injury population (e.g. Ehrlich and Barry, 1989) – unfortunately none of those that we were aware of were much help beyond providing a checklist category such as 'topic handling' to be ticked as inadequate. The major problems with currently available assessments of pragmatic disability (for a useful review see Chapter 7 of McTear and Conti-

Ramsden, 1992) are the range of phenomena that the term 'pragmatics' can be applied to, and the lack of theoretical coherence of pragmatics as an area of academic study (see the discussion in Levinson, 1983). Pragmatic ability may be seen as the ability to combine linguistic, cognitive (especially inferential), affective and social competence to be able to communicate effectively and appropriately with others. Given this breadth, it is hardly surprising that pragmatic assessment tools tend either to consist of a checklist of a wide range of heterogen-eous factors or else to sacrifice comprehensiveness to a detailed consideration of just a few key features.

Prutting and Kirchner (1987), an example of the former approach, describe their profile as a 'descriptive taxonomy', but the lack of a succinct, operational definition of pragmatics means that the checklist items are not clearly grouped together under defined superordinate categories, or differentiated in terms of their relative importance. This means, for example, that it is unclear whether poor performance with 'topic' is of more or less significance to the overall impression of dysfunction than 'inappropriate turn taking', or whether 'inappropriate turn taking' as judged on the Prutting and Kirchner scale is to be seen as similar in severity to an equivalent category in an alternative framework such as the Discourse Analysis Rating Scale from the Right Hemisphere Language Battery (Bryan, 1989). It could be argued that such comparisons are meaningless, in that Bryan is aiming at a focalised right hemisphere pathology, while Prutting and Kirschner apply the profile to a range of diagnostic groups, but because it is not indicated otherwise one can only assume that the same terms are intended to denote the same behaviours independently of the type of disorder. At any rate, frameworks such as that of Prutting and Kirchner are too superficial to be of use in cases like Colin's. On the other hand, profiles such as Ehrlich and Barry (1989), Bryan (1989) and the RICE (Halper et al., 1991) which use a narrower range of parameters and severity scales are still unable to provide any insight into the nature of Colin's problem. In cases such as that of Colin, there still appears to be no alternative to the more time-consuming exploratory methods illustrated in this chapter.

To turn to the theoretical significance of this study, the idea of explaining certain types of abnormal linguistic behaviour as resulting from compensatory functional communication strategies is not new. Lesser and Milroy (1993, p. 23 et seq.) review a number of cases where, for example, compulsive talking may be regarded as an attempt to hold on to the conversational turn as a means of avoiding revealing comprehension problems (Edwards and Garman, 1989) and increased use of stereotypes may be seen as a means of carrying on a conversation in spite of having problems with lexical access (Panzeri et al., 1987). However, we have not come across any attempt to explain topic bias in this way. There is little explicit reference to topic bias in the research literature. It is generally seen as a concomitant of obsessive or compulsive behaviour in conditions such as autism and schizophrenia (Wolff and Barlow, 1980; Frith, 1989b). The study that comes nearest to the view taken here is an analysis of topic bias in adults with learning difficulties (Rein and Kernan, 1989) which showed that repeated reference to the same topic appeared to be a strategy for maintaining social interactions. However, only one 'circumscribed interest' was identified for each subject as compared to the range of 'favourite' topics referred to by Colin. It may well be that topic bias, poor topic handling generally and repetitiveness of the type manifested by Colin may occur for different reasons in different types of communication disorder, and it would clearly be wrong to suggest that whenever such impairments do occur they are inevitably the result of compensatory communicative strategies. As a hypothesis, however, it would certainly be worth considering in future studies of this type of impairment.

References

Abbs, J. and Cole, K. (1982) Consideration of bulbar and suprabulbar afferent influences on speech motor co-ordination and programming. In S. Grillner, B. Lindblom, J. Lubker and A. Persson (Eds), *Speech Motor Control*. New York: Pergamon Press.

Abbs, J., Hunter, C. and Barlow, S. (1983) Differential speech-motor system impairments with supra-bulbar lesions. In M. Berry (Ed.), *Clinical Dysarthria*. San Diego: College Hill Press.

Adams, M. and Reis, R. (1971) The influence of the onset of phonation on the frequency of stuttering. *Journal of Speech and Hearing Research*, 14, 639–644.

Albery, E. and Grunwell, P. (1993) Consonant articulation in different types of cleft lip and palate. In P. Grunwell (Ed.), *Analysing Cleft Palate Speech*. London: Whurr.

Albery, L. (1989) Approaches to the treatment of speech problems. In J. Stengelhofen (Ed.), *Cleft Palate: The Nature and Remediation of Communication Problems*. London: Churchill Livingstone.

Alderman, N. and Ward, A. (1991) Behavioural treatment of the dysexecutive syndrome: reduction of repetitive speech using response cost and overlearning. *Neuropsychological Rehabilitation*, 1, 65–80.

Alpin, D.Y. and Rowan, V.J. (1990). Psychological characteristics of children with functional hearing loss. *British Journal of Audiology*, 24, 77–87.

Altenberg, B. (1993) Recurrent verb-complement constructions in the London-Lund Corpus. In J. Aarts, P. de Haan and N. Oostdijk (Eds), *English Language Corpora: Design, Analysis and Exploitation*. Papers from the thirteenth International Conference on English Language Research on Computerized Corpora, Nijmegen 1992. Amsterdam/Atlanta: Rodopi.

Amorosa, H., von Benda, U., Wagner, E. and Keck, A. (1985) Transcribing detail in the speech of unintelligible children: a comparison of procedures. *British Journal of Disorders of Communication*, 20, 281–287.

Andrews, J. R. (1973) Oral form discrimination in individuals with normal and cleft palates. *Cleft Palate Journal*, 10, 92–98.

Arndt, W.B., Shelton, R.L., Johnson, A.F. and Furr, M.L. (1977) Identification and description of homogeneous subgroups within a sample of misarticulating children. *Journal of Speech and Hearing Research*, 20, 263–292.

Atkinson, J.M. and Heritage, J. (Eds) (1984) *Structures of Social Action: Studies in Conversation Analysis*. Cambridge: Cambridge University Press.

Atkinson, M. (1979) Prerequisites for reference. In E. Ochs and B. Schieffelin (Eds), *Developmental Pragmatics*. New York: Academic Press.

Auerbach, S.H., Allard, T., Naeser, M., Alexander, M.P. and Albert, M.L. (1982) Pure word deafness: Analysis of a case with bilateral lesions and a defect at the prephonemic level. *Brain*, **105**, 271–300.

Baken, R.J. (1987) *Clinical Measurement of Speech and Voice*. London: Taylor & Francis.

Ball, M.J. (1984) X-ray techniques. In C. Code and M.J. Ball (Eds), *Experimental Clinical Phonetics*. London: Croom Helm.

Ball, M.J. (1988a) Review article: Clinical linguistic encounters. *Clinical Linguistics and Phonetics*, **2**, 143–151.

Ball, M.J. (Ed.) (1988b) *Theoretical Linguistics and Disordered Language* London: Croom Helm.

Ball, M.J. (1989) *Phonetics for Speech Pathology* London: Whurr

Ball, M.J. and Kent, R.D. (1987) Editorial. *Clinical Linguistics and Phonetics*, **1**, 1–5.

Ball, M., Code, C., Rahilly, J. and Hazlett, D. (1994) Non-segmental aspects of disordered speech: developments in transcription. *Clinical Linguistics and Phonetics*, **8**, 67–83.

Bamford, J. and Saunders, E. (1990) *Hearing Impairment, Auditory Perception and Language Disability*, 2nd edn. London: Whurr.

Barden, H. (1985) Dentition and other aspects of growth and development. In D. Lane and B. Stratford (Eds), *Current Approaches to Down's Syndrome*. London: Holt, Rhinehart & Winston.

Baron-Cohen, S., Leslie, A. M. and Frith, U. (1985) Does the autistic child have a 'theory of mind'? *Cognition*, **21**, 37–46.

Bates, E., Camaioni, L. and Volterra, V. (1979) The acquisition of performatives prior to speech. In E. Ochs and B. Schieffelin (Eds), *Developmental Pragmatics*. New York: Academic Press.

Bates, E., Bretherton, I. and Snyder, L. (1988) *From First Words to Grammar: Individual Differences and Dissociable Mechanisms*. Cambridge: Cambridge University Press.

Bates, E., Dale, P.S. and Thal, D. (1995) Individual differences and their implications for theories of language development. In P. Fletcher and B. MacWhinney (Eds), *The Handbook of Child Language*. Oxford: Blackwell.

Baum, S.R. and McNutt, J.C. (1990) An acoustic analysis of frontal misarticulation of /s/ in children. *Journal of Phonetics*, **19**, 177–192.

Bayles, K.A., Tomoeda, C.K. and Kaszniak, A.W. (1985) Verbal perseveration of dementia patients. *Brain and Language*, **25**, 102–116.

Behrens, S.J. and Blumstein, S.E. (1988) Acoustic characteristics of English voiceless fricatives: a descriptive analysis. *Journal of Phonetics*, **16**, 295–298.

Beresford, R. (1987) What kind of phonological description is clinically the most useful? *Clinical Linguistics and Phonetics*, **1**, 35–90.

Bernhardt, B. (1992a) Developmental implications of nonlinear phonological theory. *Clinical Linguistics and Phonetics*, **6**, 259–282.

Bernhardt, B. (1992b) The application of nonlinear phonological theory to intervention with one phonologically disordered child. *Clinical Linguistics and Phonetics*, **6**, 283–316.

Bernhardt, B. and Ball, M. (1993) Characteristics of atypical speech currently not included in the Extensions to the IPA. *Journal of the International Phonetic Association*, **23**, 35–38.

Bernhardt, B. and Gilbert, J. (1992) Applying linguistic theory to speech-language pathology: the case for nonlinear phonology. *Clinical Linguistics and Phonetics*, **6**, 123–146.

Bernhardt, B. and Stoel-Gammon, C. (1994) Nonlinear phonology: Introduction and clinical application. *Journal of Speech and Hearing Research*, 37, 123–143.

Berry, M. (Ed.) (1983) *Clinical Dysarthria* . San Diego: College Hill Press.

Best, W. and Howard, D. (1994) Word sound deafness resolved? *Aphasiology*, 8, 223–256.

Biber, D. and Finegan, E. (1991) On the exploitation of computerized corpora in variation studies. In K. Aijmer and B. Altenberg (Eds), *English Corpus Linguistics: Studies in Honour of Jan Svartvik*. London: Longman.

Bishop, D.V.M. (1983) *Test for Reception of Grammar*. Published by the author at MRC Applied Psychology Unit, 15 Chaucer Road, Cambridge, CB2 2EF, UK.

Bishop, D.V.M. (1989) *Test for the Reception of Grammar*, revised edn. Published by the author at MRC Applied Psychology Unit, 15 Chaucer Road, Cambridge, CB2 2EF, UK.

Bishop, D.V.M. and Adams, C. (1989) Conversational characteristics of children with semantic pragmatic disorder II: What features lead to a judgement of inappropriacy? *British Journal of Disorders of Communication*, 24, 241–263.

Bladon, R.A.W. and Nolan, F. (1977) A video-fluorographic investigation of tip and blade alveolars in English. *Journal of Phonetics*, 5, 185–193.

Blank, M., Gessner, M. and Esposito, A. (1979) Language without communication: A case study. *Journal of Child Language*, 6, 329–52.

Bloom, L. (1991) *Language Development from Two to Three*. Cambridge: Cambridge University Press.

Bloomer, H.H. (1971) Speech defects associated with dental malocclusions and related abnormalities. In P. Travis (Ed.), *Handbook of Speech Pathology and Audiology*. New York: Appleton-Century-Crofts.

Blumstein, S.E., Cooper, W.E., Goodglass, H., Statlender, S. and Gotlieb, J. (1980) Production deficits in aphasia: a voice-onset-time analysis. *Brain and Language*, 9, 153–170.

Boone, D.R. and McFarlane, S.C. (1988) *The Voice and Voice Therapy* , 4th edn. Englewood Cliffs, NJ: Prentice Hall.

Borden, G. and Harris, K. (1980) *Speech Science Primer*. Baltimore: Williams & Wilkins.

Borden, G.J. and Gay, T. (1978) On the production of low tongue tip /s/: a case report. *Journal of Communication Disorders*, 11, 425–431.

Bosma, J. (1967) *Symposium on Oral Sensation and Perception*. Springfield: Charles Thomas.

Bowman, J. (1971) *The Muscle Spindle and Neural Control of the Tongue*. Springfield: Charles Thomas.

Brewster, K. (1989) Assessment of prosody. In K. Grundy (Ed.), *Linguistics in Clinical Practice*. London: Taylor & Francis.

Brinton, B. and Fujuki, M. (1982) A comparison of request–response sequences in the discourse of normal and language disordered children. *Journal of Speech and Hearing Research*, 47, 57–62.

Brinton, B. and Fujiki, M. (1984) Development of topic manipulation skills in discourse. *Journal of Speech and Hearing Research*, 27, 350–358.

Brinton, B., Fujuki, M., Frome-Loeb, D. and Winkler, E. (1986) Development of conversational repair strategies in response to requests for clarification. *Journal of Speech and Hearing Research*, 29, 75–81.

Brodal, A. (1973) Self observations and neuro-anatomical considerations after a stroke. *Brain* , 96, 675–694.

Brown, G. and Yule, G. (1983) *Discourse Analysis*. Cambridge: Cambridge University Press.

Brown, R. (1973) *A First Language: The Early Stages*. London: Allen & Unwin.

Bryan, K. (1989) *Right Hemisphere language Battery*. London: Whurr.

Buchman, A.S., Garron, D.C., Trost-Cardamone, J.E., Wichter, M.D. and Schwartz, M. (1986) Word deafness: one hundred years later. *Journal of Neurology, Neurosurgery and Psychiatry*, 49, 489–499.

Buckingham, H. (1988) Phonological paraphasia. In C. Code (Ed) *Characteristics of Aphasia*. London: Taylor & Francis.

Burger, L.H., Wertz, R.T. and Woods, D. (1983) A response to treatment in a case of cortical deafness. In R.H. Brookshire (Ed.), *Clinical Aphasiology Conference Proceedings*. Minneapolis: BRK.

Bush, C. et al (1973) On specifying a system for transcribing consonants in child language: a working paper with examples from American English and Mexican Spanish. Unpublished paper, Child Language Project, Stanford University. Cited in Ingram (1976)

Butcher, A. (1989) Measuring coarticulation and variability in tongne contact patterns. *Clinical Linguistics and Phonetics*, 3, 39–47.

Butcher, A. and Weiher, E. (1976) An electropalatographic investigation of coarticulation in VCV sequences. *Journal of Phonetics*, 4, 59–74.

Button, G. and Lee, J.R.E. (Eds) (1987) *Talk and Social Organization*. Clevedon: Multilingual Matters.

Byers Brown, B. and Edwards, M. (1989) *Developmental Disorders of Language*. London: Whurr.

Byng, S. (1988) Sentence processing deficits: theory and therapy. *Cognitive Neuropsychology*, 5, 629–676.

Byng, S. and Coltheart, M. (1986) Aphasia therapy research: Methodological requirements and illustrative results. In E. Hjelmquist and L.G. Nilsson (Eds), *Communication and Handicap*. Amsterdam: Elsevier Science.

Byng, S. and Coltheart, M. (1989) A treatment for surface dyslexia. In X. Seron and G. Deloche (Eds), *Cognitive Approaches in Neuropsychological Rehabilitation*. Hillsdale, NJ: Lawrence Erlbaum Associates.

Byng, S., Kay, J., Edmunson, A. and Scott, C. (1990) Aphasia tests reconsidered. *Aphasiology*, 4, 67–91.

Canning, B. and Rose, M. (1974) Clinical measurement of the speed of tongue movement in British children with normal speech. *British Journal of Disorders of Communication*, 9, 45–50.

Caplan, D. (1992) *Language Structure, Processing and Disorders*. Cambridge, MA: MIT Press.

Caplan, D. and Utman, J.A. (1994) Selective acoustic phonetic impairment and lexical access in an aphasic patient. *Journal of the Acoustical Society of America*, 95, 512–517.

Caramazza, A. (1984) The logic of neuropsychological research and the problem of patient classification in aphasia. *Brain and Language*, 21, 9–20.

Caramazza, A. (1989) Cognitive neuropsychology and rehabilitation: An unfulfilled promise? In X. Seron and G. Deloche (Eds), *Cognitive Approaches in Neuropsychological Rehabilitation*. Hillsdale, NJ: Lawrence Erlbaum Associates.

Carr, J. (1985) The development of intelligence. In D. Lane and B.Stratford (Eds), *Current Approaches to Down's Syndrome*. London: Holt, Rhinehart & Winston.

Catalanotto, F.A. and Moss, J.L. (1973) Manual and oral stereognosis in children with cleft palate, gonadal dysgenesis, pseudohypoparathyroidism, oral facial digital syndrome and Kallman's syndrome. *Archives of Oral Biology*, **48**, 1227–1232.

Catford, J.C. (1977) *Fundamental Problems in Phonetics*. Edinburgh: Edinburgh University Press.

Chapman, R.S. (1981) Exploring children's communicative intents. In J.F. Miller (Ed.), *Assessing Language Production in Children: Experimental Procedures*. Baltimore: University Park Press.

Cherney, L.R. (1991) Cognitive–linguistic problems associated with traumatic brain injury: a perspective. In A.S. Halper, L.R. Cherney and T.K. Miller (Eds), *Clinical Management of Communication Problems in Adults with Traumatic Brain Injury*. Rockville: Aspen.

Chiat, S. (1989) The relation between prosodic structure, syllabification and segmental realisation: evidence from a child with fricative stopping. *Clinical Linguistics and Phonetics*, **3**, 223–242.

Chomsky, N. (1986) *Knowledge of language: Its Nature, Origin and Use*. New York: Praeger.

Christman, S.S. (1992) Uncovering phonological regularity in neologisms: contributions of sonority theory. *Clinical Linguistics and Phonetics*, **6**, 219–247.

Code, C. and Ball, M. (1982) Fricative production in Broca's aphasia: a spectrographic analysis. *Journal of Phonetics*, **10**, 325–331.

Code, C. and Ball, M. (Eds) (1984) *Experimental Clinical Phonetics: Investigatory Techniques in Speech Pathology and Therapeutics*. London: Croom Helm.

College of Speech and Language Therapists (1991) *Communicating Quality*. London: The College of Speech and Language Therapists.

Colton, H. and Cooker, H.S. (1968) Perceived nasality in the speech of the deaf. *Journal of Speech and Hearing Research*, **2**, 553–559.

Comb, M.L. and Slaby, D.A. (1977) Social skills training with children. In B.B. Lahey and A.E. Kazdin (Eds), *Advances in Clinical Child Psychiatry*, Vol. 1. London: Plenum Press.

Compton, A.J. and Hutton, J.S. (1978) *Compton–Hutton Phonological Assessment*. San Francisco: Carousel House.

Connery, V., Boardman, C., Bray, D., Coburn, A., Combes, C., Hammond, C., Hareker, K., Henry, C., Hoad, H., Nicholls, S., Reilly, J., Sharples, K., Stephens, H., Webb, S., Williams, P., Wilson, J. and Winfield, V. (1992) *Nuffield Centre Dyspraxia Programme*. London: The Miracle Factory.

Conti-Ramsden, G. (1990) How can we study pragmatic disabilities? In K. Mogford-Bevan and J. Sadler (Eds), *Child Language Disability* Vol II: *Semantic and Pragmatic Difficulties*. Clevedon: Multilingual Matters.

Conti-Ramsden, G. and Friel-Patti, S. (1983) Mother's discourse adjustments to language-impaired and non language-impaired children. *Journal of Speech and Hearing Disorders*, **48**, 360–367.

Conti-Ramsden, G. and Gunn, M. (1986) The development of conversational disability: A case study. *British Journal of Disorders of Communication*, **21**, 339–351.

Cooper, J., Moodley, M. and Reynell, J. (1978) *Helping Language Development*. London: Edward Arnold

Cornwell, A. (1974) Development of language abstraction and numerical concept formation in Down's Syndrome children. *American Journal of Mental Deficiency*, **79**, 179–190.

Couper-Kuhlen, E. (1986) *An Introduction to English Prosody*. Tübingen: Max Niemeyer-Verlag.

Courchesne, E. (1988) Physioanatomical consideration in Down Syndrome. In L. Nadel (Ed.), *The Psychobiology of Down Syndrome*. London: MIT Press.

Craig, H.K. and Evans, J.L. (1989) Turn exchange characteristics of SLI children's simultaneous and nonsimultaneous speech. *Journal of Speech and Hearing Disorders*, 54, 334–47.

Craig, H.K. and Gallagher, T.M. (1979) The structural characteristics of monologues in the speech of normal children: Syntactic non-conversational aspects. *Journal of Speech and Hearing Research*, 22, 46–62.

Crary, M. (1993) *Developmental Motor Speech Disorder*. Singular Publications Group. Distributed by Whurr.

Creech, C., Wertz, R. and Rosenbek, J. (1973) Oral sensation and perception in dysarthric adults. *Perceptual Motor Skills*, 37, 167–172.

Cromer, R.F. (1979) The strengths of the weak form of the cognition hypothesis for language acquisition. In V. Lee (Ed.), *Language Development*. London: Croom Helm.

Cruttenden, A. (1986) *Intonation*. Cambridge: Cambridge University Press.

Crystal, D. (1972) The case for linguistics: a prognosis. *British Journal of Disorders of Communication*, 7, 3-16.

Crystal, D. (1981) *Clinical Linguistics,* 1st edn. Vienna: Springer-Verlag.

Crystal, D. (1982) Terms, time and teeth. *British Journal of Disorders of Communication,* 17, 3–19.

Crystal, D. (1984) *Linguistic Encounters with Language Handicap*. Oxford: Blackwell.

Crystal, D. (1987a) *Clinical Linguistics* , 2nd edn. London: Whurr.

Crystal, D. (1987b) Meeting the need for case studies. *Child Language Teaching and Therapy*, 3, 305–310.

Crystal, D. (1987c) Towards a 'bucket' theory of language disability: Taking account of interaction between linguistic levels. *Clinical Linguistics and Phonetics*, 1, 7–22.

Crystal, D. (1991) *A Dictionary of Linguistics and Phonetics*, 3rd edn. Oxford: Blackwell.

Crystal, D. (1992) *Profiling Linguistic Disability*, 2nd edn. London: Whurr.

Crystal, D. and Varley, R. (1993) *Introduction to Language Pathology*, 3rd edn. London: Whurr.

Crystal, D., Fletcher, P. and Garman, M. (1989) *Grammatical Analysis of Language Disability*, 2nd edn. London: Whurr.

Cunningham, C. (1988) *Down's Syndrome: An Introduction for Parents*, 2nd edn. London: Souvenir Press.

Cutler, A. (1980) Errors of stress and intonation. In V.A. Fromkin (Ed.), *Errors in Linguistic Performance*. New York: Academic Press.

Cutler, A. (1992) Psychology and the segment. In G.J. Docherty and D.R. Ladd (Eds), *Papers in Laboratory Phonology II: Gesture, Segment, Prosody*. Cambridge: Cambridge University Press.

Dabul, B. (1978) *Apraxia Battery for Adults*. Tigard: C.C. Publications.

Dalton, P. and Hardcastle, W. (1989) *Disorders of Fluency*. London: Whurr.

Damico, J. (1985) Clinical discourse analysis: A functional approach to language assessment. In C. Simon (Ed.), *Communication Skills and Classroom Success*. San Diego: College Hill Press.

Daniloff, R., Wilcox, K. and Stephens, M. (1980) An acoustic-articulatory description of children's defective /s/ productions. *Journal of Communication Disorders*, 13, 347–363.

Darley, F., Aronson, A. and Brown, J. (1975) *Motor Speech Disorders*. Philadelphia: W.B. Saunders.

Darwin, C. (1877) A biographical sketch of an infant. *Mind*, 2, 285–294.

Davies, B. (1985) Hearing problems. In D. Lane and B. Stratford (Eds), *Current Approaches to Down's Syndrome*. London: Holt, Rhinehart & Winston.

Dean, E., Howell, J., Hill, A. and Waters, D. (1990) *Metaphon Resource Pack*. Windsor: NFER-Nelson.

Demetras, M.J., Nolan-Post, K. and Snow, C.E. (1986) Feedback to first language learners: The role of repetition and clarification questions. *Journal of Child Language*, 13, 275–292.

Denes, G. and Semenza, C. (1975) Auditory modality-specific anomia: Evidence from a case of pure word deafness. *Cortex*, 11, 401–411.

Dent, H., Gibbon, F. and Hardcastle, W.J. (1992) Inhibiting an abnormal lingual pattern in a cleft palate child using Electropalatography. In M.M. Leahy and J.K. Kallen (Eds), *Interdisciplinary Perspectives in Speech and Language Pathology*. Dublin: School of Clinical Speech and Language Studies.

Deutsch, S. (1984) Oral stereognosis. In C. Code and M.J. Ball (Eds), *Experimental Clinical Phonetics*. London: Croom Helm.

Docherty, G. and Fraser, H. (1993) On the relationship between acoustic and electropalatographic representations of speech. *Work in Progress*, 7, 8–25. Speech Research Laboratory University of Reading.

Docherty, G. and Ladd, D.R. (Eds) (1992) *Papers in Laboratory Phonology II: Gesture, Segment, Prosody*. Cambridge: Cambridge University Press.

Dollaghan, C. and Kaston, N. (1986) A comprehension monitoring program for language impaired children. *Journal of Speech and Hearing Disorders*, 51, 264–271.

Donahue, M., Pearl, R. and Bryan, T. (1980) Learning disabled children's conversational competence: Responses to inadequate messages. *Applied Psycholinguistics*, 1, 387–403.

Drew, P. (1990) Conversation analysis: Who needs it? *Text*, 10, 27–35.

Duchan, J.F. and Katz, J. (1983) Language and auditory processing: Top down plus bottom up. In E. Lasky and J. Katz (Eds), *Central Auditory Processing Disorders: Problems of Speech, Language and Learning*. Baltimore. University Park Press

Duckworth, M., Allen, G., Hardcastle, W. and Ball, M. (1990) Extensions to the International Phonetic Alphabet for the transcription of atypical speech. *Clinical Linguistics and Phonetics*, 4, 273–280.

Duffy, J. R. and Gawle, C. A. (1984) Apraxic speakers' vowel duration in consonant-vowel-consonant syllables. In J.C. Rosenbek, M.R. McNeil and A.E. Aronson (Eds), *Apraxia of Speech: Physiology, Acoustics, Linguistics, Management*. San Diego: College Hill Press.

Durand, J. (1990) *Generative and Non-linear Phonology*. London: Longman.

Dustman, R. and Callner, D. (1979) Cortical evoked responses and response decrement in non-retarded and Down Syndrome individuals. *American Journal of Mental Deficiency*, 83, 391–397.

Eastwood, P. (1981) *The Sheffield Computerized Articulation Test*. Unpublished paper, Department of Linguistics, University of Sheffield.

Edgerton, R. (1967) *The Cloak of Competence*. California: University of California Press.

Edwards, J.A. (1991) Transcription in discourse. In W. Bright (Ed.), *Oxford International Encyclopedia of Linguistics*, Vol. 1, pp. 367–371. Oxford: Oxford University Press.

Edwards, J.A. (1993) Principles and contrasting systems of discourse transcription. In J.A. Edwards and M.D. Lampert (Eds), *Talking Data: Transcription and Coding in Discourse Research*. Hillsdsale, NJ: Lawrence Erlbaum.

Edwards, M. (1983) Issues in phonological assessment. *Seminars in Speech and Language*, 4, 351–374.

Edwards, M. (1984) *Disorders of Articulation*. New York: Springer Verlag

Edwards, S. and Garman, M. (1989) Case study of a fluent aphasic: the relation between linguistic assessment and therapeutic intervention. In P. Grunwell and A. James (Eds), *The Functional Evaluation of Language Disorders*. London: Croom Helm.

Edwards, S. and Miller, N. (1989) Using EPG to investigate speech errors and motor agility in a dyspraxic patient. *Clinical Linguistics and Phonetics*, 3, 111–126.

Ehrlich, J. and Barry, P. (1989) Rating communication behaviours in the head-injured adult. *Brain Injury*, 3, 193–198.

Ellis, A. W. and Young, A. W. (1988) *Human Cognitive Neuropsychology*. Hove: Lawrence Erlbaum.

Enderby, P. (1983a) *Frenchay Dysarthria Assessment*. San Diego, CA: College Hill Press.

Enderby, P. (1983b) The standardised assessment of dysarthria is possible. In W. Berry (Ed.), *Clinical Dysarthria*. San Diego, CA: College Hill Press.

Enderby, P. and Philipp, R. (1986) Speech and language handicap: towards knowing the size of the problem. *British Journal of Disorders of Communication*, 21, 151–165.

Ervin-Tripp, S. (1977) Wait for me, roller skate. In S. Ervin-Tripp and C. Mitchell-Kernan (Eds), *Child Discourse*. New York: Academic Press.

Espir, M. and Rose, C. (1983) *Basic Neurology of Speech and Language*, 3rd edn. London: Blackwell Scientific Press.

Evarts, E. (1982) Analogies between central motor programmes for speech and for limb movements. In S. Grillner, B. Lindblom, J. Lubker and A. Persson (Eds), *Speech Motor Control*. New York: Pergamon Press.

Faircloth, M.A. and Faircloth, S.R. (1970) An analysis of the articulatory behaviour of a speech-defective child in connected speech and in isolated-word responses. *Journal of Speech and Hearing Disorders*, 35, 51–61.

Fant, G. (1960) *Acoustic Theory of Speech Production*. The Hague: Mouton.

Ferguson, A. (1994) The influence of aphasia, familiarity and activity on conversational repair. *Aphasiology*, 8, 143–158.

Fey, M.E. and Leonard, L.B. (1983) Pragmatic skills of children with specific language impairment. In T.M. Gallagher and C.A. Prutting (Eds), *Pragmatic Assessment and Intervention Issues in Language*. San Diego, CA: College Hill Press

Flege, J.E., Fletcher, S.G. and Homiedan, A. (1988) Compensating for a bite block in /s/ and /t/ production: Palatographic, acoustic and perceptual data. *Journal of the Acoustical Society of America*, 83, 212–228.

Fletcher, P. and Garman, M. (1994) Transcription, segmentation and analysis: corpora from the language-impaired. In G. Leech, J. Thomas and G. Myers (Eds), *Spoken English on Computer: Transcription, Mark-Up and Application* London: Longman.

Fletcher, S.G. (1989) Palatometric specification of stop, affricate and sibilant sounds. *Journal of Speech and Hearing Research*, 32, 736–748.

Ford, C.E. (1993) *Grammar in Interaction: Adverbial Clauses in American English Conversation*. Cambridge: Cambridge University Press.

Foster, T.D. (1990) *A Textbook of Orthodontics*. Oxford: Blackwell.

Franklin, S. (1989) Dissociations in auditory word comprehension: Evidence from nine fluent aphasic patients. *Aphasiology*, 3, 189–207.

Franklin, S., Turner, J. and Ellis, A. (1992) *ADA Comprehension Battery*. London: Action for Dysphasic Adults. Available from Action for Dysphasic Adults, Canterbury House, Royal Street, London, SE1 7LL.

Frith, C.D. and Done, D.J. (1990) Stereotyped behaviour in madness and in health. In S.F. Cooper and C.T. Dourish (Eds), *The Neurobiology of Behavioural Stereotypy* . Oxford: Oxford University Press.

Frith, U. (1980) Unexpected spelling problems. In U. Frith (Ed.), *Cognitive Processes in Spelling*. London: Academic Press.

Frith, U. (1989a) A new look at language andcommunication in autism. *British Journal of Disorders of Communication*, 24, 123–151.

Frith, U. (1989b) *Autism: Explaining the Enigma*. Oxford: Blackwell.

Frome Loeb, D. and Leonard, L.B. (1988) Specific language impairment and parameter theory. *Clinical Linguistics and Phonetics*, 2, 317–327.

Fry, D.B. (1979) *The Physics of Speech.* Cambridge: Cambridge University Press.

Gallagher, T.M. (1977) Revision behaviours in the speech of normal children developing language. *Journal of Speech and Hearing Research*, 20, 303–318.

Gallagher, T.M. and Darnton, B.A. (1978) Conversational aspects of the speech of language disordered children: revision behaviours. *Journal of Speech and Hearing Research*, 21, 118–135

Garliner, D. (1981) Recognition and diagnosis of orofacial muscle imbalance. In D. Garliner (Ed.), *Myofunctional Therapy* . Philadelphia: Samuels.

Garman, M. (1990) *Psycholinguistics*. Cambridge: Cambridge University Press.

Garrett, M. F. (1980) Levels of processing in sentence production. In B. L. Butterworth (Ed.), *Language Production*, Vol. 1: *Speech and Talk*. London: Academic Press.

Garvey, C. and Berninger, G. (1981) Timing and turn taking in children's conversations. *Discourse Processes*, 4, 27–57.

Gelman, R. and Cohen, N. (1988) Qualitative differences in the way Down Syndrome and normal children solve a novel counting problem. In L. Nadel (Ed.), *The Psychobiology of Down Syndrome*. London: MIT Press.

Gibbon, F. (1994) A description of affricate production in a group of speech-disordered children using electropalatography (EPG). In R. Aulanko and A-M. Korpijaakko-Huuhka (Eds), *Proceedings of the Third Congress of the International Clinical Phonetics and Linguistics Association*, vol. 39, pp. 35–42. Helsinki: Publications of the Department of Phonetics, University of Helsinki.

Gibbon, F. and Hardcastle, W.J. (1987) Articulatory description and treatment of 'lateral /s/' using electropalatography: a case study. *British Journal of Disorders of Communication*, 22, 203–217.

Gibbon, F. and Hardcastle, WJ. (1989) Deviant articulation in a cleft palate child following late repair of the hard palate: a description and remediation procedure using electropalatography. *Clinical Linguistics and Phonetics*, 3, 93–110.

Gibbon, F., Hardcastle, W.J. and Moore, A. (1991) Modifying abnormal tongue patterns in an older child using electropalatography. *Child Language Teaching and Therapy*, 6, 227–245.

Gibbon, F., Dent, H. and Hardcastle, W. J. (1993) Diagnosis and therapy of abnormal alveolar stops in a speech-disordered child using EPG. *Clinical Linguistics and Phonetics*, 7, 247–268.

Gibson, D. (1978) *Down's Syndrome: The Psychology of Mongolism*. Cambridge: Cambridge University Press.

Gielewski, E. (1989) Acoustic analysis and auditory retraining in the remediation of sensory aphasia. In C. Code and D.J. Müller (Eds), *Aphasia Therapy*, pp. 138–145. Whurr, London.

Gimson, A.C. (1989) *An Introduction to the Pronunciation of English*, 4th edn, revised by S. Ramsaran. London: Arnold.

Goldsmith, J.A. (1990) *Autosegmental and Metrical Phonology*. London: Blackwell.

Goldstein, P., Ziegler, W., Vogel, M. and Hoole, P. (1994) Combined palatal-lift and EPG-feedback therapy in dysarthria: a case study. *Clinical Linguistics and Phonetics*, **8**, 201–218.

Goodglass, H. and Kaplan, E. (1972, 1983) *Assessment of Aphasia and Related Disorders*. Philadelphia: Lea & Febinger.

Goodwin, C. and Duranti, A. (1992) Rethinking context: an introduction. In: A. Duranti and C. Goodwin (Eds), *Rethinking Context: Language as an Interactive Phenomenon*. Cambridge: Cambridge University Press.

Gourlay, S. (1988) Treatment of 'lateral /s/': a conventional approach. *Bulletin of the College of Speech Therapists*, June, p. 5.

Gracco, V.L. (1994) Some organisational characteristics of speech movement control. *Journal of Speech and Hearing Research*, **37**, 4–27.

Greenlee, M. (1981) Learning to tell the forest from the trees: Unravelling discourse features of a psychotic child. *First Language*, **2**, 83–102.

Grodzinsky, Y. (1990) *Theoretical Perspectives on Language Deficits*. Cambridge, MA: MIT Press.

Grodzinsky, Y. (1994) Introduction. *Brain and Language*, **45**, 299–305.

Grube, M. and Smith, D. (1989) Paralinguistic intonation-rhythm intervention with a developmental stutterer. *Journal of Fluency Disorders*, **14**, 185–208.

Grube, M., Spiegel, B., Buchhop, N. and Lloyd, K. (1986) Intonation training as a facilitator of intelligibility. *Human Communication Canada*, **13**, 210–217.

Grundy, K. (Ed.) (1989) *Linguistics in Clinical Practice*. London: Whurr.

Grunwell, P. (1985a) Comment on the terms 'phonetics' and 'phonology' as applied in the investigation of speech disorders. *British Journal of Disorders of Communication*, **20**, 165–170.

Grunwell, P. (1985b) *PACS Phonological Assessment of Child Speech*. Windsor, Berks: NFER-Nelson.

Grunwell, P. (1987) *Clinical Phonology*, 2nd edn. London: Croom Helm.

Grunwell, P. (1990) *Developmental Speech Disorders*. London: Churchill Livingstone.

Grunwell, P. (1993) Assessment of articulation and phonology. In J.R. Beech and L. Harding (Eds), *Assessment in Speech and Language Therapy*. London: Routledge.

Grunwell, P. and Huskins, S. (1979) Intelligibility in acquired dysarthria – a neurophonetic approach. *Journal of Communication Disorders*, **12**, 9–22.

Grunwell, P. and James, A. (Eds) (1989) *The Functional Evaluation of Language Disorders*. London: Croom Helm.

Grunwell, P. and Russell, J. (1988) Phonological development in children with cleft lip and palate. *Clinical Linguistics and Phonetics*, **2**, 75–96

Hagen, C. (1981) Language disorders secondary to closed head injury: diagnosis and treatment. *Topics in Language Disorders*, **1**, 73–87.

Hale, S.T., Kellum, G.D., Richardson, J.F., Messer, S.C., Gross, A.M. and Sisakun, S. (1992) Oral motor control, posturing, and myofunctional variables in 8-year-olds. *Journal of Speech and Hearing Research*, **35**, 1203–1208.

Halliday, M.A.K. (1975a) Relevant models of language. In S. Rogers (Ed.), *Children and Language: Readings in Early Language and Socialisation*. London: OUP.

Halliday, M.A.K. (1975b) *Learning How to Mean*. London: Edward Arnold.

Halliday, M.A.K. and Hasan, R. (1985) *Language, Context and Text: Aspects of Language in a Social–Semiotic Perspective*. Deakin University.

Hallidie-Smith, K. (1985) The heart. In L. Nadel (Ed.), *The Psychobiology of Down Syndrome*. London: MIT Press.

Halper, A.S., Burns, M.S., Cherney, L.R. and Mogil, S.I. (1991) *Rehabilitation Institute of Chicago Evaluation of Communication Problems in Right Hemisphere Dysfunction – 2 (RICE–2)*. Aspen Systems Corporation.

Hambly, R. and Farmer, A. (1982) An analysis of vowel duration in a group of language-disordered children exhibiting the open syllable pattern. *Folia Phoniatrica*, 34, 65–70.

Hamlet, S. (1988) Speech compensation for prosthodontically created palatal asymmetries. *Journal of Speech and Hearing Research*, 31, 48–53.

Hamlet, S.L., Bunnell, H.T. and Struntz, B.G. (1986) Articulatory asymmetries. *Journal of the Acoustical Society of America*, 65, 1276–1285.

Happé, F.G.E. (1993) Communicative competence and theory of mind in autism: A test of relevance theory. *Cognition*, 48, 101–119.

Hardcastle, W. (1976) *Physiology of Speech Production*. New York: Academic Press.

Hardcastle, W.J. (1987) Electropalatographic study of articulation disorders in verbal dyspraxia. In J. Ryalls (Ed.), *Phonetic Approaches to Speech Production in Aphasia and Related Disorders*. San Diego: College Hill.

Hardcastle, W.J. and Edwards, S. (1992) EPG-based description of apraxic speech errors. In R. Kent (Ed.), *Intelligibility in Speech Disorders: Theory, Measurement and Management*. Philadelphia: John Benjamins.

Hardcastle, W.J., MorganBarry, R.A. and Clark, C. (1985) Articulatory and voicing characteristics of adult dysarthric and verbal dyspraxic speakers: an instrumental study. *British Journal of Disorders of Communication*, 20, 249–270.

Hardcastle, W.J., Jones, W., Knight, C., Trudgeon, A. and Calder, G. (1989a) New developments in electropalatography: A state-of-the-art report. *Clinical Linguistics and Phonetics*, 3, 1–38.

Hardcastle, W.J., MorganBarry, R. and Nunn, M. (1989b) Instrumental articulatory phonetics in assessment and remediation: case studies with the electropalatograph. In J. Stengelhofen (Ed.), *Cleft Palate: The Nature and Remediation of Communication Problems*. London: Churchill Livingstone.

Hardcastle, W.J., Gibbon, F.E. and Jones, W. (1991) Visual display of tongue–palate contact: Electropalatography in the assessment and remediation of speech disorders. *British Journal of Disorders of Communication*, 26, 41–74.

Harris, J. and Cottam, P.J. (1985) Phonetic features and phonological features in speech assessment. *British Journal of Disorders of Communication*, 20, 61–74.

Harris, M. and Coltheart, M. (1986) *Language Processing in Children and Adults*. London: Routledge.

Hawkins, P. (1985) A tutorial comment on Harris and Cottam. *British Journal of Disorders of Communication*, 20, 75–80.

Henderson, S.E, Morris, J. and Frith, H. (1981) The motor deficit in Down's Syndrome children: A problem of timing? *Journal of Child Psychology and Psychiatry*, 22, 233–245.

Henry, C.E. (1990) The development of oral diadochokinesia and non-linguistic rhythmic skills in normal and speech-disordered young children. *Clinical Linguistics and Phonetics*, 4, 121–137.

Heritage, J.C. (1984a) *Garfinkel and Ethnomethodology*. Cambridge: Polity Press.

Heritage, J.C. (1984b) A change-of-state token and aspects of its sequential position. In J.M. Atkinson and J.C. Heritage (Eds), *Structures of Social Action*. Cambridge: Cambridge University Press.

Heritage, J.C. (1989) Current developments in conversation analysis. In D. Roger and P. Bull (Eds), *Conversation: An Interdisciplinary Perspective*. Clevedon: Multilingual Matters.

Heselwood, B.C., Bray, M. and Crookston, I. (1995) Juncture, rhythm and planning in the speech of an adult with Downs syndrome. *Clinical Linguistics and Phonetics*, in press.

Hewlett, N. (1985) Phonological versus phonetic disorders: some suggested modifications to the current use of the distinction. *British Journal of Disorders of Communication*, **20**, 61–54.

Hewlett, N. (1987) Review of Grunwell, P. (1985b) *PACS Phonological Assessment of Child Speech. Clinical Linguistics and Phonetics*, **1**, 191–194.

Hewlett, N. (1988) Phonetic and phonological differences between adult and child speech: A proposed model. In G. Collis, A. Lewis and V. Lewis (Eds), *Proceedings of the Child Language Seminar*, pp. 1–11. University of Warwick.

Hewlett, N. (1990) Processes of development and production. In P. Grunwell (Ed.), *Developmental Speech Disorders*. London: Churchill Livingstone.

Hiki, S. and Itoh, H. (1986) Influence of palate shape on lingual articulation. *Speech Communication*, **5**, 141–158.

Hochberg, I. and Kabnecell, J. (1967) Oral stereognosis in normal and cleft palate individuals. *Cleft Palate Journal*, **4**, 47–57.

Holland, A. (1991) Pragmatic aspects of intervention in aphasia. *Journal of Neurolinguistics*, **6**, 197–211.

Hoole, P., Ziegler, W., Hartmann, E. and Hardcastle, W.J. (1989) Parallel electropalatographic and acoustic measures of fricatives. *Clinical Linguistics and Phonetics*, **3**, 59–69.

Howard, D. and Hatfield, F.M. (1987) *Aphasia Therapy: Historical and Contemporary Issues*. Hove: Lawrence Erlbaum.

Howard, D. and Patterson, K. (1992) *The Pyramids and Palm Trees Test: A Test of Semantic Access from Words and Pictures*. London: Thames Valley Test Co.

Howard, D., Patterson, K.E., Franklin, S., Orchard-Lisle, V.M. and Morton, J. (1985) The treatment of word retrieval deficits in aphasia; a comparison of two therapy methods. *Brain*, **108**, 817–829.

Howard, S.J. (1993) Articulatory constraints on a phonological system: a case study of cleft palate speech. *Clinical Linguistics and Phonetics*, **7**, 299–318.

Howard, S.J. (1994) Spontaneous phonetic reorganisation following articulation therapy: An electropalatographic study. In R. Aulanko and A-M. Korpijaakko-Huuhka (Eds), *Proceedings of the Third Congress of the International Clinical Linguistics and Phonetics Association* vol. 39, pp. 67–74. August 1993, Helsinki. Helsinki: Publications of the Department of Phonetics, University of Helsinki.

Howard, S.J., Clark, R. and Whiteside, S. (1994) The perception of sibilant fricatives: an electropalatographic and acoustic study. Paper presented at the 1994 ASHA Convention, New Orleans.

Howard, S.J., Hartley, J. and Muller, D. (1995) The changing face of child language assessment: 1985–1995. *Child Language Teaching and Therapy*, **11**, 7–22.

Howell, J. and Dean, E. (1991) *Treating Phonological Disorders in Children: Metaphon –Theory to Practice*. Kibworth, Leics: Far Communications.

Huffman, A.L. (1978) Biofeedback treatment of orofacial dysfunction: a preliminary study. *American Journal of Occupational Therapy*, **32**, 149–154.

Huskie, C.F. (1989) Assessment of speech and language status: subjective and objective approaches to appraisal of vocal tract structure and function. In J. Stengelhofen (Ed.), *Cleft Palate: The Nature and Remediation of Communication Problems*. London: Churchill Livingstone.

Hyde-Wright, S. and Cray, B. (1990) A teacher's and a speech therapist's approach to management. In K. Mogford-Bevan and J. Sadler (Eds), *Child Language Disability*, Vol. II: *Semantic and Pragmatic Difficulties*. Clevedon: Multilingual Matters.

Ingram, D. (1975) The acquisition of fricatives and affricates in normal and linguistically deviant children. In A. Caramazza and E. Zuriff (Eds), *The Acquisition and Breakdown of Language*. Baltimore: Johns Hopkins University Press.

Ingram, D. (1976) *Phonological Disability in Children*. London: Arnold.

Ingram, D., Christensen, L., Veach, S. and Webster, B. (1980) The acquisition of word-initial fricatives and affricates in English by children between 2 and 6 years. In G. Yeni-Komshian, J.F. Kavanagh and C.J. Ferguson (Eds), *Child Phonology*, Vol.1: *Production*. New York: Academic Press.

International Phonetic Association (1993) *The International Phonetic Alphabet* (IPA). Revised to 1993. Leeds: IPA.

Itoh, H., Matsuda, Y., Sugawara, J., Fujita, Y., Kanuma, A. and Yamashita, S. (1980) Observation of articulation by using EPG of adult with malocclusion. *Journal of Dental Research*, **59**, 903 (IADR Abstracts).

Itoh, M. and Sasanuma, S. (1984) Articulatory movements in apraxia of speech (1984). In J.C. Rosenbek, M. McNeil and A. Aronson (Eds), *Apraxia of Speech*. San Diego: College Hill

Itoh, M., Sasanuma, S. and Ushijima, T. (1979) Velar movements during speech in a patient with apraxia of speech. *Brain and Language*, **7**, 227–239.

Jefferson, G. (1978) Sequential aspects of story telling in conversation. In J.N. Schenkein (Ed.), *Studies in the Organization of Conversational Interaction*. New York: Academic Press.

Jeffree, D.M. and McConkey, R. (1976) An observation scheme for recording children's imaginative doll play. *Journal of Child Psychology and Psychiatry*, **17**, 189–197.

Joanette, Y. and Brownell, L.H.H. (Eds) (1990) *Discourse Disability and Brain Damage*. New York: Springer-Verlag.

Johnson, C. (1979) Contingent queries: The first chapter. Paper presented at Language and Social Psychology Conference, Bristol.

Johnson, D. (1981) Considerations in the assessment of central auditory disorders in learning-disabled children. In R.W. Keith (Ed.), *Central Auditory and Language Disorders in Children*. San Diego: College Hill Press.

Johnston, J.R. (1992) Cognitive abilities of language impaired children. In P. Fletcher and D. Hall (Eds), *Specific Speech and Language Disorders in Children*. London: Whurr.

Jones, E.V. (1986) Building the foundations for sentence production in a non-fluent aphasic. *British Journal of Disorders of Communication*, **21**, 63–82.

Jones, S., Smedley, M. and Jennings, M. (1986) Case study: A child with high level language disorder characterised by syntactic, semantic and pragmatic difficulties. In *Advances in Working with Language Disordered Children*. ICAN.

Kamhi, A.G. and Beasley, D.S. (1985) Central auditory processing disorder: Is it a meaningful construct or a twentieth century unicorn? *Journal of Communication Disorders*, **9**, 5–13.

Karniol, R. (1992) Stuttering out of bilingualism. *First Language*, **12**, 255–283.

Kay, J., Lesser, R. and Coltheart, M. (1992) *PALPA: Psycholinguistic Assessments of*

Language Processing in Aphasia. Hove: Lawrence Erlbaum Associates.

Keatley, M.A. and Pike, P. (1976) The automated pulmonary function laboratory: clinical use in determining respiratory variations in apraxia. In R.H. Brookshire (Ed.), *Clinical Aphasiology Conference Proceedings*. Minneapolis: BRK.

Keenan, E. (1974) Conversational Competence in Children. *Journal of Child Language*, **1**, 163–183.

Keenan, E.O. and Schieffelin, B.B. (1976) Topic as a discourse notion: a study of topic in the conversations of children and adults. In C.N. Li (Ed.), *Subject and Topic*. New York: Academic Press.

Keith, R.W. (Ed.) (1981) *Central Auditory and Language Disorders in Children*. San Diego: College-Hill Press.

Kelly, J. and Local, J. (1989) *Doing Phonology*. Manchester: Manchester University Press.

Kemper, T. (1988) Neuropathology of Down Syndrome. In L. Nadel (Ed.), *The Psychobiology of Down Syndrome*. London: MIT Press.

Kent, R. and Rosenbek, J. (1982) Prosodic disturbance and neurologic lesion. *Brain and Language*, **15**, 259–291.

Kent, R.D. and Rosenbek, J.C. (1983) Acoustic patterns of apraxia of speech. *Journal of Speech and Hearing Research*, **26**, 231–249.

Kent, R., Netsell, R. and Abbs, J. (1979) Acoustic characteristics of dysarthria associated with cerebellar disease. *Journal of Speech and Hearing Research*, **22**, 627–648.

Kertesz, A. (1990) What should be the core of aphasia tests? *Aphasiology*, **4**, 97–101.

Kingston, J. and Beckman, M.E. (Eds) (1990) *Papers in Laboratory Phonology I: Between the Grammar of Physics and Speech*. Cambridge: Cambridge University Press.

Kirk, S.A., McCarthy, J.J. and Kirk, W.D. (1968) *The Illinois Test of Psycholinguistic Abilities. (ITPA)*. Illinois: University of Illinois.

Kohler, K. (1992) Comments on Chapter 8. In G.J. Docherty and D.R. Ladd (Eds), *Papers in Laboratory Phonology II: Gesture, Segment, Prosody*. Cambridge: Cambridge University Press.

Kravitz, H. and Boehm, J. (1971) Rhythmic habit patterns in infancy: Their sequence, age of onset and frequency. *Child Development*, **42**, 399–415.

Ladefoged, P. (1967) *Three Experimental Areas of Phonetics*. Oxford: Oxford University Press.

Laine, T. (1986) Articulatory disorders in speech as related to size of the alveolar arches. *European Journal of Orthodontics*, **8**, 192–197.

Laine, T., Jaroma, M. and Linnasalo, A-L. (1987) Relationships between interincisal occlusion and articulatory components of speech. *Folia Phoniatrica*, **39**, 78–86.

Lambert, J. (1989) Childhood phonological disorders. In M. Leahy (Ed.), *Disorders of Communication: The Science of Intervention*. London: Taylor & Francis.

Langer, R.M. (1981) The role of orofacial muscle imbalance in speech correction. In D. Garliner (Ed.), *Myofunctional Therapy*. Philadelphia: Samuels.

LaPointe, L. and Horner, J. (1979) *Reading Comprehension Battery for Aphasia*. Texas: Pro-Ed.

Laver, J. (1980a) Monitoring systems in the neuro-linguistic control of speech production. In V. Fromkin (Ed.), *Errors in Linguistic Performance*. New York: Academic Press.

Laver, J. (1980b) *The Phonetic Description of Voice Quality*. Cambridge: Cambridge University Press.

Laver, J. (1994) *Principles of Phonetics*. Cambridge: Cambridge University Press.

Leahy, M. (Ed.) (1989) *Disorders of Communication: The Science of Intervention* London: Whurr.

Lebrun, Y. (1985) Tongue thrust, tongue tip position at rest, and sigmatism: a review. *Journal of Communication Disorders*, **18**, 305–312.

Lebrun, Y. (1986) Aphasia with recurrent utterance: a review. *British Journal of Disorders of Communication*, **21**, 11–20.

Lees, J. and Urwin, S. (1991) *Children with Language Disorders*. London: Whurr Publishers.

Lemperle, G. (1985) Plastic surgery. In D. Lane and B. Stratford (Eds), *Current Approaches to Down's Syndrome*. London: Holt, Rhinehart & Winston.

Leonard, L.B. and Frome Loeb, D. (1988) Government-Binding Theory and some of its applications: A tutorial. *Journal of Speech and Hearing Research*, **31**, 515–524.

Lesser, R. (1978) *Linguistic Investigations of Aphasia*. London: Edward Arnold.

Lesser, R. and Milroy, L. (1993) *Linguistics and Aphasia: Psycholinguistic and Pragmatic Aspects of Intervention*. London: Longman.

Leudar, I. (1989) Communication environments for mentally handicapped people. In M. Beveridge, G. Conti-Ramsden and I. Leudar (Eds), *Language and Communication in Mentally Handicapped People*. London: Chapman & Hall.

Leudar, I., Fraser, W. and Jeeves, M. (1981) Social familiarity and communication in Down Syndrome. *Journal of Mental Deficiency Research*, **25**, 133–142.

Levelt, W.J.M. (1989) *Speaking: From Intention to Articulation*. Cambridge, MA: MIT Press.

Levelt, W.J.M. (Ed.) (1993) Accessing words in speech production: stages, processes and representations. In *Lexical Access in Speech Production*. Oxford: Blackwell.

Levinson, S.C. (1983) *Pragmatics*. Cambridge: Cambridge University Press.

Lewis, V., Boucher, J. and Astell, A. (1992) The art of symbolic play in young children: A prototype test. *European Journal of Disorders of Communication*, **27**, 231–245.

Local, J. (1992) Modeling assimilation in nonsegmental, rule-free synthesis. In G.J. Docherty and D.R. Ladd (Eds), *Papers in Laboratory Phonology II: Gesture, Segment, Prosody*. Cambridge: Cambridge University Press.

Lowe, M. and Costello, A. (1976) *The Symbolic Play Test*. Windsor: NFER.

Lucas, E.V. (1980) *Semantic and Pragmatic Language Disorders: Assessment and Remediation*. Rockville: Aspen Systems.

Lum, C. and Russell, J. (1978) An investigation of the relationship between oral-stereognostic perception and type and severity of verbal dyspraxia. *Australian Journal of Hearing Comunication Disorders*, **6**, 16–22.

Luria, A.R. (1966) *Higher Cortical Functions in Man*. New York: Basic.

Luria, A.R. (1973) *The Working Brain*. Penguin, Harmondsworth.

McDonald, S. (1993) Pragmatic skills after closed head injury: ability to meet the informational needs of the listener. *Brain and Language*, **44**, 28–46.

Macken, M.A. and Barton, D. (1980) The acquisition of the voicing contrast in English: a study of voice onset time in word-initial stop consonants. *Journal of Child Language*, **7**, 41–74.

McGlone, R.E. and Profitt, W. R. (1973) Patterns of tongue contact in normal and lisping speakers. *Journal of Speech and Hearing Research*, **16**, 456–473.

McGlone, R.E. and Profitt, W. R. (1974) Comparison of lingual pressure patterns in lisping and normal speech. *Folia Phoniatrica*, **26**, 389–397.

McNeil, M.R., Rosenbek, J. and Aronson, A. (1984) *The Dysarthrias: Physiology, Acoustics, Perception, Management*. San Diego: College Hill Press.

McNeil, M.R. and Prescott, T.E. (1978.) *Revised Token Test*. Baltimore: University Park Press.

McReynolds, L.V. and Engmann, D. (1975) *Distinctive Feature Analysis of Misarticulations*. Baltimore: University Park Press.

McTear, M.F. (1985a) *Children's Conversation*. Oxford: Blackwell

McTear, M.F. (1985b) Pragmatic disorders: A case study of conversational disability. *British Journal of Disorders of Communication*, 20, 129–142.

McTear, M.F. (1990) Is there such a thing as conversational disability. In K. Mogford-Bevan and J. Sadler (Eds), *Child Language Disability*, Vol. II: *Semantic and Pragmatic Difficulties*. Clevedon: Multilingual Matters

McTear, M.F. and Conti-Ramsden, G. (1992) *Pragmatic Disability in Children*. London: Whurr.

MacWhinney, B. (1991) *The CHILDES Project: Tools for Analyzing Talk*. Hillsdale, NJ: Lawrence Erlbaum Associates.

Marchal, A. and Espesser, R. (1989) L'Asymetrie des appuis linguo-palatins. *Journal d'Acoustique*, 2, 53–57.

Marchal, A. and Hardcastle W.J. (1993) ACCOR: Instrumentation and database for the cross-language study of coarticulation. *Language and Speech*, 36, 137–153.

Marchal, A., Hardcastle, W. J., Hoole, P., Farnetani, E., Ni Chasaide, A., Schmidbauer, O., Galiano-Ronda, I., Engstrand, O. and Recasens, D. (EUR-ACCOR) (1991) The design of a multichannel database. *Proceedings of the XIIth International Congress of Phonetic Sciences*, Aix-en-Provence, August 19–24, Vol. 5, pp. 422–425.

Marshall, J.L. (1982) What is a symptom-complex? In M.A. Arbib, D. Caplan, and J.C. Marshall (Eds), *Neural Models of Language Processes*. London: Academic Press.

Marshall, J., Pring, T. and Chiat, S. (1993) Sentence processing therapy: working at the level of the event. *Aphasiology*, 7, 177–200.

Martin, A.D. (1974) Some objections to the term 'apraxia of speech'. *Journal of Speech and Hearing Disorders*, 39, 53–64.

Maxim, J., Huppert, F., Beardsall, L. and Brayne, C. (1991) Can elicited language be used to diagnose dementia? A comparison of demented, depressed, aphasic and normal elderly subjects. *National Hospital's College of Speech Sciences – Work in Progress*, 1, 13–21.

Maxwell, E. and Weismer, G. (1982) The contribution of phonological, acoustic and perceptual techniques to the characterization of a misarticulating child's voice contrast for stops. *Applied Psycholinguistics*, 3, 29–44.

Maynard, D. W. (1980) Placement of topic changes in conversation. *Semiotica*, 30, 263–290.

Menn, L. and Obler, L.K. (Eds) (1990) *Agrammatic Aphasia: A Cross-Language Narrative Sourcebook*. Amsterdam: Benjamins.

Mentis, M. and Prutting, C.A. (1991) Analysis of topic as illustrated in a head-injured and a normal adult. *Journal of Speech and Hearing Research*, 34, 583–595.

Miller, J.F. (1988) The developmental asynchrony of language development with children with Down Syndrome. In L. Nadel (Ed.), *The Psychobiology of Down Syndrome*. London: MIT Press.

Miller, J.F. and Chapman, R.S. (1982–1993) *Systematic Analysis of Language Transcripts* (SALT). Madison, WI: Language Analysis Laboratory, University of Wisconsin-Madison.

Milloy, N.R. (1991) *Breakdown of Speech: Causes and Remediation*. London: Chapman Hall.

Milroy, L. (1985) Phonological analysis and speech disorders: a comment. *British Journal of Disorders of Communication*, 20, 171–180.

Milroy, L. (1988) Profile for analysing conversational disability. Unpublished Manuscript, Department of Speech, University of Newcastle Upon Tyne.

Milroy, L. and Perkins, L. (1992) Repair strategies in aphasic discourse: towards a collaborative model. *Clinical Linguistics and Phonetics*, 6, 27–40.

Milton, S.B. (1988) Management of subtle cognitive communication deficits. *Journal of Head Trauma Rehabilitation*, 3, 1–12.

Milton, S.B., Prutting, C.A. and Binder, G.M. (1984) Appraisal of communicative competence in head-injured adults. In R.H. Brookshire (Ed.), *Clinical Aphasiology Conference Proceedings*, pp. 114–123. Minneapolis: BRK.

Mitchell, R.A. and Berger, J.J. (1975) Neural regulation of respiration. *American Review of Respiratory Disease*, 3, 206–224.

MorganBarry, R. (1987) Language use versus phonology versus prosody: a spin-off effect? *Proceedings of the Child Language Seminar*. York University.

MorganBarry, R. (1989) EPG from square one: An overview of electropalatography as an aid to therapy. *Clinical Linguistics and Phonetics*, 3, 81–91.

MorganBarry, R. (1990a) Phonetic and phonological aspects of neurological speech disorders. Unpublished PhD dissertation, University of Reading.

MorganBarry, R. (1990b) Prosodic and timing characteristics of two unusual patients. *Proceedings of the Voice Technology Conference*. London, NHCSS.

MorganBarry, R. (1993) Measuring segmental timing in pathological speech using electropalatography. *Clinical Linguistics and Phonetics*, 7, 275–284.

MorganBarry R. (1995) A comparative study of the relationship between dysarthria and verbal dyspraxia in adults and children. *Clinical Linguistics and Phonetics*, in press.

Morris, J., Franklin, S., Ellis, A.W., Turner, J. and Bailey, P. J. (1995) Remediating a speech perception deficit in an aphasic patient. *Aphasiology*, in press.

Moskowitz, B.A. (1975) The acquisition of fricatives: a study in phonetics and phonology. *Journal of Phonetics*, 3, 141–150.

Müller, D. (1985) What does a language score really mean? *Child Language, Teaching and Therapy*, 1, 38–45.

Nelson, H.E. (1991) *The National Adult Reading Test*, 2nd edn. Oxford: NFER-Nelson

Netsell, R. (1986) *A neurobiological view of Speech Production and the Dysarthrias*. San Diego: College Hill Press.

Netsell, R. and Abbs, J. (1976) Some possible uses of neuromotor speech disturbances in understanding the normal mechanism. *Dynamic Aspects of Speech Production*. US-Japan Seminar.

O'Hala, J.J. (1992) The segment: primitive or derived? In G.J. Docherty and D. R. Ladd (Eds), *Papers in Laboratory Phonology II: Gesture, Segment, Prosody*. Cambridge: Cambridge University Press.

Ochs-Keenan, E. (1977) Making it last: Repetition in children's discourse. In S. Ervin-Tripp and C. Mitchell-Kernan (Eds), *Child Discourse*. New York: Academic Press.

Ogura, T. (1991) A longitudinal study of the relationship between early language development and play development. *Journal of Child Language*, 18, 273–294.

Ohde, R. N. and Sharf, D. J. (1992) *Phonetic Analysis of Normal and Abnormal Speech*. New York: Merrill.

Oliver, R., Jones, M., Smith, S. and Newcombe, R. (1985) Oral stereognosis and diadokokinetic tests in children and yound adults. *British Journal of Disorders of Communication*, **20**, 271–280.

Ollers, D. K. and Eilers, R. E. (1975) Phonetic expectation and transcription validity. *Phonetica*, **31**, 288–304.

Olswang, L.B. and Bain, B. (1985) The natural occurrence of generalisation during articulation treatment. *Journal of Communication Disorders*, **18**, 109–129.

Panzeri, M., Semenza, C. and Butterworth, B. (1987) Compensatory processes in the evolution of severe jargon aphasia. *Neuropsychologia*, **25**, 919–933.

Paradis, C. and Prunet, J-F. (1991) *The Special Status of Coronals*. Dordrecht: Foris.

Passy, J. (1990) *Cued Articulation*. Available from The Australian Council for Educational Research Ltd., Radford House, Frederick Street, Hawthorn, Victoria 3122, Australia.

Patterson, K. and Shewell, C. (1987) Speak and spell: Dissociations and word-class effects. In M. Coltheart, G. Sartori, and R. Job (Eds), *The Cognitive Neuropsychology of Language*. London: Lawrence Erlbaum Associates.

Perkins, M.R. (1982) Review of D. Crystal (1981) *Clinical Linguistics*. *British Journal of Disorders of Communication*, **17**, 87–89.

Perkins, M.R. (1994) Repetitiveness in language disorders: A new analytical procedure. *Clinical Linguistics and Phonetics*, **8**, 321–336.

Perkins, M.R. (1995) Corpora of disordered spoken language. In G. Leech, J. Thomas and G. Myers (Eds), *Spoken English on Computer: Transcription, Mark-Up and Application*. London: Longman.

Perkins, M.R. and Varley, R. (1995) *A Machine-Readable Corpus of Aphasic Discourse*. Speech Science Unit, University of Sheffield.

Piaget, J. (1926) *The Language and Thought of the Child*. London: Routledge and Kegan-Paul.

Pisoni, D.B. and Luce, P.A. (1987) Acoustic-phonetic representations in word recognition. *Cognition*, **25**, 21–52.

Poizner, H., Bellugi, U. and Iragui, V. (1984) Apraxia and aphasia for a visual-gestural language. *American Journal of Physiology: Regulative, Integrative and Comparative Physiology*, **246**, R868–R883.

Pollack, E. and Rees, N.S. (1972) Disorders of articulation: clinical applications of distinctive feature theory. *Journal of Speech and Hearing Disorders*, **37**, 451–461.

Praamstra, P., Hagoort, P., Maassen, B. and Crul, T. (1991) Word deafness and auditory cortical function. *Brain*, **114**, 1197–1225.

Prather, E.M., Hedrick, D.L. and Kern, C.A. (1975) Articulation Development in children aged two to four years. *Journal of Speech and Hearing Disorders*, **40**, 179–191.

PRDS (1980) The phonetic representation of disordered speech. *British Journal of Disorders of Communication*, **15**, 215–220.

PRDS (1983) *The Phonetic Representation of Disordered Speech: Final Report*. London: King's Fund.

Pressel, G. and Hochberg, I. (1974) Oral form discrimination of children with cleft palate. *Cleft Palate Journal*, **11**, 66–71.

Pring, T.R. (1986) Evaluating the effects of speech therapy for aphasics: Developing the single case methodology. *British Journal of Disorders of Communication*, **21**, 103–115.

Prizant, B.M. (1983) Language acquisition and communicative behaviour in autism: toward an understanding of the 'whole' of it. *Journal of Speech and Hearing Disorders*, **48**, 296–307.

Prizant, B.M. and Schuler A.L. (1987) Facilitating communication: Theoretical foundations. In D.J. Cohen, A.M. Donellan and R. Paul (Eds), *Handbook of Autism and Pervasive Developmental Disorders*. London: Wiley.

Prutting, C.A. and Kirchner, D.M. (1987) A clinical appraisal of the pragmatic aspects of language. *Journal of Speech and Hearing Disorders*, **52**, 105–119.

Pueschel, S.M. (1988) Visual and auditory processing in children with Down Syndrome. In L. Nadel (Ed.), *The Psychobiology of Down Syndrome*. London: MIT Press.

Pye, C., Wilcox, K.A. and Siren, K.A. (1988) Refining transcriptions: the significance of transcriber 'errors'. *Journal of Child Language*, **15**, 17–37.

Rain, B.N. (1993) Paediatric neurology. In J. Walton (Ed.), *Brain's Diseases of the Nervous System*. Oxford: Oxford University Press.

Rapin, I. and Allen, D. (1983) Developmental language disorders: Nosologic considerations. In U. Kirk (Ed.), *Neuropsychology of Language, Reading and Spelling*. Academic Press: New York.

Rapin, I. and Allen, D.A. (1987) Developmental dysphasia and autism in preschool children: characteristics and subtypes. In *Proceedings of the First International Symposium of Specific Speech and Language Disorders in Children*. London: AFASIC.

Rathbone, J.S. and Snidecor J.C. (1959) Appraisal of speech defects in dental anomalies with reference to speech improvement. *Angle Orthodontics*, **29**, 54–59.

Rein, R.P. and Kernan, K.T. (1989) The functional use of verbal perseverations by adults who are mentally retarded. *Education and Training in Mental Retardation*, **24**, 381–389.

Renfrew, C. (1969) *The Bus Story*. Published by author.

Reynell, J.K (1977) *Reynell Developmental Language Scales*. London: NFER-Nelson.

Ringel, R., Burk, S. and Scott, C. (1968) Tactile perception: form discrimination in the mouth. *British Journal of Disorders of Communication*, **3**, 150–155.

Robertson, S.J. (1982) *Dysarthria Profile*. Communication Skill Builders.

Robertson, S.J. and Thompson, F. (1986) *Working with Dysarthrics*. Buckingham: Winslow Press.

Rondal, J. (1988) Down's Syndrome. In K. Mogford and D. Bishop (Eds), *Language Development in Exceptional Circumstances*. Edinburgh: Churchill Livingstone.

Rosenbek, J.C. and LaPointe, L. (1985) The dysarthrias: description, diagnosis and treatment. In Johns, D F (Ed.), *Clinical Management of Neurogenic Disorders*, 2nd edn. Boston: Little, Brown & Co.

Rosenbek, J.C. and Wertz, R.T. (1973) Oral sensation and perception in apraxia of speech and aphasia. *Journal of Speech and Hearing Research*, **16**, 22–36.

Rosenbeck, J.C., Wertz, R.T. and Darley, F.L. (1973) Oral sensation and perception in apraxia of speech and aphasia. *Journal of Speech and Hearing Research*, **16**, 22–36.

Russell, J. (1989a) Cleft palate and other craniofacial anomalies in children. In M.M. Leahy (Ed.), *Disorders of Communication: The Science of Intervention*. London: Taylor & Francis.

Russell, J. (1989b) Early intervention. In J. Stengelhofen (Ed.), *Cleft Palate: The Nature and Remediation of Communication Problems*. London: Churchill Livingstone.

Russell, J. and Grunwell, P. (1993) Speech development in children with cleft lip and palate. In P. Grunwell (Ed.), *Analysing Cleft Palate Speech*. London: Whurr.

Rutter M. (1978) Diagnosis and definition of childhood autism. *Journal of Autism and Developmental Disorders*, **8**, 139–161.

Sacks, H. and Schegloff, E. (1974) Two preferences in the organisation of reference to persons in conversation and their interactions. In N.V. Avison and R.J. Wilson (Eds), *Ethnomethodology: Labelling Theory and Deviant Behaviour*. London: Routledge & Kegan-Paul

Sacks, H., Schegloff, E.A. and Jefferson, G. (1974) A simplest systematics for the organization of turn-taking for conversation. *Language*, **50**, 696–735.

Salkie, R. (1990) *The Chomsky Update: Linguistics and Politics*. London: Unwin Hyman.

Sandson, J. and Albert, M.L. (1984) Varieties of perseveration. *Neuropsychologia*, **22**, 715–732.

Sarno, M.T. (1980) Analyzing aphasic behaviour. In M. Sarno and O. Hook (Eds), *Aphasia, Assessment and Treatment*. New York: Masson.

Sbordone, R.J. (1988) Assessment and treatment of cognitive–communicative impairments in the closed-head injury patient: a neurobehavioural–systems approach. *Journal of Head Trauma Rehabilitation*, **3**, 55–62.

Schegloff, E.A. (1979a) The relevance of repair to syntax-for-conversation. In T. Givon (Ed.), *Syntax and Semantics*, Vol. XII: *Discourse and Syntax*. New York: Academic Press.

Schegloff, E.A. (1979b) Identification and recognition in telephone conversation openings. In G. Psathas (Ed.), *Everyday Language: Studies in Ethnomethodology*. New York: Irvington.

Schegloff, E.A. (1982) Discourse as an interactional achievement: some uses of 'uh huh' and other things that come between sentences. In D. Tannen (Ed.), *Analyzing Discourse: Text and Talk*. Washington DC: Georgetown University Press.

Schegloff, E.A. (1987a) Analyzing single episodes of interaction: an exercise in conversation analysis. *Social Psychology Quarterly*, **50**, 101–114.

Schegloff, E.A. (1987b) Some sources of misunderstanding in talk-in-interaction. *Linguistics*, **25**, 201–218.

Schegloff, E.A. (1992) Repair after next turn: the last structurally provided defense of intersubjectivity in conversation. *American Journal of Sociology*, **97**, 1295–1345.

Schegloff, E.A. and Sacks, H. (1973) Opening up closings. *Semiotica*, **6**, 344–377.

Schegloff, E.A., Jefferson, G. and Sacks, H. (1977) The preference for self-correction in the organization of repair in conversation. *Language*, **53**, 361–382.

Schiffrin, D. (1994) *Approaches to Discourse*. Oxford: Basil Blackwell.

Schlobinski, P. and Schütze-Coburn, S. (1992) On the topic of topic and topic continuity. *Linguistics*, **30**, 89–121.

Schmidt, R.A. (1975) A schema theory of discrete motor skill learning. *Psychological Review*, **82**, 225–260.

Schwartz, M. (1984) What the classical aphasia categories can't do for us, and why. *Brain and Language*, **21**, 3–8.

Selkirk, E.O. (1984) *Phonology and Syntax*. Cambridge, MA: MIT Press.

Shankweiler, D., Harris, K.S. and Taylor, M.L. (1968) Electromyographic studies of articulation in aphasia. *Archives of Physical Medicine and Rehabilitation*, **49**, 1–8.

Shewan, C.M. and Bandur, D.L. (1986) *Treatment of Aphasia: A Language Oriented Approach*. London: Taylor & Francis.

Shindo, M., Kaga, K. and Tanaka, Y. (1991) Speech discrimination and lip reading in patients with word deafness or auditory agnosia. *Brain and Language*, **40**, 153–161.

Shoumaker, R.D., Ajax, E.T. and Schenkenberg, T. (1977) Pure word deafness (auditory verbal agnosia). *Diseases of the Nervous System*, 38, 293–299.

Shriberg, L.D. and Kent, R. (1982) *Clinical Phonetics*. New York: Macmillan.

Shriberg, L.D. and Lof, G. L. (1991) Reliability studies in broad and narrow phonetic transcription. *Clinical Linguistics and Phonetics*, 5, 225-279.

Shriberg, L. and Smith, A.J. (1983) Phonological correlates of middle-ear involvement in speech-delayed children: a methodological note. *Journal of Speech and Hearing Research*, 26, 293–297.

Shriberg, L. D., Kwiatkowsi, J. and Hoffman, K. (1984) A procedure for phonetic transcription by consensus. *Journal of Speech and Hearing Research*, 27, 456–465.

Shriberg, L.D., Hinke, R. and Trost-Steffen, C. (1987) A procedure to select and train persons for narrow phonetic transcription by consensus. *Clinical Linguistics and Phonetics*, 1, 171–189.

Silverman, S.R. and Kricos, P.B. (1990) Speech reading. *The Volta Review*, 92, 4.

Sinclair, J. (1991) *Corpus, Concordance, Collocation*. Oxford: Oxford University Press.

Siren, K.A. and Wilcox, K.A. (1990) The utility of phonetic versus orthographic transcription methods. *Child Language, Teaching and Therapy*, 6, 127–139.

Smit, A. and Bernthal, J. (1983) Voicing contrasts and their phonological implications in the speech of articulation-disordered children. *Journal of Speech and Hearing Research*, 26, 486–500.

Smith, B.R. and Leinonen, E. (1992) *Clinical Pragmatics: Unravelling the Complexities of Communicative Failure*. London: Chapman & Hall.

Smith, G.F. and Berg, J.M. (1976) *Down's Anomaly*. Edinburgh: Churchill Livingstone.

Smith, N.V. (1973) *The Acquisition of Phonology: A Case Study*. Cambridge: Cambridge University Press.

Snow, K. (1961) Articulation proficiency in relation to certain dental abnormalities. *Journal of Speech and Hearing Disorders*, 26, 209–212.

Spencer, A. (1984) A non-linear analysis of phonological disability. *Journal of Communication Disorders*, 17, 325–348.

Spencer, A. (1986) Towards a theory of phonological development. *Lingua*, 68, 3–38.

Sperberg-McQueen, C.M. and Burnard, I. (1994) *Guidelines for Electronic Text Encoding and Interchange*. Chicago: Text Encoding Initiative.

Spreen, O. and Benton, A.L. (1969) *Neurosensory Center Comprehensive Examination for Aphasia*. Victoria, University of Victoria.

Stackhouse, J. and Wells, B. (1993) Psycholinguistic assessment of developmental speech disorders. *European Journal of Disorders of Communication*, 28, 331–348.

Starkweather, C.W. (1987) *Fluency and Stuttering*. Englewood Cliffs: Prentice-Hall.

Starkweather, C.W. and Gottwald, S. (1990) The demands and capacities model II: Clinical applications. *Journal of Fluency Disorders*, 15, 143–157.

Stech, E.L. (1982) The analysis of conversational topic sequence structures. *Semiotica*, 39, 75–91.

Stengelhofen, J. (Ed.) (1989) The nature and causes of communication problems in cleft palate. In *Cleft Palate: The Nature and Remediation of Communication Problems*. London: Churchill Livingstone.

Stephens, H. and Elton, M. (1986) A description of the systematic use of articulograms in the treatment of children with severe developmental speech disorders. *College of Speech Therapists Bulletin*, December.

Stephens, M.I. and Daniloff, R.G. (1977) A methodological study of factors affecting the judgment of misarticulated /s/. *Journal of Communication Disorders*, **10**, 207–220.

Stephens, M.I., Hoffman P.R. and Daniloff R.G. (1986) Phonetic characteristics of delayed /s/ development. *Journal of Phonetics*, **14**, 247–256.

Stone, M., Faber, A., Raphael, L.J. and Shawker, T.H. (1992) Cross-sectional tongue shape and linguopalatal contact patterns in /s/, /ʃ/ and /ʎ/. *Journal of Phonetics*, **20**, 253–270.

Stubbs, M. (1986) *Educational Linguistics*. Oxford: Blackwell.

Stuffins, G.M. (1989) The use of appliances in the treatment of speech problems in cleft palate. In J. Stengelhofen (Ed.), *Cleft Palate: The Nature and Remediation of Communication Problems*. London: Churchill Livingstone.

Sugishita, M., Konno, K., Kabe, S., Yunoki, K., Togashi, O. and Kawamura, M. (1987) Electropalatographic analysis of apraxia of speech in a left-hander and in a right-hander. *Brain*, **110**, 1393–1417.

Svartvik, J. (1992) Corpus linguistics comes of age. In J. Svartvik (Ed.), *Directions in Corpus Linguistics: Proceedings of Nobel Symposium '82*, Stockholm, 4–8 August 1991. Berlin/New York: Mouton de Gruyter.

Tait, M. and Shillcock, R. (1993) Research in progress: Syntactic theory and the characterization of dysphasic speech. *Clinical Linguistics and Phonetics*, 7, 237–239.

Taylor, T.J. (1992) *Mutual Misunderstanding*. North Carolina: Duke University Press.

Travis, L.E. (Ed.) (1971) *Handbook of Speech Pathology and Audiology*. Englewood Cliffs, NJ: Prentice-Hall.

Van Lancker, D. (1987) Nonpropositional speech: neurolinguistic studies. In A. W. Ellis (Ed.), *Progress in the Psychology of Language*, Vol. 3. London: Lawrence Erlbaum Associates.

Van Riper, C. and Irwin, J. (1958) *Voice and Articulation*. Englewood-Cliffs, NJ: Prentice-Hall.

Vance, J. (1994) Prosodic deviation in dysarthria: a case study. *European Journal of Disorders of Communication*, **29**, 61–76.

Vygotsky, L. (1986) *Thought and Language*. London: MIT Press.

Warren, D.W., Nelson, G.R. and Allen, G. (1980) Effects of increased vertical dimension on size of constriction port and fricative sound intelligibility. *Journal of the Acoustical Society of America*, **67**, 1828–1831.

Warren, D.W., Allen, G. and King, H.A. (1984) Physiologic and perceptual effects of induced anterior open bite. *Folia Phoniatrica*, **36**, 164–173.

Washino, K., Kasai, Y., Uchida, Y. and Takeda, K. (1981) Tongue movement during speech in a patient with apraxia of speech: a case study. In F.C. Peng (Ed.), *Current Issues in Neurolinguistics: Proceedings of the 2nd ICU Conference of Neurolinguistics*. Tokyo: International Christian University.

Waterson, N (1971) Child phonology: a prosodic view. *Journal of Linguistics*, 7, 179–211.

Wechsler, D. (1981) *Wechsler Adult Intelligence Scale*, revised UK version. London: Harcourt Brace Jovanovich.

Weismer, G. and Elbert, M. (1982) Temporal characteristics of 'functionally' misarticulated /s/ in 4- to 6-year old children. *Journal of Speech and Hearing Research*, **25**, 275–287.

Weismer, G., Dinnsen, D. and Elbert, M. (1981) A study of the voicing distinction associated with omitted, word-final stops. *Journal of Speech and Hearing Research*, **46**, 320–327

Weniger, D. (1990). Diagnostic tests as tools of assessment and models of information processing: a gap to bridge. *Aphasiology*, **4**, 109–113.

Wertz, R.T. (1985) Neuropathologies of speech and language: an introduction to patient management. In S.L. Johns (Ed.), *Clinical Management of Neurogenic Disorders*, 2nd edn. Boston: Little, Brown & Co.

Wertz, R.T., LaPointe, L.L. and Rosenbek, J.C. (1984) *Apraxia of Speech in Adults*. Orlando: Grune & Stratton.

Wilcox, K.A., Stephens, M.I, And Daniloff, R.G. (1985) Mandibular position during children's defective /s/ productions. *Journal of Communication Disorders*, **18**, 273–283.

Wilkinson, R. (1995) The application of conversation analysis to the assessment of aphasic talk-in-interaction. PhD thesis, University of Central England, Birmingham.

Wilson, B. and Patterson, K. (1990) Rehabilitation for cognitive impairment: does cognitive psychology apply? *Applied Cognitive Psychology*, **4**, 247–260.

Wilson, B., Cockburn, J. and Baddeley, A. (1991) *Rivermead Behavioural Memory Test*. Bury St Edmonds: Thames Valley Test Company.

Wilson, W.R. and Morton, K. (1990) Reconsideration of the action-theory perspective on speech motor control. *Clinical Linguistics and Phonetics*, **4**, 341–362.

Wing L. (1981) Asperger's syndrome: A clinical account. *Psychological Medicine*, **11**, 115–130.

Wing, L. (1988) The continuum of autistic characteristics. In E. Schopler and G. B. Mesibov (Eds), *Diagnosis and Assessment in Autism*. New York: Plenum.

Wingate, M. (1985) Stuttering as a prosodic disorder. In R.F. Curlee and W.H. Perkins (Eds), *Nature and Treatment of Stuttering: New Directions*. London: Taylor & Francis.

Wolff, S. and Barlow, A. (1980) Schizoid personality in childhood: a comparative study of schizoid, autistic and normal children. In S. Chess and A. Thomas (Eds), *Annual Progress in Child Psychiatry and Child Development*. New York: Brunner/Mazel.

Yairi, E (1981) Disfluencies of normally speaking two year old children. *Journal of Speech and Hearing Research*, **24**, 1490–495.

Yamashita, Y., Michi, K., Imai, S., Suzuki, N. and Yoshida, H. (1992) Electropalatographic investigation of abnormal lingual–palatal contact patterns in cleft palate speakers. *Clinical Linguistics and Phonetics*, **6**, 201–217.

Yoder, D. and Miller, J. (1972) What we may know and what we can do: input toward a system. In J. McLean, D. Yoder and R. Schiefelbusch (Eds), *Language Intervention with the Retarded: Developing Strategies*. Baltimore: University Park Press.

Yorkston, K. and Beukelman, D. (1978) A comparison of techniques for measuring intelligibility of dysarthric speech. *Journal of Communication Disorders*, **11**, 499–512.

Yorkston, K. and Beukelman, D. (1981) *Assessment of Intelligibility of Dysarthric Speech*. Oregon: CC Publications.

Yorkston, K., Beukelman, D., Minifie, F. and Sapir, S. (1984) Assessment of stress patterning. In M.R. McNeil, J. Rosenbek and A. Aronson (Eds), *The Dysarthrias: Physiology, Acoustics, Perception, Management*. San Diego: College Hill Press.

Young, E.C. (1991) An analysis of young children's ability to produce multisyllabic English nouns. *Clinical Linguistics and Phonetics*, **5**, 297–316.

Ziegler, W. and von Cramon, D. (1986) Spastic dysarthria after acquired brain injury: an acoustic study. *British Journal of Disorders of Communication*, **21**, 173–187.

Index